Generative AI-Enhanced Science Education From Early Childhood to Higher Education

Michail Kalogiannakis
https://orcid.org/0000-0002-9124-2245
University of Thessaly, Greece

Dimitrios Sotiropoulos
https://orcid.org/0000-0001-7367-5760
University of Thessaly, Greece

IGI Global Scientific Publishing
Publishing Tomorrow's Research Today

Vice President of Editorial	Melissa Wagner
Director of Acquisitions	Mikaela Felty
Director of Book Development	Jocelynn Hessler
Production Manager	Mike Brehm
Cover Design	Jose Rosado

Published in the United States of America by
IGI Global Scientific Publishing
701 East Chocolate Avenue
Hershey, PA, 17033, USA
Tel: 717-533-8845 | Fax: 717-533-7115
Website: https://www.igi-global.com E-mail: cust@igi-global.com

Library of Congress Cataloging-in-Publication Data

No LCCN (CIP Data Pending)
ISBN13: 979-8-3373-9074-1
Isbn13Softcover: 979-8-3373-9075-8
EISBN13: 979-8-3373-9076-5

British Cataloguing in Publication Data
A Cataloguing in Publication record for this book is available from the British Library.

Table of Contents

Detailed Table of Contents

running on the R program was used; publication trends, keyword frequencies, citation analyses, author and institution collaborations, and scientific mapping techniques were utilized. The analysis findings show that academic interest in productive artificial intelligence tools has increased significantly between 2021 and 2025. The study also systematically identifies key trends, application areas, and research gaps related to the integration of these technologies into educational processes.

This study examines the process through which preschool teachers utilize an AI-supported digital interface to assess children's scientific process skills within the scope of early childhood science education, employing a Design-Based Research (DBR) approach.The AI-supported system enabled teachers to systematically record classroom observations, generate automated reports, and receive individualized activity recommendations. The study was conducted with three preschool teachers and fourteen children aged 4–5 years in their respective classrooms. Following science activities implemented by the teachers, observation data were entered into the system, and qualitative data regarding the usability and functionality of the program were collected. In conclusion, the developed digital interface emerges as an innovative, practical, and supportive tool for assessment processes in early childhood education.

This study explores the integration of Artificial Intelligence (AI) in early childhood education (ECE), highlighting its pedagogical potential, ethical challenges, and practical implications. Through a scoping review of recent scholarly literature and international reports, the paper outlines how AI technologies are increasingly shaping educational experiences for young learners. While AI presents promising avenues for enhanced assessment, inclusive learning, and reduced teacher workload, concerns regarding data privacy, reduced human interaction, and algorithmic bias remain significant. The paper emphasizes the importance of transparent, equitable, and developmentally appropriate implementation of AI in ECE. Recommendations include strengthening teacher training, designing locally relevant AI applications, and

Preface

In recent years, generative artificial intelligence (GenAI) has been one of the most impactful technological innovations. Like so many other areas of society and the world, GenAI is changing how we think about and interact within education systems, as well as in different places. Technology will continue to advance exponentially and has the potential to change every area of society. Within this vast spectrum of innovations, GenAI technology is exciting to those researching, developing, and implementing science- and STEM-related strategies.

At this time, numerous conferences and forums worldwide are discussing the best ways to understand, design, and integrate GenAI technologies into education. The goal of this edited volume is to provide a means for researchers to participate in an ongoing discussion regarding what is being learned from the empirical research, the theoretical basis of GenAI technology, and the practical use of GenAI in the areas of science/STEM education, early childhood education, higher education, and climate change education.

This volume discusses the design and development of GenAI-supported learning experiences; areas of research related to STEM in Early Childhood Education; issues of AI literacy and ethics for students in the early grades; the use of GenAI to assess student development of scientific process skills; how students are using GenAI in Engineering Education; what influences instructors to adopt or avoid the use of GenAI; and how GenAI can lead to climate literacy and a greater understanding of the connection between humans and their environment.

Although there is increasing awareness of the possibilities that GenAI offers in education, there remains a gap between the theoretical opportunities it provides and its actual use in real-life learning contexts! This book explicitly addresses this gap by presenting studies and analyses that include examples of good practice in using GenAI for home-based Parent-Child Co-Engagement in Preschool/Kindergarten and Early Childhood Science Assessment, Project-Based Learning in Higher Education, and Teaching Practice within Higher Education. These chapters also encourage critical thinking about the relationship between the extensive use of AI tools and enhanced learning outcomes, with additional emphasis placed on the need for careful instructional design and evidence-based interpretation of these tools.

The various contributors to this volume present examples of how GenAI can help develop scientific concepts, promote creativity and engagement through storytelling and multimodal design, and create more responsive learning and assessment processes. Moreover, this volume challenges us to consider critical issues regarding responsible use (for example, developmental appropriateness for young learners; data privacy/safety; content safety; bias; transparency) and the need for educators and parents to facilitate GenAI use with their children.

The book encompasses design-based research, bibliometric mapping, scoping review work, case study research in higher education, and mixed-method modelling approaches that combine predictive machine learning and structural equation modelling. This methodological diversity is intended to provide both a robust view of current evidence and actionable implications for educational design, professional education, and policy.

A broad audience of scholars, STEM educators, educational technologists, researchers, and policymakers will benefit from this volume, as all seek a clear conceptual framework and guidance on how to use GenAI to design curricula, provide instructional guidance, assess students, and create learning environments.

The technological capabilities of GenAI continue to grow at an unprecedented rate as this book goes to press; the technologies presented here (e.g., from large language models to purpose-built educational software) are merely representative of the state of the art in 2025.

Nevertheless, the pedagogical commitments emphasised in this volume extend beyond any single tool: human-centred design, developmentally appropriate practice, cultural responsiveness, and evidence-based decision-making remain essential as new capabilities emerge.

As editors, we hope this collection serves as a timely and valuable reference for readers seeking to understand, critically evaluate, and responsibly harness the transformative potential of generative artificial intelligence in science and STEM education, both now and in the years ahead.

ORGANIZATION OF THE BOOK

Chapter 1 presents the development process of a GenAI-powered digital story creation application designed to support preschool parent–child interaction. It documents the design process and reports parent and child perspectives on the application's educational and emotional affordances, while explicitly addressing ethical issues such as privacy, bias, and age-appropriate content moderation.

Chapter 2 presents bibliometric research on scientific trends in the area of Generative AI Tools used for STEM Education in Early Childhood and identifies the mapping process, the issue(s) being addressed, publication characteristics, and patterns of influence; finally, Emerging Themes were identified from the collected data.

Chapter 3 examines the use of AI-supported assessment methods to evaluate young children's scientific process skills. It describes a learning activity in which children explore liquid buoyancy and discusses how an AI-supported, observation-based assessment system can support developmentally appropriate evaluation in early childhood science.

Chapter 4 synthesises emerging challenges and opportunities related to artificial intelligence literacy in Early Childhood Education (ECE). Findings were grouped according to their implications for ECE experiences, curriculum development, and responsible classroom practice, as guided by the emerging use of Artificial Intelligence literacy models for young learners.

Chapter 5 investigates the extent to which students use generative AI tools (GenAI) to support their learning within a university-level mechatronics course and highlights connections between GenAI usage and students' approaches to project-based engineering learning. This analysis includes students' self-assessments of the perceived relationship between GenAI use and computational thinking (CT), indicating a neutral effect of GenAI use on CT skill development.

Chapter 6 uses a mixed-methods approach to examine how various factors shape Moroccan higher education faculty members' use of GenAI tools. The study includes both quantitative (large-sample) and qualitative data and applies predictive machine learning and structural equation modelling to complement the survey results. In addition, interview data help identify key characteristics that affect an instructor's willingness and ability to adopt GenAI tools, informing recommendations for institutional support and professional development.

Chapter 7 focuses on how GenAI has the potential to enhance pedagogy regarding educating about climate change. The chapter addresses how climate literacy, learner engagement, and various pedagogical methods - such as storytelling, personalisation, and participatory learning - can be employed to increase engagement with learners in both formal and informal settings.

Chapter 8 describes how GenAI can support the long-term development of climate change education in STEM, including engineering and science disciplines. The chapter discusses AI-enabled simulations, adaptive learning supports, and creative content generation (e.g., narratives and activities) as approaches for strengthening climate literacy, sustainability-oriented problem-solving, and learner engagement, while also considering the ethical and equity implications of implementation.

CONCLUSION

With this edited book coming to an end, we have reviewed all the perspectives, methodologies, and ideas from the various authors who contributed to the research on Generative Artificial Intelligence (GenAI) in education, specifically in relation to the STEM disciplines and sciences. All of the chapters indicate that GenAI is NOT a neutral technology or a single solution; instead, the value of GenAI as an educational tool is dependent upon the design of the tool to fit the intended use and the thoughtful and critical ways in which it is used to support the pedagogical goals of teaching and learning.

The findings presented within the pages of this text show that GenAI can help to enhance science education by adding value to the inquiry processes, increasing student interest and engagement, creating developmentally appropriate approaches that utilise narrative and multimodal formats, improving the way assessment and feedback are provided, and creating additional avenues to educate about climate change and sustainability. However, as evidenced through these findings, there should be a great deal of caution when adopting GenAI without effort and attention to ethical considerations, equitable accessibility, and privacy for all users of the technology, as well as with regard to the validity of assessments and evaluations of learning outcomes based solely upon the implementation of GenAI.

This volume contributes to closing the gap between theory and practice through examples of how practitioners at different levels have incorporated the benefits of evidence-based decision-making into their everyday practice through implementation and critical analysis of existing research in early childhood education, home-based parent-child interaction, and post-secondary education settings, thereby providing practitioners with evidence-based examples of what is available in practical application, including both strengths and limitations of evidence-based decision-making methods. The contradictory findings identified in this volume create a space for more advanced dialogue about the application of GenAI alongside practitioner-developed, evidence-based practices.

Additionally, this volume provides insight into the potential future direction of research and practice. Given the rapid pace at which GenAI technology develops, there is an immediate need for longitudinal studies and research that combine design-thinking with representatives from various disciplines; longitudinal studies will help to capture how GenAI technologies influence scientists' thinking, changes in practice over time, as well as, ultimately, what GenAI tools will lead to in terms of increased success and improvement in student learning outcomes. Furthermore, the need for ongoing development of ethical frameworks, professional development models, and institutional policies governing the proper use of GenAI technologies across all contexts remains a priority, especially in early childhood education, the parent-child relationship, and educational decision-making.

The chapters in this book conclude that actual transformative change will occur only when GenAI is integrated into learning environments that reflect the importance of 3 core tenets — inquiry, equity, and human agency. We hope this book serves as both a reference and a starting point for establishing meaningful conversations, partnerships, and innovative approaches to continue developing education as we move toward an increasingly AI-integrated global society.

ADDITIONAL READING

Kalogiannakis, M., & Sotiropoulos, D. (Eds.). (2026). *Harnessing Generative Artificial Intelligence for Science Education*. IGI Global Scientific Publishing., https://doi.org/10.4018/979-8-3373-2913-0

Kalogiannakis, M., Papakonstantinou, N., & Sotiropoulos, D. (2025). From Support Tool to Learning Partner: A Systematic Review of GenAI Integration in University Science Labs. *Creative Education, 16*, 1364–1401. https://doi.org/10.4236/ce.2025.169083

Meletiou-Mavrotheris, M., & Sotiropoulos, D. (2025). Educator Perspectives on AI in STEAM Education: Insights from a Four-Semester Study in a Graduate Level Teacher Education Course. In: A. Garfield, K. Gamage, K. & N. Gordon (Eds.), *Proceedings of the 6th International Conference on Education Development and Studies 2025. ICEDS 2025. Lecture Notes in Educational Technology*. Springer, Singapore. https://doi.org/10.1007/978-981-95-5234-4_20

Sotiropoulos, D., Raikou, N., & Kalogiannakis, M. (2025). Views of future Special Education teachers on teaching Natural Sciences during Practicum. *Review of Science. Mathematics and ICT Education, 19*(2), 137–159. https://doi.org/10.26220/rev.5423

Sotiropoulos, D., Xenakis, C., Xenakis, A., & Kalogiannakis, M. (2026). GenAI and Ancient Greek Natural Philosophy: Exploring the Foundations of Science Concepts Through Interactive Dialogues. In Kalogiannakis, M., & Sotiropoulos, D. (Eds.), *Harnessing Generative Artificial Intelligence for Science Education* (pp. 69–102). IGI Global Scientific Publishing., https://doi.org/10.4018/979-8-3373-2913-0.ch003

Sotiropoulos, D., & Kalogiannakis, M. (2025). Using GenAI Tools to Enhance Teaching and Learning in Science. In *Proceedings of the 14th Hybrid Edition of the International Conference New Perspectives in Science Education*, 293-301, Italy-Florence: Filodiritto-Pixel, 19-21 March 2025, https://doi.org/10.26352/L319_2420-9732

Sotiropoulos, D., & Meletiou-Mavrotheris, M. (2025). Postgraduate student teachers' perspectives concerning AI and its integration into STEAM teaching and learning. In Papadakis, S. (Ed.), *AI roles and responsibilities in education* (pp. 3–21). Springer., http://doi.org/10.1007/978-3-031-96855-6_1

Spasopoulos, T., Sotiropoulos, D., & Kalogiannakis, M. (2025). Generative AI in Pre-Service Science Teacher Education: A Systematic Review. *Advances in Mobile Learning Educational Research, 5*(2), 1501–1523. https://doi.org/10.25082/AMLER.2025.02.007

Uğraş, H., Uğraş, M., Papadakis, S., & Kalogiannakis, M. (2025). Innovative early childhood STEM education with ChatGPT: Teacher perspectives. Technology. *Knowledge and Learning*, *30*(2), 809–831. https://doi.org/10.1007/s10758-024-09804-8

Uğraş, M., Çakır, Z., Zacharis, G., & Kalogiannakis, M. (2025). ChatGPT in Early Childhood Science Education: Can It Offer Innovative Effective Solutions to Overcome Challenges? *Computers*, *14*(9), 368. https://doi.org/10.3390/computers14090368

Xenakis, A., Dimos, I., Feidakis, M., Sotiropoulos, D., Kalovrektis, K., & Nikolaou, G. (2025). An LLM-based smart repository platform to support educators with computational thinking, AI, and STEM activities. In *Empowering STEM educators with digital tools* (pp. 107–136). IGI Global Scientific Publishing., http://dx.doi.org/10.4018/979-8-3693-9806-7.ch005

Chapter 1
AI-Powered Storytelling App for Preschool Parent-Child Interaction Development Process and Parent-Child Perspectives

Ali İbrahim Can Gözüm
https://orcid.org/0000-0002-7765-4403
Kafkas University, Turkey

Nalan Özbey
https://orcid.org/0000-0001-7849-5689
Dede Korkut Faculty of Education, Kafkas University, Turkey

ABSTRACT

This study used a Design-Based Research (DBR) approach to develop and evaluate a generative AI-powered digital story app for young children and their parents. DBR integrates iterative design, implementation, evaluation, and redesign of educational interventions in real settings. The study aimed to digitalize story creation to support cognitive, affective, and language development, enhance parent-child interaction, and explore AI's educational potential. Five phases were conducted: literature review, prototype design with text/voice commands and personalized story generation, pilot testing with preschoolers aged 4–5 and parents, qualitative feedback analysis, and final re-implementation. Data from interviews and observations focused on usability, engagement, and developmental outcomes. Participants were purposively selected

DOI: 10.4018/979-8-3373-9074-1.ch001

from a public preschool in eastern Turkey, with ethical measures ensuring confidentiality. Findings highlighted children's creative story generation and parents' views of AI-supported storytelling as an educational tool.

1. INTRODUCTION

The growing exposure of children to digital environments from an early age has significantly expanded both the risks and opportunities associated with technology use in family life. As digital tools become increasingly integrated into children's daily routines, there is a growing need for families not only to protect their children from potentially harmful content but also to guide their digital practices through active mediation and meaningful co-engagement (Churchill, 2016; Gözüm, 2022; Hobbs, 2017). Especially in the preschool period-when the foundations for cognitive, social, and emotional development are being established-strengthening child-parent communication through collaborative digital experiences holds transformative potential (Pahl, 2011; Vasalou, Kalantari, Kucirkova, & Vezzoli, 2020).

Digital storytelling technologies (DSTs), which combine multimodal and multimedia elements such as text, image, sound, and video (Agnese et al., 2020), offer promising avenues for such engagement. These platforms foster digital literacy, narrative thinking and emotional expression through a non-linear, child-centered learning process often described as a "spiral of empowerment" (Churchill, 2016; Hobbs, 2017). When co-designed and co-experienced by families, such tools can facilitate self-expression, support family identity construction and transform how children and parents view each other (Bruner, 2003; Liaqat, Axtell, & Munteanu, 2021).

In light of this, the present study introduces a generative artificial intelligence (GenAI)-powered digital story creation application designed specifically to support parental mediation strategies and foster collaborative engagement between children and parents. The application enables users to create personalized narratives based on co-selected characters, settings, and temporal structures. It integrates science-based content aligned with national preschool curricula, targeting the development of children's early scientific reasoning, inquiry skills, and conceptual understanding. Importantly, the design process was informed by early childhood education experts to ensure pedagogical alignment with age-appropriate developmental and cognitive benchmarks (Rubegni & Landoni, 2014; Gözüm,2022).

The primary aim of this research is twofold: (1) to document the design process of the GenAI-powered story creation application and (2) to explore parent and child perspectives on its educational, emotional and technological affordances. Through structured interviews and task-based interactions, the study investigates how the application supports digital literacy, parental mediation, child engagement, and concept learning in science (Gözüm & Kandır, 2021; Gözüm, 2022). Prior work has shown that children benefit cognitively, socially, and emotionally when engaged in collaborative digital storytelling experiences (Di Blas et al., 2010; Rutta et al., 2020), yet relatively few studies have examined these dynamics in the home setting or within early childhood populations.

Initial findings indicate that parents appreciated the app's capacity to promote guided technology use, support shared storytelling experiences, and foster their children's curiosity about scientific topics. Children reported the app as fun, creative, and empowering—particularly valuing the opportunity to shape their own stories and interact with their parents during the process. As research in DST increasingly emphasizes the importance of child agency and meaningful parent involvement (Vasalou et al., 2020), this study contributes to a growing body of evidence supporting the home-based, co-constructive use of digital storytelling tools in early education.

Within the scope of the study, ethical issues such as children's data privacy, algorithmic bias, and age-appropriate content moderation were taken into consideration; the aim was to create a safe digital environment under the guidance of parents.

The findings suggest that GenAI-powered interactive storytelling platforms can serve as both developmental and relational assets for families with preschool-aged children. The implications extend beyond individual learning outcomes to include broader considerations for the design of inclusive, engaging, and educationally robust digital tools for early childhood.

2. LITERATURE REVIEW

2.1 Generative Artificial Intelligence

Artificial intelligence is one of the most important tools that transform educational practices by creating revolutionary changes in the field of education, become dynamic in the teaching and learning process, and are used to meet the changing needs of contemporary education.

Artificial intelligence, coined in 1956, has since been an attempt to understand how a machine can simulate intelligent human behavior or intelligence (Oliveira, 2017). AI encompasses not only machine learning and data processing but also complex problem-solving and decision-making capabilities, encompassing terms such as algorithms, data mining, and neural networks, demonstrating intelligence (Baker et al., 2019; Moya et al., 2023; Zawacki-Richter et al., 2019). Since its inception, artificial intelligence has experienced significant growth with advances in artificial neural networks and deep learning, and after 2022, a field of artificial intelligence called generative artificial intelligence (GenAI) has emerged, which uses deep learning models to predict and combine large datasets, learning patterns, and sequences to generate new content in the form of images, text, audio or other formats (Hashmi & Bal, 2024; García-Peñalvo et al., n.d.; Lim et al., 2023; Martineau, 2021; Muller et al., 2022). Representing a significant advancement in artificial intelligence technology, genAI is one of the most transformative technologies of the digital age, characterized by its ability to create original content from large amounts of data. This feature has generated significant interest, especially in the education sector (Cordero et al., 2025) and people have speculated that genAI could lead to the evolution of the education system (Firat, 2023). To this end, GenAI has begun to be integrated into education as it generates content based on patterns learned from training data, fostering a student-based learning paradigm that can significantly enhance both teaching and learning experiences.

2.2 Generative Artificial Intelligence in Early Childhood Education

Early childhood education is one of the educational levels where genAI technology is being integrated. GenAI has rapidly emerged as a powerful tool for transforming educational practices, particularly in early childhood education (Harrison & Shazaad, 2025). However, because AI curricula for young children were designed in recent years, they have still not been sufficiently researched in early childhood education (Kanders et al., 2024; Su et al., 2023; Yu et al., 2025). According to Edwards (2023), those working in early childhood research and practice should not only be aware of the terminology but also consider the impact of new technologies and their integration with various knowledge and practices. Understanding how generative AI (GenAI) technology is used in practice and the opportunities for innovation and change it presents is crucial (Luo et al., 2024). Furthermore, teachers' integration of technology into educational processes will help students increase their technological literacy and minimize the challenges they may face in future educational settings (Kurniah et al., 2023). Integrating AI into educational environments, especially early childhood education, transforms traditional pedagogical methods and interactions within the classroom. AI technologies offer unprecedented opportunities for personalized learning, cognitive development and accessibility (Elbanna & Armstrong, 2024; Su & Yang, 2022, Wu, 2024).

In early childhood education, generative AI tools can be used to enhance and encourage instruction in various fields, including lecturing (using genAI tools to create personalized and interactive lessons tailored to students' level and interests), discussion and chat (using genAI tools to prompt questions and lead discussions, encouraging students' thinking and communication skills and providing feedback on students' answers, helping them think deeply), reading guidance (creating reading experiences for students through virtual reality and augmented reality technologies, increasing motivation and emotional awareness), practice (providing students with opportunities to practice in virtual and simulated environments), demonstration (helping students produce demonstrations and providing demonstration platforms and opportunities) and discovery (emphasizing students' learning and development through self-directed exploration and inquiry) (Zhao et al., 2024). Therefore, by using genAI tools that provide comprehensive learning experiences in early childhood, the learning experiences of children, whose cognitive abilities and learning styles differ greatly from those of adults, can be diversified and their development supported.

GenAI enables teachers to dynamically organize and customize instructional resources, contributing to the accurate and effective presentation of complex concepts, particularly for children. Capable of generating a wide range of engaging educational materials, from interactive simulations to personalized digital story content, GenAI can alleviate teachers' burdens on lesson preparation while also increasing overall teaching effectiveness (Chen, 2023; Guettala et al., 2024). Furthermore, GenAI supports teachers in adapting to curriculum changes and current learning standards, enabling them to produce digital story content aligned with existing curricula and appropriate for children's developmental levels (Yu & Guo, 2023). In this respect, AI-powered digital story creation applications can make teaching processes more flexible, interactive and child-centered. However, the accuracy and reliability of the content generated by GenAI models is a significant topic of discussion, especially in situations where information reliability is critical in education. GenAI's potential to occasionally produce false or misleading information necessitates meticulous content control and teacher guidance in digital story applications developed for children (Ansari et al., 2024).

Educators have begun using various pedagogical strategies to promote children's genAI literacy and enhance their learning experiences (Ng et al., 2022). One of these strategies is integrating interactive digital stories into the educational process using genAI technologies. The use of digital story creation in the classroom provides children with a personalized learning experience (Raffone, 2022) and contributes to the development of written expression, critical thinking and creative expression skills (Fang et al., 2023; Isaac et al., 2024; Nurlaela et al., 2022). Moreover, such practices support children's 21st-century skills (Isaacs et al., 2024; Niemi et al., 2019) and strengthen their motivation by increasing their digital literacy levels (Liu et al., 2018).

2.3 Generative Artificial Intelligence-Powered Digital Story Creation Application

GenAI can create personalized digital story content based on children's individual learning pace, needs and learning styles (Bura & Myakala, 2024; Chan & Hu, 2023). This allows the complexity and narrative pace of stories to be adjusted to suit the child's developmental level (Nguyen et al., 2019). Thus, GenAI technology enables the development of adaptable story creation application tailored to children's interests and learning needs.

These genAI-powered applicationlications make children's educational processes more effective by supporting their imagination and creative thinking skills (Kong & Yang, 2024). Furthermore, by simulating real-world concepts through digital stories, they help children reinforce theoretical knowledge with concrete experiences. Digital storytelling can be used as an important tool to deepen conceptual understanding, especially in STEM fields, at an early age (Cheng et al., 2024).

Digital story creation integrates language, communication and technology skills within an interdisciplinary approach, enabling children's literacy development within an inquiry-based pedagogical framework (Ng et al., 2022). In this context, GenAI-powered digital story creation stands out as a powerful teaching strategy that not only meets individual learning needs but also enables children to develop emotional connections and insights.

Because genAI models are trained on large datasets, they can generate contextual and meaningful stories, enabling educational content to be engaging and tailored to children's developmental characteristics (Vidrih & Myahi, 2023). GenAI-powered digital story creation experiences, particularly those offered in early childhood, support cognitive and emotional development, laying a solid foundation for children's future academic success (Chen, 2024). Furthermore, these child-oriented apps offer interactive and personalized learning environments, enabling educational opportunities that are adaptable to different developmental levels.

Another area where GenAI, which has a transformative impact in the educational context, is assessment. GenAI is used to evaluate teaching effectiveness by providing automated grading, providing detailed feedback, assessing children's understanding and engagement, ensuring academic integrity, and helping to grade assignments more efficiently (Holmes et al., 2022; Huang et al., 2023; Luckin, 2017). Therefore, thanks to the assessment tools offered by GenAI, teachers and parents can monitor children's cognitive development, learning differences, strengths and areas for improvement through diagnostic, formative and summative assessments. These assessment processes can also be used in genAI-powered digital story creation applications, contributing to the delivery of developmentally appropriate content and enriching learning experiences for children.

A review of the literature reveals that digital story creation is being used as a pedagogical tool to improve artificial intelligence literacy among primary school students (Ng et al., 2022; Wu & Chen, 2020). Another study conducted at the primary school level investigated the benefits that GenAI systems could offer to teachers and students (Han et al., 2024). The intersection of genAI tools and digital story creation in the context of teaching English as a foreign language at different educational levels has been examined (Belda-Medina & Goddard, 2024; Cheung & Shi, 2025) and the relationships between GenAI strategies and the development of 21st-century skills have been analyzed (Chen, 2024; Cheung & Shi, 2025; Isaacs et al., 2024; Niemi et al., 2019; Yang et al., 2020). Additionally, various findings have been obtained on the effects of digital story projects on speaking proficiency (Al-Amri, 2020; Harji & Gheitanchian, 2017; Yang et al., 2020) and the potential advantages and limitations of digital story creation with GenAI at different educational levels (Chen, 2024; Fang et al., 2023; Han et al., 2023). Furthermore, "AI for children" curriculums have been developed to help young children learn about AI (Yang, 2022) and potential use cases, opportunities and risks related to the implementation of genAI in early childhood have been discussed (Kander et al., 2024).

However, considering the developmental needs of children in early childhood and how GenAI can transform early education experiences, there are limited studies in the literature on how these tools can complement or integrate into existing pedagogical practices. Furthermore, research addressing the potential impact of GenAI tools on parent-child interaction processes is also lacking.

This study aims to bridge the gap between technology and education. It examines the development process of an genAI-powered digital story creation application developed by researchers to clarify how generative AI technologies can be adapted through digital story creation applications for children in early childhood, how these tools can contribute to children's development, and how they can strengthen parent-child interactions. Indeed, during the development of this tool, the suitability of the application for its intended purpose was discussed, as well as the parent-child interaction itself. In this context, the application developed with parents and children was first examined to determine its true educational applicability.

2.4. Generative Artificial Intelligence and Ethical Issues

The transformative opportunities offered by Generative Artificial Intelligence (GAI) in the field of education also bring along significant ethical issues that need to be carefully managed, especially in a developmentally critical stage such as the preschool period. Systematic reviews conducted in recent years show that in AI applications for preschool children, fundamental risks such as data privacy, algorithmic bias, developmental appropriateness, and content safety stand out (Tırpan,

2024). These studies reveal that among ethical principles, the theme of "equality and justice" is most frequently emphasized; whereas the principles of "solidarity" and "dignity" are addressed in a more limited manner. This situation shows that ethical frameworks regarding the use of GAI in early childhood education have not yet fully matured.

In this context, the main ethical issues that could be encountered specifically in our GAI-assisted digital storytelling application and solution suggestions can be evaluated as follows:

Preschool children are one of the most vulnerable groups in the context of digital data protection. Digital storytelling applications often collect sensitive information such as children's voice recordings, the stories they create, and usage data. Although regulations like GDPR partially provide protection, they do not fully meet the unique needs of the early childhood context (Berson et al., 2025). The fact that children do not have the capacity to cognitively comprehend data use or give consent requires developers to meticulously implement measures such as transparent data policies, data minimization, and parental consent. GAI models can unintentionally reproduce cultural or societal biases due to the limitations of the datasets they are trained on. This situation can lead to the formation of characters or plotlines that reinforce stereotypes in storytelling applications (Tırpan, 2024). To reduce this risk, which could have negative effects on identity formation in early childhood, it is important to observe the principles of diversity, inclusivity, and cultural sensitivity from the design process of the application onwards. Furthermore, it is necessary for the generated content to be regularly audited.

In the preschool period, learning occurs largely through social interaction, sensory experience, and imaginative play. Therefore, it is important that GAI tools are positioned not in a way that reduces children's human interactions, but in a way that supports them. An application design that encourages parent-child interactions through joint media engagement will be healthier from both pedagogical and relational perspectives (Su et al., 2023). Additionally, it is an important ethical principle for the application to support children's creativity but not restrict their imagination. GAI carries the risk of producing unpredictable or age-inappropriate content. Existing regulatory frameworks can be fragmented and insufficient in the face of rapid technological developments in this regard (Berson et al., 2025). Therefore, it is necessary for the application to include multi-layered content filtering mechanisms, parental controls, and human-supervised approval processes.

Screen time balance is important in terms of maintaining the balance between the developmental benefits of digital tools and traditional learning experiences such as physical activity, face-to-face social interaction, and imaginative play. Parent-child co-use and mediated engagement play a key role in achieving this balance (Gözüm, 2022).

In this context, it is of great importance that AI applications designed for preschool children are developed within an ethical framework, a child-centered approach is adopted, and parents' active participation in the process is ensured. Future studies should develop comprehensive solution suggestions for these ethical problems and examine long-term developmental effects.

3. METHOD

3.1. Research Design

This study employed a Design-Based Research (DBR) design to examine and develop the use of an genAI-powered digital story creation application with children and parents in early childhood. The DBR approach is a method that focuses on the design, implementation, evaluation and iterative development of an educational product or intervention in real-life contexts, aiming to bridge the gap between practice and theory (Design-Based Research Collective, 2003).

Design-Based Research (DBR) is a flexible and collaborative research approach that aims to develop, implement, evaluate, and cyclically redesign innovative interventions in educational practices in real-life contexts (Anderson & Shattuck, 2012, p. 17). The DBR approach also incorporates mixed-method features, allowing for the combined use of various data collection tools and analysis techniques.

Figure 1. Design-based research

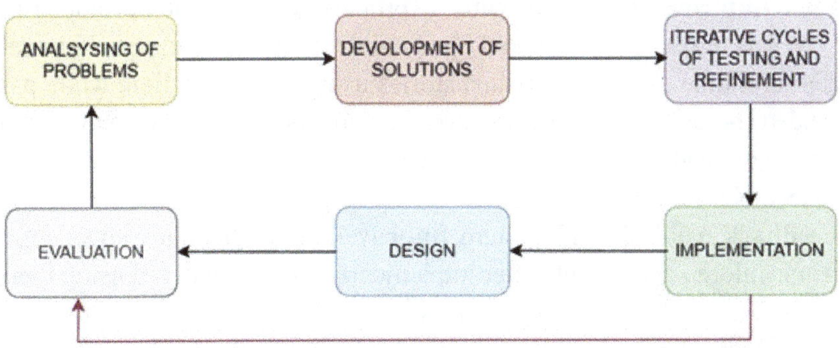

According to Figure 1, DBR requires the holistic and interactive execution of the analysis, design, implementation, evaluation, and redesign phases of an intervention developed to solve an educational problem (Wang & Hannafin, 2005).

In this study, the DBR approach was chosen to develop a generative AI-supported digital story creation application and to evaluate its usability with children and their parents in early childhood. The primary motivation for this study is to digitalize story creation processes to support the cognitive, affective and language development of early-age children, strengthen parent-child interactions and investigate the pedagogical applicability of GenAI technology.

This research was conducted within the framework of the Design-Based Research (DBR) approach, in the following five phases (Design-Based Research Collective, 2003; Anderson & Shattuck, 2012):

- **Literature Review and Creation of the Theoretical Framework:** A comprehensive literature review was conducted in the areas of storytelling in early childhood, generative AI applications, digital literacy, child-parent interaction and personalized learning (Kaptan & Çakır, 2025; Su, Ng, & Chu, 2023; Sun et al., 2024). A review of the literature revealed that studies on the pedagogical functions of generative AI tools, particularly in early childhood, are limited (Kaptan & Çakır, 2025).
- **Application Design and Prototype Development:** In line with theoretical insights obtained from the literature, a GenAI-powered digital story creation application was designed, featuring features such as voice commands, concept identification, character selection, a test module and personalized story generation. Care was taken to ensure that the application was user-friendly, interactive and developmentally appropriate (Sun et al., 2024).
- **Pilot Implementation and Initial Data Collection:** The developed prototype was tested with preschool-aged children and their parents in a real-life setting (home). Children created stories using the application, while parents guided the process. Data collection was conducted through semi-structured interviews and direct observation forms covering child and parent experiences (Su, Ng, & Chu, 2023).
- **Feedback Analysis and System Improvements:** Qualitative data collected from children and parents after implementation was analyzed using thematic analysis. Based on user experiences, suggestions such as increasing character variety, adding read-alouds to the test module and incorporating musical feedback were integrated into the system, and technical and pedagogical improvements were made (Anderson & Shattuck, 2012).
- **Re-Implementation of the Revised Application and Final Evaluation:** The updated applicaton was implemented with a second group of users, and

child and parent feedback was collected again. In this phase, children's learning motivation, attitudes toward the application and parents' assessments of the app's developmental contributions were analyzed. Additionally, the system's capacity to strengthen parent-child interaction, support creativity and provide personalized learning experiences has been extensively evaluated (Kaptan & Çakır, 2025; Su, Ng, & Chu, 2023; Sun et al., 2024).

3.2. Participants

The participants in this study consisted of four parents and four children actively involved in a Design-Based Research (DBR) process. Participants were selected through a purposive sampling method from among children and their parents attending a public preschool in eastern Turkey during the spring semester of the 2024-2025 academic year (Yıldırım & Şimşek, 2013).

The selection of participating parents was based on volunteering. Criteria included their openness and interest in technological tools, their ability to interact with their children at a level that allows for digital content creation, and their willingness and time to actively participate in the research process. The child participants were in the 4-5 age group, encompassing children with the developmental capacity to actively participate in the digital story creation process and generate creative ideas.

During the research process, parents and children jointly experienced a digital story creation application developed with generative artificial intelligence technology. During the story creation process, different sections of the application (home page, story plot, character addition, concepts to be taught, and test module) were explored together. Following the implementation, data were collected from both parents and children through semi-structured interviews. Children's opinions were collected within the framework of pedagogical research ethics, using age-appropriate question formats and a game-based interview environment (Patton, 2015).

The children's identities were kept confidential and informed consent forms were obtained from parents in accordance with ethical guidelines. The research was structured to understand both how children interact with a genAI-powered application and how parents experience this process (Yıldırım & Şimşek, 2013).

The participant profile provided a rich and holistic context for evaluating the application's developmental appropriateness, ease of use, pedagogical contributions and aspects that support parent-child interaction. In this context, the research provided insights into children's creative story creation processes, as well as parents' attitudes and evaluations toward digital tools and comprehensive analysis was conducted.

Within the scope of the research's ethical dimensions, the data security of child participants was ensured, the application content was filtered to be age-appropriate, and the active participation of parents in the process was encouraged.

3.3. Development of a Generative Artificial Intelligence-Powered Digital Story Application

In this research, an genAI-powered digital story creation application was developed to support children's cognitive, affective and language development in early childhood and to strengthen parent-child interactions. The application utilizes genAI technologies to generate personalized stories guided by children and includes various interactive components such as voice commands, character selection, concept identification and quiz sections.

The application development process was multi-stage, practical and feedback-oriented, in accordance with the principles of the Design-Based Research (DBR) approach. The technological infrastructures used in the development process are as follows:

- Interactive web-based user interfaces developed using HTML, CSS, and JavaScript;
- SQL-based data management systems for secure and systematic storage of user input.

The digital story creation process consists of four basic design components: 1) User management system 2) Digital story creation criteria selection interface 3) Digital story reading or audio listening interface and 4) Evaluation.

1. **User management system:** This section contains the user's membership information, favorite digital stories and evaluations.
2. **Digital story creation criteria selection interface:** This interface includes entering a digital story plot (written and audio), selecting characters or adding special characters, selecting the concepts to be covered within the story, which are the learning outcomes of the digital story, and creating a digital story by specifying the story length (short, medium, long) and language level (easy, intermediate).
3. **Digital story reading, audio listening and downloading interface:** This section allows the parent or program to read the digital story created with the generative artificial intelligence program to the child. The digital story creation program is integrated with generative artificial intelligence and generative artificial intelligence designs a digital story based on criteria determined by the parent and child. This designed digital story can be read aloud to the child by the parent or if the child's literacy level is considered low, it can be read aloud by the genAI tool. There is also an option to download it for rereading at different times.

4. **Evaluation:** This is the evaluation phase of the story read to the child by the parent or the genAI program. During the evaluation phase, the child answers 10 multiple-choice questions related to the story generated by the genAI. Feedback is then provided on the answers, aiming to help the child acquire the concepts identified at the outset as the learning outcome.

The app's genAI infrastructure can transform children's words into contextually relevant and developmentally meaningful narratives, providing a learning environment that is both educational and interactive during the story-writing process conducted with parents.

Throughout the development process, the application prioritized:

- Designing for children's ages,
- Offering flexibility for independent use with parental guidance,
- Supporting language development, conceptual learning, and creativity,
- Increasing accessibility with audio guidance, visual support, and a simple interface.

The application was revised based on parent and child feedback from the pilot studies, particularly by increasing the variety of characters and concepts in the user interface and adding music to the homepage and audio to the buttons. This digital story creation application tool has become an innovative application that allows young children to interact with genAI to create creative content, engage in shared digital experiences with their parents, and create personalized learning scenarios that support their literacy development.

3.4. Data Collection Tools

This study used two different data collection tools to comprehensively examine the use experiences and interaction processes of an genAI-powered digital story creation application by children and parents:

1. **Observation Form:** A structured observation form, developed by the researchers, was used to systematically record parents' behaviors, interaction styles and in-app reactions while using the application with their children. This form focuses on criteria such as how children use the application, parents' level of guidance and collaboration within the application.
2. **Semi-Structured Interview Form:** The semi-structured interview form, used in one-on-one interviews with parents after the application, aimed to provide an in-depth exploration of participants' opinions about the application, their

challenges, positive experiences and suggestions. The interview form consisted of open-ended questions and its flexible structure allowed for the discovery of specific details about the participants' experiences.

3.5. Validity and Reliability of Data Collection Tools

Various methods were adopted to ensure the validity and reliability of the data collection tools used in the study.

To ensure the content validity of the data collection tools, the form and interview questions were sent to three academics with expertise in the relevant field, and necessary corrections and improvements were made based on expert opinions (Yıldırım & Şimşek, 2013). Furthermore, the observation form and interview form items were prepared based on a literature review in the fields of early childhood education, digital learning tools, and generative artificial intelligence applications. Preliminary data collected during the pilot study were analyzed to assess the items' suitability and clarity and revisions were made if necessary (Miles & Huberman, 1994). These processes supported the content and face validity of the tools (Lincoln & Guba, 1985).

To increase the reliability of the observation form, inter-coder reliability was ensured among the researchers. Twenty percent of the observational data collected in the study was independently coded by two researchers and the agreement between the coding results was measured using Cohen's Kappa. The Kappa value obtained was found to be 0.85, indicating a high level of reliability (Miles & Huberman, 1994).

To ensure the reliability of the interview data, the interview recordings were fully transcribed and analyzed separately by two researchers. Coding schemes were compared during the analysis process and agreement was reached on potential differences. Furthermore, interview summaries were shared with the participants and the accuracy of their statements was verified (member checking) (Lincoln & Guba, 1985).

Finally, screenshots were supplemented with triangulation to ensure the mutual accuracy of information obtained from different data sources, thus strengthening the internal validity of the study (Patton, 2015). This holistic approach allowed the data collection tools used in the study to collect both valid and reliable data.

4. FINDINGS

Face-to-face interviews were conducted to gather child and parent feedback regarding the development of a generative AI-powered digital story creation application designed to strengthen parent-child interaction in the preschool period.

Children were coded as C1, C2, C3, and C4, while parents were coded as E1, E2, E3, and E4. The app's interface, developed based on data obtained from children and parents during the app's development process, is as follows:

4.1 Findings Regarding the "Home Page" of the Story Creation Application

The responses of children and parents to the first question, "How did you find the "home page" of the story creation application?", were analyzed under categories, subcategories, and codes, and the findings are shown in Table 1.

Table 1. Findings regarding the "home page" of the story creation application

Category	Subcategory	Codes	Participants
Design	Visuality	The photo is beautiful	C1, C3, C4, E4
		The photo is realistic	E1
		Liking the colors	C1, C4, E1
		Liking the toys in the photo	C1
		Liking the colors of the buttons	C2
		Liking the shapes of the buttons	C2,
	Button interactivity and usability	The buttons are eye-catching	C2
		The buttons are easy to use	E4
		The buttons are functional	E2, E4
Emotional Responses	Interest and likeability	Fun	C2, C3
		Wanting to write a story right away	C3, C4
	Access	Wanting to log in to the app every day	C1
Recommendation	Music	Background music	C4
	Sound	Button sounds	C2
	Vibrantness	Moving objects	E3

As seen in Table 1, three of the children said they liked the background photo and two said they loved the colors. Two children found the page entertaining, and two said they wanted to write a story right away. In addition, one child each liked the toy picture and the button colors and shapes, respectively. They found the buttons eye-catching and wanted to access the application every day. Two children suggested that the background of the page should include music and sounds on the buttons. One parent found the photo on the homepage appealing, one said the photo was realistic and one liked the colors. One parent stated that the buttons on the page were functional. One parent also suggested that the page include animated objects. An examination of Table 1 indicates that children and parents generally liked the app's homepage. Some of the statements children and parents made about the app's homepage are as follows:

"The cover page of this program is beautiful, I loved it. I really liked the colors. There are also toys on the page. Can I open this page every day?" (C1)

"The buttons are like candy; there were buttons shaped like stars and hearts, and I pressed them right away. It was so fun. But I wish the buttons would play sounds when I pressed them." (C2)

"When my mom opened this page, the picture in front of me was beautiful. There are children like me who live with their mothers; they are so sweet. The page is so fun. Can I write a story right away?" (C3)

"I was so happy when I saw the page. The colors and the photos were beautiful and I wanted to write a story right away. I wish the page also played children's music." (C4)

"The colors on the home page are beautiful and the pictures are so realistic." (E1)

"When you click the buttons on the page, the corresponding pages immediately open." (E2)

"There could have been moving objects on the home page. This would have attracted children's attention more." (E3)

"The photo on the page perfectly matches the program. Furthermore, all the buttons on the homepage are very easy to use and serve their purpose." (E4)

Based on interviews with children and parents, findings from the homepage were reviewed and adjustments were made to the story creation application homepage. The interface of the digital story creation application for children consists of a title, login, sign up, favorites, leaderboard and create story buttons (Figure 2).

Figure 2. Digital story creation application interface

The user first clicks the "Sign Up" button and becomes a member by entering their membership information. Then, they click the "Log In" button to log in to the system with their email address and password (Figure 3).

Figure 3. User membership and app login interface

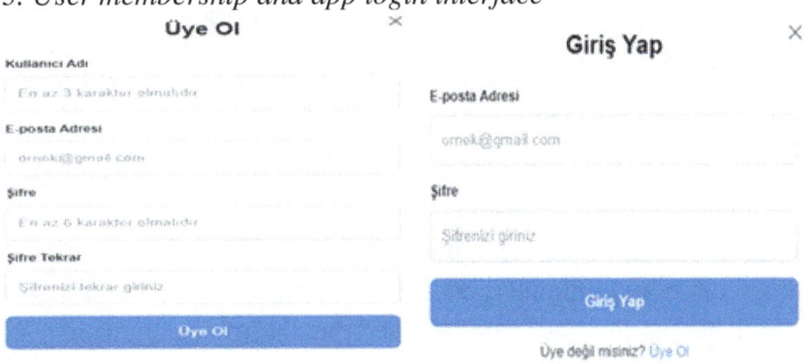

After logging in to the system with their membership information, the user is presented with a story creation interface consisting of six sections. The first section of the app is "Story Plot Entry".

4.2 Findings From the "Story Plot Entry " Section of the Story Creation App

The responses of children and parents to the second question, "What do you think about the story plot entry section of the story creation app?" are categorized, subcategorized, and coded. The findings are shown in Table 2.

Table 2. Findings from the "story plot entry" section of the story creation app

Category	Subcategory	Codes	Participants
User Experience and Ease of Use	Written expression	Mother's use of the keyboard	C1, C2, C3,
		No problems with writing	E4
	Voice expression	Child uses the microphone	C1,C3, C4
		Child and parent use the microphone together	C2
	Independent use	Can be used without a parent	C4
	Voice commands	Ease of using the microphone	E1, E2, E3, E4
		Advantage due to lack of literacy	E1
	Error-free operation	No errors in written and spoken use	C2, E2
	Simple interface	Simple interface	E4
Emotional Response	Entertainment and enjoyment	Fun app	C1, C2, E3
	Excitement and appreciation	Exciting app	E3
Request	Desire to participate	Child's desire to use the app	C1, C3

As seen in Table 2, three of the children stated that their mothers used the keyboard, three used the microphone themselves and one story plot entry using voice commands with her parent. Four parents stated that the voice command feature was easy to use, one said it was advantageous due to low literacy levels and one parent said the interface was quite simple. One child said she could use it independently without a parent, two children and one parent said they enjoyed the app and one parent said it was exciting. Two children stated that their mothers generally wanted to use the app and expressed their desire to participate in the process. An examination of Table 2 suggests that both children and parents generally appreciated the story plot entry section of the app. Some of the statements made by children and parents regarding the story plot entry of the app are as follows:

"I told my mother to write but she writes very slowly and wouldn't let me write. Then we tried voice recording and I told her and my tablet recorded what I said. I really enjoyed it that way." (C1)

"I started the story and my mother wrote it. The next time we wrote a story, we used our voices. It was more enjoyable that way. My mother said she wrote exactly what I said. My computer is very smart." (C2)

"My mother wouldn't let me start telling the story. She creates and writes stories in her own head. Then I pressed the microphone and I started telling the story." (C3)

"I used this part very easily; I can create stories without my mother. I just pressed the microphone." (C4)

"The microphone recording feature is very nice. My reading and writing skills aren't very high, so I would have struggled." (E1)

"We used this part without any problems. I think the keyboard operation and voice command feature are very well thought out." (E2)

"I was so excited when I wrote the story's plot. Things like this didn't exist back then. I created the first two stories. I really enjoyed it. It was very easy to use." (E3)

"The story plot entry part was very simple and easy to use." (E4)

Based on interviews with children and parents, findings from the story plot entry section were reviewed and adjustments were made to the story-adding feature of the story creating app. Users can add an introductory section to a story using either the keyboard or voice commands (Figure 4).

Figure 4. Story plot entry interface

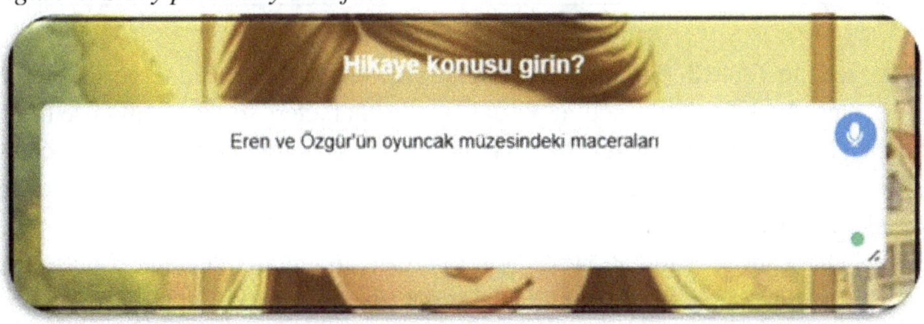

The second section of the story creation app is adding story characters.

4.3 Findings From the "Character Addition" Section of the Story Creation App

The responses of children and parents to the third question, "What do you think about the "character addition" section of the story creation app?", are analyzed under categories, subcategories and codes and the findings are shown in Table 3.

Table 3. Findings from the "character addition" section of the story creation app

Category	Subcategory	Codes	Participants
Interest in characters	Liking the characters	Wanting all characters to be included in the story	C1
		Finding the characters appealing	C1
	Number of characters	Wanting more characters	C2
Usability	Visual deficiencies	Adding visuals to characters for those who don't know how to read	C3
	Customization opportunities	Having a section for adding special characters	C4
	Error-free	The section for adding characters doesn't hinder use	E3, E4
Usage experience	Character placement	The added characters are included in the story	E1
	Number of characters	Allowing the addition of any number of characters	E1
Educational and emotional contribution	Real-life connection	The characters fit the child's life and foster emotional connection	E2

As seen in Table 3, one child liked the characters, and one said there should be more. One child suggested adding visuals to the characters so they could use them independently without a parent and one said it made sense to have a special character section. One parent stated that the desired number of characters were added and all the selected characters were included in the story. One parent stated that the special character addition allowed them to create an emotional connection to the story by adding characters related to real life. One child stated that there should be more characters and one child stated that visuals should be added to the characters so they could use them independently. When Table 3 is examined, it can be said that both children and parents generally liked the character addition of the app. Some of the statements made by children and parents regarding the character addition of the app are as follows:

"I wanted to choose all the characters. They're all so beautiful; I wanted them all." (C1)
"It would have been better if you added more characters because I couldn't think of them." (C2)
"My mom told me the characters and I chose the ones I wanted. But I wish those buttons had pictures on them so I could use them without my mom." (C3)
"It's good that we can add characters whenever we want. My mom and I added so many characters. Our story is going to be so beautiful." (C4)
"My son and I added so many characters to the story. We were so surprised that he included all the characters we added in the story." (E1)
"The fact that the characters were connected to his own life made him love the story so much. That's why adding characters made so much sense." (E2)
"We added characters very easily and without any problems. I read them and we decided together to create the characters." (E3)
"The add character and add special character buttons worked flawlessly." (E4)

Based on interviews with children and parents, findings from the character addition section were reviewed and adjustments were made to the story creating app's character addition feature. After entering the story plot into the app, the user selects the characters they want to include in the story or adds a character of their choice (Figure 5).

Figure 5. Interface for selecting characters to be included in the story

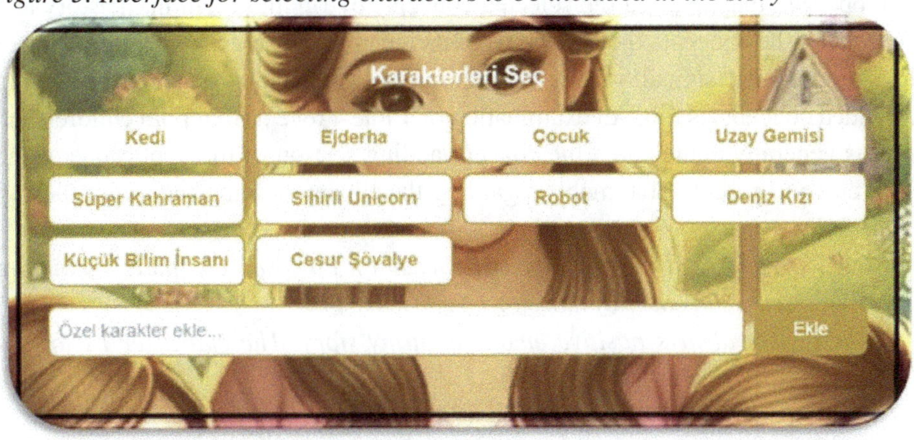

The concept list interface, which is included in the preschool curriculum and also covers the science field of this program, has been added to the story to be created in the third part of the application.

4.4 Findings From the "Concepts to be Taught" Section of the Story Creation Application

The responses of children and parents to the fourth question, "What do you think about the concepts to be taught in the story creation application?" are discussed under categories, subcategories and codes and the findings are shown in Table 4.

Table 4. Findings from the "concepts to be taught" section of the story creation app

Category	Subcategory	Codes	Participants
Educational contribution	Conceptual learning	Learning seasonal concepts through stories	C1
		Conceptualizing emotions	C2
	Concept discovery activity	Trying to find selected concepts in the story	C4
	Learning through fun	Learning concepts in a fun way	E1
	Surprise learning effect	Reflecting concepts in the story	E3
User experience	Layout of concepts	Including added concepts in the story	C3
	Additive design structure	Including the part where you add the desired concept	E2, E4

As seen in Table 4, two of the children learned the concepts of season and emotion, one said they learned the selected concepts by finding them in the story and one said all the concepts they added were included in the story. Two parents stated that the additive design allows for the addition of desired concepts and that learning the added concepts is fun. An examination of Table 4 reveals that both children and parents generally appreciated the concept-adding section of the app. Some of the children's and parents' statements regarding the concept-adding section of the app are as follows:

"I've learned about the seasons with this story. For example, there's a picture of summer on the cover of this story, right?" (C1)

"There were always positive emotions in my story. The character I chose, a unicorn, was always happy." (C2)

"All the concepts my mother and I chose were in my story." (C3)

"My mother wanted me to listen to the story carefully. She asked me to find the words we chose in the story. It was so much fun." (C4)

"We both had fun and learned." (E1)

"It made sense to have an addition section under each concept, just like the character addition section. But we were so excited that we immediately continued creating the story by selecting existing concepts." (E2)

"I didn't think the concepts we chose would actually make it into the story. I was really surprised and excited." (E3)

"It was great that we could add new concepts in addition to the existing concepts. My child got even more excited when we added concepts based on the characteristics of the characters we initially identified." (E4)

Based on interviews with children and parents, findings from the "concepts to be taught" section were reviewed, and adjustments were made to the "concepts to be taught" section of the story creation application. A concept list interface covering the science domain of the preschool curriculum was added to the story creation application (Figure 6).

Figure 6. Interface of concepts to be included in the story

The user will be able to select the concepts child wants to include in the story and learn by the child using the story creation application and will also be able to add the concept child wants to the concept category covering that area (Figure 7).

Figure 7. Example category interface in the concept list

The fourth section of the story is where the story's length and language level are adjusted. The story length is set at 250 characters for short stories, 500 for medium-length stories, and 750 for long stories (Figure 8).

Figure 8. The interface where the story settings are made.

After completing the story settings, click the "Story creation" button (Figure 9).

Figure 9. The story creation button

After clicking the "story create" button, the story creation application works in integration with generative artificial intelligence, enabling the genarative AI program to create a story according to specified criteria. After this stage, the fifth section of the story includes options such as "add to favorites" to add the created story to your favorites, "view story" to see the story created by the generative AI program on the screen, "listen to the story" voiced by the generative AI program, and "download story" to save the story (Figure 10).

Figure 10. The option interface for the created story

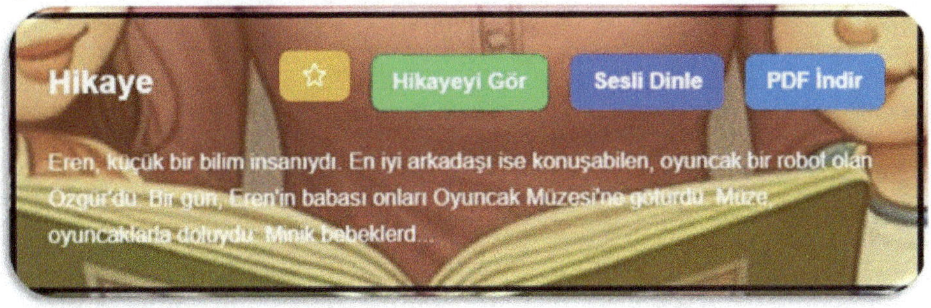

When the user clicks the star icon that represents their favorites, the stories created by the generative artificial intelligence program appear. In this sixth section of the story creation application, the user can give the story a name, rearrange it as desired, and take a quiz related to the story (Figure 11).

Figure 11. Interface of the story added to favorites

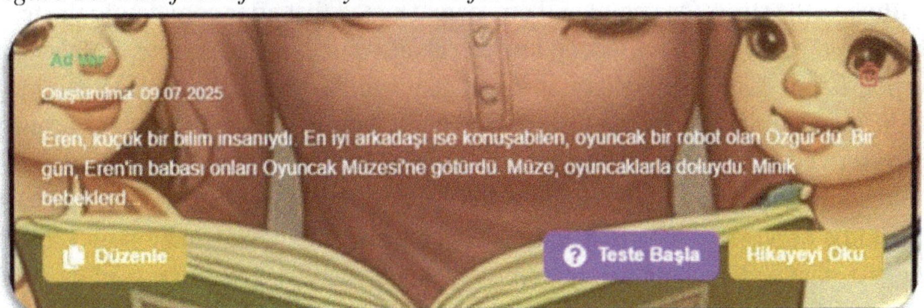

When the user clicks on the "My Favorites" option, there is a test section in the interface that appears.

4.5 Findings From the "Test" Section of the Story Creation App

The responses of children and parents to the fifth question, "What do you think about the test part of the story creation app?" are discussed under categories, subcategories and codes, and the findings are shown in Table 5.

Table 5. Findings from the "test" section of the story creation app

Category	Subcategory	Codes	Participants
Feedback	Gamification elements	Earning rewards for correct answers	C1
	Correct/incorrect indicator	Colorful display of correct and incorrect answers	E1
Accessibility	Statistical information	Comparison of correct and incorrect answers with solution time	C4, E2
Scope	Voice feedback suggestion	Adding audio for correct and incorrect answers	E4
	Independent use	Inability to answer the test without a parent's presence	C3
Emotional support	Test scope	Including test questions in the story	C2
Feedback	Positive response to failure	Maintaining motivation despite incorrect answers	E3

As seen in Table 5, one child stated that all the test questions were prepared according to the story. One child and one parent stated that after completing the test, they saw the number of correct and incorrect answers, the success rate, and the test response time. One parent also stated that displaying correct and incorrect answers in different colors was an advantage. One child, however, stated that child wanted the test to be audio-visual because child could not use it without a parent, and one child stated that rewards should be given for correct answers and audio feedback should be provided for correct and incorrect answers. An examination of Table 4 suggests that children and parents generally appreciated the test section of the app. Some of the statements made by children and parents regarding the test section of the app are as follows:

"It would have been better if we could have gotten balloons or candies or even characters when we answered the questions correctly." (C1)

"All the test questions at the end of the story I wrote were in the story itself, and they were very simple; I didn't have any trouble." (C2)

"I wish the test questions were audio; I couldn't read them without my mother." (C3)

"I solved the questions for my first story very quickly. I was so excited when I had time." (C4)

"It was great that it showed our mistakes in red when the test was completed. Otherwise, I would have had a hard time. Maybe my child wouldn't have learned the correct answer." (E1)

"The test showed the number of correct and incorrect answers. We also looked at the times to see which story took the shortest time to answer the questions." (E2)

"The story was so well-crafted and exciting that even my daughter's incorrect answers didn't upset her." (E3)

"Audio can be added to the tests for correct and incorrect answers. This way, children who can't read can more easily distinguish between correct and incorrect answers." (E4)

Based on interviews with children and parents, findings from the test section were reviewed, and adjustments were made to the story creation app's testing. After answering the test questions, the user sees the correct answers and also sees the correct answers for any incorrect answers. Furthermore, after answering, the time it took to complete the exam, the number of correct answers, and the success rate are analyzed (Figure 12).

Figure 12. Analysis of the solved test

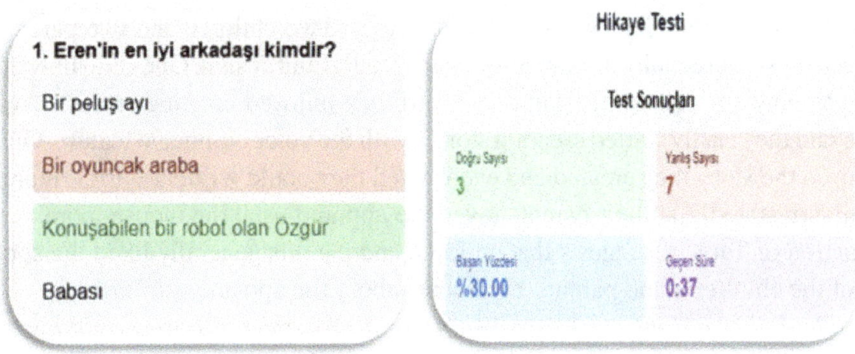

Finally, the child and parents were consulted regarding the overall story development process, and the final version of the process was developed accordingly.

4.6 Findings Regarding the Overall Story Creation App

The responses of children and parents to the sixth question, "Would you evaluate the story ceration app in general?" are presented in Table 6, broken down into categories, subcategories and codes.

Table 6. Findings regarding the overall story creation app

Category	Subcategory	Codes	Participants
Ease of use	Fast and simple use	Easy story creation	C1, C4, E3, E4
	Use of buttons	Ease of button use	E3
Fun and play	Game-like experience	Story creation is like a game	C2
Imagination and motivation	A writer's dream	Support for finding one's own story valuable and becoming a writer	C3
Family communication	Shared activity	Collaboration with parents	C3, C4, E3
Content and completeness	Reflection of story elements	Complete inclusion of added characters and concepts	E1, E2
Visual support	Background and design	Liking the background	C1,C3,E2,E3
Auditory support	Voice command suggestion	Advantage of audio storytelling	E1, E2
Parental control/ dominance	Parent's request for use	Parent's ability to guide the app more than the child	C3, C4

As seen in Table 6, the story creation app is easy and quick to use, fostering shared time and fostering family communication. Parents noted that the app's content accurately reflects the elements added to the story. Two children and two parents expressed their appreciation for the story's background and design. One child likened the app to playing a computer game and said they enjoyed creating stories. Two parents said they easily started creating stories with the voice command feature. One child loved the story they created and even stated they could write it. Furthermore, two children stated that their parents loved the app and used the mouse more. An examination of Table 6 suggests that children and parents generally liked the app. Some of the children's and parents' comments about the app are as follows:

"You told us about the story creation program. We created stories right away, easily. I loved this page and want to use it every day. The pictures are beautiful." (C1)

"It's like playing a game on the computer. Creating a story is like playing a game." (C2)

"The pictures on the page were beautiful. My mom and I made stories together and it was wonderful. I'm going to be a story writer when I grow up. I create wonderful stories. But my mom used it a lot. I want to use it too." (C3)

"I had a great time with my mom. The homepage was beautiful. We easily created beautiful and entertaining stories in a very short time. But I wish I had used the mouse more." (C4)

"Sounds can be added to the buttons in the program. It created a perfect story based on the concepts and characters we added. Audio storytelling is very advantageous for people with low literacy levels. The added characters were included in the story without any missing parts." (E1)

"I really liked the visuals of the program. There was a lovely picture in the background. All the characters and concepts we added were fully present in the story. Also, as I mentioned before, starting the story with voice commands is very easy." (E2)

"My child and I had a lot of fun. The buttons in the program were very useful. The program was easy to use. We also really liked the background." (E3)

"This application was very easy to use and we had no trouble at all. Once the story was complete, we were excited to create it again." (E4)

5. DISCUSSION

This study's findings suggest that the generative AI-powered storytelling application developed to enhance parent-child interaction during early childhood serves as a successful example of interactive digital storytelling (IDS), rather than traditional digital storytelling. Unlike conventional digital storytelling, which typically presents linear narratives with limited user control (Lambert, 2013), interactive digital storytelling allows children and families to navigate and influence the narrative flow based on their choices. As child C3 noted, *"I started telling the story by pressing the microphone... My mom writes her own stories, but this time I created mine."* This autonomy aligns with the interactive structure emphasized by Alexander (2011) and Erstad (2011), which positions the learner as an active decision-maker in a dynamic multimedia environment.

Unlike traditional digital storytelling, which may position children as passive consumers of narrative, the app supports active, individualized story construction, offering multimedia tools such as voice input, concept tagging, and character customization. These features not only enhance usability but also promote creativity, critical thinking, and emotional expression—competencies emphasized in the literature (Chen & Lee, 2023; Kaya & Yılmaz, 2022; Shelton et al., 2016).

From a family interaction perspective, the findings highlight both shared and individualistic storytelling dynamics. While children and parents engaged in co-use, such as jointly selecting characters or concepts, parents often assumed a facilitative rather than co-creative role. This finding contrasts with earlier empirical research on family digital storytelling, where identity negotiation between parent and child was observed (Kalantari, Rubegni, Benton, & Vasalou, 2023; Liaqat et al., 2021;; Pahl, 2011; Vezzoli, Kalantari, Kucirkova, & Vasalou, 2020). In our case, children's narratives appeared either child-centric, focused on their personal interests and imagination (e.g., unicorns, summer), or family-centric, reflecting shared experiences (e.g., holidays, pets). As Bruner (2003) suggests, both narrative forms contribute to children's understanding of selfhood and relational identity within the family.

Notably, family-centric stories often re-ignited affective bonds and recalled shared memories—such as C1's remark, *"There's a picture of summer on the cover of this story, right?"*, revealing the emotional connection built through narrative. Similarly, children expressed joy in co-creating stories with parents, as in C4's case: *"I had a great time with my mom... we created beautiful and entertaining stories."* These examples support the view that digital storytelling serves as a socio-emotional tool, capable of deepening intergenerational bonds through shared narratives, even if identity negotiation does not occur explicitly.

Vasalou et al. (2020b) observed that even in the absence of explicit identity negotiation, digital storytelling can support both self-expression and family belonging. In our findings, child-centric stories—while more autonomous—still played a transformative role by revealing what mattered to the child, thereby enhancing parental empathy and awareness, particularly in cases where children are reluctant to share emotions directly (Kalantari et al. 2023).

In terms of parental involvement, the results resonate with Yen et al. (2018), who cautioned against prescribing fixed parental roles and encouraged exploration of meaningful and flexible interactions in digital environments. In our study, parents were frequently involved before or after story creation, guiding the child, managing interface navigation, or helping with voice inputs. This facilitative role aligns with the idea that designing DSTs to capture parental prompts or memories—such as meaningful objects, past events, or photos (as suggested by Liaqat et al., 2021)-could allow children to incorporate those elements creatively, maintaining their agency while still honoring family narratives.

Furthermore, the current application reflects the transformative potential of interactive digital storytelling in science education, particularly in early childhood. Many children reported learning concepts like seasons or emotions (e.g., *"I've learned about the seasons with this story"* – C1). The design also allowed for exploration-based concept discovery, where children identified embedded concepts within the story—a technique that mirrors constructivist science learning approaches (Demir, 2023; Kaya & Yılmaz, 2022). Compared to traditional digital storytelling, which presents concepts statically, IDS engages children in searching, hypothesizing, and reflecting on content.

While international studies on IDS in science education are increasing (Murray, 2024; Poonsawad, Srisomphan, & Sanrach, 2022), its application in Türkiye remains scarce, with Demir (2023) conducting one of the few empirical studies. His findings—reporting significant gains in academic achievement and attitudes—are mirrored in our early childhood context through observed improvements in engagement, autonomy, and emotional investment in learning activities.

Finally, features such as interactive testing, gamification (e.g., rewards, visual feedback), and audio-visual scaffolds supported not only the learning of content but also the development of visual literacy, narrative sequencing, and metacognition. The desire for more audio-based feedback from children who couldn't read independently (e.g., *"I wish the test questions were audio; I couldn't read them without my mother"* – C3) reveals a strong case for integrating universal design for learning (UDL) principles in future versions.

This study contributes to the growing understanding of how interactive digital storytelling tools powered by generative AI can foster autonomous learning, strengthen emotional bonds, and scaffold family communication. The emphasis on co-constructed narratives aligns with prior research demonstrating that storybooks and mediated storytelling interactions function as powerful scaffolding tools that enhance children's language skills, receptive vocabulary, and communicative competence within adult–child exchanges (Aktulun et al., 2024). By supporting both child-centric creativity and family-centric memory sharing, the app presented in this study offers a versatile and developmentally meaningful model for early childhood education. Moreover, it invites future research to examine how such platforms can balance children's agency with parental scaffolding, ensuring that joint engagement is culturally responsive and supportive of diverse family interaction patterns.

This study reveals the potential of generative AI-assisted digital storytelling to enrich learning in the preschool period, while also shedding light on the aspects of current applications that require ethical development. The literature indicates that issues such as data privacy, algorithmic bias, and content safety constitute a central area of risk in GAI use, particularly within the early childhood context (Tırpan, 2024). Therefore, it is crucial for future research to develop concrete design principles aimed at making the data processing practices of applications more transparent and secure. Furthermore, it is emphasized that ethical guidelines safeguarding children's rights must be established to enable the responsible use of AI in early childhood education (Berson et al., 2025). In addition, more comprehensive models that include variables such as AI literacy, joint media engagement, and parent-child interaction should be developed to understand preschool children's interactions with artificial intelligence (Su et al., 2023). Longitudinal studies examining the long-term effects of GAI-assisted digital storytelling on key areas like creativity, language development, and social-emotional learning will provide more robust evidence regarding the pedagogical value of this technology. Finally, cross-cultural comparative research will offer valuable insights into how digital storytelling applications function across different socio-cultural contexts and will contribute to the development of more inclusive, adaptable, and universal design principles.

6. CONCLUSION

This study explored the experiences of preschool-aged children and their parents using a generative AI-powered interactive digital storytelling (IDS) application designed to support narrative construction, early learning, and parent-child interaction. The results revealed that the app was perceived as highly engaging, user-friendly, and developmentally appropriate. Both children and parents reported positive emotional responses to various interface elements such as the homepage visuals, interactive buttons, customizable characters, and audio-visual feedback mechanisms. Notably, the integration of voice commands, gamified test features, and concept-based storytelling enhanced children's autonomy and learning while also facilitating joint activities with caregivers.

Children demonstrated strong enthusiasm for storytelling, with several participants expressing a desire to continue creating stories independently or with parental support. The app not only promoted imagination and creativity but also served as a tool for emotional expression and science concept acquisition—particularly regarding seasonal knowledge, emotions, and everyday experiences. Parents valued the app's accessibility, functional design, and its ability to reflect the elements they and their children selected together, which strengthened their perceived connection to the child's narrative world.

Overall, the study confirms the educational and relational potential of generative AI-driven interactive storytelling environments in early childhood. It also demonstrates that when digital tools are carefully designed with multimodal features and flexible interaction paths, they can successfully support both child agency and collaborative family engagement-without requiring rigid co-creation roles.

REFERENCES

Agnese, A., De Donato, R., Palmieri, G., Pellegrino, M. A., Petta, A., Scarano, V., & Serra, L. (2020). Visual storytelling by novelette. In *2020 24th International Conference Information Visualisation* (Vol. IV, pp. 723–728). IEEE. https://doi.org/ DOI: 10.1109/IV51561.2020.0012

Aktulun, Ö. U., Gözüm, A. İ. C., Kaya, Ü. Ü., Papadakis, S., & Kalogiannakis, M. (2024). Storybooks as a scaffolding tool in teacher–child interaction: The mediating role of vocabulary and receptive language in the investigation of the relationship between teacher attitude and children's language skills. In Papadakis, S., & Kalogiannakis, M. (Eds.), *Education, development and intervention* (pp. 25–48). Springer., DOI: 10.1007/978-3-031-60713-4_2

Al-Amri, H. M. (2020). Digital storytelling as a communicative language teaching-based method in EFL classrooms. *Arab World English Journal, 11*(1), 270–281. DOI: 10.24093/awej/vol11no1.20

Alexander, B. (2011). *The new digital storytelling: Creating narratives with new media*. Praeger. DOI: 10.5040/9798216979456

Anderson, T., & Shattuck, J. (2012). Design-based research: A decade of progress in education research? *Educational Researcher, 41*(1), 16–25. DOI: 10.3102/0013189X11428813

Ansari, A. N., Ahmad, S., & Bhutta, S. M. (2024). Mapping the global evidence around the use of ChatGPT in higher education: A systematic scoping review. *Education and Information Technologies, 29*(9), 11281–11321. DOI: 10.1007/s10639-023-12223-4

Baker, T., Anissa, N., & Smith, L. (2019). *Educ-AI-tion rebooted? Exploring the future of artificial intelligence in schools and colleges*. Nesta Foundation. https://media.nesta.org.uk/documents/Future_of_AI_and_education_v5_WEB.pdf

Belda-Medina, J., & Goddard, M. B. (2024). AI-driven digital storytelling: A strategy for creating English as a foreign language (EFL) materials. *International Journal of Linguistics Studies, 4*(1), 40–49. DOI: 10.32996/ijls.2024.4.1.4

Berson, I. R., Berson, M. J., & Luo, W. (2025). Innovating responsibly: Ethical considerations for AI in early childhood education. *AI Brain Child, 1*(2), 2. Advance online publication. DOI: 10.1007/s44436-025-00003-5

Bruner, J. S. (2003). *Making stories: Law, literature, life*. Harvard University Press.

Bura, C., & Myakala, P. K. (2024). Advancing transformative education: Generative AI as a catalyst for equity and innovation (No. arXiv:2411.15971). *arXiv*. https://doi.org//arXiv.2411.15971DOI: 10.48550

Chan, C. K. Y., & Hu, W. (2023). Students' voices on generative AI: Perceptions, benefits, and challenges in higher education. *International Journal of Educational Technology in Higher Education, 20*(1), 1–18. DOI: 10.1186/s41239-023-00411-8

Chen, G. (2024). The impacts of AI-driven storytelling applications on language acquisition and literacy development in early childhood education: A systematic review. *Asian Journal of Advanced Research and Reports, 18*(10), 1–12. DOI: 10.9734/ajarr/2024/v18i11770

Chen, L., & Lee, J. (2023). The effect of digital storytelling on secondary school students' perception of environmental behaviour and affective dispositions. *Research in Science Education, 54*(2), 89–105.

Chen, S. Y. (2023). Generative AI, learning and new literacies. *Journal of Educational Technology Development and Exchange, 16*(2), 1–19. DOI: 10.18785/jetde.1602.01

Cheng, Y., Pedaste, M., Bardone, E., & Huang, Y. (Eds.). (2024). *Innovative technologies and learning: 7th International Conference, ICITL 2024, Tartu, Estonia, August 14–16, 2024, Proceedings, Part I* (Vol. 14785). Springer Nature.

Cheung, L. M. E., & Shi, E. (2025). Co-creating stories with generative AI: Reflections from undergraduate students of a storytelling service-learning subject in Hong Kong. *Australian Review of Applied Linguistics, 47*(4), 259–283. Advance online publication. DOI: 10.1075/aral.24101.che

Churchill, N. (2016). Digital storytelling as a means of supporting digital literacy learning in an upper-primary-school English language classroom (Doctoral dissertation). Edith Cowan University. https://ro.ecu.edu.au/theses/1774

Cordero, J., Torres-Zambrano, J., & Cordero-Castillo, A. (2025). Integration of generative artificial intelligence in higher education: Best practices. *Education Sciences, 15*(1), 32. DOI: 10.3390/educsci15010032

Demir, İ. C. (2023). Ortaokul 6. sınıf "Dolaşım Sistemi" konusunun öğretiminde interaktif dijital öyküleme kullanımının öğrencilerin akademik başarı ve tutumlarına etkisi [Unpublished master's thesis]. Ordu University.

Design-Based Research Collective. (2003). Design-based research: An emerging paradigm for educational inquiry. *Educational Researcher, 32*(1), 5–8. DOI: 10.3102/0013189X032001005

Di Blas, N., Paolini, P., & Sabiescu, A. (2010). Collective digital storytelling at school as a whole-class interaction. In *Proceedings of the 9th International Conference on Interaction Design and Children* (pp. 11–19). ACM. DOI: 10.1145/1810543.1810546

Edwards, S. (2023). Early childhood education and care, artificial intelligence and the postdigital. *Australasian Journal of Early Childhood, 48*(3), 179–181. DOI: 10.1177/18369391231198910

Elbanna, S., & Armstrong, L. (2024). Exploring the integration of ChatGPT in education: Adapting for the future. *Management & Sustainability: An Arab Review, 3*(1), 16–29. DOI: 10.1108/MSAR-03-2023-0016

Erstad, O. (2011). Digital storytelling in education: Creative expression, narrative, and technology. *Learning, Media and Technology, 36*(2), 157–162. DOI: 10.1080/17439884.2011.579000

Fang, X., Ng, D. T. K., Leung, J. K. L., & Chu, S. K. W. A. (2023). Systematic review of artificial intelligence technologies used for story writing. *Education and Information Technologies, 28*(11), 1–37. DOI: 10.1007/s10639-023-11741-5

Firat, M. (2023). What ChatGPT means for universities: Perceptions of scholars and students. *Journal of Applied Learning and Teaching, 6*(1), 57–63. DOI: 10.37074/jalt.2023.6.1.22

García-Peñalvo, F. J., Llorens Largo, F., & Vidal, J. (n.d.). The new reality of education in the face of advances in generative artificial intelligence. *Revista Iberoamericana De Educación a Distancia, 27*(1), 9–39. DOI: 10.5944/ried.27.1.37716

Gözüm, A. İ. C. (2022). Digital games for STEM in early childhood education: Active co-playing parental mediation and educational content examination. In Papadakis, S., & Kalogiannakis, M. (Eds.), *STEM, robotics, mobile apps in early childhood and primary education* (pp. 355–375). Springer., DOI: 10.1007/978-981-19-0568-1_21

Gözüm, A. İ. C., & Kandır, A. (2021). Digital games pre-schoolers play: Parental mediation and examination of educational content. *Education and Information Technologies, 26*(3), 3293–3326. DOI: 10.1007/s10639-020-10382-2

Guettala, M., Bourekkache, S., Kazar, O., & Harous, S. (2024). Generative artificial intelligence in education: Advancing adaptive and personalized learning. *Acta Informatica Pragensia, 13*(3), 460–489. DOI: 10.18267/j.aip.235

Han, A., & Cai, Z. (2023). Design implications of generative AI systems for visual storytelling for young learners. In *Proceedings of the 22nd Annual ACM Interaction Design and Children Conference* (pp. 470–474). Chicago, IL, USA. DOI: 10.1145/3585088.3593867

Han, A., Zhou, X., Cai, Z., Han, S., Ko, R., Corrigan, S., & Peppler, K. (2024). Teachers, parents, and students' perspectives on integrating generative AI into elementary literacy education. In *Proceedings of the CHI Conference on Human Factors in Computing Systems*. ACM. DOI: 10.1145/3613904.3642438

Harji, B. M., & Gheitanchian, M. (2017). Effects of multimedia task-based teaching and learning approach on EFL learners' accuracy, fluency and complexity of oral production. *The Turkish Online Journal of Educational Technology*, *16*(2), 25–34.

Harrison, R., & Shazaad, K. (2025). Generative AI in early childhood education: Designing culturally responsive curriculums with ChatGPT. DOI: 10.13140/RG.2.2.15237.26082

Hashmi, N., & Bal, S. (2024). Generative AI in higher education and beyond. *Business Horizons*, *67*(5), 607–614. DOI: 10.1016/j.bushor.2024.05.005

Hobbs, R. (2017). *Create to learn: Introduction to digital literacy*. John Wiley & Sons. DOI: 10.1002/9781394260201

Holmes, W., Porayska-Pomsta, K., Holstein, K., Sutherland, E., Baker, T., Shum, S., Santos, O., Rodrigo, M., Cukurova, M., Bittencourt, I., & Koedinger, K. (2022). Ethics of AI in education: Towards a community-wide framework. *International Journal of Artificial Intelligence in Education*, *32*(3), 504–526. DOI: 10.1007/s40593-021-00239-1

Huang, A. Y., Lu, O. H., & Yang, S. J. (2023). Effects of artificial intelligence-enabled personalized recommendations on learners' learning engagement, motivation, and outcomes in a flipped classroom. *Computers & Education*, *194*, 104684. DOI: 10.1016/j.compedu.2022.104684

Isaacs, M., Tondeur, J., Howard, S., Claro, M., & Braak, J. (2024). Digital storytelling as a strategy for developing 21st-century skills: A systematic review of qualitative evidence. *Technology, Pedagogy and Education*, *33*(5), 573–593. DOI: 10.1080/1475939X.2024.2343929

Kalantari, S., Rubegni, E., Benton, L., & Vasalou, A. (2023). "When I'm writing a story, I am really good": Exploring the use of digital storytelling technology at home. *International Journal of Child-Computer Interaction*, *38*, 100613. DOI: 10.1016/j.ijcci.2023.100613

Kanders, K., Stupple-Harris, L., Smith, L., & Gibson, J. L. (2024). Perspectives on the impact of generative AI on early-childhood development and education. *Infant and Child Development*, *33*(4), e2514. DOI: 10.1002/icd.2514

Kaptan, E., & Cakir, R. (2025). The effect of digital storytelling on digital literacy, 21st century skills and achievement. *Education and Information Technologies, 30*(8), 11047–11071. DOI: 10.1007/s10639-024-13287-6

Kaya, A., & Yılmaz, R. (2022). The effect of digital story applications on academic achievement in science education. *International Journal of Educational Research, 11*(3), 112–130.

Kong, S. C., & Yang, Y. (2024). A human-centred learning and teaching framework using generative artificial intelligence for self-regulated learning development through domain knowledge learning in K–12 settings. *IEEE Transactions on Learning Technologies, 17*, 1588–1599. DOI: 10.1109/TLT.2024.3392830

Kurniah, N., Agustriana, N., & Sapri, J. (2023). Integration of scientific literacy and technology in designing early childhood learning. *Indonesian Journal of Early Childhood Education Studies, 12*(2), 204–210. DOI: 10.15294/ijeces.v12i2.75634

Lambert, J. (2013). *Digital storytelling: Capturing lives, creating community.* Routledge. DOI: 10.4324/9780203102329

Liaqat, A., Axtell, B., & Munteanu, C. (2021). Participatory design for intergenerational culture exchange in immigrant families: How collaborative narration and creation fosters democratic engagement. In *Proceedings of the ACM on Human-Computer Interaction, 5*, 1–40. CSCW1. DOI: 10.1145/3449172

Lim, W. M., Gunasekara, A., Pallant, J. L., Pallant, J. I., & Pechenkina, E. (2023). Generative AI and the future of education: Ragnar¨ok or reformation? A paradoxical perspective from management educators. *International Journal of Management Education, 21*(2), 100790. Advance online publication. DOI: 10.1016/j.ijme.2023.100790

Lincoln, Y. S., & Guba, E. G. (1985). *Naturalistic inquiry.* Sage Publications. DOI: 10.1016/0147-1767(85)90062-8

Liu, K. P., Tai, S. J. D., & Liu, C. C. (2018). Enhancing language learning through creation: The effect of digital storytelling on student learning motivation and performance in a school English course. *Educational Technology Research and Development, 66*(4), 913–935. DOI: 10.1007/s11423-018-9592-z

Luckin, R. (2017). Towards artificial intelligence-based assessment systems. *Nature Human Behaviour, 1*(3), 0028. DOI: 10.1038/s41562-016-0028

Luo, W., He, H., Liu, J., Berson, I. R., Berson, M. J., Zhou, Y., & Li, H. (2024). Aladdin's genie or Pandora's box for early childhood education? Experts chat on the roles, challenges, and developments of ChatGPT. *Early Education and Development, 35*(1), 96–113. DOI: 10.1080/10409289.2023.2214181

Miles, M. B., & Huberman, A. M. (1994). *Qualitative data analysis: An expanded sourcebook* (2nd ed.). Sage Publications.

Moya, B., Badías, A., González, D., Chinesta, F., & Cueto, E. (2023). Computational sensing, understanding, and reasoning: An artificial intelligence approach to physics-informed world modeling. *Archives of Computational Methods in Engineering, 31*(4), 1897–1914. DOI: 10.1007/s11831-023-10033-y

Muller, M., Chilton, L. B., Kantosalo, A., Maher, M. L., Martin, C. P., & Walsh, G. (2022). GenAICHI: Generative AI and HCI. *Conference on Human Factors in Computing Systems - Proceedings*. DOI: 10.1145/3491101.3503719

Murray, J. T. (2024). *Interactive storytelling*. Springer Nature.

Ng, D. T. K., Luo, W., Chan, H. M. Y., & Chu, S. K. W. (2022). Using digital story writing as a pedagogy to develop AI literacy among primary students. *Computers and Education: Artificial Intelligence, 3*, 100054. DOI: 10.1016/j.caeai.2022.100054

Nguyen, H., Pham, V., Tran, D., & Le, T. (2019). Intelligent tutoring chatbot for solving mathematical problems in high school. *2019 11th International Conference on Knowledge and Systems Engineering*, 1–6. DOI: 10.1109/KSE.2019.8919396

Niemi, H., Niu, S. J., Li, B., & Vivitsou, M. (2019). Supporting student learning toward 21st-century skills through digital storytelling. In Yu, S., Niemi, H., & Mason, J. (Eds.), *Shaping future schools with digital technology* (pp. 95–112). Springer., DOI: 10.1007/978-981-13-9439-3_6

Nurlaela, M., Ilham, J., & Lisabe, C. M. (2022). The effects of Storyjumper on narrative writing ability of EFL learners in higher education. *Journal of Education, 8*(14), 1641–1647.

Oliveira, A. (2017). *Mentes digitais, a ciência redefinindo a humanidade*. IST Press.

Pahl, K. (2011). My family, my story: Representing identities in time and space through digital storytelling. *Teachers College Record, 113*(13), 17–39. DOI: 10.1177/016146811111301302

Patton, M. Q. (2015). *Qualitative research & evaluation methods* (4th ed.). Sage Publications.

Poonsawad, A., Srisomphan, J., & Sanrach, C. (2022). Synthesis of problem-based interactive digital storytelling learning model under gamification environment promotes students' problem-solving skills. [iJET]. *International Journal of Emerging Technologies in Learning, 17*(5), 103–119. DOI: 10.3991/ijet.v17i05.28181

Raffone, A. (2022). Gamifying English language learning through interactive storytelling and MALL technologies. *Language Teaching Research*. Advance online publication. DOI: 10.1177/13621688221102

Rubegni, E., & Landoni, M. (2014). Fiabot!: Design and evaluation of a mobile storytelling application for schools. In *Proceedings of the 2014 conference on Interaction Design and Children* (pp. 165–174). DOI: 10.1145/2593968.2593979

Rutta, C. B., Schiavo, G., Zancanaro, M., & Rubegni, E. (2020). Collaborative comic-based digital storytelling with primary school children. In *Proceedings of the Interaction Design and Children Conference* (pp. 426–437). DOI: 10.1145/3392063.3394433

Shelton, C. C., Warren, A. E., & Archambault, L. M. (2016). Exploring the use of interactive digital storytelling video: Promoting student engagement and learning in a university hybrid course. *TechTrends, 60*(5), 465–474. DOI: 10.1007/s11528-016-0082-z

Su, J., Ng, D. T. K., & Chu, S. K. W. (2023). Artificial intelligence (AI) literacy in early childhood education: The challenges and opportunities. *Computers and Education: Artificial Intelligence, 4*, 100124. DOI: 10.1016/j.caeai.2023.100124

Su, J., Ng, D. T. K., & Chu, S. K. W. (2023). Artificial intelligence (AI) literacy in early childhood education: The challenges and opportunities. *Computers and Education: Artificial Intelligence, 4*, 100124. DOI: 10.1016/j.caeai.2023.100124

Su, J., & Yang, W. (2022). Artificial intelligence in early childhood education: A scoping review. *Computers and Education: Artificial Intelligence, 3*, 100049. DOI: 10.1016/j.caeai.2022.100049

Sun, Y., Chen, J., Yao, B., Liu, J., Wang, D., Ma, X., & He, L. (2024). Exploring parents' needs for children-centered AI to support preschoolers' interactive storytelling and reading activities. *Proceedings of the ACM on Human-Computer Interaction, 8*(CSCW2), 1–25.

Tırpan, C. (2024). *The ethical issues in generative artificial intelligence: A systematic review*. bmij, 12(4), 729–747.

Vasalou, A., Kalantari, S., Kucirkova, N., & Vezzoli, Y. (2020a). Designing for oral storytelling practices at home: A parental perspective. *International Journal of Child-Computer Interaction, 26*, 100214. Advance online publication. DOI: 10.1016/j.ijcci.2020.100214

Vezzoli, Y., Kalantari, S., Kucirkova, N., & Vasalou, A. (2020b). Exploring the design space for parent-child reading. In *Proceedings of the 2020 CHI Conference on Human Factors in Computing Systems* (pp. 1–12). DOI: 10.1145/3313831.3376696

Vidrih, M., & Myahi, S. (2023). Generative AI-driven storytelling: A new era for marketing. https://doi.org//arXiv.2309.09048DOI: 10.48550

Wu, J., & Chen, D. T. V. (2020). A systematic review of educational digital storytelling. *Computers & Education, 147*, 103786. DOI: 10.1016/j.compedu.2019.103786

Wu, Y. (2024). Is early childhood education prepared for artificial intelligence?: A global and US policy framework literature review. *Open Journal of Social Sciences, 12*(8), 127–143. DOI: 10.4236/jss.2024.128010

Yang, W. (2022). Artificial intelligence education for young children: Why, what, and how in curriculum design and implementation. *Computers and Education: Artificial Intelligence*, *3*, 100061. DOI: 10.1016/j.caeai.2022.100061

Yang, Y. T. C., Chen, Y. C., & Hung, H. T. (2020). Digital storytelling as an interdisciplinary project to improve students' English speaking and creative thinking. *Computer Assisted Language Learning*, *35*(4), 840–862. DOI: 10.1080/09588221.2020.1750431

Yen, K., Chen, Y., Cheng, Y., Chen, S., Chen, Y.-Y., Ni, Y., & Hiniker, A. (2018). Joint media engagement between parents and preschoolers in the U.S., China, and Taiwan. *Proceedings of the ACM on Human-Computer Interaction*, *2*(CSCW), 1–19. DOI: 10.1145/3274461

Yıldırım, A., & Şimşek, H. (2013). *Sosyal bilimlerde nitel araştırma yöntemleri* (9. Baskı). Seçkin Yayıncılık.

Yu, H., & Guo, Y. (2023). Generative artificial intelligence empowers educational reform: Current status, issues, and prospects. *Frontiers in Education*, *8*, 1183162. DOI: 10.3389/feduc.2023.1183162

Yu, S., Hou, Y., & Li, H. (2025). Suitability of Chinese GenAI platforms for early childhood education: A multifaceted evaluation. https://doi.org/DOI: 10.21203/rs.3.rs-6300153/v1

Zawacki-Richter, O., Marín, V., Bond, M., & Gouverneur, F. (2019). Systematic review of research on artificial intelligence applications in higher education: Where are the educators? *International Journal of Educational Technology in Higher Education*, *16*(1), 9. Advance online publication. DOI: 10.1186/s41239-019-0171-0

Zhao, Y., Yusof, S. M., Hou, M., & Li, Z. (2024). How can generative artificial intelligence help teachers in early childhood education with their teaching? Analyses from the perspective of teaching methods. *International Journal of Academic Research in Progressive Education and Development*, *13*(1). Advance online publication. DOI: 10.6007/IJARPED/v13-i1/20958

Chapter 2
Scientific Trends Towards the Use of Generative Artificial Intelligence Tools in Early Childhood STEM Education:
A Bibliometric Analysis

Zehra Çakır
Bayburt University, Turkey

Mustafa Uğraş
https://orcid.org/0000-0001-6921-0178
Fırat University, Turkey

Dimitrios Sotiropoulos
http://orcid.org/0000-0001-7367-5760
University of Thessaly, Greece

Michail Kalogiannakis
http://orcid.org/0000-0002-9124-2245
University of Thessaly, Greece

ABSTRACT

This study aims to analyze scientific publications on the use of productive artificial intelligence tools in STEM education during early childhood between 2021 and 2025 using bibliometric methods. In this context, the international literature published during the relevant period was examined to identify scientific production trends,

DOI: 10.4018/979-8-3373-9074-1.ch002

prominent authors, influential studies, institutional and international collaboration networks, and thematic focuses. A total of 1,224 documents were included in the analysis. During the data analysis process, the Bibliometrix (Biblioshiny) software running on the R program was used; publication trends, keyword frequencies, citation analyses, author and institution collaborations, and scientific mapping techniques were utilized. The analysis findings show that academic interest in productive artificial intelligence tools has increased significantly between 2021 and 2025. The study also systematically identifies key trends, application areas, and research gaps related to the integration of these technologies into educational processes.

INTRODUCTION

Today, the dizzying pace of technological developments has brought about radical changes and transformations in education systems. In education, AI has begun to attract attention by offering easier and more enjoyable learning environments for subjects such as mathematics, science, engineering, and technology (STEM disciplines), which are important for the future of society but are often avoided by individuals due to their perceived difficulty (Demircioğlu & Demir, 2024). Artificial Intelligence has revolutionised education for students who feel anxious, prejudiced, or develop negative attitudes towards these subjects (M. Uğraş, 2024). In order to eliminate negative attitudes toward these fields and increase interest, STEM education has been implemented in early childhood in developed and developing countries in recent years. However, with the impact of developing technology, various challenges have begun to be encountered in STEM education implemented in early childhood (Uğraş et al., 2024). For example, teachers' ability to plan different STEM activities, their competence in implementing these activities, evaluating the activities carried out, time, material and space constraints (Al Darayseh & Mersin, 2025), and developmental issues such as young children's inability to understand abstract concepts are some of the challenges that can arise. Moreover, these challenges in STEM education have been exacerbated by current global events that have disrupted education. At this point, the continuous renewal of technology and its development in areas such as artificial intelligence have provided opportunities for different perspectives in education systems and for overcoming challenges. It has added a new dimension to STEM education in early childhood in both literature and practice (Lin et al., 2025). Artificial intelligence has shown rapid growth and change in many fields of study, such as STEM, robotics, coding, education, and autonomous driving (Uğraş & Uğraş, 2025). This transformation process is not limited to changes made by a specific stakeholder or a single education programme. On the contrary, it has brought about comprehensive innovations in different disciplines and age groups, from preschool to higher education, and from social sciences such as history to mathematics and science (Demircioğlu & Demir, 2024). The fundamental aim of these changes in the education system, which are linked to technological developments, is to support social development and raise the overall level of development of the country, as is the case with every change (Yılmaz, 2023). Artificial intelligence has become an important focus in early childhood education research by supporting teachers in various areas such as managing STEM assessment processes, data collection, planning the teaching process, and developing innovative teaching strategies (Uğraş & Uğraş, 2025). Studies in the field emphasise that the use of artificial intelligence technologies in educational institutions will facilitate learning processes and that research should focus on this area (El Fathi et al., 2025; Lin et al., 2025; Uğraş et al., 2025; Xu & Ouyang, 2022). It is also stated that these technologies have the potential to offer STEM education tools tailored to each student's individual learning style (Uğraş and Uğraş, 2025;) and that AI-supported tools are expected to be used more widely and competently in educational environments in the future (Duralar, 2024; İşler & Kılıç, 2021; Zhai et al., 2021). In today's world, the scarcity of longitudinal studies in the literature on the long-term effects of AI in early childhood is striking (UNICEF Innocenti, 2023). The vast majority of studies focus on higher education and vocational education levels (Chen et al., 2020). Research on early childhood and primary education levels is more limited. This imbalance creates a serious gap in understanding the pedagogical and ethical effects of artificial intelligence at an early age. Bibliometric analyses are needed to systematically identify where these gaps exist (e.g., in which educational levels, countries, neglected areas such as early childhood STEM), the most studied themes, and country and institutional collaborations, and to accelerate work in these areas to fill the gaps (Donthu et al., 2021). Artificial intelligence offers powerful opportunities for personalization, accessibility, and teacher support in early childhood education. In particular, the effects of generative AI applications on children's trust development, language acquisition, and identity perception are a new area of research. There are also gaps in local studies on how cultural contexts modify these effects. STEM education in early childhood, one of the most dynamic areas of education, aims to develop students' scientific thinking, problem-solving, and questioning skills for the welfare of society because it is an area related to scientifically researchable questions or technological problems that can be solved through engineering and design (Van Keulen, 2018). In this regard, STEM has the potential to directly benefit from the opportunities offered by artificial intelligence technologies, creating a new and easy dimension in early childhood STEM education (Al Darayseh & Mersin, 2025; Uğraş & Uğraş, 2025; Xu & Ouyang, 2022). Therefore, identifying the relevant gaps and increasing efforts in the specified areas will contribute to society.

WHAT IS ARTIFICIAL INTELLIGENCE IN EDUCATION?

The term artificial intelligence was first used in 1956 in a project study conducted by John McCarthy at Dartmouth College in the United States (Kutlucan & Seferoğlu, 2024). During the same period, Herbert A. Simon, Cliff Shaw, and Allen Newell developed the Logic Theorist programme, which is considered the first artificial intelligence programme. The English abbreviation for artificial intelligence is AI (Artificial Intelligence) (Holmes et al., 2019). The purpose of artificial intelligence is to produce computers and machines that mimic human-like intelligence, thinking, skills, learning, and decision-making (Kutlucan & Seferoğlu, 2024) (Kutlucan & Seferoğlu, 2024). Russell and Norvig (2021) define artificial intelligence as the ability of an agent to perceive data from its environment and make rational decisions based on that information (Russell & Norvig, 2010). In this context, it is emphasised that artificial intelligence systems must not only perform predefined tasks but also adapt to changing conditions and respond autonomously (independently) (Uğraş & Uğraş, 2025). Machine commands, natural language processing, data mining, artificial neural networks, and algorithms are fundamental areas directly related to artificial intelligence (Smith, 2019). Through these fields, artificial intelligence is currently being utilised in various applications such as image and speech recognition (Hwang et al., 2020), healthcare, decision support systems, language translation, computer programming, control systems, and robot technologies (Zhu, 2020). These types of applications reveal that artificial intelligence also has significant potential in the context of education (Uğraş & Uğraş, 2025). Artificial intelligence has a highly effective potential to offer innovative and rapid solutions to teaching processes, especially in learning areas such as language, science, engineering, and mathematics (Ouyang et al., 2023). The main goal of AI is to make processes faster and more efficient, analyse big data in detail and accurately, and improve human-machine interactions (Bibri & Jagatheesaperumal, 2023). This focuses on imitating cognitive processes such as thinking, problem solving, learning and decision making (Kutlucan & Seferoğlu, 2024). Intelligent teaching systems analyse students' learning speeds, knowledge levels and deficiencies, providing personalised content and increasing the effectiveness of the learning process (Ouyang et al., 2023). In addition, virtual laboratories and simulations make abstract concepts more concrete and accessible (Chen et al., 2020). In this context, AI aims to develop systems that not only perform pre-programmed tasks but also learn from experience, extract meaning from complex data sets, and adapt to new situations (Arı, 2024). Artificial intelligence applications in education provide significant benefits for both teachers and students by enabling personalisation and automation of the teaching process. In particular, the ability to monitor students' performance levels in real time and provide adaptive content accordingly makes the teaching process more dynamic and effective. This allows teachers to free themselves from repetitive tasks and devote more time to creative teaching methods and one-on-one interaction with students (Uğraş, 2024). Various studies have shown that AI-supported intelligent teaching systems facilitate learning by visualising complex concepts, particularly in science and mathematics, and increase student motivation (Gülbahar & Kalelioğlu, 2018). Especially in early childhood, it has become possible to support students' developmental skills through artificial intelligence applications appropriate to their developmental level (Uğraş et al., 2025). In this context, the role of artificial intelligence in education has not been limited to a merely instrumental function but has gained importance as an innovative element that transforms pedagogical design (Temur, 2025).

THE ETHICAL AND PEDAGOGICAL EFFECTS OF ARTIFICIAL INTELLIGENCE ON CHILDREN

In recent years, the use of artificial intelligence (AI) has become increasingly widespread due to the opportunities it offers in the field of education. This prevalence has been particularly noticeable in higher education. On the other hand, there are serious gaps in early childhood (0–8 years), which is the critical period when cognitive, emotional, and social development occurs most rapidly in education and training. The significant impact of basic education on individuals' lives and society makes it crucial to focus on integrating current educational models into this field. However, this focus brings with it not only the pedagogical opportunities offered by AI applications but also challenges. When looking at the challenges of AI, the most fundamental issue that arises is that of "privacy and data protection." AI toys, language learning applications, and learning analytics tools developed for the early age group generally collect voice, image, or behavioral data. The misuse of such sensitive data poses risks that could threaten the child's safety and future rights (UNICEF, 2020). International organizations recommend that child rights-centered policy frameworks be taken into account in this regard (UNICEF, 2021; UNESCO, 2021; OECD, 2021). Due to children's lack of capacity to give informed consent, transparency and parental consent may be made mandatory for the collection of such data. Another ethical issue arises with the concepts of "bias and fairness." When AI systems are designed with unbalanced educational data, they can produce discrimination based on a child's socioeconomic, linguistic, or cultural differences. A child labeled as "failing" or "underachieving" at this age may have their education and learning path misdirected. This situation may apply to both developed and developing countries, as well as to the opportunities available in the environment where children live within a country. A third risk is commercialization and manipulation. Advertising, attention-grabbing strategies, and data trading in digital products aimed at children can lead to unethical outcomes. Generative AI-based chatbots or gamified content, in particular, can exploit children's trust and convey misinformation (UNICEF Innocenti, 2023). On the other hand, if not used in a balanced manner in education, increased screen exposure at an early age poses risks in terms of children's socio-emotional development areas, such as hindering the development of face-to-face communication, play, and empathy skills. When all these risks are given due consideration and boundaries and frameworks are established, AI also offers noteworthy opportunities from a pedagogical perspective. Especially since we live in an evolving era and must adapt to it, providing individuals with opportunities for training in this field will benefit both society and the individual. It will provide facilitating opportunities in educational settings. AI offers the possibility of creating a personalized learning environment tailored to the individual pace, interests, and needs of children, especially those with special needs. Furthermore, AI assists teachers in identifying the needs of the classroom. Thus, AI takes on the role of a complementary tool that supports the pedagogical process; it should not replace human interaction; teaching should be used within certain boundaries in a way that supports play-based pedagogy.

STEM EDUCATION AND ARTIFICIAL INTELLIGENCE IN EARLY CHILDHOOD

In the rapidly digitalising world of the 21st century, education systems have also had to keep pace with this transformation. Technological developments have not only changed the ways of accessing information; they have also radically transformed learning environments, methods and tools (Demircioğlu & Demir, 2024). This transformation has led to the reshaping of education systems; STEM education, which encompasses science, technology, engineering, and mathematics, has become an important tool for imparting the advanced cognitive and productive skills required by contemporary individuals (Van Keulen, 2018). STEM education aims to prepare children for future careers and social life by instilling fundamental competencies such as problem solving, design-oriented thinking, interdisciplinary connections, and productivity at an early age (Van Keulen, 2018). At this point, a critical objective emerges at the intersection of artificial intelligence technologies and STEM education. In recent years, rapid advances in artificial intelligence (AI) technologies have led to new applications in education. Artificial intelligence is a tool that is frequently used in our social lives and various industries (Uğraş et al., 2024). In a world where what we see, hear, and learn is often determined by algorithms, artificial intelligence has become increasingly important (Su, 2018; Uğraş et al., 2025). Uğraş (2024) reported that our children decide what to watch based on AI recommendations or use AI tools to help them with their homework. Generative AI tools, in particular, have the potential to make early childhood STEM learning processes more interactive and creative through text generation, visual creation, storytelling, and personalised content production for children (M. Uğraş, 2024; Xu & Ouyang, 2022). Thanks to these tools, children can take an active and enjoyable role in learning environments as producers rather than just consumers (Temur, 2025). The literature also indicates that the innovative opportunities offered by artificial intelligence tools are highly compatible with the nature of STEM education and provide ease of application (Al Darayseh & Mersin, 2025; Uğraş & Uğraş, 2025; Xu & Ouyang, 2022). Functions such as text production, visual creation, modelling, coding, and personalised learning scenarios make early childhood STEM applications more accessible, interactive, and creative (Van Keulen, 2018). This aspect of artificial intelligence that supports productivity enables students to grow as individuals who not only consume information but also produce it. We see that artificial intelligence has come to the fore alongside Industry 4.0 within the education vision of many countries. Within this education vision, emphasis is placed on the relationship between humans and technology, and the aim is to equip the new generation of teachers and students with productivity, entrepreneurship, scientific reasoning, lifelong learning and digital skills (Bayram & Çelik, 2023). The 11th Development Plan (2019-2023) includes among its goals, in line with global developments, the adoption of an interdisciplinary approach that integrates science, mathematics, engineering, and technology into education to develop individuals' problem-solving and creativity skills, and to raise individuals who are proficient in technology use, innovative, and entrepreneurial individuals (KANDIR & TEMEL, 2025). Early childhood is a developmental stage when individuals are most open to learning and innovation (Van Keulen, 2018). Therefore, the experiences provided during this period shape children's mental structures, problem-solving approaches, productivity, and the other characteristics mentioned above. In this context, integrating early childhood STEM education with productive artificial intelligence tools will be effective in facilitating the acquisition of interdisciplinary thinking skills and transforming technology into an active learning tool (Uğraş et al., 2025). It will enable children to use their imagination to create tangible products and produce creative solutions to problems.

Among the views and findings in the literature on the use and dissemination of artificial intelligence in education, it has been observed that some UNESCO Member States have developed national artificial intelligence programmes. Many countries, including the United States, Canada, the United Kingdom, and Finland, have also promoted STEAM education at the early childhood and high school levels by integrating artificial intelligence knowledge into existing subjects such as science and technology (Lin et al., 2025). Therefore, there is a greater need for research on artificial intelligence instructional design that has the flexibility and adaptability to integrate artificial intelligence knowledge into existing education programmes (KANDIR & TEMEL, 2025). In line with these needs, research has focused on the use of artificial intelligence technologies to improve the quality of teaching and learning in early childhood STEM education. To provide an example of how artificial intelligence tools can be used in STEM education in early childhood in alternative areas such as sound, visuals, and language, a teacher could use ChatGPT or a similar AI tool in class to create a problem situation based on a STEM-focused visual story, such as "The spaceship is broken. What can we do to fix it?" Then, students could be asked to create designs using STEM materials to solve the problem. Finally, the designs can be discussed and compared with different alternative designs offered by AI tools. AI-supported education presented in this way contributes to the development of children's learning processes, such as language development, creativity skills, productivity, and developing different perspectives, in an easier, more enjoyable, and technological environment.

In conclusion, the integration of AI into STEM education provides a learning environment that responds to students' individual learning needs, develops critical thinking and problem-solving skills, supports equality in education, provides support for challenges in STEM applications, and prepares students for the workforce of the future. Based on all this information, the study conducted a bibliometric analysis of academic publications from 2021 to 2025 related to the use of generative AI tools in early childhood STEM education, as found in the existing literature.

METHOD

Bibliometric analysis of studies on STEM education in early childhood not only reveals the intellectual structure of knowledge fields, but also offers important opportunities for determining the current status of research topics, prominent current issues, and future trends (Arora & Chakraborty, 2021; Kapoor et al., 2018; Rejeb et al., 2022). This method is a powerful analytical tool that enables the identification of research areas across different disciplines and the quantitative and objective examination of development models related to these areas (Song et al., 2019). Researchers frequently use bibliometric analysis methods to evaluate the development process of a specific topic across different scientific fields (Dao et al., 2023). According to Zupic and Čater (2015), the scientific mapping process based on bibliometric approaches consists of five stages: study design, data collection, data analysis, data visualisation, and interpretation, and this process is carried out systematically (Zupic & Čater, 2015) (Figure 1).

Figure 1. The process of mapping science

The research design constitutes the first stage, in which the fundamental elements of the research, such as its purpose, scope, and method, are determined. At this stage, the general framework of the research is outlined, and a methodological roadmap is created. The data collection process involves systematically obtaining relevant scientific sources (articles, theses, etc.) from various academic databases in line with the defined research topic. The aim of this stage is to access qualified and reliable sources that are appropriate for the purpose of the study. The collected data is analysed using bibliometric techniques, thereby identifying prominent trends, effective studies, important researchers and key concepts. The analysis process aims to reveal the current structure and dynamics of the research field. In the data visualisation stage, the analysis findings are presented using graphs, maps, and other visual tools to make the data clearer and more understandable. This stage contributes to users' ability to interpret the data quickly and effectively. The final stage, interpretation, involves making sense of the findings and evaluating them in the context of scientific developments in the relevant field. This process completes the overall integrity of the study, allowing the data obtained to be considered in context and conclusions to be drawn. All of these stages ensure that bibliometric research is conducted systematically and contribute to the scientific depth and clarity of the results obtained.

In this context, the aim of this study is to conduct a bibliometric analysis of studies on the use of generative artificial intelligence tools in early childhood STEM education. In line with this aim, the following research questions are addressed:

- What are the most cited journals, most influential authors, most productive countries, and most productive institutions in studies on the use of generative artificial intelligence tools in early childhood STEM education?
- What are the dominant themes that emerge from title, abstract, and keyword analyses of studies on the use of generative AI tools in early childhood STEM education, and how have these themes changed over time?

DATA ANALYSIS

Within the scope of this research, studies conducted between 2021 and 2025 (including 17 July 2025) on the use of productive artificial intelligence tools in STEM education in early childhood were examined. No restrictions were imposed in terms of the language of publication. The sample includes journal articles, book chapters, conference proceedings, and early access publications, which are assumed to be the source of the most recent findings and empirical data (Dinić & Jevremov, 2021). The studies included in the review were selected through careful keyword selection based on predefined search terms and criteria to minimise selection bias and access the largest possible number of studies related to the topic. The search process was conducted using the keywords ('generative artificial intelligence' OR 'generative AI' OR 'ChatGPT' OR 'large language model*') AND ('STEM' OR "STEAM") AND ('early childhood education' OR 'preschool education' OR 'early years education'). As a result of this query, a total of 1,224 studies were identified in the Web of Science (WOS) database. During the data analysis process, the Biblioshiny interface was used with the R programme to systematically answer the research questions. In this context, various analyses were conducted, including annual publication trends, keyword frequency, publishing journals and institutions, citation analysis, bibliographic links, co-author analysis, keyword distribution, and current topic trends (Aria & Cuccurullo, 2017). Within the scope of the study, both performance analysis and scientific mapping techniques were utilised in line with bibliometric methodology (Donthu et al., 2021). This methodological approach aims to comprehensively reveal the structural patterns and development trends in the literature.

Table 1. Main information about the data field of use of generative artificial intelligence tools in early childhood STEM education

Description	Results
Timespan	2021:2025
Sources (Journals, Books, etc)	342
Documents	1224
Keywords Plus (ID)	1041
Author's Keywords (DE)	3361
Authors	3743
Authors of single-authored docs	182
Single-authored docs	190

continued on following page

Table 1. Continued

Description	Results
Co-Authors per Doc	3,44
International co-authorships %	20,26

Table 1 provides basic information about the data field on the Use of Generative Artificial Intelligence Tools in Early Childhood STEM Education. Between 2021 and 2025, 1,224 research papers were published in 342 document types. In the field of using productive artificial intelligence tools in early childhood STEM education, 3,743 researchers worked, 182 of whom were sole authors, and 1,041 keywords emerged in the published research papers.

Figure 2. Annual research publications in the field of using generative artificial intelligence tools in early childhood STEM education

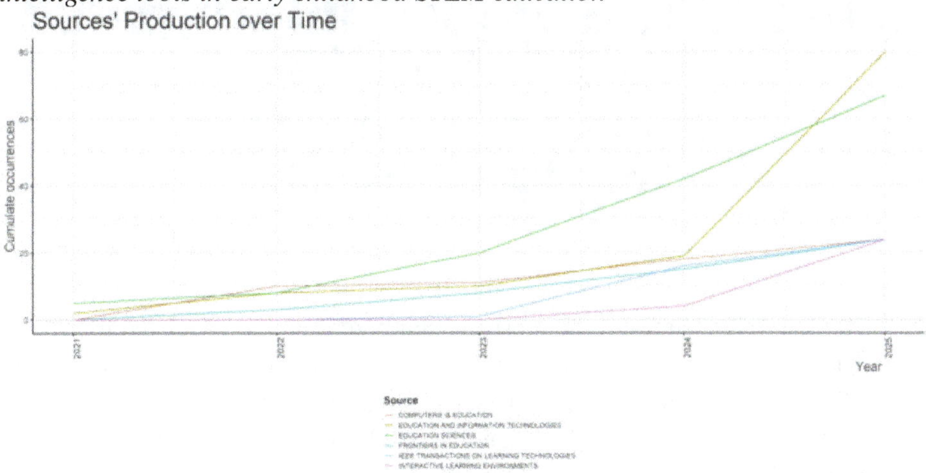

Between 2021 and 2025, a total of 443 articles were published on the use of productive artificial intelligence tools in early childhood STEM education, and the number of studies increased over the years (Figure 2). When examining the figure, a general upward trend in the number of articles published in the top six journals between 2021 and 2025 can be observed. In particular, there has been a notable increase in the journals 'Education and Information Technologies' and 'Education Sciences.' In the journal 'Education and Information Technologies,' where only two articles were published in 2021, this number rose to 80 by 2025. Similarly, the number of articles published in the journal 'Education Sciences' increased from five in 2021 to 67 in 2025. The 'Computers & Education' journal has also seen a steady increase since

2022, reaching 24 articles in 2025. The 'Frontiers in Education,' 'IEEE Transactions on Learning Technologies,' and 'Interactive Learning Environments' journals have also seen a notable increase, particularly after 2023. In the 'IEEE Transactions on Learning Technologies' journal, no articles were published in 2021 and 2022, but this number increased to 16 in 2024 and 24 in 2025. These findings indicate that research on educational technologies and information technology-focused studies have been published with increasing momentum over the years in these journals, reflecting a growing interest among researchers in these fields.

Figure 3. Word cloud based on keywords related on field of use of generative artificial ıntelligence tools in early childhood STEM education

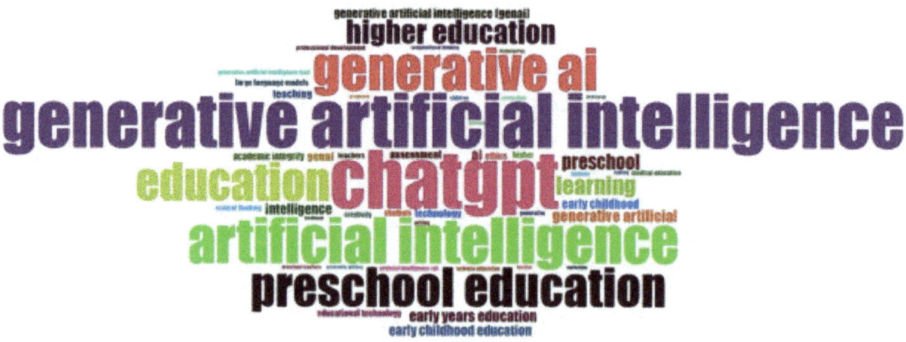

According to the findings, the most frequently repeated term related to the use of productive artificial intelligence tools in early childhood STEM education is 'ChatGPT' (201) (Figure 3). This result reveals that a large portion of recent studies are directly focused on ChatGPT. ChatGPT is followed by the terms 'Generative artificial intelligence' (190), 'Artificial intelligence' (158) and 'Generative AI' (147). These data show that artificial intelligence and, in particular, generative artificial intelligence technologies are being intensively addressed in research in the field of education. Among the terms that stand out in the context of education are 'Preschool education' (137), "Education" (133) and 'Higher education' (83). This shows that generative artificial intelligence is being addressed not only at the higher education level but also in studies targeting early age groups such as preschool education. The relatively lower frequency of the term 'learning' (65) suggests that artificial intelligence applications are being studied within the framework of specific levels and tools rather than general learning processes. Finally, partially overlapping terms such as 'preschool' (53) and 'generative artificial' (43) indicate that some key terms are written in different forms (e.g., "preschool" vs. 'preschool education'). This highlights the importance of ensuring term consistency when conducting keyword analysis. Overall, these findings reveal that research on AI applications in education is largely concentrated around ChatGPT and generative AI technologies, with this focus expanding to encompass both higher education and preschool-level applications.

Figure 4. Keywords of trend topics on research field of use of generative artificial intelligence tools in early childhood STEM education

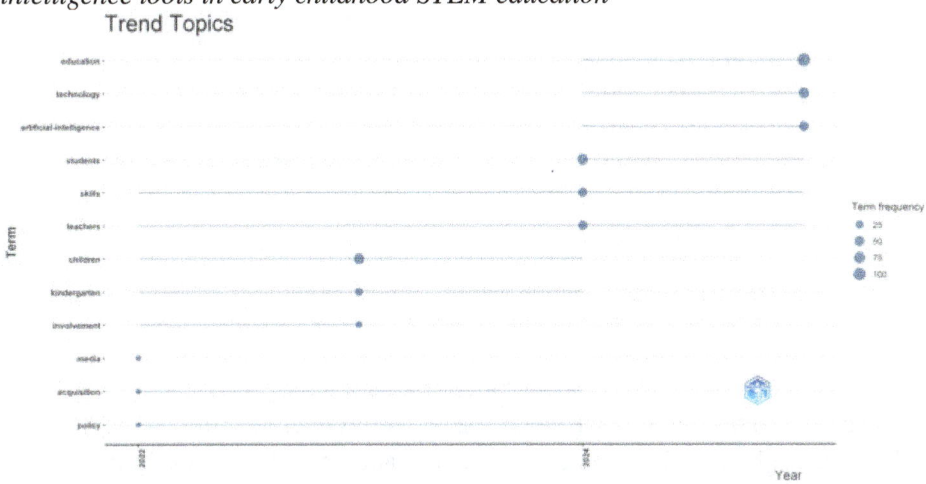

According to the findings in Figure 4, among the terms frequently used in 2022 in relation to the use of productive artificial intelligence tools in early childhood STEM education are children, kindergarten, involvement, skills, teachers, acquisition, media, and policy. These terms were used intensively in 2022 and showed a certain spread in subsequent years. In particular, terms related to early childhood education, such as 'children' (63 times) and 'kindergarten' (20 times), have been used increasingly since 2022. In 2023, the frequency of the terms *children*, *kindergarten*, and *involvement* continued, indicating that research trends on children's participation in education and early childhood education continued this year. However, there is no data indicating that new terms emerged this year; topics from the previous year continued. 2024 was a period in which the terms *students*, *skills*, *teachers*, and *education* became widespread. This year, with the prominence of the terms 'education' (111 times) and 'students' (69 times), the focus shifted to areas such as school-age education, teacher qualifications, and skill development. In 2025, the high frequency of basic terms such as *education*, *skills*, *teachers* and *students* continues. This indicates that education policies and pedagogical practices are becoming more student-centred and skill-based. In addition, terms such as *media* and *acquisition*, which appeared in previous years, have become less visible in recent years.

Figure 5. Most relevant sources on field of use of generative artificial ıntelligence tools in early childhood STEM education

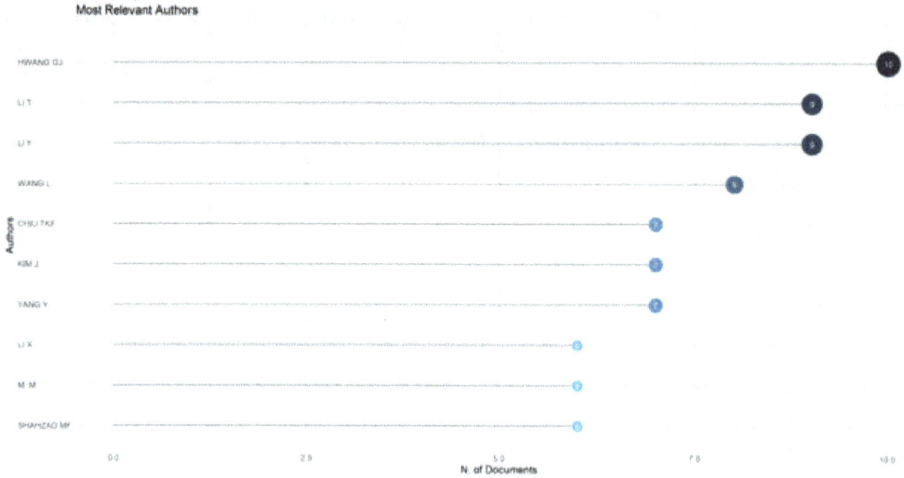

According to the author analysis on the use of productive artificial intelligence tools in early childhood STEM education, the author with the most publications is Hwang Gj with 10 articles (Figure 5). This author is followed by Lı T and Lı Y with 9 publications each, Wang L with 8 publications, Chıu Tkf, Kım J and Yang Y with 7 publications each, and Lı X, M. M and Shahzad MF with 6 publications each. This shows that certain researchers stand out in terms of publication output in the field and make important contributions that shape the field.

Figure 6. Top 10 productive institutions in the field of use of generative artificial intelligence tools in early childhood STEM education

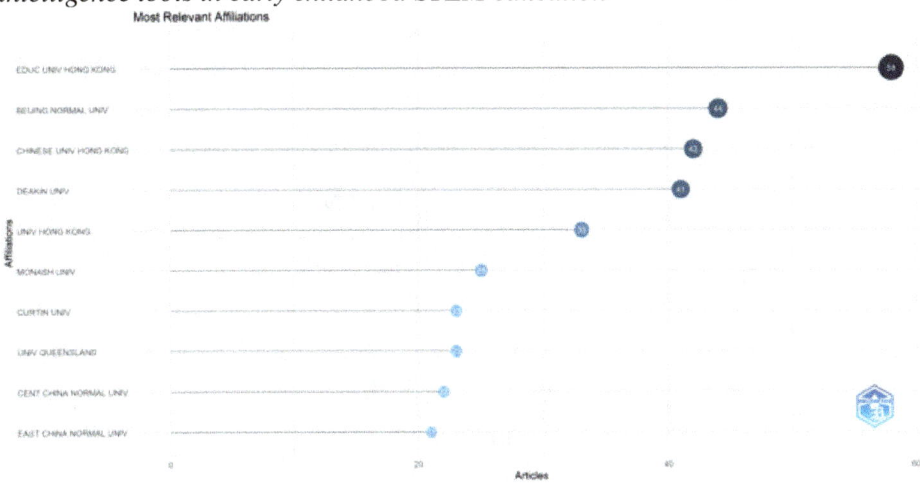

Figure 6 shows the institutions that have published the most on the use of generative artificial intelligence tools in early childhood STEM education. Findings related to institutional distribution indicate that publications on generative artificial intelligence and education are concentrated in specific universities. In this context, the institution with the most publications is The Education University of Hong Kong (n = 58). This university is followed by Beijing Normal University (n = 44), The Chinese University of Hong Kong (n = 42) and Deakin University (n = 41). It is noteworthy that these four institutions have made significant contributions to publications in the field of generative artificial intelligence and education. In addition, Australian-based universities such as The University of Hong Kong (n = 33), Monash University (n = 25), Curtin University (n = 23) and The University of Queensland (n = 23) also occupy important positions on the list. This shows that universities in both China and Australia are playing leading roles in this field. At the end of the list are Central China Normal University (n = 22) and East China Normal University (n = 21).

Figure 7. Network for inter-institutional collaboration in the field of use of generative artificial intelligence tools in early childhood STEM education

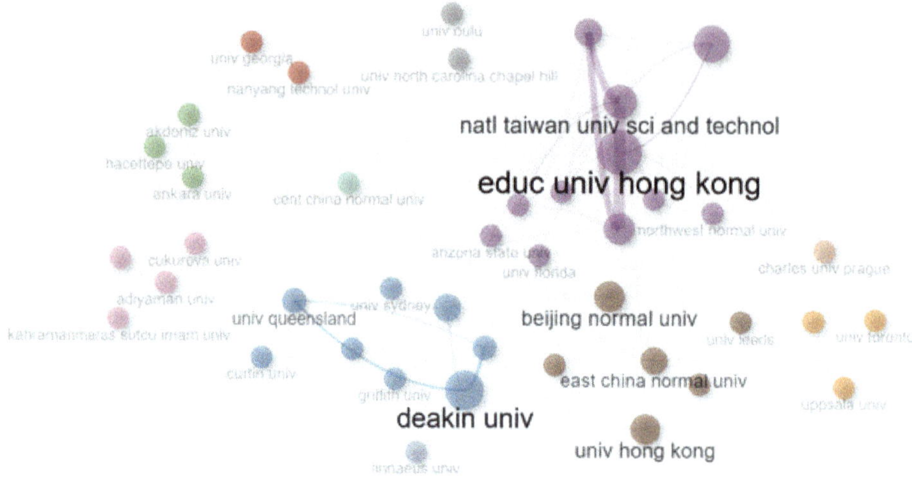

When examining inter-institutional collaborations related to research on the use of productive artificial intelligence tools in early childhood STEM education, 11 different clusters emerge (Figure 7). Cluster 1 consists of the University of Georgia and Nanyang Technological University. Cluster 2 includes Akdeniz University, Hacettepe University, and Ankara University. Cluster 3 includes Adiyaman University, Cukurova University, Gazi University, and Kahramanmaras Sütçü Imam University. Cluster 4 consists solely of Central China Normal University. Cluster 5 is represented by the University of North Carolina at Chapel Hill and the University of Oulu. Cluster 6 includes Deakin University, University of Queensland, Queensland University of Technology, Monash University, Curtin University, University of Wollongong, Griffith University, and University of Sydney. Cluster 7 consists of the Education University of Hong Kong, Chinese University of Hong Kong, National Taiwan University of Science and Technology, National Taichung University of Education, Yuan Ze University, Wenzhou University, Arizona State University, National Taiwan Normal University, Northwest Normal University, Zhejiang University, and University of Florida. Cluster 8 includes Beijing Normal University, the University of Hong Kong, East China Normal University, South China Normal University, Hong Kong Polytechnic University, and the University of Leeds. Cluster 9 comprises the University of Toronto, Uppsala University, and Harvard Medical School. Cluster 10 consists solely of Charles University in Prague. Cluster 11 is represented solely by Linnaeus University.

Figure 8. The most revelant countries field of use of generative artificial intelligence tools in early childhood STEM education

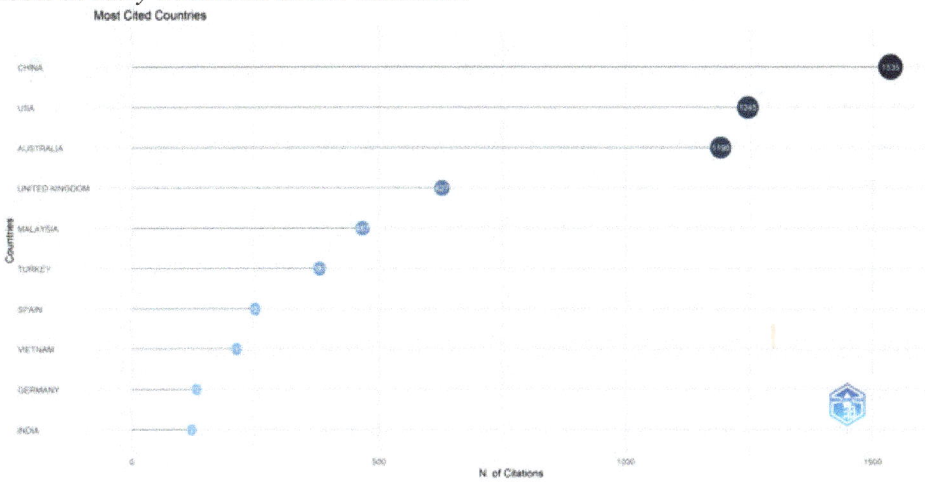

According to the data, China ranks first with 1,535 citations in the total number of citations related to the use of productive artificial intelligence tools in early childhood STEM education (Figure 8). It is followed by the United States with 1,245 citations, Australia with 1,190 citations, the United Kingdom with 627 citations, and Malaysia with 467 citations. Turkey ranks sixth with a total of 381 citations. Other countries in the ranking include Spain with 253 citations, Vietnam with 215 citations, Germany with 133 citations, and India with 123 citations.

Figure 9. Top 10 most globally cited documents field of use of generative artificial ıntelligence tools in early childhood STEM education

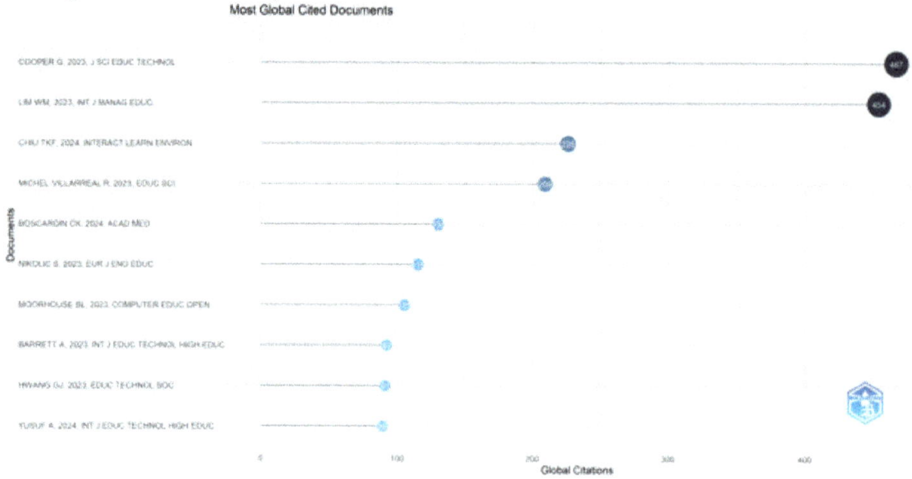

According to a citation analysis on the use of productive artificial intelligence tools in early childhood STEM education, the most cited study is the article published by Cooper G in 2023 in the Journal of Science Education and Technology, which received a total of 467 citations (Figure 9). This study is followed by Lim WM's article published in 2023 in the 'International Journal of Management Education' with 454 citations. In third place is Chiu TKF's study published in 2024 in the 'Interactive Learning Environments' journal with 226 citations. Other highly cited publications include those by Mıchel-Vıllarreal R (209 citations), Boscardin CK (130 citations), Nikolic S (115 citations), Moorhouse BL (105 citations), Barrett A (92 citations), Hwang GJ (91 citations), and Yusuf A (89 citations). These findings demonstrate that current and effective studies in the field quickly gain high levels of citations and are recognised as important reference sources by the research community.

Figure 10. Top 10 most relevant authors field of use of generative artificial ıntelligence tools in early childhood STEM education

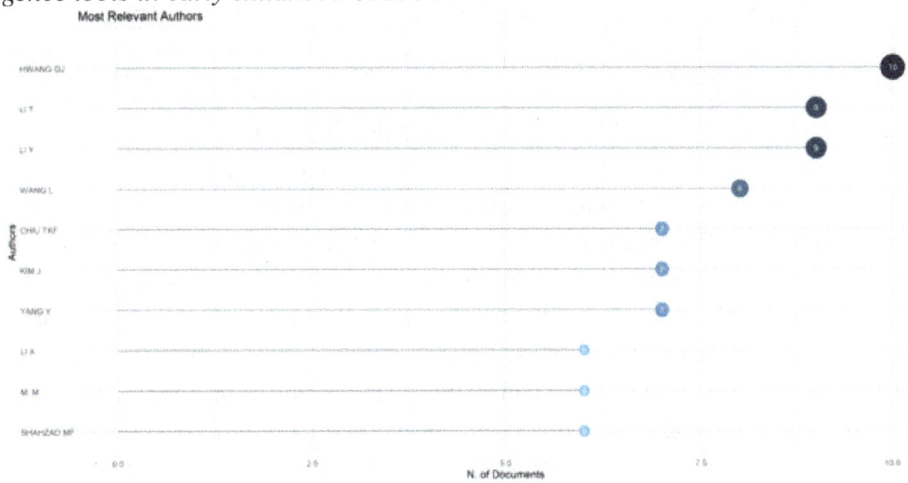

According to Figure 10, in the author analysis regarding the use of productive artificial intelligence tools in early childhood STEM education, Hwang Gj was determined to be the author who contributed the most to the field with 10 publications. This author is followed by Lı T and Lı Y with 9 publications each, Wang L with 8 publications, and Chıu Tkf, Kım J, and Yang Y with 7 publications each. Additionally, researchers Lı X, M. M, and Shahzad M.F each contributed 6 publications to the literature. These findings indicate that the aforementioned authors have played a significant role in shaping the direction of research in the field and have taken a central role in the formation of research trends.

RESULTS AND DISCUSSION

In this study, a bibliometric analysis of a total of 1,224 studies obtained from the Web of Science database on the use of productive artificial intelligence tools in early childhood STEM education was conducted. These analyses were performed using tables obtained from the analysis results menu provided by the database using the R programme and the Biblioshiny interface. In this context, studies on the use of generative artificial intelligence tools in early childhood STEM education were analysed and tabulated in each category, including annual publication trends, publishing journals and institutions, citation analysis, bibliographic links, co-author analysis, current topic trends, abstract and keyword distribution, prominent themes, and how these changed over the years. As a result of the analysis of publications on the use of productive artificial intelligence tools in early childhood STEM education, a total of 342 documents were found between 2021 and 2025. Within these sources, a total of 1,224 documents were found to have been published in this field.

The results also showed that 3,743 researchers worked in this field and 1,041 keywords were used. Looking at the 'annual publication trend' results of the study, it was seen that a total of 443 articles were written between 2021 and 2025, and that the trend of studies increased over the years. This shows that education technology and information technology-focused studies are being published in relevant journals with increasing momentum over the years and that researchers' interest in these fields is gradually increasing. With the development of technology and its widespread use in all areas of society, it is an expected result that technology, which has a significant place in education, will increase (Ersoy & Gürgen, 2021). For this reason, not only is the number of technology-related publications increasing every day (Valtonen et al., 2022), but it is also expected that there will be an increase in publications on the use of productive artificial intelligence tools in early childhood STEM education from the 2000s onwards (Ouyang et al., 2023; Temur, 2025; Yılmaz, 2023). Again, emphasising the importance of artificial intelligence, Wang and colleagues have highlighted the importance of adopting an exploratory education in artificial intelligence education and integrating it into science, mathematics, information technology and comprehensive application courses, as well as developing AI courses suitable for school conditions (Wang, 2023).

Among the most frequently repeated 'key words' in the results related to the use of productive artificial intelligence tools in early childhood STEM education, the term 'ChatGPT' comes first. This result reveals that a large part of the recent studies are directly focused on ChatGPT. The 'most frequently used terms' that stand out in the results include 'preschool,' 'child,' 'education,' 'teacher,' 'skill,' and 'higher education.' This situation shows that research on artificial intelligence applications in education is largely concentrated around ChatGPT and generative artificial intelligence technologies; that this concentration has expanded to include both higher education and preschool applications in the field of education; and that it is increasingly oriented towards student-centred and skill-based learning. ChatGPT occupies an important place in the literature on AI in education, particularly in developing conceptual understanding, reducing misconceptions in education, and increasing participation in STEM education (El Fathi et al., 2025). ChatGPT has become one of the most studied topics in the field of education due to its advantages such as being an AI tool with high accessibility potential that students are increasingly using (Cotton et al., 2024) and facilitating learning and teaching (Ateş et al., 2025; Farrokhnia et al., 2024). Zawacki-Richter et al. (2019) noted that most articles on AI applications in higher education were written in computer science and STEM disciplines (Zawacki-Richter et al., 2019).

The 'most publishing institutions' in the relevant field are generally universities in China and Australia, which have taken leading roles in this area. Again, the top two countries with the most citations in this field are China and the United States. In support of this, Un and Saleh (2024) noted that research on the application of artificial intelligence in STEM/STEAM education has shown a significant growth trend, particularly in China and the United States since 2019 (Sun & Saleh, 2024). When examining developments in the use and dissemination of artificial intelligence in national education, some UNESCO Member States such as the United States, Canada, China, and Finland have integrated artificial intelligence knowledge into existing subjects like science and technology, thereby promoting the STEAM approach at the primary and secondary education levels (Kandır & Temel, 2025; Li et al., 2020). When examining research on the use of artificial intelligence (AI)-supported tools in STEM/STEAM education from a country-specific perspective, it is evident that such research is concentrated primarily in developed countries such as the United States, Europe, and China. The economic and technological infrastructure of these countries undoubtedly plays a significant role in this development (Li et al., 2020). In other developing countries, AI-based educational applications are not widespread. This lack of widespread adoption is influenced by various structural, economic, and pedagogical limitations, such as inadequate digital infrastructure, limited internet connectivity, lack of support for AI-supported education policies, insufficient opportunities for teacher training, and lack of financial resources (OECD, 2024). This carries the risk of increasing educational inequalities between countries. Therefore, international collaborations, localized content, and strategies that strengthen teacher capacity are needed to ensure global opportunity equality in AI-based STEM education.

The authors of the most cited studies are Cooper G. (2023), Lim WM. (2024), Chiu TKF., Mıchel-Vıllarreal R, Boscardin CK., Nikolic S., Moorhouse BL., Barrett A., Hwang GJ., and Yusuf A. These findings indicate that current and effective studies in the field attract attention by receiving a high number of citations in a short period of time and are considered important reference sources by the research community. Keser Ateş, Kaleci & Erdoğan (2025) reached common conclusions in their bibliometric studies on artificial intelligence and stated that the six authors with the most citations in the relevant field are Gwo-Jen Hwang, Melissa Bond, Olaf Zawacki-Richter, Haoran Xie, Ahmed Tlili and Ronghuai Huang (Ateş et al., 2025).

The authors who have made the most significant contributions to the field of using productive artificial intelligence tools in early childhood STEM education are Hwang Gj, Li T and Li Y, Wang L, Chiu Tkf, Kim J, and Yang Y. These findings show that the authors have been influential in shaping the direction of research in this field and have played a central role in the formation of research trends.

In recent years, STEAM education has become an integral part of pre-university education, being implemented in kindergartens, primary schools, middle schools, and high schools. When we consider the supportive role of artificial intelligence as educational frameworks for students in the context of advancing technology, integrating it with STEM and increasing research in this area could contribute to a better understanding of how learning processes can be improved. Therefore, the impact of artificial intelligence tools on education needs to be further intensified and researched by more STEAM education researchers in future studies. With the rapid development of education, the STEM interdisciplinary integration model has also evolved and gained a new vitality and area of development in educational studies with the support of artificial intelligence (Wu, 2021).

REFERENCES

Al Darayseh, A., & Mersin, N. (2025). Integrating generative AI into STEM education: Insights from science and mathematics teachers. *International Electronic Journal of Mathematics Education, 20*(3), em0832.

Arı, S. (2024). Sınıf öğretmenlerinin yapay zekâ kaygılarının farklı değişkenler açısından incelenmesi. *Nevşehir Hacı Bektaş Veli Üniversitesi SBE Dergisi, 14*(4), 2393–2405. DOI: 10.30783/nevsosbilen.1519636

Aria, M., & Cuccurullo, C. (2017). bibliometrix: An R-tool for comprehensive science mapping analysis. *Journal of Informetrics, 11*(4), 959–975. DOI: 10.1016/j.joi.2017.08.007

Arora, S. D., & Chakraborty, A. (2021). Intellectual structure of consumer complaining behavior (CCB) research: A bibliometric analysis. *Journal of Business Research, 122*, 60–74. DOI: 10.1016/j.jbusres.2020.08.043

Ateş, S. K., Kaleci, F., & Erdoğan, A. (2025). Artificial intelligence in education: A bibliometric analysis. *Ahmet Keleşoğlu Eğitim Fakültesi Dergisi, 7*(1), 14–36.

Bayram, K., & Çelik, H. (2023). Yapay zekâ konusunda muhakeme ve girişimcilik becerileriyle bütünleştirilmiş sosyo-bilim etkinliği: Fen bilgisi öğretmen adaylarının görüşleri. *Fen Bilimleri Öğretimi Dergisi, 11*(1), 41–78. DOI: 10.56423/fbod.1241946

Bibri, S. E., & Jagatheesaperumal, S. K. (2023). Harnessing the potential of the metaverse and artificial intelligence for the internet of city things: Cost-effective XReality and synergistic AIoT technologies. *Smart Cities, 6*(5), 2397–2429. DOI: 10.3390/smartcities6050109

Chen, L., Chen, P., & Lin, Z. (2020). Artificial intelligence in education: A review. *IEEE Access : Practical Innovations, Open Solutions, 8*, 75264–75278. DOI: 10.1109/ACCESS.2020.2988510

Cotton, D. R., Cotton, P. A., & Shipway, J. R. (2024). Chatting and cheating: Ensuring academic integrity in the era of ChatGPT. *Innovations in Education and Teaching International, 61*(2), 228–239. DOI: 10.1080/14703297.2023.2190148

Dao, L. T., Tran, T., Van Le, H., Nguyen, G. N., & Trinh, T. P. T. (2023). A bibliometric analysis of Research on Education 4.0 during the 2017–2021 period. *Education and Information Technologies, 28*(3), 2437–2453. DOI: 10.1007/s10639-022-11211-4

Demircioğlu, E., & Demir, B. (2024). Yapay zekâ destekli matematik eğitimi: Bir içerik analizi. [JSHSR]. *International Journal of Social and Humanities Sciences Research, 11*(106), 771–785.

Donthu, N., Kumar, S., Mukherjee, D., Pandey, N., & Lim, W. M. (2021). How to conduct a bibliometric analysis: An overview and guidelines. *Journal of Business Research, 133*, 285–296. DOI: 10.1016/j.jbusres.2021.04.070

Duralar, B. (2024). *Matematik eğitiminde yapay zekâ araştırmaları: Sistematik bir inceleme.* Balıkesir Üniversitesi Fen Bilimleri Enstitüsü.

El Fathi, T., Saad, A., Larhzil, H., Lamri, D., & Al Ibrahmi, E. M. (2025). Integrating generative AI into STEM education: Enhancing conceptual understanding, addressing misconceptions, and assessing student acceptance. *Disciplinary and Interdisciplinary Science Education Research, 7*(1), 6. DOI: 10.1186/s43031-025-00125-z

Ersoy, M., & Gürgen, L. (2021). Eğitim teknolojileri ile ilgili makalelerin incelenmesi. *E-Uluslararası Eğitim Araştırmaları Dergisi, 12*(2), 1–16.

Farrokhnia, M., Banihashem, S. K., Noroozi, O., & Wals, A. (2024). A SWOT analysis of ChatGPT: Implications for educational practice and research. *Innovations in Education and Teaching International, 61*(3), 460–474. DOI: 10.1080/14703297.2023.2195846

Gülbahar, Y., & Kalelioğlu, F. (2018). Bilişim Teknolojileri ve Bilgisayar Bilimi: Öğretim Programi Güncelleme Süreci. *Millî Eğitim Dergisi, 47*(217), 5–23.

Holmes, W., Bialik, M., & Fadel, C. (2019). *Artificial intelligence in education promises and implications for teaching and learning.* Center for Curriculum Redesign.

Hwang, G.-J., Xie, H., Wah, B. W., & Gašević, D. (2020). Vision, challenges, roles and research issues of Artificial Intelligence in Education. İçinde *Computers and Education: Artificial Intelligence* (C. 1, s. 100001). Elsevier.

İşler, B., & Kılıç, M. (2021). Eğitimde yapay zekâ kullanimi ve gelişimi. *Yeni Medya Elektronik Dergisi, 5*(1), 1–11.

KANDIR, A., & TEMEL, M. (2025). OKUL ÖNCESİ DÖNEMDE YAPAY ZEKÂ OKURYAZARLIĞI EĞİTİMİNE İLİŞKİN ÖĞRETMEN GÖRÜŞLERİNİN İNCELENMESİ. *Journal of History School, 18*(LXXIV), 1–21.

Kapoor, K. K., Tamilmani, K., Rana, N. P., Patil, P., Dwivedi, Y. K., & Nerur, S. (2018). Advances in social media research: Past, present and future. *Information Systems Frontiers, 20*(3), 531–558. DOI: 10.1007/s10796-017-9810-y

Kutlucan, E., & Seferoğlu, S. S. (2024). Eğitimde yapay zekâ kullanımı: ChatGPT'nin KEFE ve PEST analizi. *Türk Eğitim Bilimleri Dergisi*, *22*(2), 1059–1083. DOI: 10.37217/tebd.1368821

Li, Y., Wang, K., Xiao, Y., & Froyd, J. E. (2020). Research and trends in STEM education: A systematic review of journal publications. *International Journal of STEM Education*, *7*(1), 1–16. DOI: 10.1186/2196-7822-1-1

Lin, C.-J., Lee, H.-Y., Wang, W.-S., Huang, Y.-M., & Wu, T.-T. (2025). Enhancing reflective thinking in STEM education through experiential learning: The role of generative AI as a learning aid. *Education and Information Technologies*, *30*(5), 6315–6337. DOI: 10.1007/s10639-024-13072-5

Ouyang, F., Dinh, T. A., & Xu, W. (2023). A systematic review of AI-driven educational assessment in STEM education. *Journal for STEM Education Research*, *6*(3), 408–426. DOI: 10.1007/s41979-023-00112-x

Rejeb, A., Abdollahi, A., Rejeb, K., & Treiblmaier, H. (2022). Drones in agriculture: A review and bibliometric analysis. *Computers and Electronics in Agriculture*, *198*, 107017. DOI: 10.1016/j.compag.2022.107017

Russell, S. J., & Norvig, P. (2010). *Artificial intelligence a modern approach.*

Smith, B. C. (2019). *The promise of artificial intelligence: Reckoning and judgment.* Mit Press. DOI: 10.7551/mitpress/12385.001.0001

Song, Y., Chen, X., Hao, T., Liu, Z., & Lan, Z. (2019). Exploring two decades of research on classroom dialogue by using bibliometric analysis. *Computers & Education*, *137*, 12–31. DOI: 10.1016/j.compedu.2019.04.002

Su, G. (2018). Unemployment in the AI Age. *AI Matters*, *3*(4), 35–43. DOI: 10.1145/3175502.3175511

Sun, N., & Saleh, S. (2024). Mapping the Landscape of AI Implementation in STEM and STEAM Education: A Bibliometric Analysis. *International Conference on Technology in Education*, 99-111. DOI: 10.1007/978-981-96-0205-6_7

Temur, S. (2025). 2000-2024 Yılları Arasında Eğitim Alanında Yapılan Yapay Zekâ Konulu Lisansüstü Çalışmaların İncelenmesi. *Dokuz Eylül Üniversitesi Buca Eğitim Fakültesi Dergisi*, *63*, 1162–1199.

Uğraş, H., & Uğraş, M. (2025). ChatGPT in early childhood STEM education: Can it be an innovative tool to overcome challenges? *Education and Information Technologies*, *30*(4), 4277–4305. DOI: 10.1007/s10639-024-12960-0

Uğraş, H., Uğraş, M., Papadakis, S., & Kalogiannakis, M. (2024). ChatGPT-supported education in primary schools: The potential of ChatGPT for sustainable practices. *Sustainability (Basel), 16*(22), 9855. DOI: 10.3390/su16229855

Uğraş, M. (2024). Evaluation of ChatGPT Usage in Preschool Education: Teacher Perspectives. *Eğitim Ve İnsani Bilimler Dergisi: Teori Ve Uygulama, 15*(30), 387–414.

Uğraş, M., Çakır, Z., Zacharis, G., & Kalogiannakis, M. (2025). ChatGPT in Early Childhood Science Education: Can It Offer Innovative Effective Solutions to Overcome Challenges? *Computers, 14*(9), 368. DOI: 10.3390/computers14090368

Valtonen, T., López-Pernas, S., Saqr, M., Vartiainen, H., Sointu, E. T., & Tedre, M. (2022). The nature and building blocks of educational technology research. *Computers in Human Behavior, 128*, 107123. DOI: 10.1016/j.chb.2021.107123

Van Keulen, H. (2018). STEM in early childhood education. *European Journal of STEM Education, 3*(3), 06.

Wang, H. (2023). Formation Mechanism and Practice Path Model of Teachers' Intelligent Literacy in the Context of Artificial Intelligence. *2023 2nd International Conference on Artificial Intelligence and Computer Information Technology (AICIT)*, 1-6.

Wu, L. (2021). Construction of STEM Interdisciplinary Integration Model Supported by Educational Artificial Intelligence. *2021 IEEE 2nd International Conference on Big Data, Artificial Intelligence and Internet of Things Engineering (ICBAIE)*, 769-772.

Xu, W., & Ouyang, F. (2022). The application of AI technologies in STEM education: A systematic review from 2011 to 2021. *International Journal of STEM Education, 9*(1), 59. DOI: 10.1186/s40594-022-00377-5

Yılmaz, A. (2023). Fen bilimleri eğitiminde dijital uygulamalar, yapay zekâ ve akıllı yazılımlar: Tehditler ve fırsatlar. A. Akpınar. *Matematik ve Fen Bilimleri Üzerine Araştırmalar-II*, 1-20.

Zawacki-Richter, O., Marín, V. I., Bond, M., & Gouverneur, F. (2019). Systematic review of research on artificial intelligence applications in higher education–where are the educators? *International Journal of Educational Technology in Higher Education, 16*(1), 1–27. DOI: 10.1186/s41239-019-0171-0

Zhai, X., Chu, X., Chai, C. S., Jong, M. S. Y., Istenic, A., Spector, M., Liu, J.-B., Yuan, J., & Li, Y. (2021). A Review of Artificial Intelligence (AI) in Education from 2010 to 2020. *Complexity, 2021*(1), 1–18. DOI: 10.1155/2021/8812542

Zhu, H. (2020). Big data and artificial intelligence modeling for drug discovery. *Annual Review of Pharmacology and Toxicology*, *60*(1), 573–589. DOI: 10.1146/annurev-pharmtox-010919-023324

Zupic, I., & Čater, T. (2015). Bibliometric methods in management and organization. *Organizational Research Methods*, *18*(3), 429–472. DOI: 10.1177/1094428114562629

Chapter 3
AI-Supported Assessment of Children's Scientific Process Skills in Exploring Liquid Buoyancy

Ali İbrahim Can Gözüm
https://orcid.org/0000-0002-7765-4403
Kafkas University, Turkey

Cansel Doymaz
https://orcid.org/0009-0006-1521-7714
Kafkas University, Turkey

ABSTRACT

This study examines the process through which preschool teachers utilize an AI-supported digital interface to assess children's scientific process skills within the scope of early childhood science education, employing a Design-Based Research (DBR) approach.The AI-supported system enabled teachers to systematically record classroom observations, generate automated reports, and receive individualized activity recommendations. The study was conducted with three preschool teachers and fourteen children aged 4–5 years in their respective classrooms. Following science activities implemented by the teachers, observation data were entered into the system, and qualitative data regarding the usability and functionality of the program were collected. In conclusion, the developed digital interface emerges as an innovative, practical, and supportive tool for assessment processes in early childhood education.

DOI: 10.4018/979-8-3373-9074-1.ch003

INTRODUCTION

The early childhood period is one of the developmental stages in which children's natural curiosity and their tendency to make sense of the world around them are most intense. This curiosity encourages them to observe, establish cause–effect relationships, and participate in simple experimental processes as part of their learning. Therefore, supporting scientific process skills through structured science activities at an early age helps children develop lasting understandings of scientific concepts and forms the foundation for more complex thinking skills that will emerge in later stages of learning (Ünal & Aral, 2014; Ay et al., 2015).

Scientific process skills are fundamental competencies that enable individuals to construct scientific thinking, conduct investigations, solve problems, and analyze and interpret the information obtained. These skills include key steps of scientific knowledge production, such as observing, formulating hypotheses, classifying, collecting and analyzing data, and making inferences. Gaining these skills starting in early childhood contributes not only to children's cognitive development but also to laying the foundations of scientific literacy (Ayas et al., 2007).

Zeidan and Jayosi (2015) emphasize that children's acquisition of scientific process skills is possible when knowledge, skills, and attitudes are supported in a holistic manner. However, teaching abstract science concepts at early ages presents various challenges. Concepts such as buoyancy, density, weight, and volume are frequently misunderstood by children, and when they are not linked to everyday experiences, conceptual misconceptions may emerge (Özsevgeç & Çepni, 2006). Basic and integrated scientific process skills play an important role in all scientific investigations conducted with children (Zeidan & Jayosi, 2015). Therefore, it is necessary to create structured and experiment-based learning environments in which abstract concepts are supported with concrete experiences. Such activities enable children to actively engage in scientific skills such as hypothesizing, observing, and collecting data (Çığrık & Özkan, 2016).

In this process, access to developmentally appropriate assessment tools is as important as teachers' pedagogical competencies. Traditional measurement methods may fall short in adequately revealing children's scientific process skills. For this reason, tools that are observation-based and process-oriented are needed (Akşin-Yavuz & Zembat, 2016). In recent years, artificial intelligence (AI) technologies have been increasingly integrated into educational settings to address this need. These technologies offer teachers the opportunity to monitor students' scientific process skills continuously, instantly, and in a more objective manner (Chiu et al., 2022). AI tools support the assessment process through functions such as structuring developmental observation records, analyzing children's responses, and generating content related to activity processes, while also providing individualized feedback for each child and reducing teachers' workload (Memarian & Doleck, 2023).

In early childhood science education, these technologies save teachers time in the evaluation of structured activities and contribute to data-driven decision-making. However, although there are studies focusing on the development of scientific process skills in early childhood (Ünal & Aral, 2014; Ay et al., 2015), the tools used to assess these skills are predominantly traditional, paper-based, and reliant on teacher observation (Akşin-Yavuz & Zembat, 2016). This increases subjectivity in the assessment process, complicates time management, and makes systematic data analysis more difficult. With the increasing use of AI-supported digital systems in education, it has been emphasized that student performance can be monitored in a more objective and individualized manner (Chiu et al., 2022; Dede, 2010).

The assessment-for-learning approach in early childhood education is based on communicating learning goals clearly to children, collecting evidence in natural environments, and interpreting these data using qualitative tools such as developmental observation forms or rubrics (Memarian & Doleck, 2023). However, most existing studies focus on higher grade levels (Alan, 2019; Çevik, 2019), and AI-supported assessment practices in preschool settings remain limited (Aşık et al., 2023).

This study presents a significant innovation by integrating an AI-supported program with an observation form developed to assess scientific process skills in early childhood education. Structured activities centered on an abstract concept such as buoyancy further enhance the system's utility by facilitating smoother assessment processes for teachers. The system provides real-time developmental reports and directly informs instructional decision-making. In this respect, the study constitutes an application-based and original research example that documents preschool teachers' experiences with technology-supported assessment tools. Moreover, by offering a model of AI-supported assessment implementation in the context of early childhood education in Türkiye, this study fills an important gap in the literature.

Research Aim and Research Questions

The primary aim of this research is to examine how an artificial intelligence (AI)–supported assessment system is used by preschool teachers to evaluate young children's scientific process skills within the scope of early childhood science education and to analyze the outputs generated by this system. In this regard, the study seeks to qualitatively evaluate the process of using the AI-supported assessment system, teachers' experiences during this process, the challenges they encountered, and the system's effectiveness in educational contexts. The research additionally aims to explore the extent to which this digital system can present children's scientific process skills accurately, systematically, and objectively; how it influences teachers' workload during the assessment process; and how it contributes to classroom practices.

Guided by these aims, the research is structured around the following questions:

- To what extent does the AI-supported assessment system present preschool children's scientific process skills accurately, systematically, and objectively?
- How does the use of the AI-supported assessment system influence teachers' workload and the way they manage the assessment process?
- What do teachers' views on the AI-supported assessment system reveal about the system's strengths, limitations, and practical functionality in classroom settings?

THEORETICAL FRAMEWORK

Pedagogical Representation of the Concept of Buoyancy and the Support of Science Process Skills

In early childhood, fostering fundamental scientific process skills that enable children to make sense of their environment is of great importance. During this period, children take their first steps into scientific thinking through basic skills such as observing, predicting, measuring, comparing, classifying, and collecting data (Husaini, Ikhsan, & Toran, 2019). Developing these skills at an early age contributes to children's growth as individuals who question, explore, and solve problems. Everyday experiences—such as ships floating on the sea, stones sinking in a stream, or a cup floating in the bathtub—provide children with initial exposure to fundamental science concepts such as buoyancy, floating, and sinking. However, these concepts are highly abstract and often difficult for young children to comprehend (Biddulph & Osborne, 1984). Research indicates that even without fully understanding abstract concepts such as density, young children are capable of predicting floating and sinking phenomena based on their observations (Özsevgeç & Çepni, 2006).

Despite this early intuition, many studies have shown that children experience significant difficulties in fully understanding these concepts, often confusing weight, volume, and density, which leads to conceptual misunderstandings (Smith et al., 1985; Carey, 1991; Özsevgeç & Çepni, 2006). Traditional instructional methods have been found insufficient in concretizing such abstract concepts and may even reinforce students' misconceptions (Loverude et al., 2003; Yin et al., 2008). For this reason, teaching science concepts such as buoyancy must go beyond transmitting conceptual knowledge; it should be supported by structured, experiment-based learning activities that promote the development of children's scientific process skills.

In science activities, these concepts should serve as tools that encourage children to actively engage in scientific skills such as observing, hypothesizing, designing experiments, and analyzing data. In this way, abstract concepts can be concretized, misconceptions can be addressed, and children's scientific thinking and problem-solving abilities can be strengthened.

The primary purpose of this study is to support the development of scientific process skills in early childhood through science activities centered on the concept of buoyancy and to evaluate this process effectively using AI-supported observation tools. This approach is critically important for fostering children's deep understanding of science and for ensuring that fundamental scientific processes are acquired as core competencies in early science education.

Assessment Processes in Early Childhood Education

Assessment is defined as the process of observing the characteristics of objects and events and expressing them through numbers or symbols. In early childhood education, it refers to procedures used to determine the extent to which children achieve specific developmental competencies. Assessment, on the other hand, is the continuous and comprehensive process of collecting and interpreting information about children's knowledge, behaviors, and skills in order to make informed decisions (Akşin-Yavuz & Zembat, 2016). In early childhood settings, this process requires a multidimensional approach that encompasses identifying children's developmental characteristics, determining their needs, planning appropriate learning activities, and providing families with meaningful feedback about their children's progress (Allen, 2007).

The assessment and evaluation process in early childhood relies on the systematic analysis of data gathered through both spontaneous and planned observations. All documents collected throughout this process play a significant role in assessing children's learning processes and developmental progress. When integrated effectively, these documents enable teachers not only to conduct internal evaluations but also to communicate transparently and evidence-based information with families regarding the child's development (Peterson & Elam, 2020). Within the scope of the present study, the use of AI-supported tools by early childhood teachers to assess children's scientific process skills becomes particularly significant. An effective assessment process should operate as a continuous, interconnected cycle between the teacher and the child. Assessment outcomes serve as guiding inputs for subsequent stages of instruction (Arnold et al., 2008). Accordingly, the functionality of the assessment process depends on the use of valid and reliable tools, as well as teachers' ability to implement these tools effectively.

Through the integration of the observation form developed in this study with an AI-supported digital application, teachers were able to systematically record and analyze their observations of children's scientific process skills and generate developmental reports. This enabled teachers to monitor children's progress more objectively and with up-to-date data while designing new instructional activities based on assessment results. Such an approach enhances the quality of the assessment-evaluation process while reducing teachers' workload (Chiu et al., 2022; Aşık et al., 2023).

Assessment methods used in preschool education must be appropriate to children's developmental levels and motivational needs. Approaches that decrease motivation, fail to capture children's interest, or harm their sense of self may reduce the effectiveness of the assessment process (Autry et al., 2009). AI-supported systems address these challenges by offering user-friendly interfaces and pedagogically appropriate designs that help teachers manage the assessment process more efficiently. The program utilized in this study enabled teachers to overcome such obstacles, allowing them to collect reliable and continuous data.

Finally, teachers' ongoing evaluation of their own practices is a critical factor in improving the quality of education (Balcı & Tezel-Şahin, 2021). AI-supported observation and assessment systems support teachers' self-evaluation processes, making the monitoring and development of children's scientific process skills more effective. In this context, the observation form and AI interface developed within this study aim to contribute to the modernization of assessment practices in early childhood education and to enhance teachers' pedagogical competencies.

Assessment Through Teacher Observation in Early Childhood Education

Measurement and assessment are indispensable tools for understanding and supporting children's development and learning processes in early childhood education. Through these processes, children's progress in knowledge, skills, and attitudes can be monitored, developmental needs can be identified, and the extent to which educational programs meet their intended goals can be evaluated (Akçadağ, 2010). In early childhood, assessment requires a multidimensional approach that considers children's holistic developmental characteristics, ensures continuous monitoring of the learning environment, and enables timely interventions when necessary (Acar, 2008).

Assessment in early childhood should focus not only on outcomes but also on the learning process itself, and it should be conducted continuously in ways that encompass children's social, emotional, cognitive, and motor development (Çoruhlu et al., 2008). In many early childhood classrooms, assessment practices remain limited. This gap may stem from teachers' lack of awareness regarding available assessment tools or insufficient competence in implementing them. Observation is therefore essential for helping teachers understand how children learn and enabling them to plan learning outcomes tailored to children's needs and embed these into daily classroom experiences (Thornton-Lang, 2012). The qualitative data teachers obtain by observing children play a foundational role in understanding individual differences and supporting developmental progress.

However, in traditional approaches, assessment often relies heavily on teachers' subjective judgments, resulting in insufficient measurement of deeper learning dimensions such as children's thinking processes, problem-solving abilities, and scientific process skills (Akçadağ, 2010). Furthermore, early childhood teachers use observation-based assessment to track children's developmental levels, organize learning environments appropriately, and provide individualized support to children (Çoruhlu et al., 2009). Teachers also play a crucial role in supporting children's understanding of science concepts and guiding them in developing scientific process skills. In particular, the observation phase enables children to use their senses to explore their environment, think analytically, and make decisions based on their observations (Maraisane, Jita, & Jita, 2024). Additionally, the systematic recording and analysis of teachers' observations are vital for ensuring the reliability and effectiveness of the assessment process (Çepni & Çoruhlu, 2010).

In early childhood education programs grounded in constructivist learning theory, measurement and assessment processes have been redesigned to support children's active learning. As a result, process-oriented assessment methods have become increasingly prominent (Gömleksiz & Bulut, 2007).

In the context of science education, teacher observation is an effective method for understanding children's use of scientific process skills and their development of curiosity and inquiry-oriented attitudes. The acquisition of scientific process skills through structured learning experiences in early childhood not only enhances children's ability to make sense of the world around them but also supports their capacity to produce creative solutions to the problems they encounter. Learning these skills at an early age strengthens children's scientific thinking abilities and contributes to the development of positive attitudes toward science. Therefore, educational environments that offer a supportive teaching approach and provide guidance from the outset of the learning process are essential for helping children internalize these skills (Maraisane, Jita, & Jita, 2024).

Teachers can monitor children's understanding of scientific concepts and their progress in scientific process skills by observing their behaviors during experiments, group activities, and everyday learning experiences (Kocaarslan, 2012). Through these observations, teachers can identify children's learning styles, strengths, and areas in need of improvement, enabling them to plan appropriate feedback and supportive activities (Gömleksiz & Bulut, 2007).

Teacher observation–based assessment in early childhood provides opportunities not only to monitor academic gains but also to track the development of children's scientific thinking skills, problem-solving abilities, and scientific attitudes. This process is critical for enhancing the effectiveness of instructional strategies and developing approaches that are responsive to children's learning needs (Çepni & Çoruhlu, 2010). Moreover, the systematic recording and analysis of observation data using AI-supported tools offers innovative and reliable methods for assessing scientific process skills in early childhood education.

Science Education and Artificial Intelligence–Supported Assessment Approaches

With the rapid advancement of technology, the field of education has undergone significant transformations, and science education has been particularly influenced by these changes. Artificial intelligence has emerged as a prominent technology that supports and enhances learning processes in science education (Sevgi & Yılmaz, 2023). Curiosity is an innate human trait; young children, driven by this curiosity, explore their surroundings and unknowingly employ scientific process skills in the process (Roberts, 2021). Science education in early childhood aims to develop students' scientific thinking skills, increase their interest in science, and enable them to integrate scientific knowledge into their daily lives (Agnoli et al., 2018). However, traditional instructional methods often fall short in capturing children's attention and fail to fully stimulate curiosity and motivation toward science. At this point, AI-supported interactive simulations and personalized learning environments facilitate children's understanding of abstract science concepts by making them more concrete (Sevgi & Yılmaz, 2023; Chan & Yuen, 2014).

Early childhood science education and AI-supported assessment processes—the central focus of this study—play a significant role in observing and fostering children's scientific process skills. AI-supported assessment systems contribute to teachers' instructional decision-making processes by taking into account individual differences in early learning. These systems provide data based on children's developmental levels, varying learning paces, and individual needs, allowing teachers to guide the learning process more objectively. The analysis of children's responses during activities through AI algorithms helps teachers identify children's strengths while also highlighting areas in need of developmental support (Vasconcelos, Rodrigues, & dos Santos, 2023). Thus, the assessment process becomes not only outcome-oriented but also process-oriented and child-centered. AI technologies adapt to children's individual learning rates and needs and provide teachers with data-driven analytics, enabling the monitoring of developmental progress and the design of new instructional activities (Casal-Otero et al., 2023). In this regard, the

AI-supported observation interface developed in this study supports teachers in systematically monitoring and evaluating scientific process skills.

On the other hand, important debates exist regarding the use of artificial intelligence in science education. One major concern relates to its potential effects on students' creativity and capacity for original thinking. Since AI operates within predefined algorithms, some argue that it may restrict children's ability to generate original ideas and may standardize learning environments (Sevgi & Yılmaz, 2023; Chan & Yuen, 2014). For this reason, AI applications in science education should be designed to support creativity and should be integrated with pedagogical approaches that encourage children's original thinking (Ayyıldız & Yılmaz, 2021; Baer & Kaufman, 2008).

Creativity in science education is a critical skill that forms the foundation of scientific discoveries and innovations. Supporting this skill at an early age contributes to children's development in problem-solving, critical thinking, and scientific process skills (Slade & Prinsloo, 2013). In AI-supported science education, monitoring children's individual performance and providing personalized feedback offer valuable opportunities for fostering these creative processes (Casal-Otero et al., 2023).

In conclusion, AI-supported assessment approaches in early childhood science education hold great potential for enhancing the quality of learning processes and supporting the development of scientific process skills. The AI-supported observation form and interface developed in this study serve as concrete examples of this technological transformation, enabling teachers to evaluate children's competencies in science more effectively and systematically.

Future Perspectives on Artificial Intelligence in Early Childhood Education

In today's world, developments in artificial intelligence (AI) are rapidly increasing, and these advancements are creating new opportunities for children as well. In their study, Chen and Li (2025) discuss these emerging possibilities and emphasize that AI presents a dual reality in early childhood education. This dual reality encompasses both learning opportunities for young children and potential ethical challenges. They highlight the need for future research focusing on parent-, child-, and educator-centered co-design processes, the integration of privacy considerations into these design processes, the development of age-appropriate adaptations for early childhood, and investigations across diverse educational contexts.

A review of various studies indicates that AI curricula have also been found effective in early childhood education. These curricula contribute to children's cognitive skills as well as their understanding of AI-related concepts such as artificial intelligence and machine learning (Chen & Li, 2025). Additionally, Kewalramani et al. (2021) suggest that researchers working in this field could design engaging activities in which children interact with AI robots to help develop their thinking about AI concepts.

The literature further shows that AI has increasingly been examined in the context of early childhood and that its effectiveness has been supported through empirical findings. The integration of AI into different phases of education also suggests that it is becoming a component of broader educational practices. When examining existing studies, it becomes evident that understanding how the concept of AI should be approached and the extent to which educators possess knowledge and competence regarding AI are of critical importance. Findings in the literature indicate that although AI is becoming more visible in early childhood education, applications related to assessment processes remain limited and open to further development.

Accordingly, the methodology followed in this study is presented in detail below to explain how the research was structured.

METHOD

In this study, a design-based research (DBR) approach was adopted to examine the functioning of an artificial intelligence–supported digital interface used by preschool teachers to assess children's scientific process skills in early childhood science education.

the first phase of the research, an observation form based on seven scientific process skills was developed: observation, classification, prediction, data collection, inference, measurement, and problem solving. These seven skills were also transferred to the machine learning model as training data. The developed form was integrated into a digital environment, and a machine learning–based AI-supported assessment interface was designed.

The interface enabled teachers to systematically record their observations following buoyancy (floating–sinking) activities and automatically generate reports regarding children's developmental progress. While the numerical scores entered by teachers were processed by machine learning algorithms, the Natural Language Processing (NLP) component analyzed teachers' free-text notes and produced additional meaningful data to support the evaluation process.

The data collection process progressed through the implementation of science activities by teachers, the entry of their observations into the digital interface, and the examination of the system-generated reports. During the data analysis and system development stages, qualitative analysis methods were employed, focusing on teacher experiences, system functionality, and challenges encountered throughout the process.

The algorithmic classifications and interpretive outputs produced by the system were evaluated for accuracy by an expert preschool teacher (Teacher 3). This expert validation played a critical role in verifying the decisions of the machine learning model and increasing the reliability of the system.

This process aimed not only to contribute theoretically to educational practice but also to support the development of effective and applicable AI-supported assessment tools within the context of early childhood science education.

RESEARCH DESIGN

Figure 1. Concept map of design-based research

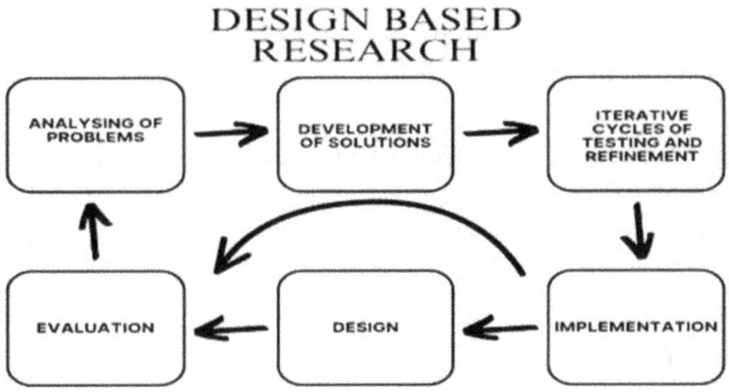

According to Figure 1, the Design-Based Research (DBR) approach is a cyclical, flexible, and collaborative research methodology used to solve an educational problem and to develop an innovative intervention within a real-life context (Wang & Hannafin, 2005). In this approach, the processes of analysis, design, implementation, evaluation, and redesign are carried out interactively. As Anderson and Shattuck (2012, p. 17) explain, DBR also encompasses a mixed-methods perspective in which multiple data collection tools and techniques are used simultaneously.

In this study, the DBR approach was adopted to effectively teach an abstract science concept such as buoyancy at the preschool level and to develop an AI-supported digital interface for assessing children's scientific process skills.

The development process of the study was carried out through the following steps:

- **Literature Review:** A comprehensive theoretical framework was established on early childhood science education, scientific process skills, AI-supported assessment systems, and teacher observations.

- **Initial Design and Material Development:** An observation form based on scientific process skills was developed and integrated into an AI-supported digital interface.
- **Pilot Implementation:** The developed interface was used by teachers in the classroom. Predetermined science activities were implemented, and observations related to the children were recorded in the system.
- **Collecting Feedback:** Qualitative data were gathered from teachers regarding system use, functionality, and the observation process. Based on this feedback, revisions were made to the digital system both technically and pedagogically.
- **Reimplementation and Final Evaluation:** The revised system was used by teachers once again, and the automatically generated reports were examined. The extent to which these reports contributed to teachers' planning of new activities was evaluated.

Throughout this process, the collected data were analyzed using qualitative analysis techniques. Teachers' experiences, the strengths and weaknesses of the system, and its potential for use within the context of early childhood education were assessed.

PARTICIPANTS AND CONTEXT

The participants of this study consisted of three preschool teachers working at an independent public preschool located in Kars, a province in Türkiye's Eastern Anatolia Region, and a total of 14 children aged 4–5 years in their classrooms. The teachers voluntarily took part in the study and met the required criteria for participation, including experience in implementing structured science activities, willingness to use digital tools, and competence in observing young children. The children's identifying information was kept confidential, and informed consent was obtained from their families in accordance with ethical guidelines.

Table 1 presents detailed information about the characteristics of the participants and the school in which the study was conducted.

Table 1. Participant and context characteristics

Category	Characteristics
Teachers	• Three female preschool teachers • Ages 27–31 years • Teaching experience: two teachers with 4 years, one teacher with 2 years • Employed at an independent public preschool • Hold a bachelor's degree in preschool education • Completed coursework on early childhood science education • Experienced in implementing structured science activities • Willing to use digital tools • Competent in observing young children • Voluntary participation
Children	• Total of 14 children • Ages 48–60 months (4–5 years) • 9 boys and 5 girls • Enrolled in a half-day preschool program • All children attending preschool for the first time • Identifying information kept confidential • Informed consent obtained from families in accordance with ethical guidelines
School and Context	• Study conducted in an independent public preschool in Kars, Eastern Anatolia, Türkiye • Children generally come from middle- and high-socioeconomic-status families • Classrooms include science learning centers where children can conduct individual science activities • Teachers plan and implement activities aligned with nationally defined early childhood science skills
Physical Environment	• Classroom setting suitable for structured science activities • Experimental materials (objects of varying density, water containers, different liquids, etc.) readily available in the classroom

This information may provide a general framework for understanding the conditions under which the study was conducted and may assist in interpreting the subsequent sections.

Development of the Artificial Intelligence Supported Digital Assessment Interface

The AI-supported digital assessment system was designed to analyze the data collected through teacher observations and to generate reports regarding children's developmental levels in scientific process skills, while also providing teachers with instructional recommendations.

The technological infrastructure used during the system development process included:

- Natural language processing (NLP) and classification algorithms developed using the Python programming language,

- SQL-based systems for database management,
- HTML, CSS, and JavaScript components for the web-based user interface,
- Dynamic user screens that allow teachers to enter data and access analysis results.

The system processes the observation data entered by teachers, matches these data with predefined indicators of scientific process skills, and accordingly:

- Provides individual, small-group, and whole-group activity suggestions,
- Generates automated reports regarding the extent to which children have achieved specific learning outcomes.

Throughout this process, revisions were made to both the interface design and the underlying algorithms based on user feedback to ensure that the system aligned with teachers' practical experiences. As a result, the system evolved into a holistic structure that not only met teachers' practical needs but also offered an innovative contribution to pedagogical assessment processes.

In this study, an artificial intelligence–supported digital interface was developed to assess children's scientific process skills within the scope of early childhood science education. The development of the interface was conducted in accordance with the principles of the Design-Based Research (DBR) approach, following a multi-stage, systematic, and practice-oriented process. Throughout the development, teachers' classroom applications, observations, and feedback were taken into consideration, and the functionality of the interface was continuously improved.

Design and Digitization of the Observation Form

In the first phase, an observation form containing scientific process skills that can be observed during science activities in preschool settings was developed by the researchers. The form was created by taking into account the fundamental scientific process skills frequently emphasized in the literature—such as observing, classifying, predicting, inferring, measuring, collecting data, and drawing conclusions—and aligning them with the learning outcomes and indicators of the preschool education curriculum developed by the Ministry of National Education of Türkiye. The form was structured in a clear and straightforward format that allowed teachers to record children's observable behaviors during structured science activities.

In the second phase, the developed form was transferred into a digital environment and configured to operate with artificial intelligence algorithms. During the digitization process, a user-friendly, simple, and accessible interface design was adopted. The system was structured so that teachers could easily enter data without requiring any technical expertise.

Technical Infrastructure and Functioning of the Artificial Intelligence Supported Digital Program

The Artificial Intelligence–Supported Digital Program was structured as a platform that enables teachers to enter their observation data into the system. Each observation form was programmed to be analyzed at the level of individual learning outcomes, and based on the levels selected by the teachers, the system automatically generates both individual and classroom-level reports. The AI algorithm embedded in the interface analyzes the data entered by teachers and identifies each child's performance level for each scientific process skill, allowing developmental progress to be monitored over time.

The system is also supported by a recommendation engine designed to assist teachers in generating post-assessment activity suggestions. Through this feature, teachers can plan new science activities that target children's areas of need or skills requiring further development.

Pilot Implementation and Revision Process

The first version of the Artificial Intelligence–Supported Digital Program was tested in a small-scale pilot study conducted in the classrooms of three preschool teachers. During the implementation process, the teachers actively used the interface, and the challenges they encountered, their suggestions, and their user experiences with the system were collected as qualitative data. Based on this feedback, the user interface of the system was simplified, data entry fields were clarified, and the reporting section was made visually more comprehensible. Additionally, the system was optimized to align with children's attention spans, the duration of observable behaviors, and the teacher's classroom interaction time; thus, processing time, data entry functions, and feedback generation were refined accordingly. However, because these improvements fell outside the primary aim of the study, they were not reported in detail within the findings section.

Final Implementation and Reporting

The revised Artificial Intelligence–Supported Digital Program was used by the teachers during the science activities conducted within the scope of the research implementation. At the end of the implementation, the system generated individual assessment reports for each child, detailing their scientific process skills, and these reports were shared with the teachers. These reports were designed to help teachers document their observations more systematically, track children's developmental progress, and develop new instructional strategies.

The developed AI-supported digital assessment program provides teachers with the advantage of systematically recording their observations, thereby making teacher observation–based assessment processes in early childhood education more objective, systematic, and data-driven. Furthermore, to reduce teachers' workload in preparing developmental reports for each child, facilitate decision-making processes, and support more effective pedagogical planning, the final version of the program was updated in alignment with teacher feedback.

DATA COLLECTION

The data for this study were obtained through the implementation of three different experimental phases conducted in a preschool classroom located in an independent kindergarten in the city of Kars. The school's relatively favorable physical and technical infrastructure, along with the generally middle-to-high socioeconomic status of the families, were factors that facilitated the implementation process.

During the data collection process, the three structured experiments were administered by two preschool teachers according to a predetermined plan and were carried out over the course of two consecutive weeks. The third teacher contributed to the process by comparing both the observational data obtained from the experiments and the evaluation outputs generated by the AI-supported system.

Teacher views were collected using a semi-structured interview form developed by the researchers. These interviews were conducted to gain a deeper understanding of teachers' experiences related to the implementation process.

Data Collection Tools

In this study, a developmentally appropriate assessment form based on scientific process skills, document analysis, and semi-structured interview techniques were used together as data collection tools.

As the first data collection technique, the documents generated automatically by the AI-supported digital assessment tool—based on the observation data entered by the teachers—were examined. These reports included outputs derived from teachers' observations of children's scientific process skills and enabled the objective documentation of the assessment process. The reports were analyzed in detail using document analysis techniques. The second data collection technique consisted of semi-structured individual interviews. These interviews were conducted to understand how teachers interpreted the reports generated by the system, how they integrated these reports into the assessment process, and their experiences regarding the effectiveness of the AI-supported system. In this way, the contribution of the system to teachers' instructional practices was evaluated holistically, both through the content of the digital outputs and through teachers' perspectives.

Content and Structure of the Assessment Form

The assessment form was designed to systematically observe preschool children's scientific process skills and was integrated into the artificial intelligence–supported digital assessment system. The form covers three fundamental experimental situations through which children explore the concept of buoyancy:

- **Situation 1 (S1):** Floating/sinking behavior of different objects in the same liquid.
- **Situation 2 (S2):** Floating/sinking behavior of the same object in different liquids.
- **Situation 3 (S3):** Floating/sinking behavior of different objects in different liquids.

Figure 2. Model representation of the experimental situations

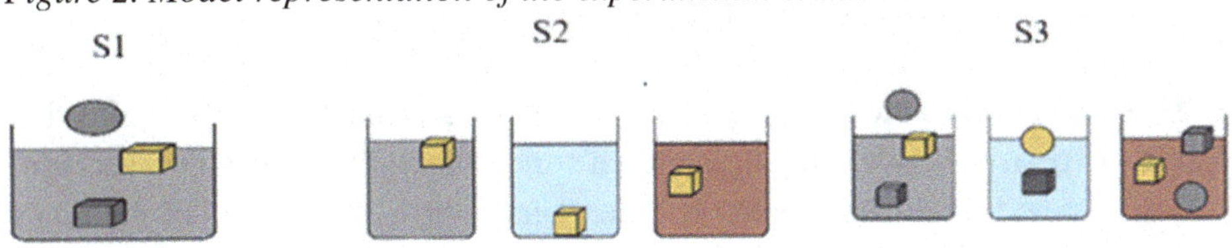

These situations were integrated into structured science activities designed to activate children's scientific thinking processes. Through the form, scientific process skills (observing, classifying, predicting, collecting data, inferring, measuring, and problem solving) are systematically observed. The observation scores for each skill are analyzed by the artificial intelligence–supported system and reported at both the general and individual levels. These reports include:

- Child-specific mean scores for each scientific process skill,
- Comparative performance means for each experimental situation (S1, S2, S3),
- Children's individual strengths and areas requiring further development,

- Personalized assessment insights and activity recommendations for teachers.

These recommendations are automatically generated by the system based on each child's observation data and guide teachers toward different types of instructional activities. In this way, the assessment form not only systematizes the observation process but also directly supports teachers' instructional planning.

Artifical Intelligence-Supported Data Analysis and Activity Recommendations

The data obtained from the form are analyzed through the developed artificial intelligence–supported digital assessment program. The digital assessment program processes the observation data entered by teachers, determines children's skill levels, and provides tailored instructional recommendations accordingly. Based on each child's performance profile, the AI algorithms generate the following types of recommendations:

- **Individual activity recommendations:** Designed specifically for the skills that require improvement or further support.
- **Small-group activity recommendations:** Structured to allow children with similar skill levels to work together.
- **Whole-group activity recommendations:** Intended for class-wide reinforcement or review of targeted skills.

These recommendations help teachers plan more targeted, flexible, and effective learning experiences while taking children's individual differences into account. They also provide important feedback for teachers in terms of monitoring children's development, identifying their needs, and personalizing the educational process.

This data collection system is structured in alignment with an authentic assessment approach suitable for early childhood education, serving as an example of technology-supported pedagogical decision-making processes.

Validity and Reliability of the Data Collection Tool

The data collection tool used in this study is an observation form developed to assess scientific process skills in early childhood. The validity and reliability procedures of the form are explained below.

Validity Study

The content validity of the form was ensured through a review of the relevant literature and expert evaluations. First, frequently assessed skills within the scope of scientific process skills (such as observing, predicting, establishing cause–effect relationships, classifying, communicating, collecting data, and inferring) were identified, and the form items were designed based on these skills.

The draft version of the form was sent to five academics specializing in early childhood education, science education, and educational measurement and evaluation. Experts were asked to provide feedback regarding the content validity, appropriateness, alignment with the target age group, and adequacy of the form for assessing the intended skills. Based on the expert feedback, several items were revised to improve clarity and simplicity.

Reliability Study

The reliability of the form was tested using the inter-rater reliability method, in which two teachers independently observed the same children during the same activity. The observation forms completed by both raters were compared, and Cohen's Kappa coefficient was calculated. The resulting Kappa value of .82 indicated a high level of agreement between observers and demonstrated strong reliability of the observation form (Landis & Koch, 1977).

In addition, the artificial intelligence–supported interface system produced highly similar reports when teachers entered comparable observations for the same child at different times, further demonstrating the system's reliability in terms of internal consistency.

In conclusion, the developed observation form was designed to reliably and validly monitor scientific process skills at the early childhood level. Supported by expert evaluations and inter-rater reliability analyses, the form has gained the necessary qualities to be used as a robust measurement instrument.

Data Analysis and System Development

In this study, the thematic analysis method was used to analyze the qualitative data. Thematic analysis is a qualitative approach that enables the systematic examination of data to identify recurring patterns, meaningful themes, and relational structures (Braun & Clarke, 2006). This method provided an effective framework for understanding teachers' experiences regarding the use of the digital assessment interface. The dataset consisted of activity assessment reports structured by the artificial intelligence system and teachers' interview responses.

The analysis process was carried out in the following stages:

- Reading and organizing the data and preparing it for coding,
- Conducting initial coding and generating preliminary themes,
- Reviewing, merging, or refining themes based on their relational structure,
- Defining the themes and reporting the findings.

The findings obtained through thematic analysis served as critical inputs for improving the design and functionalities of the developed artificial intelligence–supported digital assessment system.

FINDINGS

This section presents the findings obtained from (a) children's drawings and observation notes, (b) the assessment outputs of the artificial intelligence system, and (c) teachers' interpretations of these outputs. The results are organized thematically to provide a holistic understanding of children's scientific process skills and the contribution of the AI-supported system to the assessment process.

a) Findings Based on Children's Drawings and Observation Notes

In this section, examples obtained from children's drawings and observation notes collected from teachers regarding the implementation process are presented. The drawings produced by the children during the activity are valuable in demonstrating how they perceived objects, events, and relationships throughout the process. Similarly, the child expressions recorded in the researcher's notes make visible the ways in which they used their thinking strategies and established cause–effect relationships during the experiment.

Theme 1: Children's Predictions and Early Observations

Figure 3. Child 2's drawing showing observation of floating–sinking objects

During the experiment, the child made a prediction by saying, "Look, this one will sink now," as they placed an object into the water. The child then continued the activity with other objects and asked, "Teacher, can I do it again later?" while dropping them into the water and sharing the observation results with peers. These expressions indicate that the child actively participated in the process, followed it with curiosity and enthusiasm, and enjoyed the experiment.

Theme 2: Children's Explanations and Revised Understanding

Figure 4. Child 5's drawing showing observation of floating–sinking objects

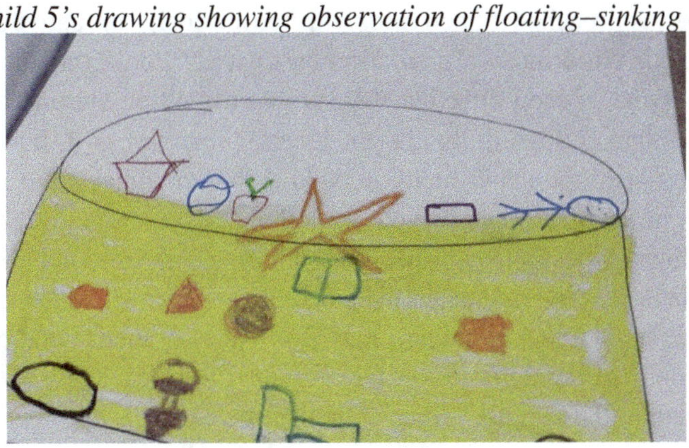

During the experiment, the child said, "I think all of them will sink." After placing the objects into the liquid, when asked, "Did all the objects sink?", the child responded, "No, this box and the ball didn't sink because they are light."

Theme 3: Testing in New Conditions and Transfer of Learning

Figure 5. Child 8's drawing showing observation of floating–sinking objects

Child 8 followed the experimental processes with great attention. During Situation 3, the child picked up an object that had sunk in water and said, "Now I want to put this in the other container; maybe it will float there." With this statement, the child tested the object in a different liquid.

When the children's expressions during the experiment are examined, it becomes evident that they approached the activities with both curiosity and active engagement. For example, one child made a prediction by saying, "Look, this one will sink," and then continued to drop different objects into the water, sharing observations with peers. Another child initially made a general prediction—"I think all of them will sink"—but after the experiment, noticed that some objects did not sink and explained this by saying, "The box and the ball didn't sink because they are light," thereby attempting to establish a cause–effect relationship. Another child, working in a multivariable setting, demonstrated a desire to test ideas further by saying, "I want to put this in the other container; maybe it will float there," and proceeded to try the object in a different liquid.

Taken together, these expressions show that the children followed the process attentively, were willing to experiment, transferred what they learned to new situations, and continually revised their predictions. This indicates that the activities not only supported children's scientific process skills but also made these skills more visible.

In the subsequent sections of the results, the analyses generated by the AI-supported system are presented together with teachers' perspectives, with the aim of providing a more holistic evaluation of children's scientific process skills.

b) Findings on the Assessment Outputs of the Artificial Intelligence System and Teachers' Responses to These Outputs

Three different experimental scenarios (Situation 1, 2, and 3) were implemented, and the artificial intelligence system analyzed students' performance in the seven core scientific process skills (Observation, Classification, Prediction, Data Collection, Inference, Measurement, and Problem Solving) using graphical representations. The teachers (T1, T2, T3) provided detailed feedback regarding these graphs and individual student profiles.

Within Situation 1, activities were conducted in which children examined the behavior of different objects placed in the same liquid (water). Based on these activities, the children's performance data for the seven scientific process skills were entered into the artificial intelligence–supported assessment system. Following the system's analysis, classwide means were calculated and visualized in Figure 1. Teacher perspectives on the system-generated report, based on the graphical data, are presented in detail below.

Figure 6. Situation 1 classwide mean of scientific process skills

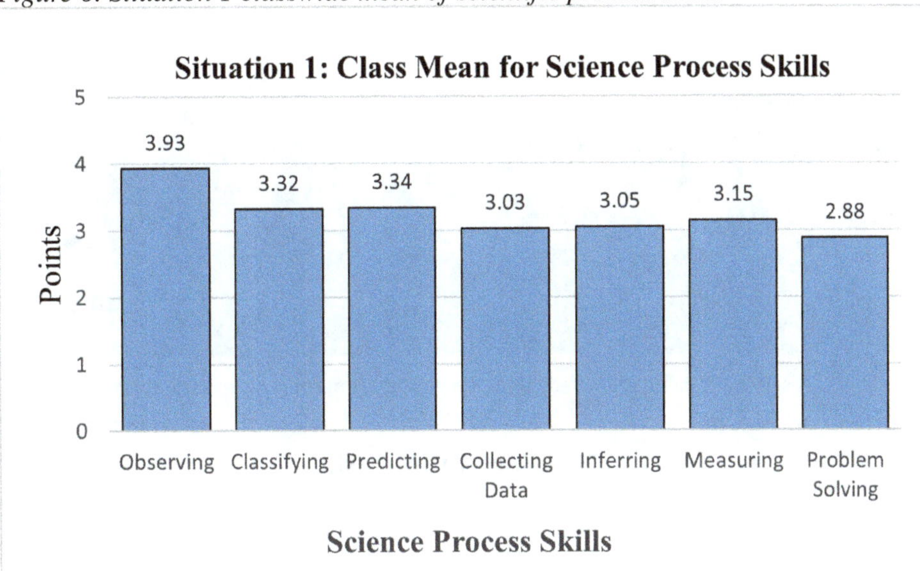

Teacher 1's views based on Figure 6: "*When examining the graph, it did not surprise me that Observation had the highest mean (x = 3.93), as the children were highly attentive to whether the objects floated or sank. Classification (x = 3.32)*

and Prediction (x = 3.34) appeared at moderate levels; some children could group objects or explain their predictions, while others struggled. More complex skills such as Data Collection (x = 3.03), Inference (x = 3.05), and Measurement (x = 3.15) were lower, and I observed that children particularly needed support in explaining the 'why' behind an event. Problem Solving showed the lowest mean (x = 2.88), as some children preferred to ask for help rather than attempt solutions. Overall, the system's detailed reports helped me identify the skills that require further support and guided how I should move children from observation toward more abstract processes like inference and problem solving."

Within Situation 2, activities were conducted in which children compared the behavior of the same object in different liquids (e.g., water, saltwater, oil). The data obtained from these activities were entered into the artificial intelligence–supported assessment system, and classwide means for the seven core scientific process skills were calculated by the system. These findings, visualized in Figure 2, are interpreted and presented below.

Figure 7. Situation 2 classwide mean of scientific process skills

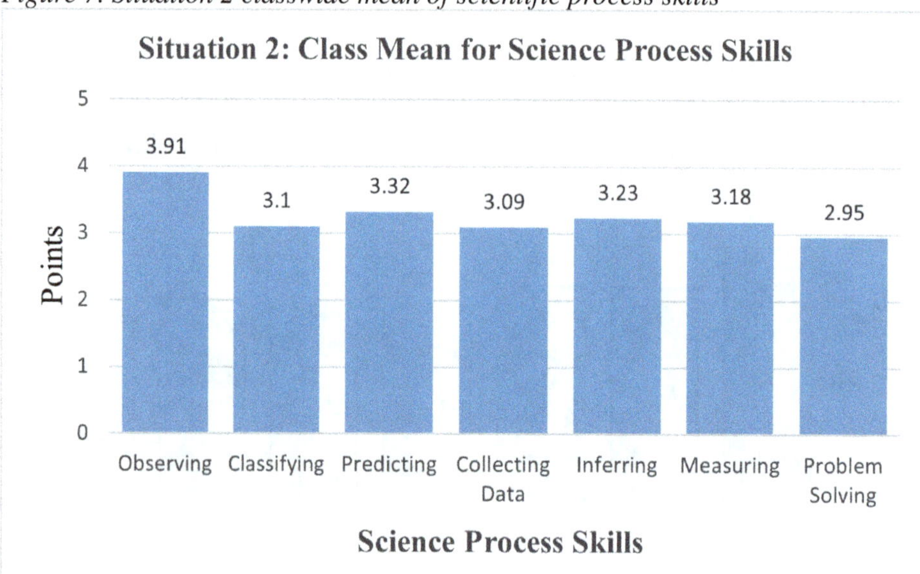

Teacher 2's views based on Figure 7 *"Seeing that Observation had the highest mean again in Condition 2 (x = 3.91) pleased me; even though we used different liquids, the children attentively monitored how the objects behaved. Prediction (x = 3.32) and Inference (x = 3.23) appeared at moderate levels; although many children could answer questions such as 'will it sink or float?', they often struggled to justify*

their reasoning. Classification (x = 3.10) and Data Collection (x = 3.09) were at low-to-moderate levels, suggesting that recording and grouping differences across liquids is not yet fully established. In Measurement (x = 3.18), children rarely used comparative expressions such as 'this one is denser'. The lowest mean emerging in Problem Solving (x = 2.95) indicates that children made limited use of their prior knowledge when a new liquid was introduced. Overall, the report clearly showed both the skills in which children are strong and the areas where further support is needed.

Within Situation 3, multivariable experimental settings were provided in which children observed the behavior of different objects in different liquids. The performance data obtained from these activities were entered into the artificial intelligence–supported assessment system, and classwide means for each scientific process skill were calculated and analyzed by the system. The findings visualized in Figure 3 are evaluated and presented below.

Figure 8. Situation 3 classwide mean of scientific process skills

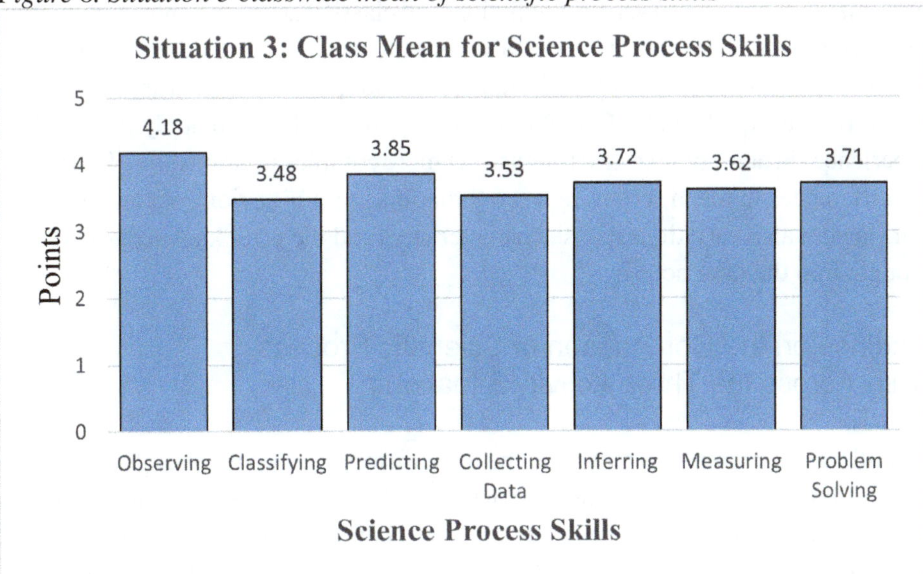

Teacher 3's views based on Figure 8:

"When examining the report for Situation 3, I saw clear improvements in the children's scientific process skills. Observation had the highest mean (x = 4.18); they were more conscious in tracking object–liquid combinations and in expressing what they observed. Problem Solving also increased (x = 3.71), showing that multi-variable environments supported their inquiry, trial-and-error, and strategy development. Prediction (x = 3.85) and Inference (x = 3.72) were strong,

as the children began making more intentional predictions and trying to justify them. Technical skills such as Measurement (x = 3.62) and Data Collection (x = 3.53) also improved, with the use of symbols and drawings becoming more apparent. Although Classification was slightly lower (x = 3.48), the increase suggests emerging multi-dimensional thinking. Overall, the report showed that the children are progressing toward higher-order skills like abstraction, causal reasoning, and strategy development—progress I could not have tracked this systematically without the AI-supported report."

To interpret this teacher's evaluation more comprehensively, it is necessary to take into account the structural differences between Situation 1 and Situation 3. These two situations differ in terms of both the level of experience they provide to children and the type of task involved. Situation 1 represents an initial phase in which children experienced the behavior of objects in water and developed preliminary understandings through basic observations. In this process, they encountered only a single-variable experimental environment, which resulted in varying mean scores across skills such as observation, prediction, and classification. In contrast, Situation 3 offered a multi-variable experimental environment in which children participated with the prior knowledge they had acquired in Situation 1. This setting, involving both different liquids and different objects, required children to apply their earlier experiences in new contexts and to construct more complex relationships. Therefore, the differences in mean scores between Situation 1 and Situation 3 reflect not only learning but also variations in task characteristics and the prior knowledge children brought into the later activity.

Findings on the Comparison of Scientific Process Skills Across the Three Activity Situations

Following the implementation of the three different experimental situations, the data from the assessment forms completed by the teacher were transferred to the artificial intelligence–supported assessment system. The system analyzed the mean scores for each scientific process skill obtained in Situation 1 (different objects in the same liquid), Situation 2 (the same object in different liquids), and Situation 3 (different objects in different liquids), and generated a comparative graph. This analysis, visualized in Figure 4, was interpreted by the system, and the findings are presented in detail below.

Figure 9. Comparison of mean scientific process skills across the three activity situations

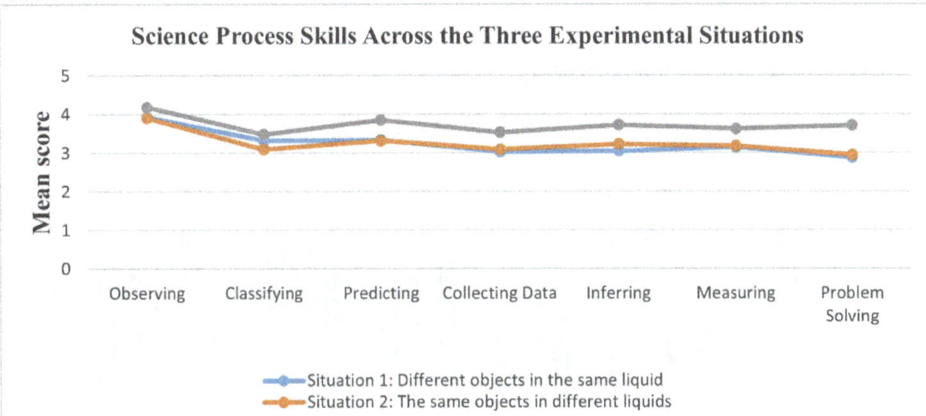

Teacher 1's views:

"When I examined the comparative graph report, I saw that the children achieved the highest means in all scientific process skills in Situation 3. It is clear that multi-variable experimental environments significantly support skills such as observation, prediction, and inference. The fact that Observation had the highest mean across all situations shows that this is the most consistent and strongest skill for the children. The increase in Prediction and Inference suggested to me that the children have begun to establish more complex relationships."

Teacher 2's Views:

"Although Problem Solving had the lowest mean across all three situations, its clear increase in Situation 3 caught my attention; this shows that the children began trying different solution strategies when faced with new conditions. There were also small but meaningful improvements in skills such as Classification, Data Collection, and Measurement. The system clearly showed these developments and guided me on which skills I should focus on in my classroom planning. Overall, I found the comparative analysis very useful; seeing how much the children progressed in each situation through a single graph provided concrete insights into how I should differentiate my instructional process."

Following the experimental activities, the individual assessment data obtained from the observation forms completed by the teachers were analyzed by the artificial intelligence–supported assessment system. The system examined each child's scores in scientific process skills and generated individual performance profiles. These profiles are intended to visualize students' strengths and areas for improvement in key skills such as observation, classification, prediction, data collection, inference, measurement, and problem solving. The individual student mean scores presented in Figure 10 were produced based on the system's assessment outputs and are supported by the interpretive comments provided below.

Figure 10. Individual student profiles

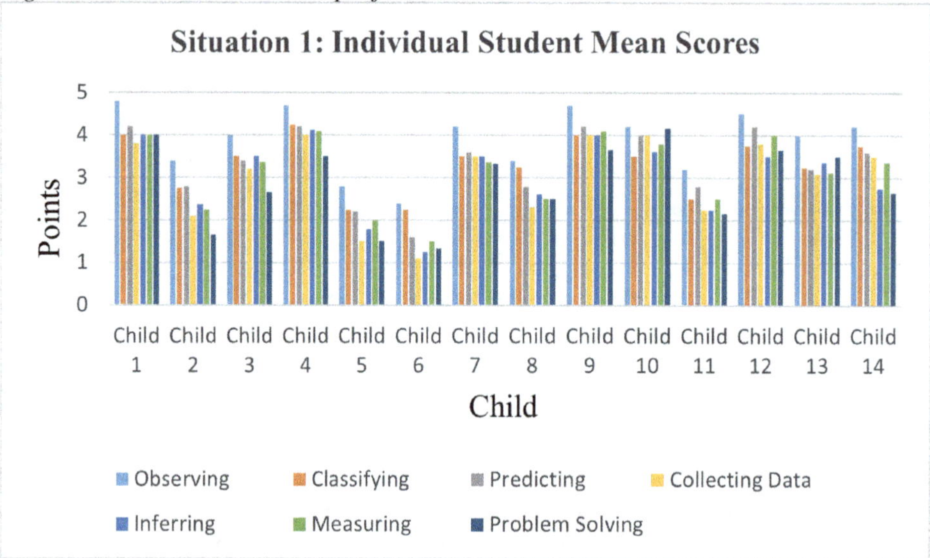

Table 2. Teachers' views on students' scientific process skills

View Area	Teacher 1's View	Teacher 2's View
Individual Differences	*"This diversity in students' skill profiles is the clearest evidence of our need to differentiate classroom activities."*	*"Each student is at a different point. This graph shows that rather than using a one-size-fits-all approach, we need to adopt a personalized instructional model."*
Observation Skills	*"Students' success in observation skills reflects their natural curiosity. We can use this strength as a springboard for developing other skills."*	*"Since observation is concrete and perceptual, our students perform better in this skill. We should turn this into an opportunity to help them build confidence."*
Problem Solving Skills	*"The low performance in p"The low performance in problem-solving skills indicates that our students need support in critical thinking and generating alternative solutions.s.*	*"Students may be hesitant to engage in trial-and-error. We can support the development of this skill by providing them with a safe environment where they feel comfortable taking risks."*
Classification & Inference	*"Some students are very good at classification and inference, while others struggle. We can encourage peer learning through group activities."*	*"We should plan more activities that include the 'predict–observe–explain' strategy for students who have difficulty establishing cause–effect relationships."*

continued on following page

Table 2. Continued

View Area	Teacher 1's View	Teacher 2's View
Data Collection & Measurement	*"Their moderate performance in data collection and measurement shows that they struggle to build a bridge between abstract recording systems and their concrete world."*	*"We should make measurement and record-keeping more concrete by using pictures, stickers, and simple charts that are meaningful for them."*
Holistic Development	*"Students who demonstrate high performance across all skills are the natural leaders of our classroom. We should encourage them with more advanced projects."*	*"Students who are strong in all areas are excellent candidates for working on complex problems. We should assign them tasks that challenge them."*
Need for Additional Support	*"Students who need support in all skills require dedicated one-on-one and structured instructional time."*	*"Breaking learning into small, manageable steps for students who struggle with basic skills is essential for building their confidence."*
General Assessment	*"This data is an invaluable guide for personalizing my instruction. It clarifies which student needs what type of support, and when."*	*"This AI-supported analysis allows me to support my teacher intuition with data, making my interventions more effective."*

As shown in Table 2, the two teachers interpret the same data with different emphases and suggestions. Although both teachers agree on the fundamental needs, their recommended solutions reflect their own pedagogical perspectives.

Following the completion of the scientific process skills assessment form—prepared for the concept of buoyancy—based on the teachers' observations, an artificial intelligence–supported assessment system generated the table presented below. The system analyzed the scores for each skill domain and calculated the child's overall performance in observation, classification, prediction, data collection, inference, measurement, and problem solving. In addition, for each skill level, it identified the appropriate type of support (individual, small group, whole group) and provided activity suggestions tailored to the child's developmental needs.

Table 3. Scientific process skills assessment and activity suggestions for child 3

Skill	Overall Score	Support Type	Activity Suggestion
Observation	4.23	Large Group	The student is highly competent in observation. As a large-group activity, different objects can be dropped into water and the class can be asked, "What did each one do?" The child can also be asked to draw their own observations and present them to their peers.
Classification	3.41	Small Group	A small-group activity can be conducted using different materials (wood, metal, sponge) and liquids. The child is given a classification responsibility (e.g., only those that float, only those that sink in oil). These groups are then compared.
Prediction	3.66	Small Group	The child's prediction skill is near good. They can participate in a planned small-group activity. Objects are shown and children are asked, "What do you think this will do?" The child's responses are recorded. Each child draws their prediction on the board using a symbol. Then the experiment is conducted and predictions are matched with outcomes.
Data Collection	3.54	Small Group	In a whole-class experiment, the child is given a task: for example, drawing the sinking objects, marking the floating ones, or recording the liquids. This supports both responsibility and collaboration.
Inference	3.62	Small Group	Cause-and-effect matching activities are conducted based on object–liquid relationships. Questions such as "Why did this sink?" and "Why is this floating?" are asked, and the child shares their answers with peers.
Measurement	3.75	Large Group	A game can be played where children measure with their fingers how much of each object sinks in water and mark it on the board. The child works with a different object than their peers and the results are discussed together.
Problem Solving	3.04	Individual	This skill needs development. The child can be given tasks like "This object sinks—how can we make it float?" Different materials are provided to encourage them to generate their own solution. Trial-and-error processes should be supported.

An examination of Table 3 shows that the student performs strongly in observation (4.23) and measurement (3.75), indicating effective attention during experiments and an ability to compare physical properties of objects. Classification, prediction, data collection, and inference skills are at a moderate level and may be strengthened through small-group activities. Problem-solving (3.04) appears relatively weaker and may benefit from individualized support and structured problem scenarios. Overall, the student demonstrates a developmental level in many scientific process skills that approaches independent performance.

Findings Regarding Teachers' Views on Their Experience Using the Artificial Intelligence System

In the preschool period, face-to-face interviews were conducted with preschool teachers to gather their views on the development process of using an artificial intelligence (AI)-supported digital interface to assess children's scientific process skills within the scope of early childhood science education. The teachers were coded as T1, T2, and T3. The data obtained from the teachers' views are presented as follows:

The qualitative data obtained from the interviews with the teachers were categorized under the themes of "form completion process," "ease of use," "assessment results," "impact on the teaching process," and "overall assessment."

Findings Regarding Teachers' Views on Completing the Assessment Form

The responses given by the teachers to the first interview question, "What do you think about the process of completing the assessment form?", were examined under the headings of category, sub-category, and codes, and the findings obtained are presented in Table 4.

Table 4. Findings regarding the artificial intelligence–supported assessment form completion process

Category	Subcategory	Codes	Participants
Content Assessment	Inclusiveness	Inclusion of sufficient information to cover all three situations	T1
	Clarity and explicitness	Items being clear, explicit, and understandable	T2, T3
	Contribution of examples	Adding sample sentences to the questions facilitates observation	T3
Applicability	Ease of completion	The form is easy to complete	T2, T3
	Flexibility	Option to complete later instead of immediately	T1, T3
	Note-taking support	Taking notes during the process makes form completion easier	T1, T3
	Need for guidance during initial use	The need for a brief user guide or example due to uncertainty during initial completion	T1
Time Management	Advantage of the digital system	Completing the form in the system saves time compared to the written version	T2

Based on Table 4, it is observed that the teachers generally found the assessment form to be clear, understandable, and sufficiently comprehensive. The teachers indicated that the items were presented with clear and easily interpretable statements. While two teachers reported that the form could be completed easily during the observation process, one teacher preferred to complete it afterwards in order to focus on guiding the children during the activity. In this regard, taking short notes during the process was stated to facilitate form completion later on. Additionally, one teacher mentioned experiencing some uncertainty when completing the form for the first time and indicated that a brief user guide or an example would have been helpful. The teachers also emphasized that presenting the form in a digital format provided a time-saving advantage. Overall, the teachers evaluated the form as functional and applicable.

Some of the teachers' statements regarding the completion of the assessment form are as follows: "*Completing the form was simple and comfortable. The items were very clear and explicit; I did not need to think about what any statement meant." (T2) "The form was prepared in a detailed manner, and the questions were short and clear. Including example sentences beside the items helped me focus on the children's statements during the activity." (T3) "Instead of filling out the form during the activity, I took notes and completed it afterwards. This made it easier for me to guide the children." (T1) "A brief guide or example would have been helpful during the first completion, as I was unsure whether I was completing it correctly." (T1)*

c) Findings Related to the "Use Process" of the Artificial Intelligence–Supported Assessment System

The teachers' views regarding their experience in using the artificial intelligence–supported assessment system were analyzed in terms of the system's functioning, ease of access, and overall user experience. The responses provided by the teachers to the second question, "What do you think about your experience using the artificial intelligence–based assessment system?" were examined under categories, subcategories, and codes. The resulting findings are presented in Table 5.

Table 5. Findings related to the use process of the artificial intelligence–supported assessment system

Category	Subcategory	Codes	Participants
Ease of Use	No Need for Technical Knowledge	Ability to use the system without requiring technical skills	T1
	Simple and Clear Interface	The system is not complex and is easy to understand	T2
	Quick Operation	Ability to make quick selections within the system	T3

continued on following page

Table 5. Continued

Category	Subcategory	Codes	Participants
User Experience	Compatibility with Digital Habits	Compatibility with mobile device and computer use	T2
	Time Efficiency	The system saves time for the teacher	T3
	Initial use experience	Need for guidance or example screens during initial use	T1
Practicality of Use	Usefulness in Large Classrooms	The system is found practical for crowded classrooms	T3

Based on Table 5, it is observed that all three teachers found the artificial intelligence–supported assessment system generally understandable and practical. Two teachers stated that the system could be used easily without requiring technical knowledge, while one teacher emphasized that it provided significant convenience, particularly in crowded classroom environments. The teachers also highlighted that the system interface was simple, that actions could be performed quickly, and that the system was compatible with both mobile devices and computers. However, one teacher noted that understanding how to proceed during the first use required some time and indicated that a brief user guide or example screen could facilitate the initial use process.

Some of the teachers' views regarding the system are presented below:

"Having the form already available in the system made the process quite easy for me. Even though I do not have much technical knowledge, I was able to use it comfortably." (T1)

"I enjoy using mobile devices and computers. I can take short notes in the classroom and enter them into the system later. The system was not complex or confusing." (T2) "I believe this system would be very useful for teachers who have large class sizes." (T3) "When using the system for the first time, I needed some time to understand how to move forward. A short guide or example screen would have made the initial use easier." (T1)

Findings Related to the "Assessment Results" of the AI-Supported Assessment System

The views regarding the assessment results presented by the artificial intelligence system—specifically the scientific process skills—were analyzed in terms of the scope of the information provided, the clarity of individual analyses, and the contribution of these results to the instructional process.

The responses given by the teachers to the third question, "What do you think about the scientific process skills assessment results presented by the artificial intelligence system?" were examined under categories, subcategories, and codes, and the findings obtained are presented in Table 6.

Table 6. Findings related to the "assessment results" of the artificial intelligence–supported assessment system

Category	Subcategory	Codes	Participants
Quality of the Information Provided	Inclusiveness and breadth of scope	Providing separate assessments for all skills	T2, T3
	Level of detail	Providing individual information and skill levels for each student	T1, T2, T3
	Rapid assessment	Completing the assessment in a very short time	T1, T2
	Classification Accuracy	AI misclassification corrected through teacher intervention.	T2
Visualization and Clarity	Graph-supported presentation	Providing an overall view of the class through graphical representation	T3
Contribution to the Teaching Process	Individual suggestions	Offering activity suggestions tailored to each student	T1, T2, T3
	Time saving	Simplifying a process that would normally take a long time	T2, T3
	Ease of integration into planning	Activity suggestions can be directly added to lesson plans	T3

Based on Table 6, it is observed that the teachers generally perceived the assessment results generated by the artificial intelligence–supported system as comprehensive, clear, and easily integrable into the teaching process. The teachers evaluated the provision of separate assessments for each skill and the detailed presentation of individual students' information and skill levels as positive features. Additionally, the system's ability to provide rapid assessment and to visually represent the overall status of the class through graphical elements was highlighted as an important advantage. The teachers also noted that the individualized activity suggestions offered for each student were time-saving and could be readily integrated into instructional planning.

However, one teacher expressed a critical view regarding classification accuracy, stating that the system occasionally misclassified certain data but corrected these errors once the teacher intervened. This suggests that although the system is generally functional, teacher verification may be necessary at times to ensure accuracy.

Some of the teachers' statements regarding the assessment results are presented below:

"I think it is quite fast. I was surprised that it provided information about the entire class as well as each of my students." (T1) "All skills were included in the assessment results. Providing separate evaluations for each skill was also

time-saving." (T2) "It provided detailed information about all scientific process skills, such as observation, prediction, and inference. It would be very difficult for me to produce this level of detail for each child individually." (T3) "When I noticed that some data were misclassified, I intervened, and the system corrected the error." (T2)

Findings Related to the Reflections of the Artificial Intelligence–Supported Assessment System on the Teaching Process

Views regarding the impact of the artificial intelligence–supported assessment results on the teaching process were analyzed in terms of individual planning, differentiation in classroom practices, and development of social skills.

The responses given by the teachers to the fourth question, "What do you think about the impact of the results produced by the artificial intelligence–supported assessment system on your teaching process?", were categorized under main categories, subcategories, and codes. The resulting findings are presented in Table 7.

Table 7. Findings related to the impact of the ai-supported assessment results on the teaching process

Category	Subcategory	Codes	Participants
Individual Planning	Guiding activity plans	Contribution of suggested activities for each child to planning	T1, T2, T3
	Addressing weaknesses	Identifying activities suitable for underdeveloped skills	T1, T2
	Possibility of periodic monitoring	Ability to record and track developmental progress	T1
In-Class Practices	Small-group planning	Ease of conducting the process by forming groups	T2, T3
	Integrating activities	Ability to combine AI suggestions with the teacher's own ideas	T3
	Alignment of suggestions with classroom conditions	Some activity suggestions not fully aligning with the classroom's physical or time constraints	T3
Social and Emotional Development	Peer interaction and recognition	Contribution of group activities to social skills	T3
	Applicability	AI recommendations being found appropriate and functional for classroom use	T3

Based on Table 7, it is observed that the teachers perceived the AI-supported assessment results as a structure that guides the instructional process, supports individualization, and is applicable in classroom practice. All three teachers stated that the activity suggestions provided for each student facilitated lesson planning and offered guidance aligned with individual needs. In addition, the system was reported to support the planning of small-group activities, promote peer interaction, and contribute positively to classroom practices in terms of social and emotional skill development.

However, one teacher expressed a critical view, noting that some of the activity suggestions did not fully align with the classroom's existing physical or time constraints and that small adaptations were needed before implementation. This finding indicates that, although the system generally supports the instructional process, the suggested activities may not always fully fit the contextual conditions of every classroom.

Some of the teachers' statements regarding the impact of the assessment results on the instructional process are as follows: *"The suggested activity types for each child can guide my future activity plans." (T1) "Proposing a separate activity type for each child greatly helps me plan the process by forming groups in the classroom." (T2) "In small-group activities, children can communicate with each other and develop their social skills." (T3) "There were instances where some activity suggestions did not fully match the physical or time conditions of my classroom; I will need to make small adaptations before applying them." (T3)*

Findings Related to General Views on the Artificial Intelligence–Supported Assessment System

General views regarding the artificial intelligence–supported assessment system were analyzed in terms of the system's overall functioning, its capacity to provide detailed data, its contribution to reducing teachers' workload, and its suitability for the preschool level.

The responses given by the teachers to the fifth question, "What do you think about the artificial intelligence–supported assessment system in general?", were examined under categories, subcategories, and codes, and the resulting findings are presented in Table 8.

Table 8. Findings regarding the overall assessment of the artificial intelligence–supported system

Category	Subcategory	Codes	Participants
Assessment Efficiency	Support for the observation process	The system detecting details that the teacher may overlook	T1, T2
	Ease and practicality	The system speeding up and simplifying the assessment process	T1, T3
Comprehensiveness and Usability	Comprehensive data presentation	The system providing detailed and rich outputs	T2, T3
	Adaptability across the process	The system being suitable for use throughout the preschool process	T3
	Digital competence differences	The system may be challenging during initial use for teachers with limited digital experience or for older teachers.	T2
Monitoring and Documentation	Development tracking	Monitoring students' development regularly through graphs	T3
	Sharing with families	Ability to provide concrete feedback to parents	T3
Potential for Wider Use	Willingness to work with the system	Desire to use it in other skill areas as well	T2

Based on Table 8, it is observed that the teachers generally viewed the AI-supported assessment system positively. The teachers stated that the system was able to capture details they might overlook during the observation process, accelerated the evaluation phase, and provided a more systematic structure. In addition, the graphical outputs offered by the system were reported to be functional both for instructional planning and for providing concrete feedback to parents. One teacher highlighted the system's potential for wider use by noting that it could be applied not only in this skill area but also across different types of skills.

However, one teacher offered a critical perspective, stating that the system may be challenging during initial use for teachers with limited digital experience or for older teachers. This finding suggests that although the system is generally functional, users with lower levels of digital competence may require additional support during the initial phase of use.

Some of the teachers' statements regarding the overall system are as follows:

"This system can identify points that I may overlook during evaluation, and it can provide quick feedback in such cases." (T1) "I think the system makes our work easier. The artificial intelligence evaluated very detailed aspects and assessed the children's process skills." (T2)"I can save the graphs provided by the system and conduct a general classroom evaluation for each month. I can give parents concrete feedback about their children's skill development." (T3)

"I think teachers with less digital experience or those who are not accustomed to using technology may find the system somewhat challenging at first." (T2)

DISCUSSION

In this study, the views of preschool teachers regarding their use of an artificial intelligence–supported digital interface to assess children's scientific process skills were examined. Based on the findings, teachers stated that the system was comprehensive in terms of content, easy to use, aligned with the instructional process, and time-saving. The statement "It was simple and comfortable to fill out the form. The items were very clear and explicit, so I did not have to wonder what they meant" (T2) indicates the system's ease of use. This highlights the increasingly significant role of artificial intelligence in instructional environments. In addition to these positive views, some teachers also expressed critical feedback: for example, Teacher 2 mentioned the need for a short user guide or sample screen due to initial uncertainty during the first use; similarly, Teacher 1 emphasized the need for guidance or an example interface during the initial implementation, and Teacher 2 reported that the AI occasionally misclassified some data, requiring teacher intervention for correction. These comments suggest that while the system offers notable advantages, certain usability and accuracy issues should be addressed to enhance its effectiveness. Thus, although teachers held positive views regarding the AI-supported system, it was observed that the teacher's role remained highly important in the interaction with artificial intelligence throughout the process.

Indeed, Huang (2018) emphasized that artificial intelligence enables the effective implementation of student-centered learning in instructional processes. Similarly, Nazaretsky et al. (2022) revealed that AI-supported assessment tools analyze students' responses, provide personalized feedback, and allow teachers to identify students' strengths and weaknesses more quickly. This aligns with the teacher perspectives obtained in our study. For example, one teacher highlighted the contribution of the AI-system to individualized planning by stating, *"Providing different activity suggestions suitable for each child can easily be integrated into the plan and implemented gradually over time" (T3)*. Another teacher confirmed the system's detailed analytical capacity by saying, *"It provided detailed information about all scientific process skills such as observation, prediction, and inference. I cannot do this individually for each child" (T3)*.

Artificial intelligence systems not only facilitate instructional processes but also strengthen teachers' assessment and planning skills (Bai et al., 2021; Cukurova et al., 2023; Wang et al., 2021, as cited in Hazzan Bishara et al., 2025). AI-supported student monitoring and assessment systems, designed to make learning more effective and efficient, track students' learning performance, offer recommendations based on individual needs, and support teachers' planning processes (Akyel & Tur, 2024).

The fact that the artificial intelligence–supported assessment tool developed in this study was found to be understandable and applicable by the teachers suggests that the integration of artificial intelligence into early childhood education may be both possible and beneficial. Evaluating the factors that influence teachers' acceptance and use of artificial intelligence tools is considered highly important for understanding how these technologies can be adapted to educational environments (Hazzan Bishara, Kol, & Levy, 2025). According to the teachers' views, the individualized reports provided by the system appeared to offer flexibility in instructional planning and seemed to support the development of specific support plans for skills in which students were lacking. The statement, "Providing a specific type of activity for each child helps me a lot in planning the process by forming groups in the classroom" (T2), illustrates this situation. This finding may align with the advantages emphasized in the literature, such as the potential of artificial intelligence systems to reduce teacher workload and allow closer monitoring of student development (Aşık et al., 2023; Arslan, 2020). The time-saving aspect of the system was also clearly expressed by the teachers: "Instead of writing everything one by one, having it in a system made it much easier and saved me time" (T2).

Supporting the development of scientific process skills in early childhood appears to play an important role in children's cognitive, social, and problem-solving abilities. The development of scientific process skills is also considered significant for societal progress, suggesting that these skills may need to be fostered during the early years of schooling (Limatahu et al., 2018). In this context, through the structured assessment form developed within the scope of this study and its digital integration, children's fundamental scientific skills—such as observing, predicting, collecting data, and making inferences—were systematically evaluated as far as possible, and their development was monitored accordingly. The findings indicated that while students seemed to be "quite strong in their observation skills," their "problem-solving skills appeared to be open to further development." Additionally, the system contributed to teachers' personalization of instruction by offering individualized, small-group, and whole-group activity suggestions based on students' developmental levels. This situation may support the potential of artificial-intelligence-based systems to create individualized educational programs (Akgün & Greenhow, 2022).

In this study, the assessment report provided by artificial intelligence offered activity suggestions at the individual, small-group, and whole-class levels, contributing to teachers' ability to plan more flexibly. It can be suggested that this may have positively influenced the applicability of the system across different learning environments and classroom structures.

Within the scope of this science-education-focused study, the integration of structured and experiment-based activities that support students' scientific process skills appears to have contributed to the early development of skills such as observing, predicting, collecting data, and making inferences.

In this context, it is noted that structured experiments may help concretize abstract concepts, may support lasting learning, and may provide opportunities for children to participate more actively in the process of acquiring scientific knowledge (Ay et al., 2015; Bozdoğan, 2017).

Some studies targeting early childhood have also shown that AI-based learning environments provide effective feedback and conceptual learning. Through the AI agent Zhorai, developed by Lin et al. (2020), children were able to comprehend concepts such as machine learning and knowledge representation and participated in the process of training the system. Similarly, Williams, Park, and Breazeal (2019) reported that preschool children learned about artificial intelligence experientially via the PopBots platform, and consequently, their perceptions of robots changed. These findings align with the teachers' statements: *"With these assessment results, I can plan separate activities for each child and integrate the activities suggested by AI with other activities" (T3).*

The use of AI-supported systems in science education can often extend beyond merely contributing to assessment processes, helping to create a more holistic learning environment that may support students' scientific thinking, problem-solving, and creative thinking skills. AI technologies tend to analyze students' learning speeds and styles and may offer personalized instructional suggestions, thereby potentially enabling many children to progress in ways that align with their individual learning journeys (Chan & Yuen, 2014; Casal-Otero et al., 2023). This feature can be considered an important advantage, particularly in early childhood instructional designs where individual differences need to be taken into account.

However, it appears that artificial intelligence may contribute not only to the learning process but also to developmental monitoring and diagnostic procedures. The systematic review conducted by Solek et al. (2025) suggested that AI-based diagnostic systems may help facilitate the early identification of developmental conditions such as Autism Spectrum Disorder (ASD) and may be able to analyze various data sources (eye movements, motor skills, genetics, etc.) with high accuracy. The teacher's statement regarding the assessment system—"It provided detailed information about all scientific process skills such as observation, prediction, and inference. I cannot do this individually for each child" (T3)—indicates that such systems may help reduce teachers' workload while providing more in-depth individual data. Furthermore, studies conducted at the higher education level have shown that AI-based systems may help make assessment and evaluation processes more data-driven and could improve the predictability of student performance. The FCN algorithm developed by Hooda et al. (2022) was able to predict student achievement with 84% accuracy and appeared to contribute to the improvement of the instructional process by offering data-driven feedback to teachers. This suggests that the present study conducted at the preschool level may provide a foundational basis for early childhood applications and that more advanced models could be developed in the future. Accordingly, AI-based systems may offer important contributions not only to assessment processes but also to the individualization of instruction. One teacher emphasized the system's flexibility for students with different learning speeds and needs by stating, "Providing different activity suggestions suitable for each child can be easily integrated into my planning" (T3). In line with this, Mena-Guacas et al. (2023) highlighted the potential of AI systems to increase student engagement, enhance teacher efficiency, and create personalized learning experiences.

In this context, Adıgüzel et al. (2023) emphasized that AI-supported applications are capable of providing personalized learning plans based on students' learning pace and developmental areas, thereby enabling individualized instruction. This aligns with preschool teachers' positive perceptions regarding the system's individualization capacity.

However, despite the advantages offered by AI systems, including efficiency, personalization, and time savings, issues such as reliability, ethical concerns, and the necessity of human oversight remain topics of debate (Grassini, 2023). Historically, assessment processes in education were predominantly teacher-centered, manual, and time-consuming (Penny & Coe, 2004). Generative AI technologies, however, overcome these traditional limitations and allow for more flexible and student-specific assessment practices (Chiu, 2024).

In this study, one teacher highlighted, "I can record the graphs provided by the system and perform a general assessment of the class for each month. I can provide concrete feedback to parents regarding students' skill development" (T3), emphasizing the contribution of AI-supported systems both to teacher planning and to parent communication. Looking ahead, AI is not expected to fully replace human-centered judgments; rather, hybrid models integrating teacher evaluations with AI-generated data are anticipated to emerge (Grassini, 2023). This transformation necessitates that teachers possess digital literacy and critical thinking skills sufficient to interpret and evaluate the data provided by AI.

Indeed, Williyan et al. (2024) noted that technology-supported assessment tools offer innovative opportunities for teachers; however, to utilize these opportunities effectively, teachers must engage with the technology not only as users but also as critical evaluators. In line with this, the teacher statement from the present study, *"Overall, while assessing, the system can detect points that I might have overlooked and provide rapid feedback" (T1)*, underscores the supportive and complementary role of AI for teachers and highlights the potential characteristics of a successful hybrid model.

Ethical concerns discussed by Berson et al. (2025) indicate that studies involving children may be exposed to certain data breaches. They also highlight that while artificial intelligence offers significant learning opportunities, it may simultaneously create risks of overreliance and potentially hinder children's independent thinking. As noted in different studies, analyses show that AI technologies may help address fundamental educational challenges; however, they also present difficulties, particularly regarding security (Liu et al., 2025).

When these findings are considered together with the results obtained in our own study, they suggest that AI-based assessment tools offer important opportunities in early childhood education, yet also involve ethical and implementation-related considerations that must be carefully managed. Therefore, future research conducted with more diverse participant groups should focus both on strengthening student data security and ethical principles, and on structuring teacher–AI interaction in a pedagogically sustainable manner.

Limitations and Challenges

The findings obtained from the artificial intelligence–supported assessment system used in this study are based on implementations conducted with a limited number of children and in the absence of a comparison group. Therefore, it is possible that different results may emerge if the study is replicated with a larger sample and with comparative groups. Additionally, the fact that the AI model's algorithms and data-processing capacity may occasionally lead to misclassifications represents another limitation that should be taken into account. The implementation was carried out over a short period of time, which restricted the ability to observe the long-term effects of AI-supported assessment. Moreover, the study was conducted in a specific city/region and school type; thus, the generalizability of the findings to all early childhood contexts may be limited. Although teachers expressed positive views regarding the use of artificial intelligence within this study, factors such as the duration of the implementation, the nature of the activity, and teachers' competencies in interacting with AI may have influenced the results. To more robustly establish the validity of these findings and to better understand the potential use of AI-supported assessment in educational settings, future studies should involve different activity types, diverse teacher competencies, and various AI applications tested across larger samples and through quantitative research designs.

In the implementation of such AI-supported assessment systems, various challenges may also emerge. First, teachers need a certain level of training and digital competence to be able to use these technologies effectively. In addition, the risk of over-reliance on artificial intelligence is another point that needs attention. Teachers' tendency to accept the analyses generated by the system as absolutely accurate may create the issue of relatively diminishing the importance of teacher observation, especially in early childhood education. Another challenge that may be encountered in the use of the system is the management of teacher–AI interaction. Working with artificial intelligence requires an approach different from traditional assessment practices, and for some teachers, this may lead to an additional adaptation process. This situation can be considered as a general phase in integrating AI with educational processes. Furthermore, it appears that teachers need a certain amount of time to interpret the reports and integrate them into pedagogical planning.

CONCLUSION AND RECOMMENDATIONS

The findings of this study indicate that artificial intelligence (AI)–supported digital assessment systems may be effectively used in early childhood education and tend to be positively received by teachers. The study suggests that such systems not only present a theoretical potential but also may serve as practical and functional tools that could contribute to reducing teachers' daily workload (Akyel & Tur, 2024; Hazzan Bishara et al., 2025). Considering that teachers' digital competencies were also regarded as an important factor in their ability to use the application in this study, it can be suggested that the study may offer guidance in this regard as well. This interpretation is also aligned with studies demonstrating that, in the context of early childhood education, teachers' levels of digital content creation and their ability to use the content they produce influence the quality of the instructional process (Doymaz & Gözüm, 2025, p. 23).

The system's contributions seem to have emerged along two main dimensions: supporting teachers and enabling personalized instruction. On one hand, the ease of use and time-saving features—illustrated by statements such as "It was simple and comfortable to fill out the form... it saved me time" (T2)—appear to have helped reduce the administrative burden in teachers' assessment processes. On the other hand, the detailed individual reports and activity suggestions provided by the system may offer a valuable data foundation for differentiated instruction, as reflected in the example "Providing a specific type of activity for each child… helps me a lot in planning the process" (T2) (Nazaretsky et al., 2022). Taken together, these insights suggest that AI may function not only as an automatic scoring tool but also as a data-informed guide that can support teachers in their pedagogical decision-making (Adıgüzel et al., 2023).

One of the other important findings of the research is that AI may play a complementary and strengthening role alongside the teacher's professional observation.

Güven and Yumugan (2025) stated that the evaluations conducted by teachers are often subjective, which may lead to certain inconsistencies in assessment results. They also noted that limited time and resources negatively affect both the quality and the reliability of these evaluations. Teachers' statements such as "The system can notice points that I might overlook while observing" (T1) suggest that these systems may help address certain human-related limitations present in traditional assessment practices (Huang et al., 2024). This indicates that teacher–AI collaboration could be valuable not only for enhancing efficiency but also for improving the depth and quality of assessment.

Artificial intelligence (AI)-supported assessment systems have the potential to both transform assessment practices and support teacher competencies in early childhood education (Mena-Guacas et al., 2023). At the same time, machine learning algorithms can offer an individualized educational approach for each child by analyzing children's performance data. (Güven & Yumugan, 2025) To fully realize this potential, the following recommendations can be proposed:

- **Dissemination and Diversification:** The use of similar AI systems should be encouraged across different developmental domains (language, motor, socio-emotional) and age groups.
- **Teacher Education:** Pre-service and in-service teacher education programs should include AI literacy and skills for effectively interpreting such systems (Williyan et al., 2024).
- **Hybrid Model Development:** Future studies should focus on hybrid assessment models that combine teachers' pedagogical expertise with AI's data analysis capabilities, integrated with ethical principles. The statement, "I think the system makes our work easier" (T2), illustrates that teachers already hold a positive perception of this collaboration, which forms the foundation for such hybrid approaches.

In this context, the steps to be taken will position artificial intelligence (AI) as a sustainable and human-centered component of the educational ecosystem, ultimately accelerating a transformation that benefits both teachers and all children. The findings of this study suggest that artificial intelligence (AI)–supported digital assessment systems may serve as an effective tool in early childhood education by helping teachers save time, supporting individualized instruction, and strengthening data-informed decision-making processes. However, for this technological transformation to progress in a sustainable and responsible way, it appears important that ethical principles remain at the center of implementation efforts.

Our study indicated that teachers may be willing to share the detailed individual reports they obtained from the system with parents. This situation suggests that AI has the potential to strengthen family–school collaboration, while also implying that systematic measures may need to be taken regarding student data privacy and security. It is important that the system's design be aligned with the principles of personal data protection and remain transparent.

Moreover, the outputs and recommendations provided by AI systems carry significant risks if assumed to be absolutely accurate without human oversight. The teachers' positive feedback, such as "The system identifies aspects I might miss while observing" (T1), demonstrates that AI functions as a complementary and supportive tool, illustrating the success of a hybrid model. Nevertheless, it is important to remember that the ultimate pedagogical decision-making and responsibility always reside with the teacher. This underscores the ethical principle of autonomy and human accountability.

Additionally, the diversity of the datasets used to train AI algorithms is vital for ensuring that the system produces fair and unbiased outcomes for all children, regardless of socio-cultural and developmental differences. To minimize potential algorithmic bias, AI systems must be tested in diverse contexts and continuously reviewed.

The integration of artificial intelligence (AI) into early childhood education is a process that must be addressed within an ethical framework. In this context, the following recommendations can be proposed:

- **Development of Ethical Guidelines:** Ethical frameworks and protocols should be established for AI-supported assessment systems based on data privacy, transparency, fairness, and human oversight.
- **Emphasis on Ethics in Teacher Education:** Teacher training programs should include topics such as the ethical use of AI systems, data literacy, and critical analysis of algorithmic decision-making processes.
- **Transparent and Participatory System Design:** Parents and educators should be informed about how the system operates and how data are used. Systems should be designed to be accountable and comprehensible.

Only with an approach built upon these ethical foundations can AI-supported systems become genuine transformative tools that empower teachers, prioritize the best interests of children, and enhance the quality of education.

REFERENCES

Agnoli, S., Vanucci, M., Pelagatti, C., & Corazza, G. E. (2018). Exploring the link between mind wandering, mindfulness, and creativity: A multidimensional approach. *Creativity Research Journal, 30*(1), 41–53. DOI: 10.1080/10400419.2018.1411423

Akçadağ, T. (2010). Öğretmenlerin ilköğretim programındaki yöntem, teknik ölçme ve değerlendirme konularına ilişkin eğitim ihtiyaçları [Training needs of teachers regarding methods, techniques, measurement, and evaluation in the primary education curriculum]. *Ahmet Yesevi Üniversitesi Mütevelli Heyet Başkanlığı, 53*, 29–50.

Akgün, S., & Greenhow, C. (2022). Artificial Intelligence in education: Addressing ethical challenges in K 12 settings. *AI and Ethics, 2*(3), 431–440. DOI: 10.1007/s43681-021-00096-7

Akşin-Yavuz, E., & Zembat, R. (2016). Dinamik değerlendirme yaklaşımı ve okul öncesi eğitimde kullanımı [Dynamic assessment approach and its use in preschool education]. *Eğitim Kuram ve Uygulama Araştırmaları Dergisi, 2*(2), 12–22.

Akyel, Y., & Tur, E. (2024). Yapay zekanın potansiyelinin ve eğitim bilimlerindeki uygulamalarının araştırılması ve araştırmalarda beklentiler, zorluklar ve gelecek yönelimleri [Investigation of the potential of artificial intelligence and its applications in educational sciences, and expectations, challenges, and future trends in research]. *Ahi Evran Üniversitesi Kırşehir Eğitim Fakültesi Dergisi, 25*(1), 1–1. DOI: 10.29299/kefad.1322341

Alan, S. (2019). Comparative ınvestigation of entrepreneurship and ınnovation perceptions of preservice teachers. International Journal of Education in Mathematics. *Science and Technology, 7*(4), 311–318.

Allen, S. F. (2007). Assessing the development of young children in child care: A research of formal assessment practices. *Early Childhood Education Journal, 34*(6), 455–465. DOI: 10.1007/s10643-007-0153-z

Anderson, T., & Shattuck, J. (2012). Design-based research: A decade of progress in education research? *Educational Researcher, 41*(1), 16–25. DOI: 10.3102/0013189X11428813

Arnold, D. H., Zeljo, A., Doctoroff, G. L., & Ortiz, C. (2008). Parent involvement in preschool: Predictors and the relation of involvement to preliteracy development. *School Psychology Review, 37*(1), 74–90. DOI: 10.1080/02796015.2008.12087910

Arslan, K. (2020). Eğitimde yapay zekâ ve uygulamaları [Artificial intelligence in education and its applications]. *Batı Anadolu Eğitim Bilimleri Dergisi, 11*(1), 71–88.

Aşık, F., Yıldız, A., Kılınç, S., Aytekin, N., Adalı, R., & Kurnaz, K. (2023). Yapay zekânın eğitime etkileri [The effects of artificial intelligence on education]. *International Journal of Social Humanities Siiences Research, 10*(98), 2100–2107. DOI: 10.5281/zenodo.8307107

Autry, M. M., Lee, J., & Fox, J. (2009). Developing a data-driven assessment for early childhood candidates. *Journal of Early Childhood Teacher Education, 30*(2), 138–149. DOI: 10.1080/10901020902885695

Ay, Y., Anagün, Ş. S., & Demir, Z. M. (2015). Sınıf öğretmeni adaylarının fen öğretiminde okul dışı öğrenme hakkındaki görüşleri [Preservice primary teachers' views on out-of-school learning in science teaching]. *Electronic Turkish Studies, 10*(15), 1109–1135. DOI: 10.7827/TurkishStudies.8702

Ayyıldız, P., & Yılmaz, A. (2021). 'Moving the kaleidoscope' to see the effect of creative personality traits on creative thinking dispositions of pre-service teachers: The mediating effect of creative learning environments and teachers' creativity fostering behavior. *Thinking Skills and Creativity, 41*(100879), 1–10. DOI: 10.1016/j.tsc.2021.100879

Baer, J., & Kaufman, J. C. (2008). Gender differences in creativity. *The Journal of Creative Behavior, 42*(2), 75–105. DOI: 10.1002/j.2162-6057.2008.tb01289.x

Balcı, A., & Tezel-Şahin, F. (2021). Okul öncesi öğretmenlerinin portfolyoya ilişkin görüşlerinin incelenmesi [Examination of preschool teachers' views on portfolios]. e-Kafkas. *The Journal of Educational Research, 8*(1), 21–44. DOI: 10.30900/kafkasegt.880423

Berson, I. R., Berson, M. J., & Luo, W. (2025). *Innovating responsibly: Ethical considerations for AI in early childhood education.* AI. *Brain and Child, 1*(1), 2. Advance online publication. DOI: 10.1007/s44436-025-00003-5

Biddulph, F., & Osborne, R. (1984). Pupils' ideas about floating and sinking. *Research in Science Education, 14*(1), 114–124. DOI: 10.1007/BF02356797

Bozdoğan, A. E. (2017). (207). Fen eğitiminde informal öğrenme ortamları dersine yönelik öğretmen adaylarının görüşleri [Pre-service teachers' views on the informal learning environments course in science education]. *Uluslararası Türk Eğitim Bilimleri Dergisi*, (8), 1–17.

Braun, V., & Clarke, V. (2006). Using thematic analysis in psychology. *Qualitative Research in Psychology, 3*(2), 77–101. DOI: 10.1191/1478088706qp063oa

Carey, S. (1991). Knowledge acquisition: Enrichment or conceptual change? İçinde S. Carey & R. Gelman (Ed.), The epigenesis of mind: Essays on biology and cognition (s. 257-291). Hillsdale.

Casal-Otero, L., Catala, A., Fernández-Morante, C., Taboada, M., Cebreiro, B., & Barro, S. (2023). AI literacy in K-12: A systematic literature review. *International Journal of STEM Education, 10*(1), 29. DOI: 10.1186/s40594-023-00418-7

Çepni, S., & Çoruhlu, T. Ş. (2010). Alternatif ölçme ve değerlendirme tekniklerine yönelik hazırlanan hizmet içi eğitim kursundan öğretime yansımalar [Reflections on teaching from an in-service training course on alternative measurement and evaluation techniques]. *Pamukkale Üniversitesi Eğitim Fakültesi Dergisi, 28*, 117–128.

Çevik, M., & Senturk, C. (2019). Multidimensional 21st century skills scale: Validity and reliability study. *Cypriot Journal of Educational Sciences, 14*(1), 11–28. DOI: 10.18844/cjes.v14i1.3506

Chan, S., & Yuen, M. (2014). Personal and environmental factors affecting teachers' creativity-fostering practices in Hong Kong. *Thinking Skills and Creativity, 12*, 69–77. DOI: 10.1016/j.tsc.2014.02.003

Chen, J. J., & Li, H. (2025). *AI and the developing child: Ethical and conceptual considerations, and practical frameworks for early childhood education.* AI, Brain and Child., DOI: 10.1007/s44436-025-00016-0

Chiu, T., Meng, H., Chai, C., King, I., Wong, S., & Yam, Y. (2022). Creation and evaluation of a pretertiary artificial intelligence (AI) curriculum. *IEEE Transactions on Education, 65*(1), 30–39. DOI: 10.1109/TE.2021.3085878

Chiu, T. K. F. (2024). Future research recommendations for transforming higher education with generative AI. *Computers and Education: Artificial Intelligence, 6*, 100197. DOI: 10.1016/j.caeai.2023.100197

Çığrık, E., & Özkan, M. (2016). Bilim merkezi'nde yürütülen öğrenme etkinliklerin öğrencilerin fen bilimleri dersindeki akademik başarılarına etkisi ve motivasyon düzeyleriyle ilişkisi [The effect of learning activities conducted in a science center on students' academic achievement in science lessons and its relation to their motivation levels]. *Uludağ Üniversitesi Eğitim Fakültesi Dergisi, 29*(2), 279–301.

Çoruhlu, Ş. T., Nas, E. S., & Çepni, S. (2008). Fen ve teknoloji öğretmenlerinin alternatif ölçme değerlendirme tekniklerini kullanmada karşılaştıkları problemler: Trabzon örneği [Problems encountered by science and technology teachers in using alternative measurement and evaluation techniques: The case of Trabzon] [EFMED]. *Necatibey Eğitim Fakültesi Elektronik Fen ve Matematik Eğitimi Dergisi, 2*(2), 1–22.

Çoruhlu, Ş. T., Nas, E. S., & Çepni, S. (2009). Fen ve teknoloji öğretmenlerinin alternatif ölçme değerlendirme tekniklerini kullanmada karşılaştıkları problemler: Trabzon örneği [Problems encountered by science and technology teachers in using alternative measurement and evaluation techniques: The case of Trabzon]. Yüzüncü yıl Üniversitesi Eğitim Fakültesi Dergisi, 6(1), 122-141.

Dede, C. (2010). Comparing frameworks for 21st century skills. İçinde J. Bellenca & R. Brandt (Ed.), 21st century skills: Rethinking how students. Solution Tree Press.

Dede, C. (2010). Technological supports for acquiring 21st century skills. *International Encyclopedia Of Education*, *3*, 158–166. DOI: 10.1016/B978-0-08-044894-7.00739-9

Design-Based Research Collective. (2003). Design-based research: An emerging paradigm for educational inquiry. *Educational Researcher*, *32*(1), 5–8. DOI: 10.3102/0013189X032001005

Doymaz, C., & Gözüm, A. İ. C. (2025). Okul öncesi öğretmenlerinin dijital içerik üretme yeterliklerinin incelenmesi: Kullanım senaryoları temelli bir uygulama [Examination of preschool teachers' digital content creation competencies: A scenario-based implementation]. In Karademir, A., Demirel, B., & Yılmaz Tam, H. B. (Eds.), *Proceedings of the 18th National Preschool Teacher Education Student Congress* (p. 25). Muş, Türkiye.

Gömleksiz, M. N., & Bulut, İ. (2007). Yeni fen ve teknoloji dersi öğretim programının uygulamadaki etkililiğinin değerlendirilmesi [Evaluation of the effectiveness of the new science and technology curriculum in practice]. *Hacettepe Üniversitesi Eğitim Fakültesi Dergisi*, *32*, 76–88.

Grassini, S. (2023). Shaping the future of education: Exploring the potential and consequences of AI and ChatGPT in educational settings. *Education Sciences*, *13*(7), 692. DOI: 10.3390/educsci13070692

Güven, G., & Yumugan, S. (2025). Artificial intelligence in preschool education: Personalized assessment and evaluation with artificial intelligence. [IJSSER]. *International Journal of Social Sciences and Education Research*, 7(12), 161–190. DOI: 10.5281/zenodo.14936787

Hazzan-Bishara, A., Kol, O., & Levy, S. (2025). The factors affecting teachers' adoption of AI technologies: A unified model of external and internal determinants. *Education and Information Technologies*, *30*(11), 15043–15069. Advance online publication. DOI: 10.1007/s10639-025-13393-z

Hooda, M., Rana, C., Dahiya, O., Shet, J. P., & Singh, B. K. (2022). Integrating LA and EDM for improving students success in higher education using FCN algorithm. *Mathematical Problems in Engineering, 2022*(1), 7690103. DOI: 10.1155/2022/7690103

Huang, R. H. (2018). The integration of artificial intelligence in education: A learner-centered approach. *International Journal of Artificial Intelligence in Education, 28*(2), 289–291.

Husaini, R., Ikhsan, Z., & Toran, H. (2019). A comprehensive 21st century child development through scientific process in early science. *Creative Education, 10*(12), 3202–3214. DOI: 10.4236/ce.2019.1012205

Kewalramani, S., Palaiologou, I., Dardanou, M., Phillipson, S., & Yang, Y. (2021). Using robotic toys in early childhood education to support children's social and emotional competencies. *Australasian Journal of Early Childhood, 46*(4), 355–369. DOI: 10.1177/18369391211056668

Kocaarslan, M. (2012). Tanılayıcı dallanmış ağaç tekniği ve ilköğretim 5. Sınıf fen ve teknoloji dersi maddenin değişimi ve tanınması adlı ünitede kullanımı [Diagnostic branched tree technique and its use in the 'change and recognition of matter' unit of 5th grade science and technology class]. *Mustafa Kemal Üniversitesi Sosyal Bilimler Enstitüsü Dergisi, 9*(18), 269–279.

Landis, J. R., & Koch, G. G. (1977). The measurement of observer agreement for categorical data. *Biometrics, 33*(1), 159–174. DOI: 10.2307/2529310

Limatahu, I., Wasis, W., Sutoyo, S., & Prahani, B. K. (2018). Development of CCDSR teaching model to improve science process skills of pre-service physics teachers. *Journal of Baltic Science Education, 17*(5), 812–827. DOI: 10.33225/jbse/18.17.812

Lin, P., Van Brummelen, J., Lukin, G., Williams, R., & Breazeal, C. (2020). Zhorai: Designing a conversational agent for children to explore machine learning concepts. *Proceedings of the AAAI Conference on Artificial Intelligence, 34*(9), 13381–13388. DOI: 10.1609/aaai.v34i09.7061

Liu, J., Chen, M., He, H., Liu, H., Luo, W., & Li, H. (2025). *Forms and functions innovation: A scoping review of digital and intelligence technologies in early childhood education practice.* AI. *Brain and Child, 1*(1), 8. Advance online publication. DOI: 10.1007/s44436-025-00010-6

Loverude, M. E., Kautz, C. H., & Heron, P. R. L. (2003). Helping students develop an understanding of Archimedes' principle. I. Research on student understanding. *American Journal of Physics, 71*(11), 1178–1187. DOI: 10.1119/1.1607335

Maraisane, L., Jita, L., & Jita, T. (2024). Engagement of science process skills for teaching science concepts in early childhood. Journal of Childhood. *Education & Society*, *5*(2), 283–293. DOI: 10.37291/2717638X.202452387

Memarian, B., & Doleck, T. (2023). A review of assessment for learning with artificial intelligence. *Computers in Human Behavior: Artificial Humans*, *1*(1), 100040. Advance online publication. DOI: 10.1016/j.chbah.2023.100040

Mena-Guacas, A. F., Urueña Rodríguez, J. A., Santana Trujillo, D. M., Gómez-Galán, J., & López-Meneses, E. (2023). Collaborative learning and skill development for educational growth of artificial intelligence: A systematic review. *Contemporary Educational Technology*, *15*(3), ep428. DOI: 10.30935/cedtech/13123

Nazaretsky, T., Dori, Y. J., & Hazzan, O. (2022). AI-based assessment tools in education: A systematic review. *Educational Technology Research and Development*, *70*(1), 123–147.

Özsevgeç, T., & Çepni, S. (2006). Farklı sınıflardaki öğrencilerin yüzme ve batma kavramlarını anlama düzeyleri [Understanding levels of students in different grades regarding the concepts of floating and sinking]. *Milli Eğitim Dergisi*, *172*, 297–311.

Penny, A. R., & Coe, R. (2004). Effectiveness of consultation on student ratings feedback: A meta-analysis. *Review of Educational Research*, *74*(2), 215–253. DOI: 10.3102/00346543074002215

Peterson, G., & Elam, E. (2020). Observation and assessment in early childhood education (Version 1.0). College of the Canyons. https://www.canyons.edu/_resources/documents/academics/earlychildhoodeducation/oer/ObservationandAssessmentinEarlyChildhoodEducation.pdf

Roberts, P. (2021). Follow the leader: Child-led inquiries to develop science learning of young children. Journal of Childhood. *Education & Society*, *2*(3), 303–313. DOI: 10.37291/2717638X.202123120

Sevgi, M., Ayyıldız, P., & Yılmaz, A. (2023). Eğitim bilimleri alanında yapay zekâ uygulamaları ve uygulamaların alana yansımaları [Artificial intelligence applications in the field of educational sciences and their reflections on the field]. İçinde Ö. Baltacı (Ed.). Eğitim bilimleri araştırmaları-IV [Educational sciences research-IV] (ss.1-18). Özgür Yayınları.

Sevgi, M., & Yılmaz, A. (2023). Yükseköğretimde dijital dönüşüm ve metaverse [Digital transformation and metaverse in higher education]. İçinde Y. Doğan & N. Şen Ersoy (Ed.), Eğitimde metaverse kuram ve uygulamalar [Metaverse in education: Theory and applications] (s.71-86). Efe Akademi Yayınları.

Slade, S., & Prinsloo, P. (2013). Learning Analytics: Ethical Issues and Dilemmas. *The American Behavioral Scientist, 57*(10), 1510–1529. DOI: 10.1177/0002764213479366

Smith, C., Carey, S., & Wiser, M. (1985). On differentiation: A case study of the development of the concepts of size, weight, and density. *Cognition, 21*(3), 177–237. DOI: 10.1016/0010-0277(85)90025-3

Solek, P., Nurfitri, E., Sahril, I., Prasetya, T., Rizqiamuti, A. F., Rachmawati, I., & Gunawan, K. (2025). The role of artificial intelligence for early diagnostic tools of autism spectrum disorder: A systematic review. *Turkish Archives of Pediatrics, 60*(2), 126–140. DOI: 10.5152/TurkArchPediatr.2025.24183

Thornton-Lang, K. M. (2012). Observation as a formal assessment tool in early childhood classrooms: A professional development module (Graduate Research Paper, University of Northern Iowa). UNI ScholarWorks. https://scholarworks.uni.edu/grp/238

Ünal, M., & Aral, N. (2014). Deney yöntemine dayalı eğitim programının 6 yaş çocuklarının problem çözme becerilerine etkisinin incelenmesi [Examination of the effect of an experiment-based education program on the problem-solving skills of 6-year-old children]. *Eğitim ve Bilim, 39*(176), 279–291. DOI: 10.15390/EB.2014.3592

Vasconcelos, M. A. R., & dos Santos, R. P. (2023). Enhancing STEM learning with ChatGPT and Bing Chat as objects to think with: A case study. *Eurasia Journal of Mathematics, Science and Technology Education, 19*(7), em2296. Advance online publication. DOI: 10.29333/ejmste/13313

Wang, F., & Hannafin, M. J. (2005). Design-based research and technology-enhanced learning environments. *Educational Technology Research and Development, 53*(4), 5–23. DOI: 10.1007/BF02504682

Williams, R., Park, H. W., & Breazeal, C. (2019, May). A is for artificial intelligence: The impact of artificial intelligence activities on young children's perceptions of robots. In *Proceedings of the 2019 CHI Conference on Human Factors in Computing Systems* (s. 1–11). DOI: 10.1145/3290605.3300677

Williyan, A., Fitriati, S. W., Pratama, H., & Sakhiyya, Z. (2024). AI as co-creator: Exploring Indonesian EFL teachers' collaboration with AI in content development. *Teaching English with Technology, 24*(2), 5–21. DOI: 10.56297/vaca6841/LRDX3699/RZOH5366

Yin, Y., Tomita, M. K., & Shavelson, R. J. (2008). Diagnosing and dealing with student misconceptions: Floating and sinking. *Science Scope, 31*(8), 34–39.

Zeidan, A. H., & Jayosi, M. R. (2015). Science process skills and attitudes toward science among Palestinian secondary school students. *World Journal of Education*, *5*(1), 13–24. DOI: 10.5430/wje.v5n1p13

Chapter 4

Navigating Artificial Intelligence Literacy in Early Childhood Education:

Emerging Future Opportunities and Challenges

Elçin Yazici Arici
https://orcid.org/0000-0002-6679-4793
Düzce University, Turkey

Nur Banu Yiğit
Duzce University, Turkey

Michail Kalogiannakis
https://orcid.org/0000-0002-9124-2245
University of Thessaly, Greece

ABSTRACT

This study explores the integration of Artificial Intelligence (AI) in early childhood education (ECE), highlighting its pedagogical potential, ethical challenges, and practical implications. Through a scoping review of recent scholarly literature and international reports, the paper outlines how AI technologies are increasingly shaping educational experiences for young learners. While AI presents promising avenues for enhanced assessment, inclusive learning, and reduced teacher workload, concerns regarding data privacy, reduced human interaction, and algorithmic bias remain significant. The paper emphasizes the importance of transparent, equitable,

DOI: 10.4018/979-8-3373-9074-1.ch004

and developmentally appropriate implementation of AI in ECE. Recommendations include strengthening teacher training, designing locally relevant AI applications, and fostering collaboration among stakeholders. The study concludes that a balanced, critically reflective, and ethically grounded approach is essential to harness the full potential of AI in promoting meaningful, inclusive, and sustainable early learning environments.

1. INTRODUCTION

Artificial Intelligence (AI), often referred to as machine intelligence, represents the capacity of computers or digital systems to carry out tasks traditionally requiring human cognitive abilities (Solanki et al., 2021). Initially developed to simulate complex mental processes such as perception, reasoning, and prediction, AI has evolved significantly since being recognized as a distinct field of academic inquiry in 1956 (Russell & Norvig, 2002; Knapp, 2006). Within educational contexts, AI has become an increasingly prominent focus, as its capacity to individualize learning pathways holds substantial promise for enhancing instructional practices. Applications range from robotic teaching assistants to automated tools for evaluating student responses, illustrating the wide scope of AI in supporting instruction, learning outcomes, and educational assessment.

While AI integration has been widely explored in the context of secondary and higher education (Su et al., 2022), its application within early childhood education (ECE), remains relatively underdeveloped. This is especially notable given that young children are growing up in environments saturated with intelligent technologies. They regularly interact with AI-enabled tools such as smart toys, voice assistants, and high-performance tablets—devices that surpass the computing power of personal computers from just a decade ago (Williams et al., 2019a). These interactions, although common, are often passive and uncritical, highlighting the need to support children's understanding of how AI works.

1.1. Artificial Intelligence in ECE

Historically, AI education began within the context of university-level computer science, requiring high-level programming knowledge that was inaccessible to young learners (Ng et al., 2021a). However, the emergence of child-friendly software and educational platforms now enables younger children to explore AI-related topics in ways suited to their developmental stage. Even so, most existing AI education research has primarily targeted middle and high school students or non-specialist undergraduates, focusing on fostering conceptual understanding and ethical awareness rather than advanced technical knowledge (Eguchi et al., 2021; Kong et al., 2022, 2023; Ng & Chu, 2021; Su et al., 2022).

In contrast, ECE settings have only recently begun incorporating AI through interactive technologies, such as programmable toys and basic coding kits, that facilitate exploration and engagement. Tools like PopBots and QuickDraw provide entry points for preschoolers to interact with supervised machine learning, knowledge representation, and generative AI (Williams, 2018; Williams et al., 2019a, 2019b). Although young children may lack the cognitive maturity to fully comprehend the inner workings of these systems, such experiences can still support the development of digital literacy and foster a sense of technological curiosity.

Some educators and scholars have questioned whether young children—especially those in kindergarten or early primary years—are developmentally ready to engage with AI concepts (Su et al., 2022). Nonetheless, a growing body of research demonstrates that AI can positively influence various dimensions of child development when introduced appropriately. These include social reasoning (e.g., theory of mind), creativity, emotional intelligence, and collaborative inquiry (Kewalramani et al., 2021; Su & Yang, 2022). For instance, Kewalramani et al. (2021) investigated the use of AI tools to promote inquiry-based learning in ECE contexts, showing promising results in supporting cognitive and social growth. These early applications of AI in ECE highlight not only the growing feasibility of introducing AI concepts to young learners but also underscore the urgent need to equip them with the foundational competencies required to understand and engage with such technologies critically what scholars now refer to as AI literacy.

1.2. Artificial Intelligence Curriculum for Kindergarten

AI education extends beyond the boundaries of traditional computational thinking by encompassing a broader understanding of how intelligent systems perceive, process, learn from, and respond to the world. This includes capabilities such as decision-making, learning, creativity, and interpretation. Given that young children are active participants in their learning and tend to think in concrete terms, hands-on and exploratory approaches are especially effective for introducing STEM-related concepts to this age group (Williams et al., 2019).

There is growing consensus that AI learning can begin as early as age three, provided it is framed in an accessible and developmentally appropriate manner (Preface, 2021). Young children are naturally inquisitive and highly responsive to new learning experiences, making early AI education both engaging and impactful when delivered with the right tools and pedagogical strategies (Preface, 2021).

1.2.1. Artificial Intelligence Literacy

The concept of AI literacy was initially introduced by Burgsteiner et al. (2016) and Kandlhofer et al. (2016), who characterized it as the ability to grasp essential knowledge and foundational principles related to artificial intelligence. Expanding on this foundation, Long and Magerko (2020) conceptualized AI literacy as a collection of competencies that empower individuals to assess AI technologies critically, communicate effectively about their functions and implications, and collaborate with AI systems across various domains—including digital platforms, domestic environments, and professional settings.

Building further, Ng et al. (2021a, 2021b) emphasized the necessity of embedding AI literacy within the broader framework of 21st-century digital skills, arguing that it should be regarded as a universal competency relevant to all learners—not solely to those in technical or computer science fields. Their instructional model integrates elements from Bloom's Taxonomy, the Technological Pedagogical Content Knowledge (TPACK) framework, and multiple dimensions of AI understanding, including conceptual foundations, practical applications, and ethical perspectives.

Finally, Kim et al. (2021) proposed a curriculum model for early childhood AI literacy that emphasizes three core goals: first, helping children recognize and name AI technologies they encounter in everyday contexts; second, providing them with basic programming abilities that allow them to interact meaningfully with AI tools; and third, cultivating an early understanding of the ethical considerations surrounding AI usage. These goals are distilled into three foundational dimensions of AI literacy: knowledge (what AI is), skills (how to use it), and attitudes (how to approach it responsibly).

1.2.1.1. Artificial Intelligence Knowledge

The AI Knowledge component is designed to provide learners with a foundational understanding of core artificial intelligence concepts (Kim et al., 2021). This competency is structured around five thematic areas: (1) definitions and classifications of AI, (2) problem-solving and search strategies, (3) reasoning processes, (4) data and machine learning, and (5) AI applications.

The first category, Definitions and Types of AI, introduces learners to the distinguishing features of AI systems in contrast to traditional algorithmic processes. It emphasizes the characteristics that define intelligent behavior in machines. The Problem-Solving and Search dimension focuses on exposing learners to various strategies used by AI systems to explore possible solutions within defined parameters.

Reasoning pertains to how computational models can replicate or simulate logical human thought processes, allowing systems to infer conclusions or make decisions. The Data and Machine Learning cluster explores how algorithms identify patterns from large datasets, offering insight into how machines "learn" from data inputs over time.

Finally, the Applications domain addresses real-world uses of AI, such as speech-to-text processing, computer vision, and machine translation. Within this domain, learners are encouraged to interact with widely available technologies—like voice assistants or optical character recognition tools—as a means to contextualize their understanding. Through experiential learning, students gain exposure to how AI functions in daily life and are empowered to apply this knowledge in practical scenarios.

Figure 1. AI4K12 proposed the five big ideas framework

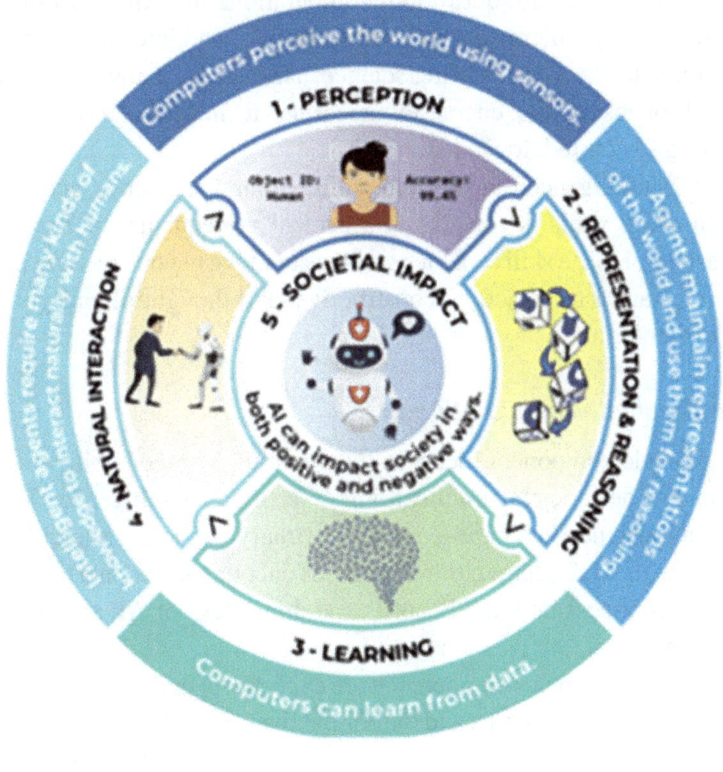

1.2.1.2. Artificial Intelligence Skill

The AI Skill domain emphasizes learners' ability to apply computational thinking and basic programming knowledge to engage with AI technologies effectively

(Kim et al., 2021). This dimension is composed of two main competencies: Using AI Tools and Computational Thinking and Programming.

Using AI Tools refers to learners' capacity to approach and solve problems by selecting and applying appropriate AI technologies. This includes making informed choices about which tools to use in specific contexts to achieve meaningful outcomes. Computational Thinking and Programming, on the other hand, involves designing and constructing simple AI systems or applications, with a particular focus on enhancing learners' ability to think logically and algorithmically.

To support this, Kim et al. (2021) incorporated the ReadyAI framework, which promotes programming skills as a foundational pathway to computational literacy. Drawing from Wing's (2006) definition, computational thinking encompasses the cognitive process of problem-solving, system design, and interpretation of human behavior through the lens of computer science. This approach involves reasoning at multiple levels of abstraction, encouraging learners to analyze and address complex problems using structured, logical strategies.

As artificial intelligence is a subfield within computer science, acquiring computational thinking skills is considered a critical prerequisite for developing AI literacy. Mastery of these skills enables students to move beyond passive interaction with AI and toward a more active, constructive, and thoughtful engagement with intelligent technologies.

1.2.1.3. Artificial Intelligence Attitude

The AI Attitude component focuses on cultivating learners' ability to critically examine the broader societal implications of artificial intelligence (Kim et al., 2021). This competency is composed of two primary elements: Social Impact and Collaboration with AI. Together, these domains encourage students to engage with ethical questions, assess both the benefits and drawbacks of AI, and reflect on its responsible use.

Students who develop this competency are expected to demonstrate awareness of how AI influences social systems and individual lives—positively and negatively. A key goal is to nurture a sense of responsibility in using AI technologies to promote collective well-being. While AI continues to drive technological progress, it also raises serious concerns related to privacy, fairness, and safety—particularly when it comes to children. Despite their high exposure to AI-enabled environments, children are often overlooked in the design, deployment, and regulation of AI systems (UNICEF, 2022).

This oversight is especially problematic, as children may lack the cognitive and communicative resources to fully grasp the consequences of AI technologies, express dissent, or seek redress when biases or harms occur. As noted by UNICEF (2022), children frequently do not have the advocacy structures necessary to protect their rights or challenge algorithmic injustices—such as biased data or unfair classifications.

The ethical risks associated with AI are already visible in real-world applications. For instance, research by Buolamwini and Gebru (2018) revealed gender and racial bias in facial recognition systems, while Manzini et al. (2019) identified discriminatory patterns in word embeddings, which can reproduce harmful stereotypes. These examples highlight the urgent need for learners to develop the capacity to evaluate the ethical dimensions of AI critically.

To support such reflection, AI literacy should equip students with the ability to adopt multiple perspectives, consider competing values, and engage in ethical reasoning. As Wong et al. (2020) emphasize, fostering a well-rounded understanding of AI involves not only technical proficiency but also an awareness of its moral and social responsibilities.

1.2.2. The Emergence of Artificial Intelligence Literacy in ECE

Recent efforts have focused on introducing age-appropriate AI concepts to preschool-aged children through playful, hands-on experiences. Foundational machine learning platforms, developmentally appropriate generative AI tools, and interactive robots like Cozmo or Jibo have served as early entry points into this domain (Druga et al., 2021; Kewalramani et al., 2021; Prentzas, 2013; Su & Yang, 2022). Experimental studies have demonstrated the feasibility of teaching basic AI principles, such as classification and prediction, through the use of AI-enabled robots (Lin et al., 2020; Vartiainen et al., 2020). These studies reveal that AI can support both cognitive development and learner engagement in ECE settings, even if children do not fully grasp the underlying algorithms (Druga et al., 2019; Ge et al., 2021; Jin, 2019; Nan, 2020; Williams et al., 2019b).

These initiatives are underpinned by a growing body of scholarship that advocates for the integration of AI literacy into early education. Yang (2022), for example, argues that the inclusion of AI in kindergarten curricula is essential for several reasons. First, understanding core AI competencies and engaging with AI applications are now fundamental for full participation in digital society (Ng et al., 2021a, 2021b). Second, children must be equipped with the skills to interpret, evaluate, and use AI technologies with critical awareness, rather than remain passive consumers of intelligent systems (Williams et al., 2019a). Third, with the increasing presence of sophisticated AI-enhanced toys in children's daily environments, there is a growing need for them to comprehend basic AI functions and the implications of their use (Kewalramani et al., 2021).

Despite the proliferation of AI in children's lives, there is still limited awareness of the importance of AI literacy for young children. As children interact with AI systems like recommendation engines and chatbots, they are rarely equipped with the knowledge to understand or critique them (Gaube et al., 2021). Misunderstandings about how AI functions—and its limitations—can lead to unrealistic expectations or unsafe interactions with technology. Therefore, it is vital to cultivate AI literacy from an early age, with a focus on ethical reasoning, technical boundaries, and foundational concepts (Kong et al., 2021, 2022; Long & Magerko, 2020; Ng et al., 2021a, 2021b).

In line with these arguments, various researchers have proposed developmentally suitable AI curricula tailored for young learners. Yang (2022) developed the "AI for Kids" curriculum, which introduces children to AI through project-based learning and embodied experiences using tools such as AI for Oceans on Code.org, Quick-Draw, and AI-enhanced educational robots like PopBots and Zhorai. The goal is to help children recognize the role of AI in daily life and to build foundational understanding through hands-on interaction. Similarly, Williams et al. (2019a) designed AI-robot interfaces that allow children to explore supervised machine learning, knowledge-based systems, and generative AI through activities like rock-paper-scissors, food classification, and music remixing. These playful, interactive tasks provide meaningful learning experiences that promote both conceptual knowledge and ethical reflection.

AI literacy has recently emerged as a key component of 21st-century digital skills. Scholars emphasize that it should not be limited to adults or older students but should include young children who are increasingly navigating AI-rich environments (Ng et al., 2021a, 2021b). Rather than positioning children as passive users of technology, educational initiatives aim to equip them with the ability to engage critically, collaborate meaningfully, and interact responsibly with AI systems (Burgsteiner et al., 2016; Kandlhofer et al., 2016; Steinbauer et al., 2021). Among the available tools, QuickDraw and other AI-driven platforms allow young learners to explore knowledge representation, basic algorithms, and data-driven logic in playful ways (Williams, 2018; Williams et al., 2019b).

To clarify the scope of AI literacy, several scholars have proposed conceptual models. One influential framework, proposed by Touretzky et al. (2019), outlines five core principles of AI understanding: (1) computers use sensors to gather input from their environment, (2) intelligent agents maintain internal models to reason about the world, (3) developing socially compatible AI systems is a complex challenge, (4) AI can learn from data, and (5) AI technologies influence society in both beneficial and harmful ways. Building on this foundation, Ng et al. (2021b) introduced a more comprehensive model that integrates AI with computational thinking (CT), emphasizing machine learning, model training, collaboration, and communication as critical dimensions of learning.

1.2.3. Tools and Resources for Artificial Intelligence at the Kindergarten Level

To support students and educators in engaging meaningfully with artificial intelligence and understanding its foundational principles, a wide array of supplementary resources has recently emerged. These tools are designed to make AI education more accessible to younger audiences. Touretzky (2017) compiled a comprehensive set of platforms and aids that serve as effective entry points into AI learning for both students and instructors. These include:

- **Cognimates** (Druga et al., 2018), an extension for Scratch that allows learners to interact with application programming interfaces (APIs) to perform tasks such as voice generation, speech-to-text recognition, text classification, object detection, and robot programming. [https://cognimates.me]
- **eCraft2Learn** (Kahn & Winters, 2017), a toolkit integrated into the Snap! programming environment that offers similar AI functionalities tailored for student exploration. [https://ecraft2learn.github.io/ai/]
- **Machine Learning for Kids**, a user-friendly online platform that enables children to train AI classifiers via Scratch extensions or web interfaces. [https://machinelearningforkids.co.uk/]
- **Cozmo**, a small-scale, cost-efficient mobile robot embedded with computer vision capabilities, including facial recognition, marker tracking, object manipulation, path planning, and speech output.
- **Calypso for Cozmo** (Touretzky, 2017), a visual, rule-based programming environment designed for the Cozmo robot. It includes functionalities such as voice command recognition, map-based navigation, state machine programming, and global scene awareness. [https://Calypso.software]
- **Google AI Experiments**, such as *Teachable Machine* and *QuickDraw*, which provide interactive demonstrations of neural networks in action—allowing users to train models or test sketch recognition systems. [https://experiments.withgoogle.com/collection/ai]
- **Google AIY Kits** (short for "AI and You"), which offer low-cost voice and vision modules powered by Raspberry Pi Zero. The voice kit connects with Google Assistant, while the vision kit uses machine learning classifiers for image recognition.
- **TensorFlow Playground**, an interactive browser-based application that allows high school and undergraduate students to experiment with artificial neural networks and observe the dynamics of backpropagation learning. [https://playground.tensorflow.org]

Alongside these technological resources, Weintrop et al. (2016) developed a detailed taxonomy to guide the integration of computational thinking into mathematics and science instruction. To establish and validate this framework, they drew on three main sources: (1) Classroom practices in science and mathematics education, (2) Established concept inventories and national/international curricular standards, and (3) Expert interviews with practicing scientists and mathematicians. Building upon this foundation, the taxonomy was organized into four major thematic domains: (1) Data Practices, which include the collection, generation, modification, analysis, and visualization of data; (2) Modeling and Simulation Practices, which involve using computational models to explain phenomena, test hypotheses, and design simulations, as well as evaluating and constructing models; (3) Computational Problem Solving, covering activities such as preparing problems for computational solutions, programming, selecting appropriate tools, evaluating solution alternatives, constructing modular code, creating abstractions, and debugging; (4) System Thinking, which refers to understanding and modeling complex systems, identifying relationships between components, reasoning across multiple levels of abstraction, communicating system behaviors, and handling system-level complexity.

This taxonomy reflects the essential cognitive and technical skills needed to bridge computational thinking with subject-specific learning in mathematics and science. Moreover, it offers a foundation for developing AI-related pedagogical strategies grounded in authentic disciplinary practices.

In parallel, Lin and Weintrop (2021) reviewed various computing curricula that utilize block-based programming (BBP) tools in both formal classroom and informal educational settings. Examples include *Exploring Computer Science*, *Scratch Encore*, *Beauty and Joy of Computing*, and the diverse set of resources from Code.org. Earlier findings by Weintrop and Wilensky (2015) revealed that learners perceived visual programming environments as more accessible due to their intuitive graphical layout, drag-and-drop features, and the ease with which commands could be identified and integrated into programs. These affordances not only facilitated understanding but also increased learners' motivation and engagement. The study also emphasized the significance of user motivation and interest in shaping the effectiveness of these tools.

Insights from these studies provide educators with a deeper understanding of how various elements—such as user interface design, learner characteristics, and instructional context—affect the successful integration of AI tools in K–12 education.

Despite the abundance of tools and pedagogical models, prior research has largely concentrated on generalized AI learning environments (Kafai & Burke, 2014), the integration of AI into specific subject areas (Weintrop et al., 2016; Hasib et al., 2022), or programming education within secondary-level contexts (Lin & Weintrop, 2021). Although these studies offer meaningful insights regarding learner needs and instructional efficacy, a standardized, in-depth framework for designing and evaluating AI curricula at the preschool level is still lacking.

Existing early childhood AI initiatives—such as those involving PopBots—primarily focus on familiarizing children with basic AI ideas like supervised learning, generative models, and rule-based systems (Williams, 2018; Williams et al., 2019a, 2019b). However, these programs often do not address larger questions regarding curriculum coherence, instructional quality, and measurable outcomes for learners in early childhood settings.

To address this gap, further investigation is needed to explore how AI can be systematically integrated into early childhood education, including the development, implementation, and assessment of comprehensive curricula. The present study seeks to respond to that need by enhancing the research base on curriculum design and offering pedagogical guidance for educators who aim to foster AI literacy from the earliest stages of learning.

2. OPPORTUNITIES OF ARTIFICIAL INTELLIGENCE LITERACY IN EARLY CHILDHOOD EDUCATION

Over the past decade, digitalisation has played a pivotal role in driving innovation within classroom practices (Vincent-Lancrin et al., 2019). While earlier innovations largely revolved around the integration of computers and internet technologies into teaching and learning, the forthcoming transformative phase is anticipated to be shaped by artificial intelligence and its convergence with other emerging technologies. Within educational contexts, AI is increasingly embedded in tools that offer functions such as learning analytics, personalized recommendations, and diagnostic assessments—each serving different pedagogical and administrative purposes (Ng et al., 2022c; Vincent-Lancrin, S. & van der Vlies, 2020).

Although many AI-based applications in education are still in early stages of development and typically confined to experimental or localized implementations, a growing body of promising practices hints at AI's potential to reshape learning environments in the coming decades. These developments may influence all levels of the education system, benefiting a diverse set of stakeholders including learners, educators, school leaders, families, and policymakers alike (Vincent-Lancrin, S. & van der Vlies, 2020).

AI holds particular promise in advancing several of the objectives set forth in Sustainable Development Goal 4 (SDG 4), which seeks to "ensure inclusive and equitable quality education and promote lifelong learning opportunities for all." Reflecting the spirit of the first G20 AI Principle, the integration of AI in education can contribute to meaningful outcomes that support human flourishing and planetary well-being. These include enhancing human potential, fostering creativity, promoting the participation of marginalized groups, narrowing socio-economic and gender disparities, and safeguarding natural resources—ultimately contributing to inclusive growth, sustainable development, and societal well-being (Vincent-Lancrin, S. & van der Vlies, 2020).

2.1. Artificial Intelligence Applications for Instruction

2.1.1. Personalizing Learning with Artificial Intelligence

One of the most significant potentials of artificial intelligence in education lies in its capacity to tailor instruction and learning resources to meet individual learners' needs. Personalized learning, an approach that adapts educational content to the unique strengths and challenges of each student, is increasingly supported by AI technologies. These systems can analyze learners' performance data to generate predictions, suggest instructional strategies, and guide the next steps in learning. AI-enabled tools allow students to progress at their own pace while simultaneously offering teachers actionable insights on how to better support them. This individualized approach to instruction holds particular relevance not only for G20 nations but also in broader global contexts. Traditional methods, such as the "Teach at the Right Level" initiative, have long addressed differentiated instruction without technological assistance; however, AI introduces new avenues to close learning gaps, particularly in foundational areas like literacy and numeracy (Ng et al., 2021c; Vincent-Lancrin, S. & van der Vlies, 2020).

Although still emerging, some educational institutions have already been leveraging such AI-driven innovations. In the United States, for instance, the Teach to One: Math program by New Classrooms began implementation in 2012 across select schools in cities like Chicago, New York, and Washington D.C. Designed for lower-secondary mathematics, the program integrates daily assessments with algorithmic decision-making to generate personalized instructional pathways. Students engage in varied learning formats, including direct instruction, peer collaboration, and adaptive educational software. The system continuously collects and analyzes data to identify learning gaps on non-linear skill maps—such as understanding mathematical relations involving ratios or rational numbers. Learners receive customized dashboards each day, outlining their progress and offering targeted learning tasks. Based on this feedback loop, personalized learning schedules are updated daily and structured into two-week instructional cycles. Teachers also benefit from real-time, data-informed dashboards that enhance their ability to provide timely, differentiated support (Kewalramani et al., 2021; Vincent-Lancrin, S. & van der Vlies, 2020). Although this model targets older learners, its adaptive structure offers valuable implications for early childhood contexts. Similar AI-driven feedback mechanisms can be simplified and embedded into playful, developmentally appropriate tools that personalize early literacy and numeracy experiences for children aged 3–8.

Similar AI applications have emerged outside formal school systems as well. In China, the TAL Education Group has developed several AI-based solutions aimed at improving university entrance exam preparation. Their "Adaptive Test and Learning Plan" platform, for example, analyzes large datasets of test items to deliver personalized questions aligned with each student's current level of understanding. The platform not only identifies suitable offline courses but also crafts individualized study plans, sharing progress insights with both students and their parents (Vincent-Lancrin, S. & van der Vlies, 2020). While primarily focused on exam preparation for older students, the adaptive algorithms underlying such systems can inform early learning designs that dynamically adjust to a preschooler's pace, attention, and preferences—thereby modeling how AI can personalize instruction in developmentally responsive ways.

While these innovations have largely focused on secondary education and test preparation, the integration of AI into early childhood education is also gaining momentum. AI-based tools designed for preschoolers—such as PopBots and QuickDraw—introduce fundamental AI concepts through interactive, play-based experiences. These technologies enable children to engage with simple machine learning principles, develop early computational thinking, and foster digital curiosity in developmentally appropriate ways (Williams et al., 2019a; Druga et al., 2019). For example, AI-assisted storytelling applications or robotics kits are being used in preschool classrooms to support emergent literacy and problem-solving, encouraging young learners to explore cause-effect relationships and pattern recognition through guided experimentation. Such tools not only lay the groundwork for future digital literacy but also support social-emotional learning and collaborative inquiry. As these AI-driven experiences continue to evolve, they offer new opportunities to rethink early learning environments and pedagogies in more inclusive and responsive ways.

2.1.2. Supporting Students with Special Needs with Artificial Intelligence

Ensuring equitable access to education remains a persistent global challenge, particularly in under-resourced regions. One of the core aims of Sustainable Development Goal 4 is to promote inclusive education by guaranteeing equal opportunities at all levels of learning, especially for individuals with disabilities. Artificial intelligence (AI) technologies have already demonstrated potential in advancing this objective by supporting learners with various impairments—ranging from visual and auditory challenges to difficulties in language, communication, or social interaction. AI-driven tools, such as wearable devices, assist visually impaired students by enabling them to interpret printed texts and recognize facial features, thereby enhancing both learning and social participation. Similarly, text-to-speech and speech-to-text applications are increasingly used to bridge communication gaps, especially for students with reading or expressive language difficulties (Ng et al., 2021b; Vincent-Lancrin, S. & van der Vlies, 2020).

Beyond these assistive applications, AI has been embedded in immersive technologies like augmented and virtual reality (AR/VR) and robotics to support learners with cognitive and emotional needs. Such tools facilitate engagement and learning for students experiencing mental health issues or developmental delays. For example, children on the autism spectrum benefit from interacting with virtual characters and digital environments designed to foster social communication skills and collaborative behaviors. These innovations are particularly impactful in early education contexts, where AI-powered toys and interactive platforms introduce foundational social-emotional and communication skills in playful, developmentally appropriate ways (Ng et al., 2022a; Vincent-Lancrin, S. & van der Vlies, 2020).

Since 2016, some universities such as Beijing Union University have implemented intelligent speech recognition systems that convert instructors' spoken words into real-time subtitles displayed on large screens. This multimodal approach—which combines sign language, audio, captions, and printed materials—allows students with diverse needs to access information through multiple sensory channels. Although such tools are most visible in secondary or higher education, similar adaptive technologies are now being piloted in early childhood classrooms, where AI-integrated smart boards, interactive storytelling applications, and speech-enhancing games help scaffold language development for children with speech or language delays (Ng et al., 2022b; Vincent-Lancrin, S. & van der Vlies, 2020).

Moreover, diagnostic tools powered by AI are increasingly being employed to identify learning difficulties such as dyslexia, dyscalculia, and ADHD (Drigas & Ioannidou, 2013). These technologies analyze behavioral patterns and performance indicators to provide early and accurate identification, enabling timely intervention. While most prominently used in school-aged populations, their integration into preschool settings holds promise for early detection and support during the critical years of development, aligning with the broader goal of fostering truly inclusive education systems from the earliest stages of learning (Ng et al., 2022b).

2.1.3. Some Other Applications

AI leverages pattern recognition to deliver tailored advice and support for students, teachers, and families:

- **In online and hybrid learning environments, AI chatbots simulate human tutors:** providing 24/7 access to homework help, personalized guidance, and real-time performance insights. A systematic review finds that learners gain from AI chatbots through enhanced study support, individualized pacing, and skill development, while educators benefit from pedagogical efficiencies and reduced workload (Labadze et al., 2023). These tools are especially useful for reserved learners, who may not pose questions in class but engage more freely through chat interfaces.
- **In classroom observation, sensor-based systems and AI-guided cameras track engagement, attention, and group dynamics:** offering teachers data-driven, real-time or retrospective insights. For example, recent research deploying multimodal sensor setups in preschool settings has generated meaningful data on peer collaboration and attention patterns, helping educators refine instructional strategies (Cha & Park, 2025).
- **In language acquisition, AI-powered speech analysis tools help educators correct pronunciation and fluency, supplementing human instruction:** Early childhood environments benefit from voice-enabled AI toys that offer corrective feedback when children practice vocabulary, fostering both language and oral-motor development (Vincent-Lancrin, S. & van der Vlies, 2020).
- **AI chatbots function as virtual tutors, answering questions anytime and alleviating reliance on teacher availability:** They are particularly beneficial for shy students, allowing them to ask without fear of judgment and gradually build confidence before engaging in class. AI also unlocks creative potential across subjects—supporting tasks from research (e.g., platforms like Perplexity and Scite help students explore topics and verify sources) to creative production. For instance, children hesitant to engage in art or music can use AI-generated images, music, or storytelling prompts to express their ideas and build confidence (British Council, n.d.).
- **AI can shoulder repetitive administrative and planning tasks, freeing educators to focus on teaching:** Suggesting lesson activities and unit plans; Refining instructional language and clarity; Generating model texts or feedback comments; Analyzing learner data to identify trends or common misconceptions. By automating these supports, AI enhances pedagogical efficiency while enabling educators to design richer learning experiences tailored to children's needs (British Council, n.d.).

In summary, AI's expanding capabilities—from personalized tutoring and creative expression to teacher support and emotional development—are enhancing educational quality across all age groups. In early childhood contexts especially, AI offers innovative pathways to nurture foundational academic, social, and emotional skills in developmentally appropriate and inclusive ways. However, the design and deployment of these tools must remain informed by rigorous academic research, ensuring they complement—rather than replace—the essential human elements of early learning.

2.2. Artificial Intelligence Applications for System and School Management

Artificial intelligence's computational capabilities are increasingly being harnessed to develop predictive and diagnostic systems that assist decision-making and offer timely feedback across various educational levels, from individual institutions (e.g., schools, universities) to broader systemic structures (e.g., districts, regions, or national systems). AI is playing a pivotal role in enhancing the completion rates of high-quality primary and secondary education, as well as in modernizing standardized assessment tools. These advancements enable a more comprehensive evaluation of diverse skill sets and foster greater alignment between assessment practices and the competencies required in an increasingly digital World (Ng et al., 2023; Vincent-Lancrin, S. & van der Vlies, 2020).

2.2.1. Reducing Dropout with the Help of Artificial Intelligence

School dropout remains a pressing concern for education policy worldwide, though the specific age groups affected often vary depending on a country's socio-economic status. For instance, in 2015, 60% of youth of upper-secondary school age in low-income nations were not attending school. By 2018, the global completion rates for primary, lower secondary, and upper secondary education were 68%, 44%, and 21% respectively—figures that fall significantly short of the target for universal completion by 2030. Policymakers and educators continue to search for effective indicators and strategies to identify and address dropout risks. AI technologies offer promising solutions to strengthen early warning systems by leveraging emerging longitudinal datasets in the education sector. While detecting at-risk students does not automatically resolve their challenges, AI-driven tools equip school leaders with novel ways to interpret existing data and craft more effective preventative measures (Vincent-Lancrin, S. & van der Vlies, 2020).

In countries like the United States, AI-based early warning systems have gained substantial traction, with various providers delivering platforms that support real-time dropout prevention efforts for schools and district administrators. One of the notable benefits of these systems is their capacity to provide timely feedback that allows for proactive intervention. Typically, these tools are deployed as interactive dashboards that help visualize students at risk of leaving school and offer tailored recommendations for support (Vincent-Lancrin, S. & van der Vlies, 2020).

Similarly, in lower-income contexts such as India, dropout rates also remain problematic. Pilot programs employing early warning systems and targeted interventions—some incorporating technological elements—have been developed and tested. While the nature of the underlying data may differ from that used in more affluent settings, the essential goal remains consistent: utilizing AI to identify and address dropout risks effectively (Vincent-Lancrin, S. & van der Vlies, 2020).

Despite their potential, early warning systems are still in a developmental phase and not yet fully mature. Ongoing research seeks to refine the indicators most predictive of dropout and to evaluate which intervention methods yield the most favorable outcomes. These tools highlight both the promise and the current limitations of AI in education: their shortcomings often stem not from harmful design but from missed opportunities to assist students who might have otherwise benefited from timely support (Vincent-Lancrin, S. & van der Vlies, 2020).

2.2.2. Assessing New Skills Sets Thanks to Artificial Intelligence

Standardized testing remains a prominent element in many educational systems, often shaping pedagogical strategies and contributing to considerable stress among students. However, there is growing consensus among policymakers and employers that assessment frameworks should extend beyond content knowledge and logical reasoning to capture more nuanced, 21st-century competencies such as critical thinking, collaborative problem-solving, and socio-emotional skills—competencies emphasized in the G20 AI Principles as fundamental to the evolving landscape of work and civic life (Vincent-Lancrin, S. & van der Vlies, 2020).

Artificial intelligence has begun to open new possibilities for assessing such complex skills. One notable development is the emergence of embedded assessment mechanisms, which enable real-time, ongoing evaluation of learner performance within digital learning environments. These AI-powered systems are capable of determining mastery of subject matter and simultaneously offering tailored, formative feedback grounded in continuous learner data. By tracking students' progression over time, such systems can adjust content delivery and feedback in a manner aligned with individual needs (Vincent-Lancrin, S. & van der Vlies, 2020).

Furthermore, AI-enhanced assessments aim not only to measure outcomes but also to capture the processes by which learners engage with tasks. Technologies such as natural language processing and speech recognition, in combination with behavioral analytics, allow for the examination of cognitive strategies and learning behaviors as students interact with educational content. This form of process-oriented assessment provides deeper insight into how students approach, adapt to, and internalize new information (Vincent-Lancrin, S. & van der Vlies, 2020).

In addition, game-based assessments and simulations present innovative avenues for evaluating higher-order skills in immersive and interactive contexts. These tools integrate assessment components into gamified environments, thereby encouraging learners to demonstrate their competencies in ways that are both engaging and authentic. Game-based assessments, often utilizing augmented or virtual reality in tandem with AI's adaptive functions, have proven effective in formative assessment contexts and are increasingly being used for summative purposes as well. Within STEM fields, such as medicine and engineering, simulations have become an established mode of evaluation—for example, through virtual surgical procedure assessments in medical education (Ng et al., 2021c; Vincent-Lancrin, S. & van der Vlies, 2020).

Importantly, the integration of these advanced assessment models is not without its challenges. The implementation of AI-driven evaluations in high-stakes settings continues to generate skepticism and technical concerns. The notion that assessments may vary across individuals yet still maintain reliability and fairness poses a fundamental challenge to widely held conceptions of equity. This underscores the dual nature of AI's impact—not only technological but also sociocultural and ethical (Ng et al., 2022b; Vincent-Lancrin, S. & van der Vlies, 2020).

In early childhood education, the application of AI in assessment is still emerging but shows significant promise. Rather than relying on formal testing methods, AI is being explored as a tool for observational assessment in preschool settings. For example, machine learning systems can analyze children's verbal expressions, gestures, and peer interactions during play to infer developmental competencies in communication, emotional regulation, or problem-solving. These systems support educators in identifying individual learning needs at a very early stage without interrupting the natural learning environment. Moreover, interactive educational games designed for preschoolers increasingly include built-in AI algorithms that adjust difficulty levels and track fine motor skills, attention span, and learning preferences—all of which provide valuable, developmentally appropriate insights that traditional assessments may overlook (Ng et al., 2022; Su & Yang, 2022).

Through such innovations, AI offers the potential to transform assessment practices across age groups, promoting more equitable and personalized learning experiences from early childhood through to tertiary education.

3. CHALLENGES OF ARTIFICIAL INTELLIGENCE LITERACY IN EARLY CHILDHOOD EDUCATION

The integration of artificial intelligence into educational settings presents a series of emerging challenges for both educators and policy makers. Central among these is the need to foster and uphold trust in AI technologies. In alignment with the core principles outlined by the G20 on responsible AI use, it is essential that AI systems in education be transparent, interpretable, and accountable—particularly given education's significant influence on learners' future career prospects and life trajectories (Vincent-Lancrin, S. & van der Vlies, 2020).

Another major concern revolves around safeguarding human-centered values through the responsible management of personal data. Ensuring that AI applications prioritize privacy and data protection is vital, as educational environments often handle sensitive information. This demands robust mechanisms to secure learners' personal data and prevent misuse, reinforcing ethical obligations toward student well-being and dignity (Vincent-Lancrin, S. & van der Vlies, 2020).

A third critical issue is the potential for excessive reliance on technology. As AI tools become increasingly embedded in instructional practices, there is a growing risk that human interaction within classrooms may diminish. Over-dependence on AI could inadvertently reduce meaningful face-to-face engagement between educators and learners, potentially undermining the relational and social aspects of learning that are especially crucial in early education. This overreliance not only shifts the pedagogical balance but may also hinder the development of communication, empathy, and interpersonal skills in young children (British Council, n.d.).

3.1. Trust in Artificial Intelligence

Realizing the full benefits of artificial intelligence in education hinges on the cultivation of trust among policymakers, educators, and other relevant stakeholders, as underscored by the G20 AI Principles. This trust is especially critical in educational contexts, where AI technologies may influence high-stakes decisions—such as school admissions or the allocation of academic and financial support—decisions that can significantly shape students' futures (Dyrbye et al., 2009; Vincent-Lancrin, S. & van der Vlies, 2020).

Trust in AI within education is multidimensional. It involves not only confidence in the system's ability to function as intended, but also in the responsible and equitable use of its outputs by human actors. For instance, AI-based early warning systems that identify students at risk of dropping out must not only demonstrate reliable accuracy but also be used with integrity. If such systems fail to identify the right students, or if their predictions are used to exclude rather than support vulnerable learners, the trustworthiness of the system is compromised. The risk lies not solely in the technology itself but also in the broader human-AI interaction. Effective interventions following AI identification must aim to reduce inequity and promote educational justice, not reinforce exclusionary practices—especially in systems where school performance metrics may incentivize the removal of underperforming students (Lin et al., 2020; Vincent-Lancrin, S. & van der Vlies, 2020).

In some instances—though still uncommon—AI applications are beginning to make or heavily influence automated decisions, such as school or university admissions. While these systems may correct certain biases present in traditional methods and enhance objectivity, they also introduce new risks. Without transparency about the algorithms used and clarity regarding their decision-making processes, such systems can inadvertently undermine fairness. For example, deep learning models may lack explainability due to their inherent complexity, making it difficult for educators, parents, or students to understand how decisions are made. In response, some governments, like France, have limited the use of opaque algorithmic models in public education due to concerns about public accountability. Strategies to build trust vary across regions: China emphasizes mutual trust and social harmony, while the EU promotes transparency and traceability, encouraging that users be informed when they interact with AI systems and fully understand their capabilities and limitations. The United States likewise supports the development of AI that is robust, safe, and trustworthy through continued research efforts (Ng et al., 2023; Vincent-Lancrin, S. & van der Vlies, 2020).

These concerns are particularly salient when AI systems are used with younger learners, including those in early childhood education. At this developmental stage, children are more vulnerable to potential harms, and less able to comprehend the implications of AI-mediated decisions. For example, facial recognition technologies or behavior-predictive tools used in preschool settings to monitor attention, or social interactions may be useful in supporting developmental progress. However, without careful oversight and ethical use, such technologies can pose significant privacy and fairness concerns. Therefore, it is critical that AI applications in early childhood settings are not only technically sound but are also implemented with transparency, sensitivity, and a commitment to protecting children's rights and well-being (Laato et al., 2020 as cited in Su et al., 2023))

3.2. Dealing with Privacy and Security Related to Artificial Intelligence

The integration of artificial intelligence into education presents numerous benefits, including enhanced learning outcomes and preparation for a technology-driven society. However, it also brings forth critical challenges related to data privacy and digital security—issues that are especially pressing given that educational data often involve minors. Two primary concerns emerge in this context: the risk of inappropriate access to and use of students' personal information, and the potential for algorithmic bias stemming from flawed or unrepresentative data inputs (Vincent-Lancrin, S. & van der Vlies, 2020; Yang, 2022).

AI systems in education frequently rely on extensive data collection to tailor learning experiences and predict student needs. Yet, the accumulation and storage of such data raise important ethical and legal questions. Families worry that archived student information might be used in future decisions by schools or even employers, thus highlighting the need to determine what data should be retained, for how long, and under what conditions they can be accessed. Another concern involves the commercialization of educational data—where learners' personal information might be repurposed for profit in an environment that is traditionally safeguarded from commercial influence (Vincent-Lancrin, S. & van der Vlies, 2020).

These issues tie into broader debates about the human-centered nature of trustworthy AI. As algorithmic technologies become more embedded in educational settings, it becomes essential to preserve fundamental rights such as the ability to maintain privacy, avoid continuous surveillance, and ensure that one's future is not unjustly shaped by outdated or irrelevant personal records. Questions around consent, autonomy, and the ethical use of AI tools become particularly salient when those tools are applied to vulnerable populations, such as children (Vincent-Lancrin, S. & van der Vlies, 2020).

Various nations have introduced regulatory measures to address these challenges. The European Union's General Data Protection Regulation (GDPR) enforces strict guidelines concerning the handling of personal data, emphasizing transparency, data minimization, and accountability. In the United States, the Family Educational Rights and Privacy Act (FERPA) provides a legal framework specifically tailored to protect students' educational records. Similarly, China's Governance Principles for Responsible AI stress the importance of respecting individual privacy, ensuring informed consent, and enhancing the transparency and reliability of AI systems (Vincent-Lancrin, S. & van der Vlies, 2020).

These privacy considerations are particularly crucial in early childhood education, where young children often lack the cognitive maturity to comprehend or consent to data practices. AI applications used in preschool contexts—such as tools that track play behavior or assess socio-emotional development—must be carefully monitored to ensure they do not compromise children's rights or well-being. For example, multi-object tracking systems that analyze toddlers' social interactions may offer developmental insights but also carry significant risks if the data are mishandled or used beyond their intended purpose. Thus, safeguarding data privacy and ensuring ethical usage are foundational to deploying AI responsibly across all educational levels, especially in early learning environments (Laato et al., 2020 as cited in Su et al., 2023))

3.3. Overreliance and Dependency

As artificial intelligence becomes more deeply embedded in educational settings, a significant concern is the potential for overreliance on these tools, especially in ways that may unintentionally erode human interaction in the classroom. While AI offers valuable support in areas such as personalized learning, real-time feedback, and administrative assistance, excessive dependence on these technologies can compromise essential relational and developmental aspects of learning—particularly for younger children (British Council, n.d.).

In early childhood education, meaningful interactions with teachers and peers form the foundation for cognitive, emotional, and social development. Face-to-face communication fosters skills such as empathy, cooperation, and language acquisition—skills that cannot be fully nurtured through interaction with AI systems alone. When AI begins to dominate instructional delivery or problem-solving processes, children may become passive recipients of information, losing opportunities to engage in rich, human-centered learning experiences. For example, if a preschooler frequently interacts with a voice-activated tutor rather than a caregiver or peer, their capacity to navigate social cues, express emotions, or negotiate in collaborative tasks may be diminished (Su & Yang, 2022).

Moreover, for learners of all ages, heavy reliance on AI for completing tasks—such as using chatbots to generate answers or write assignments—may reduce the depth of understanding. Rather than engaging in reflective thinking, students might begin to outsource cognitive labor to AI systems, resulting in surface-level knowledge that hinders long-term academic growth. As noted in recent studies (Labadze et al., 2023), students who routinely depend on AI for answers often struggle to build on foundational concepts in more complex learning scenarios. This challenge is particularly concerning in early education, where foundational skills in reasoning, imagination, and metacognition are still forming.

However, eliminating AI from classrooms is not the solution. Instead, educators must be intentional about how they integrate these tools. Framing AI as a scaffold—rather than a replacement—for human cognition is essential. For instance, children can be encouraged to use AI tools to brainstorm ideas or explore creative representations (e.g., through image generation or speech tools), but the interpretation, extension, and presentation of those ideas should remain learner driven. Teachers play a critical role in guiding students to question, reflect, and critique the outputs produced by AI, fostering both digital literacy and independent thinking (British Council, n.d.).

In sum, while AI can enhance educational efficiency and access, it is crucial to maintain a balance between technological facilitation and human connection. Particularly in early childhood settings, where developmental outcomes are closely tied to social interaction, AI integration must be approached with caution. Educators and policymakers should promote strategies that encourage AI-supported learning without compromising interpersonal development, critical thinking, or the emotional richness of the classroom environment.

4. METHODS

This chapter adopts a scoping review approach to synthesize recent research and policy discussions on artificial intelligence (AI) literacy in early childhood education (ECE). To identify relevant studies, we searched four academic databases—ERIC, PsycINFO, Scopus, and Web of Science—using the keywords "artificial intelligence literacy," "AI literacy," "AI education," and "early childhood" OR "preschool." Studies were included if they (a) examined AI-related learning experiences for children aged 3–8, (b) discussed teacher preparation or curriculum models in ECE, or (c) addressed ethical or pedagogical implications of AI use in early learning contexts. Reports focusing exclusively on secondary or higher education were excluded unless they provided transferable insights for early childhood education.

In addition to peer-reviewed journal articles, policy reports and frameworks (e.g., UNICEF, OECD, AI4K12, ReadyAI) were reviewed to situate the findings within global educational and ethical perspectives. This process aimed to ensure comprehensive coverage and provide a coherent synthesis of the state of AI literacy in early learning environments.

5. CONCLUSION

The integration of artificial intelligence into early childhood education presents both transformative opportunities and significant challenges. As explored throughout this chapter, AI technologies can support inclusive learning environments, facilitate the development of foundational AI literacy, personalize instruction, enhance assessment practices, and offer targeted interventions to prevent dropout—when applied ethically and effectively. In the context of ECE, tools such as AI-enabled robots, adaptive platforms, and game-based assessments have already demonstrated promise in fostering engagement, scaffolding socio-emotional skills, and supporting young learners with diverse needs. However, these innovations also require educators and policymakers to critically reflect on issues of data privacy, algorithmic bias, transparency, and the risk of overdependence on AI that may compromise human-centered pedagogical relationships.

Realizing the full potential of AI in early education demands a cautious, inclusive, and evidence-based approach. Teachers must be equipped with the competencies to use AI not as a replacement, but as a facilitator of developmentally appropriate, interactive, and meaningful learning experiences. Similarly, the design and deployment of AI systems should remain transparent, explainable, and anchored in human values—especially when engaging with young children. Trust in AI must extend beyond its technical performance to include its ethical use, cultural relevance, and capacity to support equity and justice in early education. Moving forward, collaborative efforts among educators, researchers, developers, and families will be essential to ensure that AI not only augments early learning but also safeguards the developmental integrity of childhood in an increasingly digital world.

6. RECOMMENDATIONS

To ensure the effective and ethical integration of artificial intelligence in early childhood education (ECE), a series of strategic recommendations can guide stakeholders in educational practice, research, and policy development. These recommendations aim to enhance instructional quality, support teacher preparedness, and foster developmentally appropriate AI literacy among young learners.

- **Enhancing Educator Preparedness through Continuous Professional Learning:** Early childhood educators should be provided with opportunities to deepen their understanding of AI through sustained and flexible professional development. Online platforms, open-access digital modules, and micro-credentialing systems may serve as accessible means for educators to engage with contemporary developments in AI at their own pace. This approach ensures that teachers are equipped to integrate AI tools meaningfully into pedagogical practices without imposing rigid time constraints.
- **Developing Holistic and Adaptive AI-Integrated Teaching Frameworks:** Instructional design involving AI should be constructed through an integrated lens that considers learner-centeredness, teacher-student interaction, AI competency development, and the pedagogical impact of AI tools. These elements should be interwoven into cohesive instructional models that are sensitive to the developmental needs of young children and that support human interaction rather than replacing it.
- **Creating Developmentally Appropriate AI-Enriched Content and Experiences:** AI-based learning activities should be tailored specifically

to the early childhood context. Engaging, age-appropriate resources such as playful learning applications, interactive storybooks, and intelligent toys can help familiarize children with basic AI concepts through experiential learning. These resources should promote curiosity, creativity, and problem-solving, while avoiding cognitive overload or passive consumption.

- **Leveraging the TPACK Framework to Guide AI Integration in Teacher Practice:** The Technological Pedagogical Content Knowledge (TPACK) model can provide a robust conceptual foundation for supporting educators in balancing their subject expertise, pedagogical strategies, and AI-based tools. By aligning AI integration with existing curricular goals and classroom dynamics, TPACK-informed approaches can ensure that technology enhances, rather than disrupts, the learning experience.
- **Contextualizing AI Use to Support Localized Educational Goals and Practice:** Rather than applying generalized AI models, AI systems should be adapted to align with local cultural, linguistic, and curricular contexts. This includes the use of AI to assist educators in curriculum planning, classroom management, and the provision of personalized, formative feedback. Local adaptation enhances relevance and acceptance, particularly in under-resourced or diverse educational environments.
- **Encouraging Empirical Evaluation of AI-Interactive Tools in ECE Settings:** There is a pressing need for further empirical research evaluating the cognitive, social, and emotional effects of AI-embedded tools in early learning environments. Future studies should explore the efficacy of AI-powered robots, educational games, and adaptive learning applications in supporting skill development among preschool-aged children. Longitudinal and mixed-method designs may provide nuanced insights into how these tools influence learning trajectories over time.

By implementing these recommendations, educational stakeholders can promote a balanced, inclusive, and evidence-informed adoption of AI in early childhood education—ensuring that technological advancements support, rather than replace, the relational and developmental foundations of early learning.

REFERENCES

British Council. (n.d.). *AI in education: How to navigate the opportunities and challenges*. https://internationalschools.britishcouncil.org/blog/ai-in-education-how-to-navigate-the-opportunities-and-challenges

Buolamwini, J., & Gebru, T. (2018, January). Gender shades: Intersectional accuracy disparities in commercial gender classification. In *Conference on fairness, accountability and transparency* (pp. 77–91). PMLR.

Burgsteiner, H., Kandlhofer, M., & Steinbauer, G. (2016). Irobot: Teaching the basics of artificial intelligence in high schools. *Proceedings of the AAAI Conference on Artificial Intelligence, 30*(1), 4126–4127. DOI: 10.1609/aaai.v30i1.9864

Cha, K., & Park, J. (2025). Automated analysis of preschoolers' play and social behaviors using multi-object tracking technology: An exploratory approach. *Educación XX1, 28*(2). https://doi.org/DOI: 10.5944/vol28n2a206

Drigas, A., & Ioannidou, R. (2013). A review on artificial intelligence in special education. In *Information Systems, E-learning, and Knowledge Management Research, Communications in Computer and Information Science*. Springer., DOI: 10.1007/978-3-642-35879-1_46

Druga, S., & Ko, A. J. (2021). How do children's perceptions of machine intelligence change when training and coding smart programs? In *Interaction design and children* (pp. 49–61). DOI: 10.1145/3459990.3460712

Druga, S., Vu, S., Likhith, E., Oh, L., Qui, T., & Breazeal, C. (2018). *Cognimates*. http://cognimates.me/home

Druga, S., Vu, S., Likhith, E., & Qiu, T. (2019). Inclusive AI literacy for kids around. the world. *Proceedings of the FabLearn,* 104–111. DOI: 10.1145/3311890.3311904

Eguchi, A., Okada, H., & Muto, Y. (2021). Contextualizing AI education for K-12 students to enhance their learning of AI literacy through culturally responsive approaches. *KI- Künstliche Intelligenz,* 35(2), 153–161.

Gaube, S., Suresh, H., Raue, M., Merritt, A., Berkowitz, S. J., Lermer, E., Couhlin, J., Guttang, J., Colak, E., & Ghassemi, M. (2021). Do as AI say: Susceptibility in deployment of clinical decision-aids. *NPJ Digital Medicine, 4*(1), 1–8. DOI: 10.1038/s41746-021-00385-9 PMID: 33608629

Ge, D., Wang, X., & Liu, J. (2021). A teaching quality evaluation model for preschool teachers based on deep learning. *International Journal of Emerging Technologies in Learning, 16*(3), 127–143. DOI: 10.3991/ijet.v16i03.20471

Hasib, K. M., Rahman, F., Hasnat, R., & Alam, M. G. R. (2022, January). A machine learning and explainable AI approach for predicting secondary school student performance. In 2022 *IEEE 12th Annual computing and communication workshop and conference* (CCWC) (pp. 399–405). IEEE. DOI: 10.1109/CCWC54503.2022.9720806

Jin, L. (2019). Investigation on potential application of artificial intelligence in preschool children's education. In *The 5th annual international conference on network and information systems for computers* (ICNISC2019). DOI: 10.1088/1742-6596/1288/1/012072

Kafai, Y. B., & Burke, Q. (2014). *Connected code: Why children need to learn programming*. Mit Press. DOI: 10.7551/mitpress/9992.001.0001

Kandlhofer, M., Steinbauer, G., Hirschmugl-Gaisch, S., & Huber, P. (2016). Artificial intelligence and computer science in education: From kindergarten to university. In *2016 IEEE frontiers in education conference* (FIE) (pp. 1–9). IEEE.

Kewalramani, S., Kidman, G., & Palaiologou, I. (2021). Using artificial intelligence (AI)- interfaced robotic toys in early childhood settings: A case for children's inquiry literacy. *European Early Childhood Education Research Journal, 29*(5), 652–668. DOI: 10.1080/1350293X.2021.1968458

Kim, S., Jang, Y., Kim, W., Choi, S., Jung, H., Kim, S., & Kim, H. (2021, May). Why and what to teach: AI curriculum for elementary school. *Proceedings of the AAAI Conference on Artificial Intelligence, 35*(17), 15569–15576. DOI: 10.1609/aaai.v35i17.17833

Knapp, S. (2006). *Artificial intelligence: Past, present, and future.* VOX of Dartmouth.

Kong, S. C., Cheung, W. M. Y., & Zhang, G. (2021). Evaluation of an artificial intelligencE literacy course for university students with diverse study backgrounds. *Computers & Education. Artificial Intelligence, 2*, 100026.

Kong, S. C., Cheung, W. M. Y., & Zhang, G. (2022). Evaluating artificial intelligence literacy courses for fostering conceptual learning, literacy and empowerment in university students: Refocusing to conceptual building. *Computers in Human Behavior Reports, 7*, 100223. DOI: 10.1016/j.chbr.2022.100223

Kong, S. C., Cheung, W. M. Y., & Zhang, G. (2023). Evaluating an artificial intelligence literacy programme for developing university students' conceptual understanding, literacy, empowerment and ethical awareness. *Journal of Educational Technology & Society*, *26*(1), 16–30.

Labadze, L., Grigolia, M., & Machaidze, L. (2023). Role of AI chatbots in education: Systematic literature review. *International Journal of Educational Technology in Higher Education*, *20*(1), 56. DOI: 10.1186/s41239-023-00426-1

Lin, P., Van Brummelen, J., Lukin, G., Williams, R., & Breazeal, C. (2020). Zhorai: Designing a conversational agent for children to explore machine learning concepts. *Proceedings of the AAAI Conference on Artificial Intelligence*, *34*(9), 13381–13388. DOI: 10.1609/aaai.v34i09.7061

Lin, Y., & Weintrop, D. (2021). The landscape of Block-based programming: Characteristics of block-based environments and how they support the transition to text-based programming. *Journal of Computer Languages,* 67, Article 101075.

Long, D., & Magerko, B. (2020). What is AI literacy? Competencies and design considerations. In *Proceedings of the 2020 CHI conference on human factors in computing systems* (pp. 1–16). DOI: 10.1145/3313831.3376727

Manzini, T., Lim, Y. C., Tsvetkov, Y., & Black, A. W. (2019). Black is to criminal as caucasian is to police: Detecting and removing multiclass bias in word embeddings. *arXiv Preprint arXiv:1904.04047.* DOI: 10.18653/v1/N19-1062

Nan, J. (2020). Research of application of artificial intelligence in. Preschool education. In *The 2020 international symposium on electronic information technology and communication engineering*. Jinan, China.

Ng, D. T., Leung, J. K., Su, J., Ng, R. C., & Chu, S. K. (2023). Teachers' AI digital competencies and twenty- first-century skills in the post-pandemic world. *Educational Technology Research and Development*, *71*(1), 137–161. DOI: 10.1007/s11423-023-10203-6 PMID: 36844361

Ng, D. T. K., Lee, M., Tan, R. J. Y., Hu, X., Downie, J. S., & Chu, S. K. W. (2022c). A review of AI teaching and learning from 2000 to 2020. *Education and Information Technologies*, *28*(7), 8445–8501. DOI: 10.1007/s10639-022-11491-w

Ng, D. T. K., Leung, J. K. L., Chu, K. W. S., & Qiao, M. S. (2021a). AI literacy: Definition, teaching, evaluation and ethical issues. *Proceedings of the Association for Information Science and Technology*, *58*(1), 504–509. DOI: 10.1002/pra2.487

Ng, D. T. K., Leung, J. K. L., Chu, S. K. W., & Qiao, M. S. (2021b). Conceptualizing AI literacy: An exploratory review. *Computers & Education. Artificial Intelligence, 2*, 100041.

Ng, D. T. K., Leung, J. K. L., Su, M. J., Yim, I. H. Y., Qiao, M. S., & Chu, S. K. W. (2022b). AI Literacy Education in Early Childhood Education. In *AI Literacy in K-16 Classrooms* (pp. 63–74). Springer International Publishing. DOI: 10.1007/978-3-031-18880-0_5

Ng, D. T. K., Luo, W., Chan, H. M. Y., & Chu, S. K. W. (2022a). Using digital story writing as a pedagogy to develop AI literacy among primary students. *Computers and Education. Artificial Intelligence, 3*, 100054. DOI: 10.1016/j.caeai.2022.100054

Preface. (2021). *The ultimate guide for artificial intelligence (AI) for kids.* https://www.preface.ai/blog/kids-learning/ai-for-kids

Prentzas, J. (2013). Artificial intelligence methods in early childhood education. In *Artificial Intelligence, evolutionary computing and metaheuristics* (pp. 169–199). Springer. DOI: 10.1007/978-3-642-29694-9_8

Russell, S., & Norvig, P. (2002). *Artificial intelligence: A modern approach.* https://storage.googleapis.com/pub-tools-public-publication-data/pdf/27702.pdf

Solanki, S. L., Pandrowala, S., Nayak, A., Bhandare, M., Ambulkar, R. P., & Shrikhande, S. V. (2021). Artificial intelligence in perioperative management of major gastrointestinal surgeries. *World Journal of Gastroenterology, 27*(21), 2758–2770. DOI: 10.3748/wjg.v27.i21.2758 PMID: 34135552

Steinbauer, G., Kandlhofer, M., Chklovski, T., Heintz, F., & Koenig, S. (2021). A differentiated discussion about AI education K-12. *Kunstliche Intelligenz, 35*(2), 131–137. DOI: 10.1007/s13218-021-00724-8 PMID: 34007103

Su, J., Ng, D. T. K., & Chu, S. K. W. (2023). Artificial intelligence (AI) literacy in Early Childhood education: The challenges and opportunities. *Computers and Education. Artificial Intelligence, 4*, 100124. DOI: 10.1016/j.caeai.2023.100124

Su, J., & Yang, W. (2022). Artificial intelligence in early childhood education: A scoping review. *Computers and Education: Artificial Intelligence, 3*, 100049. DOI: 10.1016/j.caeai.2022.100049

Su, J., Yu, C., & Ng, D. T. K. (2022). A meta-review of literature on educational approaches for teaching AI at the K-12 levels in the Asia-Pacific region. *Computers and Education: Artificial Intelligence,* Article 100065.

Touretzky, D., Gardner-McCune, C., Martin, F., & Seehorn, D. (2019). Envisioning AI for K-12: What should every child know about AI? *Proceedings of the AAAI Conference on Artificial Intelligence, 33*(1), 9795–9799. DOI: 10.1609/aaai.v33i01.33019795

Touretzky, D. S. (2017). *Computational thinking and mental models: From Kodu to Calypso. In 2017 IEEE blocks and beyond workshop (B&B).* IEEE.

UNICEF. (2022). *AI for children.* https://www.unicef.org/globalinsight/featured-projects/ai-children

Vartiainen, H., Tedre, M., & Valtonen, T. (2020). Learning machine learning with very young children: Who is teaching whom? *International Journal of Child-Computer Interaction, 25*, 100182. DOI: 10.1016/j.ijcci.2020.100182

Vincent-Lancrin, S., J. Urgel, S. Kar, and G. Jacotin (2019), *Measuring Innovation in Education 2019: What Has Changed in the Classroom?* Educational Research and Innovation, OECD Publishing. DOI: 10.1787/9789264311671-en

Vincent-Lancrin, S., & van der Vlies, R. (2020). *Trustworthy artificial intelligence (AI) in education: Promises and challenges.* OECD Publishing., DOI: 10.1787/a6c90fa9-

Weintrop, D., Beheshti, E., Horn, M., Orton, K., Jona, K., Trouille, L., & Wilensky, U. (2016). Defining computational thinking for mathematics and science classrooms. *Journal of Science Education and Technology, 25*(1), 127–147. DOI: 10.1007/s10956-015-9581-5

Weintrop, D., & Wilensky, U. (2015). To block or not to block, that is the question: Students' perceptions of blocks-based programming. In *Proceedings of the 14th international conference on interaction design and children* (pp. 199–208). DOI: 10.1145/2771839.2771860

Williams, R. (2018). *PopBots: Leveraging social robots to aid preschool children's artificial intelligence education* (Doctoral dissertation, Massachusetts Institute of Technology). Massachusetts Institute of Technology.

Williams, R., Park, H. W., & Breazeal, C. (2019b). A is for artificial intelligence: The impact of artificial intelligence activities on young children's perceptions of robots. In *Proceedings of the 2019 CHI conference on human factors in computing systems* (pp. 1–11). DOI: 10.1145/3290605.3300677

Williams, R., Park, H. W., Oh, L., & Breazeal, C. (2019a). Popbots: Designing an artificial intelligence curriculum for early childhood education. In *Proceedings of the AAAI Conference on Artificial Intelligence,* 33 pp. 9729–9736), 1. DOI: 10.1609/aaai.v33i01.33019729

Wing, J. M. (2006). Computational thinking. *Communications of the ACM*, *49*(3), 33–35. DOI: 10.1145/1118178.1118215

Wong, G. K., Ma, X., Dillenbourg, P., & Huan, J. (2020). Broadening artificial intelligence education in K-12: Where to start? *ACM Inroads*, *11*(1), 20–29. DOI: 10.1145/3381884

Yang, W. (2022). Artificial Intelligence education for young children: Why, what, and how in curriculum design and implementation. *Computers & Education. Artificial Intelligence*, •••, 100061.

KEY TERMS AND DEFINITIONS

AI Literacy: The ability to understand, critically evaluate, and responsibly use AI technologies. In early childhood settings, this also includes fostering foundational concepts through playful and age-appropriate interactions.

Artificial Intelligence (AI): A branch of computer science focused on developing machines and systems capable of performing tasks that typically require human intelligence, such as learning, reasoning, and problem-solving. In education, AI supports personalized learning and automates instructional decisions.

Data Privacy in Education: The protection of learners' personal and sensitive data collected through digital educational platforms, ensuring ethical data use, secure storage, and informed consent—particularly crucial for minors in ECE.

Early Childhood Education (ECE): An educational framework encompassing the care and instruction of children from birth to age eight, emphasizing holistic development—including cognitive, social, emotional, and physical growth—within age-appropriate contexts.

Educational Innovation: The introduction of new methods, tools, or approaches—often driven by technology—that aim to improve educational outcomes and adapt to the changing needs of society.

Inclusive Education: An approach that ensures equitable access to quality learning experiences for all children, including those with diverse abilities or vulnerabilities. AI tools can enhance inclusivity through assistive technologies and differentiated instruction.

Personalized Learning: A pedagogical approach where content, pace, and learning strategies are tailored to meet the unique needs, strengths, and interests of individual learners, often facilitated by adaptive AI technologies.

Trustworthy AI: A set of principles and practices aimed at ensuring that AI systems are reliable, transparent, and aligned with human values. In educational settings, this involves accountability in decision-making and the protection of students' rights.

Chapter 5

Using Generative AI at the University: Do ChatGPT and Other AI Tools Promote Computational Thinking?

Avraam Chatzopoulos
https://orcid.org/0000-0002-2569-4147
University of West Attica, Greece

ABSTRACT

Every day, more and more people use Artificial Intelligence (AI) for everyday tasks related to work and entertainment. But what about the use of AI in education? This paper aims to investigate whether university students (and future engineers) use Generative AI tools for their academic obligations and to determine whether these tools can contribute positively to the development of their Computational Thinking skills. For this reason, a case study based on a STEM educational approach in a Mechatronics course is presented. It was investigated to what extent the students who attended the course used and utilized AI tools such as ChatGPT, DeepSeek, Gemini, Copilot, etc., for the completion of their STEM projects. The results showed that a vast majority of students responsibly use the AI tools in their everyday academic tasks, but these do not substantially affect their Computational Thinking skills. While the existing literature abundantly confirms the above, further research needs to be done in the future in the direction of the correlation of the tools with Computational Thinking.

DOI: 10.4018/979-8-3373-9074-1.ch005

1. INTRODUCTION

The use of the Generative Artificial Intelligence (AI) in an ever-wider range of tasks by an ever-wider range of people, including university students, is a common secret (Freeman, 2025; HEPI, 2025). It has a tremendous potential for both teachers (Carnegie Learning, 2024) and students (CoSN, 2025; HEPI, 2025), as its use follows an exponential trend is transforming education (Stone, 2024), raising new ethical, legal, and pedagogical questions (Stone, 2025) that extend beyond the current and previous educational technology discussions (Teamann, 2023).

At present, in most educational institutions and universities, there is a strong skepticism (Slagg, 2024) as to whether it can make a positive contribution to the learning process of learners and an equally strong concern as to how it could be used effectively for the benefit of the educational community (HEPI, 2025; Stone, 2024). To this end, this chapter seeks to investigate whether the use of Artificial Intelligence can contribute positively to the knowledge of university students (future engineers) and, in particular, to the development of their computational thinking when used at will.

The first section of the chapter introduces the reader to basic concepts and definitions necessary for understanding this paper. Consequently, it presents the concept of Computational Thinking, what STEM education is, and various definitions of artificial intelligence necessary for understanding the text. In addition, there is a quick introduction to the most popular Artificial Intelligence tools, such as ChatGPT, DeepSeek, Gemini, Claude AI, Copilot, Perplexity AI, Meta AI, MidJourney, DALL·E 3, Cursor, that can be used and contribute to education, specifically to the university education of future engineers. The first section ends with a brief review of the literature that searches the use of Artificial Intelligence applications (tools) and their exploitation in education in general and in engineering education.

The second section of the chapter presents the materials and methods of a case study conducted on students of the Department of Industrial Design and Production Engineering (IDPE) at the University of West Attica (UNIWA). This department delivers an Industrial Design and Production Engineering degree after ten semesters of taught courses. The subject of the department is the design of modern systems and services, creatively combining knowledge and methodologies from a broad spectrum of sciences, using new technologies for the design and production of innovative products, with the ultimate goal of increasing productivity and production and maintaining environmental sustainability (IDPE, 2024). In this way, its graduates must be capable of creatively using new technologies, science, and art to design solutions in the form of easy-to-use and functional products, processes, and systems in all productive sectors (IDPE, 2024).

This case study was based on the Mechatronics course, an interesting and demanding engineering course, taught in the 7th semester of the department's curriculum. Mechatronics is the intersection of multiple engineering disciplines (see § Mechatronics), where the main learning outcomes are the design, synthesis, and programming of a physical mechatronic system (IDPE, 2025). To achieve this goal, the teaching team responsible for the delivery of the course utilized STEM (§ STEM Education) and assigned a semester-long mechatronics system project to groups of students who were confronted with a multitude of engineering problems, such as:

1. the study, design, and construction of the mechatronic system mechanical prototype,
2. the design and development of the electronic part of the mechatronic system, and finally,
3. the writing of the necessary program (software) to control it.

In addition, upon completion of the project, the students had to write an accompanying technical report detailing the process and steps involved in its implementation.

The purpose of this case study was to investigate whether students used and utilized Artificial Intelligence tools to complete their mechatronic project, and whether the use of these tools contributed to the development of their Computational Thinking. As presented below (§ Computational Thinking), Computational Thinking is an important tool in solving complex problems, including engineering problems, and is an essential skill for the engineers of the future.

The third section of the chapter relates to the results of the self-assessment of the students who have used Artificial Intelligence tools, where their views are recorded. It presents how students have used Artificial Intelligence. That is, whether they have used Artificial Intelligence to easily and quickly write their assignments without delving into the results of their queries and without trying to understand the generated text of the assignment. Or, whether they have used Artificial Intelligence as a source of inspiration, as a starting point, to better understand the problem, to obtain some basic guidelines, and proceed to solve the tasks on their own, and to what extent. In conclusion, whether Artificial Intelligence helped them to develop as engineers/scientists, to develop their Computational Thinking, such as critical thinking, to learn and understand new knowledge, and whether they considered their integration in the educational process useful.

Finally, in the fourth section, we conclude and discuss the paper's findings.

This chapter contributes and could be very beneficial for all those who are involved in education, educators, researchers, and policymakers, as it gives a comprehensive look at Artificial Intelligence's use in education and explores all the benefits related to it.

Engineering Education

The first definition examined in this chapter is Engineering Education, as it is the base of every engineering department that delivers education. Engineering Education focuses on the development of technical skills and core competencies such as analytical thinking, communication, and teamwork, integrating innovative learning methods and technologies to simulate real-world engineering challenges (Cheville, 2014; Diogo et al., 2023). Therefore, students in engineering university departments such as the IDPE are trained to seek solutions to real problems related to industry and beyond. Engineering education learns them how to approach the solution of a problem and specifically to analyze it, explore hypothetical solutions, design, test, and implement applicable, feasible, and acceptable solutions (IDPE, 2023). In this context, education based on STEM (§ STEM Education) has recently gained popularity, becoming the new trend of teaching and learning, due to its proven learning value at every level of education, including higher education (G. E. Chamilothoris & Papoutsidakis, 2005; Chatzopoulos et al., 2023; Xatzopoulos et al., 2013). And, STEM teaching methods appear to help engineering students develop cognitive skills in critical thinking and problem-solving, abilities essential for developing the Computational Thinking (Chatzopoulos, Papoutsidakis, Kalogiannakis, Psycharis, et al., 2020) of the engineers of the future (Chatzopoulos et al., 2024; Dotson et al., 2020).

STEM Education

The STEM acronym is the evolution of the SMET definition (Chatzopoulos, Papoutsidakis, Kalogiannakis, & Psycharis, 2020) introduced by the National Science Foundation (NSF) in the 1990s (Chatzopoulos, Papoutsidakis, Kalogiannakis, & Psycharis, 2020). In the literature, there is a multitude of definitions relating to STEM, and due to its popularity, there is even a multitude of variations of the term STEM, including STEAM, STREAM, STM, STEMi, eSTEM, etc. (Chatzopoulos, Papoutsidakis, Kalogiannakis, et al., 2019; Kantaros et al., 2021). However, the term STEM is an acronym for the synthetic terms of Science, Technology, Engineering, and Mathematics (APS, 2017) and is a holistic, interdisciplinary framework, an educational approach integrating these disciplines to address real-world problems. As such, STEM is more than traditional teacher-centric learning that is based on lecture learning, and encourages experiential, project-based learning methods and teamwork (Pastrana et al., 2025). According to Vasquez, there are four levels of STEM integration as depicted in Figure 1, which are (Thananuwong, 2015; Vasquez et al., 2013):

1. The *disciplinary* where students learn concepts and skills separately in each discipline.
2. The *multidisciplinary* approach, where students learn concepts and skills separately in each discipline, but in reference to a common theme.
3. The *interdisciplinary* approach, where students learn concepts and skills from two or more disciplines that are tightly linked to deepen knowledge and skills.
4. The *transdisciplinary* approach, whereby, when undertaking real-world problems, students apply knowledge and skills from two or more disciplines and helps to shape the learning experience.

The use and implementation of STEM in education has multiple benefits for students, including (Chatzopoulos et al., 2021; Francis & Stephens, 2018; Ioannou & Bratitsis, 2016; Morrison & Bartlett, 2009; Radiopoulou et al., 2025):

1. It encourages students to think in different ways, to express creative ideas, and to work in teams, fostering teamwork and socialization.
2. Due to the STEM's teamwork nature, students learn how to work with others, learn from and with their teammates, and foster their sense of belonging.
3. It helps them to develop new skills, to become innovative, problem-solvers, and self-conscious, and develop their soft-skills such as critical-thinking, creativity, teamwork, communication, concentration, and cognitive–social skills.
4. It helps them to eliminate stereotypes about gender and race, and bridges ethnic and gender differences.
5. And most importantly, due to its practical application and involvement in many scientific fields, it makes education more fun and attractive and retains the students' curiosity and attention.

Figure 1. The four increasing levels of STEM approaches to curriculum integration (Thananuwong, 2015)

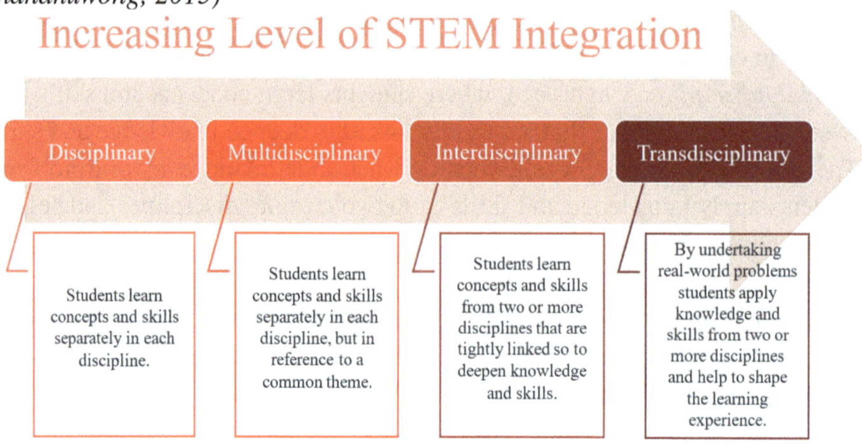

Regardless of how STEM is integrated in education (*disciplinary, multidisciplinary, interdisciplinary, transdisciplinary*), recent trends focus on assigning real, authentic projects to students, intending to develop their problem-solving skills and Computational Thinking through the acquired knowledge to solve them (Chatzopoulos et al., 2024; Sattar & Nawaz, 2023). And, the main tool in this direction is the adoption of Computational Thinking.

Computational Thinking

In general, Computational thinking (CT) is a problem-solving process that borrows concepts and skills from computer science to solve complex engineering problems (Harimurti et al., 2019). It is a way of thinking that can be used by anyone to solve everyday problems in their lives (Papadakis et al., 2016; Yadav et al., 2011). The CT term was first introduced by Seymour Papert (Papert, 1996) and later defined in depth by Jeannette Wing, who defined it as a rich set of methods for the solution of various problems (Wing, 2006). While CT's exact definition is still in debate (Ioannidou et al., 2011), in the education context, it is considered a STEM (Kanaki et al., 2025) and Engineering Design practice that helps students to ask questions on their assigned projects/problems, design their solutions, and communicate their findings (Chatzopoulos et al., 2024).

In the literature, there are references to CT's *components* (Zahilah Mohamed Zaki et al., 2019), *dimensions* (Grover, 2011; Psycharis, 2020), *concepts* (Brennan et al., 2019; Grover, 2011), *practices* (Brennan & Resnick, 2012), *perspectives* (Brennan & Resnick, 2012), *characteristics* (Harimurti et al., 2019), *spaces* (Psycharis, 2020), and other similar aspects that describe the *skills* (Kanaki et al., 2022) necessary for its implementation. On a basic level, the key skills developed by utilizing CT can be broken down into the following five essential skills (Chatzopoulos, Papoutsidakis, Kalogiannakis, Psycharis, et al., 2020) as depicted in Figure 2:

1. Decomposition (or Segmentation) that is, the ability to simplify a complex problem by breaking it down into smaller, more manageable parts.
2. Pattern Recognition (or Generalization), that is, the ability to recognize known tasks or parts of them (patterns) to use them for finding solutions more easily, which often leads to easier algorithmic thinking.
3. Abstraction, that is, the ability to focus on the essential details of the problem or a solution, and explain it by removing unimportant details. To be able to conceptualize an idea.
4. Algorithmic Thinking, that is, the ability to solve a problem by creating an ordered series of instructions, a step-by-step plan.
5. Evaluation (Debugging), that is, the ability to test the produced solution for errors, to verify whether it works as intended, and if not, to find what needs to be improved. In computer science, this step means to find and correct mistakes within a program.

Figure 2. The five essential computational thinking skills

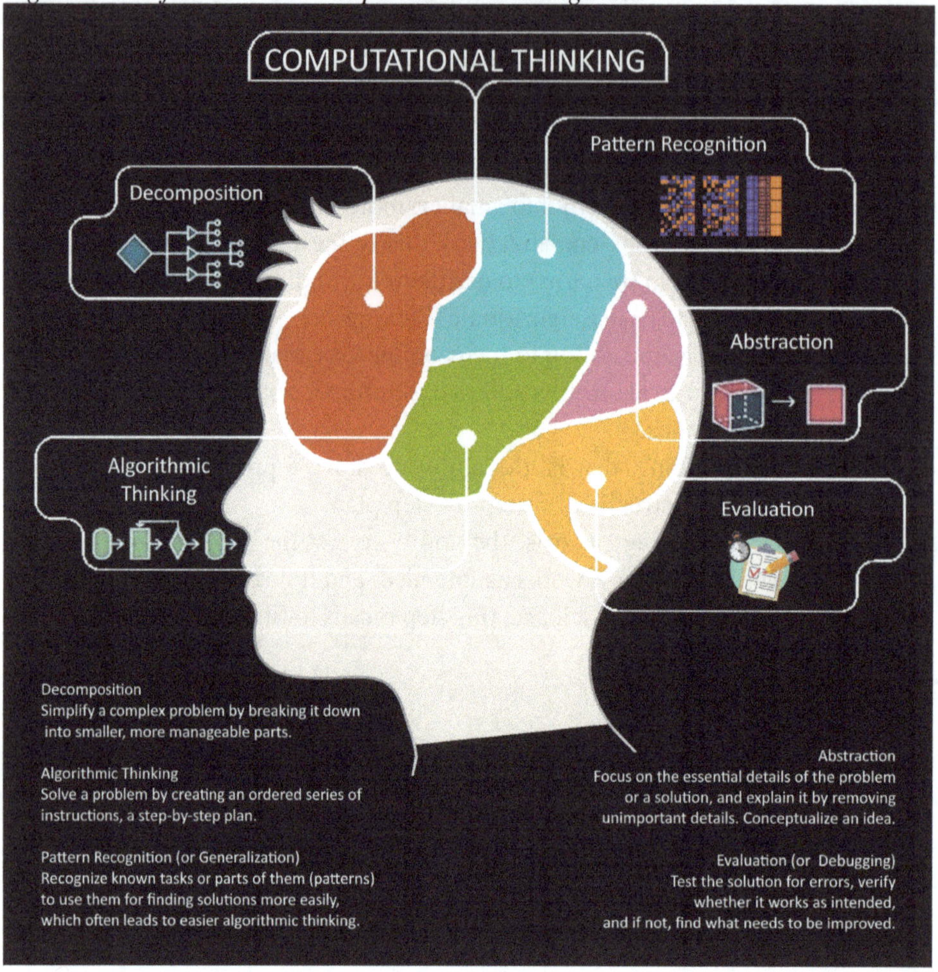

Problem-Based Learning

The implementation of the CT in practice, i.e., the assignment of a project/ problem to students and its solution, is preferably implemented in a learning environment delimited within the STEM framework and supported by the Problem-Based Learning (PBL). PBL is similar to the Challenge-Based Learning (CBL), an effective learning framework where students undertake to successfully complete a complex project, facing obstacles and challenges as they seek its solution. Similarly, over time, the differences have decreased- learning frameworks, everyone can be a Learner, Teacher/Learner, and Learner/Teacher (Nichols et al., 2016).

For a successful PBL design, Larmer and Mergendoller (Larmer & Mergendoller, 2010) detail seven basic elements every project needs to have:

1. Students have to know why they are doing this project.
2. Students have to create a "driving question" to focus their efforts on the project.
3. For making a project meaningful, students must have voice and choice.
4. The project must develop the students' 21st-century skills, such as collaboration, communication, the use of technology, critical thinking, and other essential soft skills, for their workplace and life.
5. Students engage more if they conduct a real inquiry, find information and answers to their questions, in an ongoing loop that drives them to innovation, thus a solution to the problem.
6. Student teams need to have feedback and revision between them to drive them to create high-quality solutions to the problem.
7. Finally, students need to present their work to a real audience, not just their teacher, as it is more meaningful to them. (1) A "need to know," (2) a driving question, (3) student voice and choice, (4) 21st century skills, (5) inquiry and innovation, (6) feedback and revision, and (7) a publicly presented product.

And, this leads to the five key phases or stages (Figure 3) of a successful PBL process as described below (Kember, 2005; Perkins, 2025):

1. *Project Planning,* where the teacher maps the cognitive path and thinking journey of their students. It includes the driving question, the deliverables (solutions or products of the problem), the timeline, the scaffolding, and the assessments. Everything had to be aligned with the learning goals of the course. In this phase, students are not yet active participants.
2. *Project Launch,* where the teacher announces the project to the students and invites them to be active participants. He introduces the driving question and the authentic audience, which helps to unlock their critical thinking. This leads to unpacking and modeling the list of questions they will need to know to answer the driving question.
3. *Project Implementation*, where the project has begun. The students think, learn, and make connections with content while the teacher supports, scaffolds, teaches, and engages them.

This phase could have multiple milestones depending on the project's scope and scale, and beyond discovery alone, it includes various teaching strategies.

4. *Project Conclusion*, where the project has ended, and the students prepare to present their deliverables (solutions or products) to a real audience. The teacher needs to assess each individual student for his/her learned knowledge that was intended to be taught.
5. *Project Debrief*, where the teacher reflects and considers what went well and not well in the project, what he may change if he does it again, what revisions and adjustments need to be done in future projects, etc. In addition, more feedback can be taken by asking his students to evaluate their learning and performance.

Figure 3. The five phases of the Project-Based Learning (PBL)

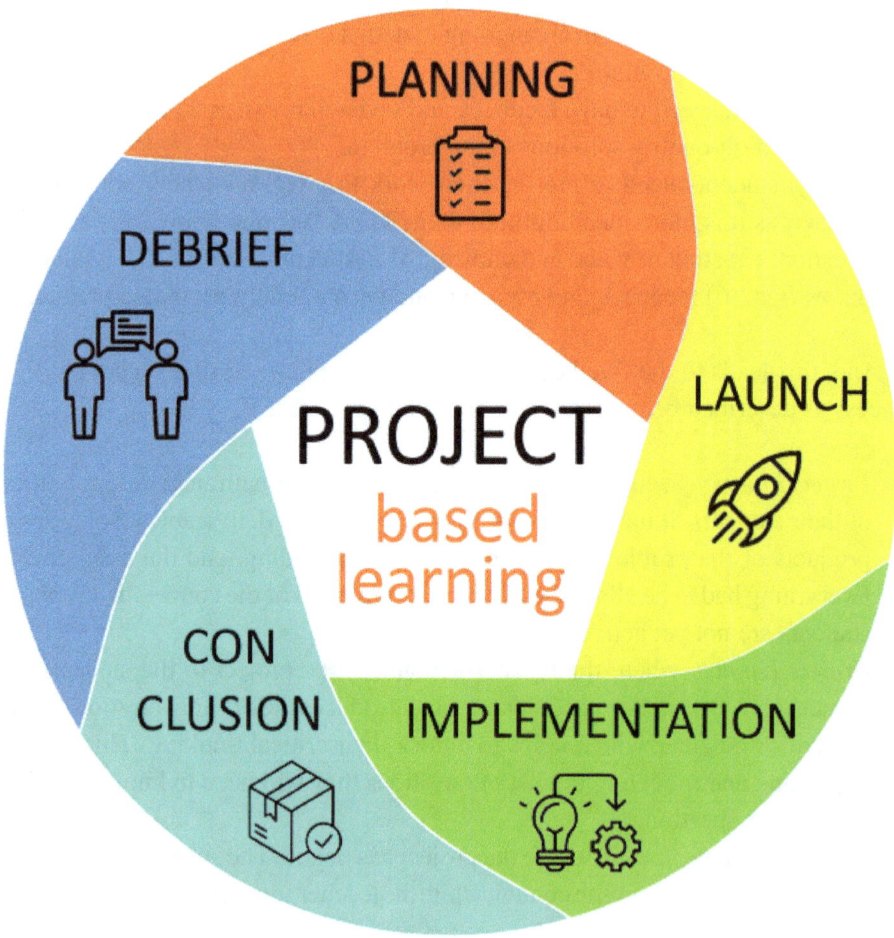

AI Definitions and Tools

Artificial Intelligence (AI)

Artificial intelligence (AI) is a term coined by John McCarthy in 1955, and it means a machine-based system that can learn through human interaction, make predictions, decisions, or recommendations when it is given a set of human-defined objectives. It includes supervised, unsupervised, reciprocal, and 'deep' learning systems to perform the following (Cardona & Rodriguez, 2024; Tzirides et al., 2023):

1. Perceive virtual and real environments,
2. analyze such perceptions and abstract them into models in an automated manner,
3. formulate information or action based on these model inferences.

Generative Artificial Intelligence (GenAI)

Generative Artificial Intelligence or Generative AI (GenAI) is a type of AI that has achieved significant success and uses sophisticated machine learning models to create new content, enabling anyone to create —such as text, images, music, audio, videos, or code—in response to a prompt or query (He et al., 2025). GenAI is distinguished from other AI forms as it generates novel output and provides insights that are not possible with other traditional tools. Under the term GenAI, there is a range of technologies delivering text, video, image, and other computer-generated digitized media (Tzirides et al., 2023). GenAI is based on a Large Language Model (LLM) that chatbots use. They sprang public attention with the launch of the well-known ChatGPT version 3.5 in November 2022. This version was a series of Generative Pre-trained Transformers (GPTs) developed by OpenAI, a start-up company founded in 2015. The first version of GPT-1 was released in 2018 (Tzirides et al., 2023). Later, in March 2024, OpenAI introduced the GPT-4 which stunned many and outperformed the older version (Rudra, 2023). Other big techs followed this path, Google announced Bard (today is named Gemini), its own AI chatbot, Microsoft first introduced Copilot in 2023 as part of its Microsoft 365 suite, Anthropic introduced Claude as a next-generation AI assistant designed to be helpful, honest, and harmless (Lindsey et al., 2025), Facebook AI Research founded Meta AI (Wiki, 2025b), etc. Today, there are thousands of GenAI tools provided free or with a subscription, suitable for everyday use (Karageorgakis, 2025) and, of course, education (Karageorgakis, 2023).

Generative AI tools in Education

Digital technology has been a significant factor in education's improvement as it enhances teacher effectiveness and increases students' academic performance (Kalogiannakis et al., 2025). AI, as a new trendy digital technology, could not be outside of this. Its tools, especially GenAI tools, have been increasingly used daily in educational practice, and they have emerged as a focal point in educational research (Kalogiannakis et al., 2025). They transform education, as they provide personalized learning, support problem-solving, and foster critical thinking (Kwid et al., 2024). With hundreds of educational AI tools in the market (Spinellis, 2025), free or with subscription (AIxploria, 2025), specialized in any field and for any educational task (Karageorgakis, 2023), educators are increasingly recognizing their potential inside the classroom (Kwid et al., 2024). These tools can be utilized to facilitate students' teaching and learning and help educators in common tasks, to name some (Karageorgakis, 2023, 2025):

1. Chatbots like ChatGPT (https://chat.openai.com), Claude (https://claude.ai), and Gemini (https://gemini.google.com) are the most publicly known GenAI tools to generate coherent and useful replies in users' prompt requests.
2. Research assistants such as NotebookLM (https://notebooklm.google/), Scispace (https://scispace.com), and Research Rabbit (https://researchrabbitapp.com) help researchers to enhance their productivity and work by providing literature review, access to scholarly articles, organizing notes, an AI writer, paraphrasing tools, and much more.
3. Data analysis AI tools like Graphy (https://graphy.app), Sheet AI (https://www.excelly-ai.io), and Excelly (https://www.sheetai.app) help to analyze data and handle multiple tables and charts.
4. Content writing, such as Grammarly (https://www.grammarly.com), Quillbot (https://quillbot.com/), and Copy.ai (https://www.copy.ai), can enhance users' writing faster, while correcting text's spelling and grammar, and more.
5. E-learning course creation, like Learning Studio (https://learningstudioai.com), Articulate 360 (https://www.articulate.com/360/), and Coursebox (https://www.coursebox.ai), are AI-based authoring tools for online course creation.
6. Teaching assistants such as MagicSchool AI (https://www.magicschool.ai), EduGPT (https://edugpt.com), and Brisk (https://www.briskteaching.com) can help educators generate classroom-related material.
7. Presentation generators like Gamma (https://gamma.app), Beautiful.ai (http://beautiful.ai), and MagicSlides (https://www.magicslides.app) can craft the presentation's outline and create the presentation's slides alone.

8. Language learning, such as Duolingo (https://en.duolingo.com), EduGPT (https://edugpt.com), and Elsa Speak (https://elsaspeak.com/en/), can work as language teachers helping students to learn foreign languages.
9. Quiz platforms to engage students by gamifying lessons and quizzes, such as Kahoot (https://kahoot.com), Quizalize (https://www.quizalize.com), and Quizziz (https://quizizz.com).
10. Text-to-speech AI tools convert text into spoken words while choosing the speaker's accent, gender, and age. Representatives of this category are Speechify (https://speechify.com), Elevenlabs (https://elevenlabs.io/), and Polly (https://aws.amazon.com/polly).
11. Other educational tools like DeepL (https://www.deepl.com), an AI translator and writer, GenType (https://labs.google/gentype), a free AI tool for preschool and language teachers and parents, and NoteGPT (https://notegpt.io), which is referred to as an AI Swiss knife with several AI tools.
12. Code programming AI tools like Cursor (https://cursor.com), GitHub Copilot (https://github.com/features/copilot), and Base44 (https://base44.com) help to write easy, fast, and better software code and applications.
13. Productivity AI tools such as Notion (https://www.notion.so), Scribe (https://scribehow.com), and Mymind (https://mymind.com) improve efficiency between different tasks, while saving time and money.
14. Image Generation, like MidJourney (https://www.midjourney.com/), DALL-E (https://chat.ai-pro.org/chat/dall-e/), Canva (https://canva.com), and Leonardo (https://leonardo.ai), allows users to create images based on their prompts and provided descriptions.
15. Video Generation tools such as Sora (https://openai.com/sora/), Pictory (https://pictory.ai), and InVideo(https://invideo.io) are fantastic AI tools that generate video content by turning scripts or text given by the user.
16. Animated graphics AI tools that help educators and students to animate static images and transform them into videos. Animated Drawings (https://sketch.metademolab.com/canvas), Animated Characters (https://www.adobe.com/express/create/animation), and Capcut (https://www.capcut.com) are some of the well-known representatives of this category.
17. Music generation to create compositions based on user prompts and defined parameters, such as genre, mode, and instrument. Suno (https://suno.ai), Musicfy (https://musicfy.lol), and Beatoven (https://www.beatoven.ai) are three representatives.

In conclusion, the entry of AI into education, in combination with these supporting AI tools, excels in multiple ways:

1. Enhancing adaptive learning and teaching.
2. Providing rich analytics based on data-driven insights.
3. Providing language support and content creation.
4. Enhancing students' accessibility and maximizing inclusivity.
5. Assisting with the educational organization administration by automating tasks and operations.

Generative AI tools

In this section, the GenAI tools used in this research are briefly presented.

ChatGPT

ChatGPT is the publicly widely known OpenAI GenAI chatbot, which introduced AI to the public in November 2022 with its version GPT 3.5 (Gill et al., 2024; Tzirides et al., 2023). It is an umbrella of GenAI tools used to respond to users' conversational writing requests to generate original text, images, and sound (OpenAI, 2025a; Rudra, 2023). ChatGPT uses and analyzes a large volume of data sources, like websites, books, and other text, to generate coherent and useful replies, responding to users' prompts, using natural language processing model algorithms and machine learning (Gill et al., 2024; Rudra, 2023). Although its first version (GPT-1) dates back to 2018, version 3.5 (GPT-3.5) was the one that caught the public's attention, including students, educators, professionals, and experts working in higher education, who quickly realized the potential and role it would play in education (Gill et al., 2024). In March 2024, version GPT-4 was introduced, which left many speechless and outperformed GPT-3.5 (OpenAI, 2024; Rudra, 2023). It provides many features to the users: (i) writes, edits, and brainstorms ideas, (ii) summarize texts (i.e. meetings) and finds new insights, (iii) writes, corrects, and debugs code, (iv) answers questions even the complex ones, (vi) searches the web, (vii) automates tasks, (viii) analyzes data and creates charts, (ix) describes and explains uploaded images, and much more (OpenAI, 2025a). The latest version of ChatGPT, GPT-5, was introduced in August 2025, which is the most useful, smartest, and fastest model with built-in thinking (OpenAI, 2025d). While the limited version of ChatGPT is free to use, there are other improved, better, pro, paid versions like ChatGPT Plus, ChatGPT Pro available to the public (OpenAI, 2025c).

DeepSeek

DeepSeek is a large language model (LLM) developed by DeepSeek AI. Like Chat-GPT, it was designed to understand and generate human-like text in response to a wide range of prompts and questions. It was introduced as DeepSeek-R1-Zero and DeepSeek-R1. DeepSeek-R1-Zero was trained via large-scale reinforcement learning (RL) without supervised fine-tuning, and it demonstrated remarkable reasoning capabilities. DeepSeek-R1 was introduced to achieve performance comparable to OpenAI on reasoning tasks. Unlike ChatGPT, DeepSeek has no paid plans, is free to use, multimodal (means to process files such as images, PDFs, Word documents, etc.), and supports the research community, as it is open-sourced: DeepSeek-R1-Zero, DeepSeek-R1, and six dense models. DeepSeek can be a daily assistant helping with tasks like answering questions, writing, analysis, coding, and more (DeepSeek-AI et al., 2025).

Gemini

Gemini AI is Google's family of AI tools (or multimodal models, as it is technically defined). These models were trained to understand text, audio, video, and images in order to develop a model with strong generalist capabilities, cutting-edge understanding, and performance in these domains. The first version of Gemini, Gemini 1.0, came into three subversions: i) Ultra, ii) Pro, and iii) Nano, each one focused on addressing different computational limitations and application requirements. At present, the last version, the Gemini 2.5, includes three major variants:

1. The Gemini 2.5 Pro, which is the most advanced model, is suitable for complex reasoning, coding, and multimodal understanding.
2. The Gemini 2.5 Flash, which is the model designed for fast, cost-efficient performance with adaptive thinking.
3. The Gemini 2.5 Flash-Lite which is a lightweight version for real-time, low-latency tasks.

Moreover, Google develops other models, Imagen for image generation, Veo for video production, and Lyria for music generation (Gemini Team et al., 2025; Google, 2025).

Claude AI

Claude AI is Anthropic's family of LLMs, designed to be helpful, honest, ethical, and safe. Claude AI is grounded in Constitutional AI, a framework that guides behavior using ethical principles rather than human feedback and ensures that outputs align with predefined ethical values and principles. Constitutional AI works by integrating a constitution, i.e., a set of principles, to guide the model's behavior during the training process. Principles include human rights protection, equality promotion, avoidance of offensive, harmful content, and they are from various sources, such as the UN Declaration of Human Rights, DeepMind's Sparrow principles, best practices from terms of service, etc. Constitutional AI is trained in two phases: first, it is trained to revise and critique, based on its principles, its own delivered responses, and second, it uses reinforcement learning to generate AI rather than human feedback. In this way, the model produced is more helpful and harmless compared to those trained with human feedback. Claude AI is very good at understanding natural language, reasoning, and aligns with safety, and it is used in research, enterprise, and consumer applications (Lindsey et al., 2025; Priyanshu et al., 2024).

Copilot

Copilot is Microsoft's GenAI assistant integrated into Microsoft 365 applications to enhance users' productivity by generating, summarizing, and analyzing content across Microsoft's office tools, Word, Excel, PowerPoint, and Outlook (Microsoft, 2025b). Its key components include natural language processing (NLP) to understand and respond to everyday language commands, and machine learning (ML) algorithms to analyze users' patterns, behaviors, and preferences, to offer more accurate responses based on previous actions (CopilotTeam, 2025). Microsoft's Copilot offers a wide range of capabilities to simplify repetitive tasks (automation) and provides contextual intelligence to help make richly informed and faster decisions. Using it, many tasks can be simplified, like: i) creating documents (e.g., reports, presentations, emails, etc.), ii) analyzing data in Excel, iii) assisting project management (e.g., track tasks, schedules, projects, etc.), and iv) enhancing communication, e.g., summarizing and drafting emails (CopilotTeam, 2025).

Perplexity AI

Perplexity AI is an AI-powered, powerful web engine that synthesizes responses based on users' queries. It combines web search, LLMs, NLP, and AI-generated content to deliver direct, fast, real-time, summarized answers, accompanied by citations and their corresponding links to sources (Aayushi, 2025; Wikipedia, 2025b). It was founded by Perplexity AI Inc. in 2022, and it is offered in two versions: a free public version and a paid pro version that has access to more advanced LLMs (Wikipedia, 2025b). The pro version provides extended features, e.g., collaboration features, and includes ChatGPT integration (Eghosa, 2025). Perplexity AI differs from other web engines in that it leverages Internet content to synthesize information, rather than returning relevant web links as the other traditional web engines do. It provides transparent responses to the users' requests with inline source links and citations

(Pageon, 2025), and it excels in technical topics and academic research (Eghosa, 2025). It focuses on safety by providing an optional private browser and end-to-end encryption, and privacy, so it's suitable for sensitive research topics. Furthermore, its mobile version surprisingly performs as well as the desktop one, so it's very practical for those who work with many devices (Eghosa, 2025). Perplexity can help students, educators, researchers, developers, tech, and business professionals to instantly gather information and gain accurate insights, so it is a useful tool in education too (Aayushi, 2025).

Meta AI

Meta AI is Meta's (formerly Facebook's) AI assistant integration within its social media platforms like Instagram, Facebook, and WhatsApp (Nolasco & Dicuangco, 2025; Wiki, 2025c). It was launched in September 2023, and it became available in April 2025 as a standalone application. It is based on Meta's Llama, which is an open-source, customized, cost-efficient family of LLMs specialized for its social media applications, that understands users' preferences and provides responses based on user accounts' data (Meta, 2025a; Wiki, 2025c). Meta AI was mainly built to generate AI for social media interactions and create content within the following Meta's range of apps and products (Meta, 2025b):

1. Social apps like Instagram, Facebook, Messenger, and WhatsApp offer content generation, chatbots, image and video creation, translation, and text analysis.
2. Meta AI app, a standalone or a web-based app to generate content, chat, and interact with a personal AI assistant, using natural language, image, and video creation, writing, and project management.
3. AI-enabled smart Meta Glasses by Ray-Ban that combine advanced AI features, i.e., voice-commands, capture photos and videos, real-time translations, managing calls and messages, etc., with wearable fashion.

Despite its limitations, Meta AI could be a valuable tool for educators by incorporating it into their learning and teaching activities, since it can generate replies very similar to human conversation and provide organized and useful information (Nolasco & Dicuangco, 2025).

MidJourney

Midjourney is a publicly known AI image generator tool, capable of generating high-quality, realistic, or highly artistic images based on users' prompts (Wiki, 2025d). Midjourney draws an image in just a few minutes by understanding the user's request written in simple words. Midjourney doesn't simply combine stored images by just making a collage of them, but it decodes the user request's words, imagines them, and converts them into a reality by synthesizing an image (Hanna, 2023). This AI tool has been compared to DALL-E, OpenAI's equivalent image generator tool; both AI models are trained on a large amount of images to be able to produce their own images, but Midjourney differentiates from the others (DALL-E, Leonardo, Adobe's Firefly, etc.) as it exists as a social app through Discord servers (Pazur, 2025; Wiki, 2025d). Midjourney can be used in two ways: (i) via the Midjourney Bot on the official Midjourney Discord server, or (ii) via the web app available at its official site www.midjourney.com. The Midjourney Bot selection allows users to see the images and the galleries of other users, too. Midjourney is not free; it needs a subscription. However, the user can try and use it for free, but there is a limit of 25 text prompts, i.e., queries and /or "imagine" command to initiate the AI's generation (Wiki, 2025d). All the images produced by Midjourney become public unless the user selects to create in stealth mode, which is included in the more expensive Pro and Mega subscription plans (Pazur, 2025).

DALL·E

DALL·E is OpenAI's legacy state-of-the-art generative AI model, similar to Midjourney, for image generation (Awan, 2025; OpenAI, 2025a). It was first introduced in January 2021 as a variant of the GPT-3 language-processing model, with its name originating from the surrealist artist Salvador Dali, and from Wall-E, the Pixar animated robot (Awan, 2025; Wiki, 2025a). In April 2022, OpenAI introduced DALL·E 2, which generated more realistic, higher-resolution images, and in September 2023, it introduced its last version, DALL·E 3, which was a significant upgrade with advanced capabilities. In February 2024, watermarks began to be added to DALL·E's generating images, alongside metadata in a promoted standard by the Content Authenticity Initiative (Wikipedia, 2025a).

DALL·E uses trained images and data to generate images from users' prompts, i.e., text descriptions, combining unrelated concepts in a fancy way, and transforming existing images (Hanna, 2023). It is equipped with a rich set of capabilities, e.g., anthropomorphized versions of objects and animals, by combining disparate ideas in often plausible, surreal, visual ways (Hanna, 2023). DALL·E is very good at generating discrete objects and close-up photographs, and it can recognize visual media and literary works, pop culture (Hanna, 2023). While it can create stunning images in multiple styles, such as photorealistic paintings, imagery, emoji, etc., widening the possibilities for creativity, education, and more, it still lacks emotional evaluation, since it can't understand what makes an image funny, important, novel, or meaningful (Slack, 2023; Wikipedia, 2025a). DALL·E 3 is now integrated into ChatGPT, so the user can ask in the main chat to create an image (OpenAI, 2025a).

Cursor

A very popular application of AI tools, especially in the programming community, is their application in writing and debugging programming code. In recent days, the LLM models have been successfully used as programming assistants, helping to complete, insert, edit, and debug code, to build software products (Jiang et al., 2024). Cursor is an AI-driven code editor designed to help write and understand code faster. It utilizes advanced LLMs like Claude, GPT-5, Gemini, and Grok to help users generate, edit, refactor, and explain codebases in natural language (Anysphere, 2025; Gurova, 2025). The users just have to describe what they want to build or change, and Cursor will generate the appropriate code for them. Cursor AI is a fork of Visual Studio Code, so it retains its user-friendly, extensive ecosystem, making it easier for programmers who are familiar with it (Aubry, 2024). On its website, Cursor AI is advertised as a new way to build software that increases users' productivity, trusted by millions of professional developers. Some of its cutting-edge features are (Anysphere, 2025):

1. Cursor AI's agents turn users' ideas into effective code.
2. Cursor AI predicts the users' next actions and autocompletes code with accuracy, speed, and precision.
3. It learn how the users' codebase works, and can completely understand it, no matter its complexity or scale.
4. Cursor AI develops enduring software by accelerating scale and secure development.
5. It has access to the best LLM models, such as those from OpenAI, Gemini, xAI, and Anthropic.

Cursor AI is offered in three versions: a free pro, a two-week trial plan version with limited completions and requests, a paid pro plan version for developers with unlimited completions and limited requests, and a business plan version with many more features (Gurova, 2025).

Sora

Sora is a text-to-video generative AI model that can form a user's prompt, generate realistic or imaginative, complex scenes accompanied by multiple characters, subjects, and background accurate details, and specific motion types (OpenAI,

2025b). Sora is not the only or the first text-to-video AI model. Other research efforts like Meta's Make-A-Video, Google's Veo 3, or Runway's Gen-2 have led to the development of LLMs generating video content. These models are derived from text-to-image models, like Sora, which is an adaptation of the DALL·E 3, making them sub-derivatives of foundational models (He et al., 2025; Wikipedia, 2025c). Sora was released by OpenAI in February 2024 and is distinguished from the previous video generation models by its ability to produce up to one-minute-long high-quality videos (Liu et al., 2024). To start using it, the user describes the desired video by providing relative text or uploads another video or image file as a starting point. In this case, the user has to confirm that he/she is the owner of the uploaded file or that he/she has the necessary rights to do so. In any case, users must not upload any video or image content of other individuals without their express written consent. Next, the user can review the desired video settings, such as the resolution, the aspect ratio, the number of desired variations, and the video's duration. After submitting the prompt with these settings, it generates the video in up to one minute (OpenAI, 2025b). Sora has a remarkable ability to understand and interpret human instructions and generate impressive, detailed scenes, including multiple characters performing specific actions in detailed backgrounds (Liu et al., 2024). This is because Sora can understand not only the user's prompt but also how those things described in the prompt exist in the physical world, discerning the elements' complicated interplay within a scenario. (Liu et al., 2024; OpenAI, 2025b). Sora was publicly released in December 2024, is not free to use, and is only available to ChatGPT paid versions, ChatGPT Plus, Business, and Pro. (Wikipedia, 2025b).

Related Work

As the use of Artificial Intelligence (AI) tools in education increases exponentially, so does the interest of the research community. There is now a wealth of research in the literature examining the use of these tools by students, teachers, and their impact on education. Similar research to the one presented in this chapter has demonstrated an ever-increasing use of AI tools by the educational community. For example, (Almassaad et al., 2024), after investigating 859 students' perceptions of GenAI tools in Saudi Arabian higher education, they revealed that they are frequently used (78.7%) to clarify and define concepts, to translate text, to generate ideas, and to summarize academic literature. While they clearly understood the benefits of these tools, they were concerned about their challenges, like the misleading information, plagiarism, and the subscription fees. In another study, (Pavlenko & Syzenko, 2024) investigated 247 random Ukrainian university students' experiences of using ChatGPT for learning purposes, and working on tasks and assignments. The findings of the study confirmed that the students used ChatGPT mostly to search for information and to improve their writing skills by helping them with text editing. Furthermore, the study's findings revealed a positive attitude towards the tool among the students, since they believed it promoted the quality of their learning. Focusing on the use of GenAI tools, (Chan & Hu, 2023) surveyed 399 university students from various disciplines, both undergraduate and postgraduate, in Hong Kong. The study revealed students' positive attitude towards these tools in learning and teaching, and it recognized their potential for brainstorming, personalized learning, writing, research, and analysis support. In the same way, (Ngo, 2023) surveyed 200 university students via an online survey and interviewed 30 more students to investigate how they were perceived using ChatGPT for learning, including benefits, barriers, and potential solutions. The study showed students had a positive opinion towards this GenAI tool, as it saved them time, while providing personalized learning and information in various thematic areas. Remarkably, (Malmström et al., 2023) surveyed 5,894 Swedish university students to investigate how they use GenAI tools and their attitudes towards them for learning purposes. Once again, the findings of their research revealed the students' positivity towards the GenAI tools in effective learning and in education in general. Almost all of them were familiar with the publicly known ChatGPT, and more than 33% used it regularly. In addition, 1,707 of the survey respondents offered comments, thoughts, and reflections about the effective and ethical use of GenAI tools in higher education. One more large-scale study was conducted by (Kelly et al., 2023) to explore the students' perspectives on the GenAI tools. In this study, 1,135 Australian university students were surveyed to investigate their views on these tools. The study revealed that students didn't have experience and confidence in using these tools, something that can be attributed to the time period in which the research was conducted (2023). It should be noted that the first and most well-known GenAI was ChatGPT, introduced to the public in November 2022.

It is noteworthy that in the literature, there are many studies related to the use of GenAI in engineering and STEM. Like the (Yabaku & Ouhbi, 2024) research, which investigated university students' perceptions and expectations of GenAI tools like ChatGPT and Copilot in software engineering. For this reason, they conducted a study of 127 students at Uppsala University (Sweden) to record their perceived benefits, challenges, motivations, and usage preferences. They found that 84% of participants have used GenAI tools, mostly ChatGPT, and they benefited from them in idea generation and code optimization, while they encountered several challenges, like understanding user intent, and inaccuracies in generated content. Furthermore, this study offered insights and suggestions on the practical use of these AI tools towards software engineering education. In this direction, (Kharrufa et al., 2024) published a study that explored the integration of GenAI tools in software engineering team projects and recorded the students' views about them. For this purpose, they surveyed 39 undergraduate students and interviewed 8 to provide their insights on the impact of GenAI tools on the students' coding experiences, self-efficacy, and learning. The study findings revealed that the use of the GenAI tools can play a role both as an assistant or an educator, and as a team member, too. The GenAI tool could be a valuable peer to help team decisions towards brainstorming, reviewing, or writing code, documentation, and other activities. Another research (Wang et al., 2025) surveyed 40 college students and 28 faculty to study how and why students used GenAI tools when they looked for support in their problem-solving STEM coursework. The research's findings revealed that students used the GenAI at high rates (92.5% used them, and only 7.5% reported no use of GenAI tools) and for several applications, like to find topics' explanations, explore related, summarize readings, and assist with questions, and the main reason was to save time. Furthermore, this research provided insights into how to guide students towards the appropriate use of these tools. In one more study (Luo et al., 2025), students and instructors were surveyed on GenAI tools usage in engineering education. Specifically, they explored usage patterns of GenAI tools and investigated perspectives and attitudes toward these tools among the two groups, students and instructors. The findings of this study reported that students were familiarized and engaged with these tools, while the instructors showed reluctance to incorporate them into the educational process, reflecting a divide between them. In a same research, the authors in (Reihanian et al., 2025) reviewed 52 papers academic papers for the use of GenAI tools (especially ChatGPT and Claude) in computer science education. It revealed that while these tools improves students' learning efficiency, and support creative work, several concerns were raised, such as error propagation, AI hallucinations, and bias.

Regarding the second part of this work, which examines the contribution of GenAI tools to the development of CT skills, there are similar, but not exactly the same, studies in the literature, such as the study of (Ruiz-Rojas et al., 2024), which examined the impact of GenAI tools on university students' critical thinking and collaboration. The findings of this research revealed that a total of 64% of the students believed that GenAI tools significantly improved their critical thinking ability and enhanced collaboration. On the same roadmap, the qualitative study of (Sánchez Muñoz et al., 2025) investigated how high-school students engaged with GenAI tools, and how this interaction influenced their computational thinking and knowledge construction. Using a critical-constructivist framework and an action-research methodology, this study revealed that while GenAI tools fostered computational fluency and creativity, they raised challenges on critical reflection, epistemic vigilance, and project feasibility. Particularly noteworthy is the study of (Gervacio, 2024), which explored how GenAI tools, and particularly ChatGPT, enhanced self-directed learning for college students. The authors of the study interviewed 15 random college students to find out that ChatGPT helped them to break down complex subjects, which is the CT's decomposition skill, to enhance self-directed learning and efficiency in completing tasks, and to improve their analytical skills. Last but not least, the authors (Aisha Irshad et al., 2025) in their study explored the impact of the GenAI tools on higher education, and the students' perspectives on the integration of these tools within the context of Education 4.0. For this reason, they conducted qualitative research and interviewed 26 undergraduate and postgraduate students of the University of Sargodha to conclude that while GenAI tools benefit students' conceptual clarity, academic results, and time management, their excessive use can have the opposite results and hinder the students' critical analysis and learning development.

2. MATERIAL AND METHODS

The second section of this chapter seeks to investigate whether the use of Artificial Intelligence (AI) can contribute positively to the knowledge of university students (and future engineers) and, in particular, to the development of their CT when used at will. For this purpose, a research based on a case study by university engineering students was conducted. The case study was held at the Department of Industrial Design and Production (IDPE) of the University of West Attica (UNIWA) and was implemented within the framework of the Mechatronics course. In this section, the research background concepts, material, and methods are thoroughly presented.

Background Concepts and Learning Objectives

This subsection focuses on the necessary background concepts and learning objectives of the Mechatronics course, as well as its relation to the system design.

A. Mechatronics

There are numerous definitions of Mechatronics; however, the most relevant is that Mechatronics is a growing interdisciplinary field (Figure 4) that integrates mechanical engineering, electrical engineering, electronics engineering, computer engineering, and control theory to create automated, intelligent, and autonomous systems and products (Awtar et al., 2002; Chatzopoulos et al., 2023). By extension, all modern autonomous or automatic physical devices that contain intelligence and specifically incorporate a microcontroller (microprocessor or microcomputer) can be considered as mechatronic systems, their design and development being the result of the convergence of the above engineering fields. In this way, teaching Mechatronics becomes a very demanding job, and it has historically been developed in many forms and contexts (Alptekin & Freeman, 1996; Amerongen, 2000; Arkin et al., 1997; G.

Chamilothoris, 2002; Lyshevski, 2002). Many studies have already documented the value of Mechatronics in the interdisciplinary context of an engineering curriculum (Brown & Brown, 2002; Carryer, 1995; Geddam, 2003; Giurgiutiu et al., 2002), which has led to the adoption of project-oriented didactics methods for teaching Mechatronics, thus project-oriented and project-based learning (Andersen et al., 2003; Bula et al., 2018; Carryer, 2002; Gardner, 2002; Xatzopoulos et al., 2013). And, STEM, due to its synthetic, holistic, interdisciplinary nature, is the most suitable educational approach to integrate Mechatronics disciplines to address real-world problems (Chatzopoulos et al., 2023, 2024; Lagogiannis & Chatzopoulos, 2025). In addition, Mechatronics, like STEM, can be a general-purpose educational tool for imparting competencies and general skills.

Figure 4. Mechatronics is an interdisciplinary field that integrates mechanical, electronics, computer engineering, and control engineering

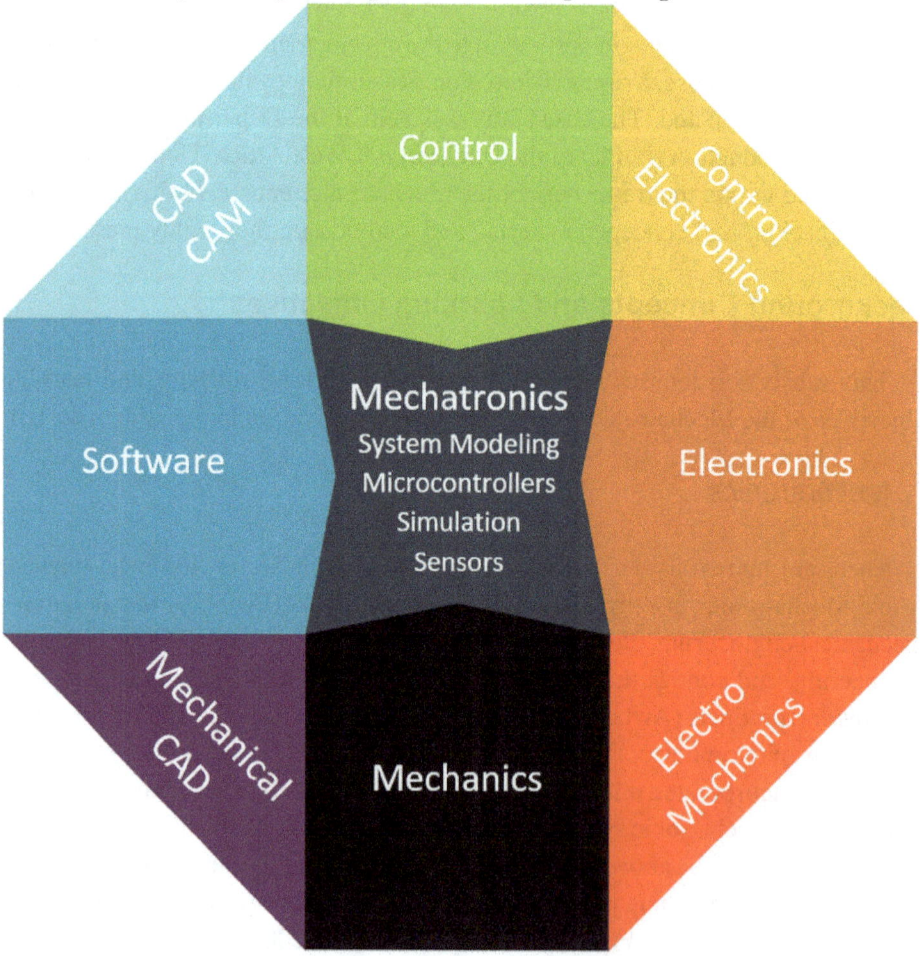

B. Learning Objectives of the Mechatronics Course

The Mechatronics course mission and purpose –similar to the IDPE department- is the design of modern mechatronic systems and products, such as these (Chatzopoulos, Papoutsidakis, Sofianos, et al., 2019; Karpuzi et al., 2019; Koikas et al., 2015; Louros et al., 2018; Minetou et al., 2024; Papoutsidakis et al., 2018; Priniotakis et al., 2015; Sigalos et al., 2019), creatively combining knowledge and methodologies from a broad spectrum of sciences and engineering (IDPE, 2025).

The learning objectives for this course are based on the specific goals of the IDPE's educational program and, among others, are (IDPE, 2025):

1. Understanding the basic architecture of a mechatronic system and its principles, thus to understand the mechanical, electrical, and electronic design of the system.
2. Sensor and actuator integration, which includes gaining knowledge about electronics components that sense and act in the environment.
3. Developing embedded systems, which include the integration of a microcontroller, microprocessor, or microcomputer into the mechatronic system.
4. Programming and controlling operation, which develops the students' algorithmic thinking and involves the ability to program and handle complex controls of the mechatronic system.
5. Communication systems, which include learning about systems-to-systems or systems-to-human communications and their protocols.
6. Power systems, which include the energy requirements of the mechatronic devices in terms of voltage/current, are provided through the use of power supplies or batteries.
7. System integration and testing, which includes the knowledge about integrating different subsystems into a cohesive mechatronic design. In addition, includes all the necessary skills to assemble, test, and debug the mechatronic system, i.e., mechanical assembly, verifying the correct operation of the system based on the initial specifications and finding related errors.
8. Designing a mechatronic system according to the Engineering Design Process.

C. Teaching for Mechatronics

To test the students' CT in practice and answer the research questions (§ Research Questions), the researcher utilized the STEM framework supported by the PBL to deliver the Mechatronics course. As noted above, PBL is an effective learning framework that assigns students to complete a complex project, in this case, a mechatronic system. In this way, students face challenges and obstacles, and they acquire knowledge as they seek the project's solution using STEM.

Following the five phases of a successful PBL process (§ Problem-Based Learning), the proposed theoretical model is based on the literature (Atmatzidou et al., 2018; Bers et al., 2014; Chatzopoulos, Papoutsidakis, Kalogiannakis, Psycharis, et al., 2020) and utilizes the *CT Skills Model* in conjunction with the *Teacher Guidance Protocol* (Atmatzidou et al., 2018). It comprises the following six stages:

1. *Challenge*. Similar to PBL's *launch phase*, the *challenge stage* is the stage where an authentic problem (which is a complex mechatronic system) is presented to the university students with the goal of accomplishing. The *didactic team*, which is responsible for the delivery of the Mechatronics course, introduces the driving question and the authentic audience. The mechatronic system is not easy to achieve, even though it seems to be feasible.
2. *Explore*. In this stage, the students use CT to inquire, think, learn, and make connections with learning content. The didactic team supports, scaffolds, teaches, engages, and leads the students to develop a problem-solving approach and find a solution by decomposing and simplifying the problem into smaller, manageable parts. The students –as future engineers- are introduced to the Engineering Design Process (Figure 5), a must-know engineering process similar to CT. After all, the CT has been based on and inspired by it (Chatzopoulos, Papoutsidakis, Kalogiannakis, Psycharis, et al., 2020; Harimurti et al., 2019; Lego, 2016).
3. *Exchange*. In this stage, the students have already inquired and found solutions for their mechatronic project. They reflect on their work, recognize known and frequently used parts, and use general pieces of learning as reusable parts of their tasks. Last but not least, they communicate their knowledge with fellow students and the didactic team, exchanging views and solutions with peers.
4. *Develop*. In this stage, the students implement their solution and develop their mechatronic system by constructing a prototype.
5. *Test*. The students' prototype is being tested and evaluated. If it meets all the mechatronic project's specifications, they move on to the next stage, which is the *conclusion*.
6. *Conclusion*. The mechatronic system (project) is finished, and the students present it to the audience, the didactic team, and other peers. The didactic team assesses each student for his/her learned knowledge that was intended to be taught.

Similar to the Engineering Design Process, this model uses a loop process, meaning that the knowledge gained by the students from the develop stage can be fed into the *exchange* (or even into the *explore*) stage, in case the mechatronic system prototype doesn't fulfil the requirements of the project. Moreover, the students' deliverables and the gained knowledge can be used by the didactic team to shape the mechatronics project requirements of the next academic year. Based on Atmatzidou's *Teacher Guidance Protocol* (Atmatzidou et al., 2018), the teaching team of the course actively participates in this model. In addition to setting learning objectives and evaluating students, it actively interacts with them, receiving feedback and revising objectives and deliverables.

Figure 5. The engineering design process of a mechatronic system

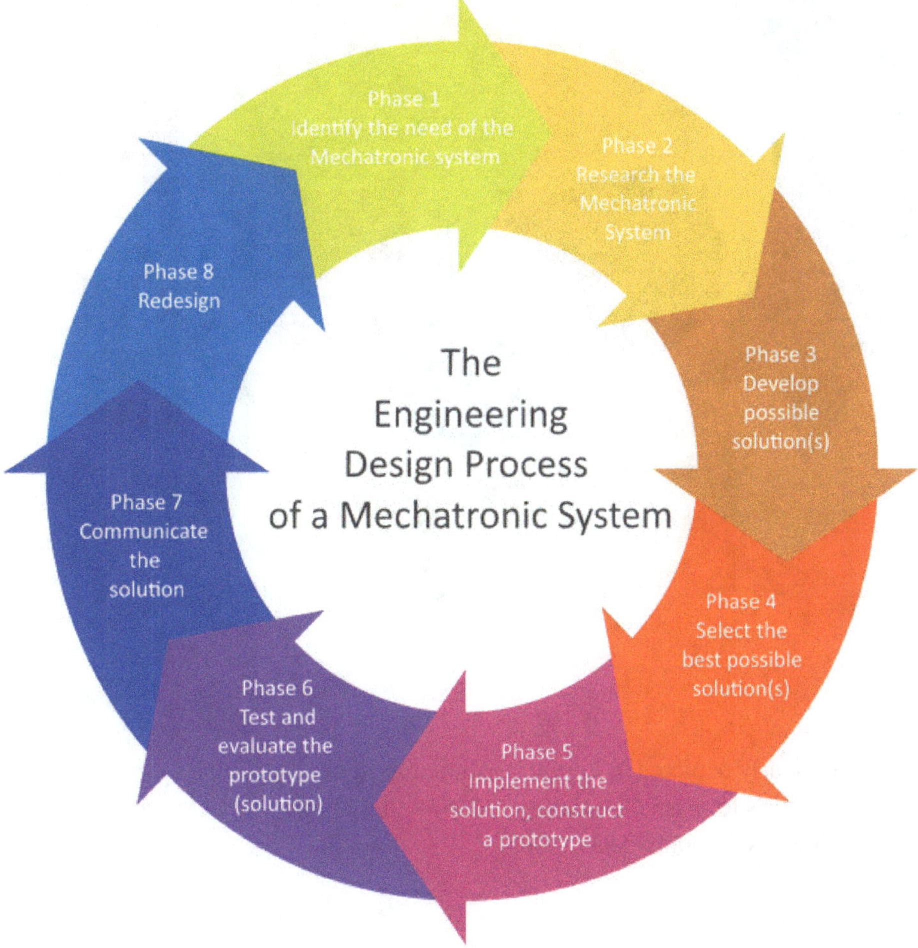

Figure 6. Teaching model for the mechatronics course

This is clearly depicted in Figure 6, where the student's internal loop is included in the educator's loop (didactic team's loop) with the following clear stages (G. E. Chamilothoris & Papoutsidakis, 2005):

1. Review didactic goals.
2. Introduce new means.
3. Receive students' feedback.
4. Appraise results.

D. The Mechatronics Project

To achieve the research objective, that is, if AI was used by the students to complete the mechatronics project assigned to them, the course didactic team formulated the following project.

1. Objective

The purpose of the mechatronics project was the construction and demonstration of the operation of a mechatronic system that controls a ball suspended in an air stream using a microcontroller (mC). The device consisted of a base that incorporated a cylinder in which the ball floated in place, as depicted in Figure 7.

Figure 7. Floating ball arrangement: The proposed mechatronic system

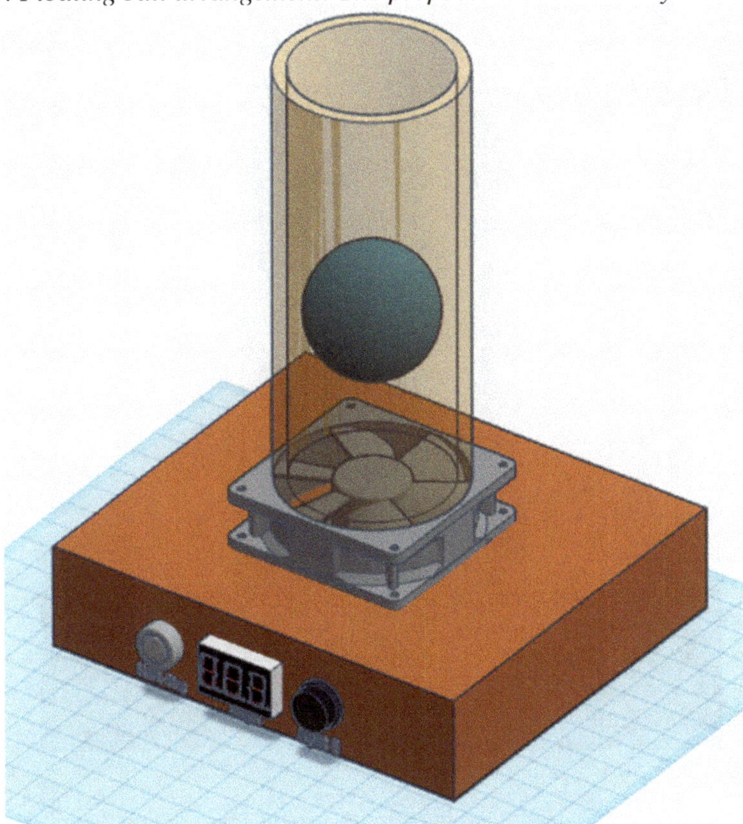

To control the floating ball, the device had to include the following components:

1. A fan driven by a DC brushed or brushless motor to supply the air flow, together with its power supply.
2. A sensor to detect the position of the ball. Position detection can be done optically, acoustically, or by other means.
3. A potentiometer to select the desired position of the ball.
4. A button for starting/stopping the operation of the device (Figure 8).
5. A display for showing the position of the ball. The display can be a 3-digit LED display or an LCD (Figure 8), or through the microcontroller's serial communication with computer software (e.g., Arduino Serial Monitor).
6. A buzzer for producing start, operation, and end audio signals.
7. An Arduino, ESP, or Raspberry Pi microcontroller/microcomputer (mC) system and the necessary electronic interfaces for connecting the mC to the components mentioned above (see Figure 9).

Figure 8. The mechatronics system device's controls

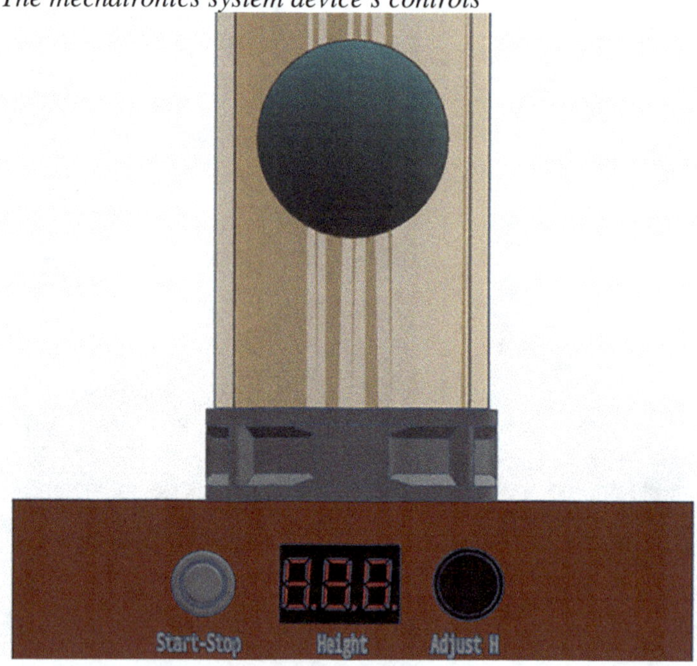

Figure 9. The microcontroller and the electronic circuitry of the proposed mechatronic system

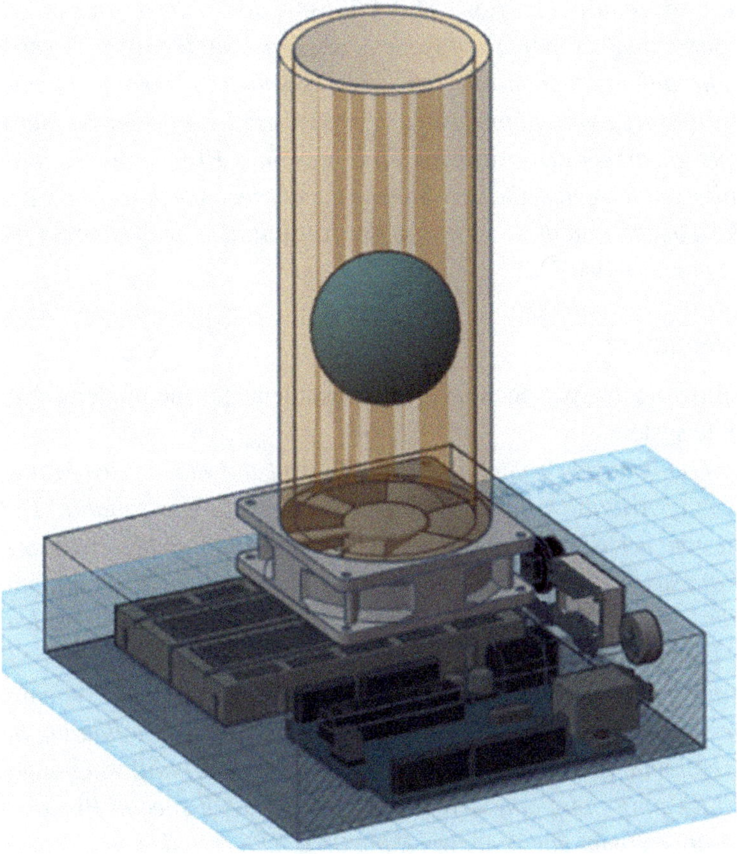

2. Specification

The purpose of the mechatronic system was to maintain a constant distance between the suspended ball and the fan by controlling the fan airflow via the microcontroller system, regardless of any external disturbances that may occur during operation.

3. Operation

The required operation of the assigned mechatronic system was the following: *"When the device is started, the buzzer emits a short beep to inform the user (student) that the device is in ball position input mode (mode 1). The user rotates the potentiometer to select the desired position value, e.g., 3cm, which is displayed on the device's screen/display. To complete the entry of the desired position, the user presses the button once, the buzzer sounds a prolonged beep, and the device switches to the floating ball control mode (mode 2). The fan then produces the required air flow to keep it suspended in the desired position, while at the same time its numerical value is displayed on the device's screen in real time. Throughout the control of the floating sphere, if there is a disturbance in its position, e.g., violent movement of the sphere by an external factor, the mC attempts to correct its position again in less than 10 seconds. To terminate the operation of the device, the user presses the button once more, the buzzer sounds two short beeps, and the device returns to the initial state of entering the position of the sphere (mode 1)."*

4. Implementation

The following instructions were given to students for the implementation of the mechatronic system:

"The mC unit must be compatible with the open and widely used Arduino system. Any type of Arduino with an operating voltage of 5V is suitable. The mC unit and the connected electronic components are available at electronics stores and also from suppliers of equipment for experimental or educational purposes. In addition, many electronic components can be recovered from obsolete or older technology IT devices, such as printers, scanners, toys, etc. No specific dimensions are given for the mechanical part of the mechatronic system, so that it can be made from a variety of materials. For example, the floating ball can be a conventional 40 mm ping-pong PP (polypropylene) ball weighing 2.7g, or a SUNFLEX ping-pong ball weighing 6g and made of special PU foam, or even a decorative 20mm pom-pom weighing 0.7g. The cylinder can be designed and printed using a 3D printer and transparent thread, or a commercially available acrylic tube made of PLEXIGLAS or PMMA can be selected. The fan can be recycled from a variety of devices, such as computer power supplies, processor cooling systems, air blowers, etc."

5. Deliverables

The project's deliverables were the construction and demonstration of the proper functioning of the mechatronic system and an accompanying technical report with clear instructions, and with the following specifications:

1. Architecture of the mechatronic system, which means to schematically present the implemented device as a "mechatronic" system, distinguishing between the processing unit, sensors, actuators, and interfaces.

2. Equipment. Lists the components (materials) that have been used and is accompanied by a brief description of their main characteristics.
3. Software structure. Describe the organization of the software (program) of the mechatronic system. List the main code structures, such as libraries or additional functions that have been used. Use a flow chart to depict the software structure of the system.
4. Program. It captures the code in Arduino C/C++ language, according to the syntax guide, and with full comments.
5. Results. Records any brief comments or observations from the application (functional test) of the mechatronic system as implemented.

Consequently, the project deliverables fulfil the achievement of the learning objectives of the Mechatronics course as described briefly above (§ Learning Objectives of the Mechatronics Course).

6. Evaluation

During the presentation of the project to the students, clear instructions were given regarding their evaluation, with detailed records of the percentages of participation of the deliverables in their final grade. The final grade included the grade of the overall layout of the mechatronic system, the evaluation of the accompanying technical report, the presentation of the system, and the answers given by each student individually during a short oral examination per group with questions related to the subject and implementation of their work.

7. Students Teams

As noted above, the case study of this research focuses on a STEM educational approach, and a fundamental aspect of STEM is teamwork. Thus, the students who attended this course participated and worked in teams of three people, where every member had a distinct role:

1. *Mechanical Engineer (MechEng)* who was responsible for the mechanical aspects of the mechatronic system, including materials selection and construction of the physical device's prototype. Some of the problems in this member relate to the 3D design and modeling, testing of the components, and, of course, the construction of the whole project.
2. *Electronic Engineer (ElecEng)* who was responsible for the electrical and electronic circuits of the mechatronic system, and the human-device/PC-device communication. This member relate to the sensors, circuitry, and communications of the system.

3. *Computer Engineer (CompEng)* who was responsible for the design and development of the software running within the mC and, by extension, was responsible for the control of the mechatronic system, e.g., controlling the ball suspended in the air stream.

Guided by the Engineering Design Process, each team member applied the CT's dimensions to find and test solutions to the problem they had been assigned. At the same time, all team members closely collaborated, and in the end, they tested and evaluated the solution to create a unified final device. Moreover, collaboration, views, and experiences exchange between the teams was encouraged, as mentioned in the Exchange stage of the Teaching model for the Mechatronics course (§ Teaching for Mechatronics). However, the teams' deliverables had not been identical or bear significant similarities, as in this case, they were disqualified. Not to mention, the formulation of the team members was in line with the learning objectives of the Mechatronics course (§ Learning Objectives of the Mechatronics Course).

8. Didactic Team

In this context, the didactic team of the Mechatronics course was responsible for fully supporting the student teams to fulfil the Mechatronics project, thus:

- To decide on the learning outcomes of the Mechatronics course and write the scenario and the specifications of the mechatronics project assigned to the students.
- To develop the Mechatronics lectures based on the learning outcomes of the course, using STEM education principles, methodologies, and practices.
- To introduce the driving question and present the assigned project to the university students with the goal of accomplishing.
- To present and explain the Engineering Design Process as a tool for mechatronic system designing.
- To deliver all the necessary, missing Mechatronics modules and recap/refresh existing knowledge, to support students' knowledge such as Microcontroller-Based System Design, Data Collection and Analysis, Automatic Control Systems, Proportional Integral, Derivative (PID) control, Pulse Width Modulation (PWM), etc.
- To provide feedback to the student teams.
- To provide additional or extraordinary lectures or support meetings if the relevant feasibility was determined.
- To inspire, engage, and help individual students and the teams.

As mentioned above (§ Teaching for Mechatronics), the proposed teaching model utilized the CT skills in conjunction with the Teacher Guidance Protocol. The Teacher Guidance Protocol (Atmatzidou et al., 2018), which is based on the Schoenfeld model (Schoenfeld, 1992), refers to all these teachers' instructional interventions for supporting the development of the students' problem-solving skills and their metacognition. According to this:

1. The teacher has the role of the facilitator and the consultant. He/she provides support in the form of feedback, prompts, hints, etc.
2. And the students are prompted to externalize their thinking through think-aloud protocols and their reflections on how they applied their strategies.

Based on this, the didactic team fulfilled all the prerequisites of the Teacher Guidance Protocol as mentioned above in section "Teaching for Mechatronics", and an additional supportive action towards the students was the provision of an indicative technical study structure with clear writing instructions.

E. Leveraging the STEM Framework

Special mention was given to the STEM adoption for this teaching model for Mechatronics. Thus, the mechatronics project assigned to the students was based on the content of STEM disciplines, aka *Science*, *Technology*, *Engineering,* and *Mathematics*, all situated in a real-world context to interconnect these subjects and enhance student learning (Lagogiannis & Chatzopoulos, 2025; Pastrana et al., 2025).

For the *Science* discipline, the didactic team covered several fundamental Mechatronics topics useful for the students to build a solid theoretical framework for understanding how to build the mechatronics project.

For the *Technology* discipline, the didactic team provided students with hands-on use of the Arduino mC, the C/C++ programming environment, and the Tinkercad simulation software. This educational content was delivered through e-class, a Learning Management System (LMS), YouTube, and on-site lectures; therefore, it was widely accessible and more interactive, and the students had the ability to explore, experiment, and adjust their self-paced learning experience according to their needs.

The *Mathematics* discipline was seamlessly integrated into the *Science* and *Technology* disciplines, as students worked on a series of equations that they had learned in theory (*Science* discipline), that was necessary for controlling the suspended ball by controlling the fan's angular speed.

Last, the *Engineering* discipline was implemented by applying the above disciplines' knowledge to the physical mechatronic system and to its relevant model in a simulator developed in Tinkercad. This step was the most important, as the students applied their knowledge by assembling the mechatronic system's physical device and its electronic circuit, and wrote the program (code) to control it. The virtual environment of Tinkercad's simulator was more suitable for quick experiments and fast code testing, but the hands-on physical system was the realistic environment that reinforced the practical application of the engineering principles within the simulations.

Together, all these STEM disciplines formed an interdisciplinary approach to STEM education, fostering a comprehensive and experiential learning process in mechatronics system design/development, as it is depicted in Figure 10.

Figure 10. The integration of the STEM disciplines in the design and development of the mechatronic system of this research

Research Questions

The research questions (RQs) of this research are the following:

RQ1. Do university students –future engineers- use Generative Artificial Intelligence to solve the problems/tasks assigned to them? And if so, how often do they use it?
RQ2. Does the use of Artificial Intelligence benefit university students in developing their Computational Thinking, such as critical thinking, to solve complex engineering problems?

Research Context and Participants

This case study was conducted at the UNIWA during the winter semester (13 weeks, October to March) in 2024 and 2025. Participants were students attending the course "Mechatronics" in the IDPE department. A total of 188 students attended the Mechatronics course; however, only 137 (73%) participated voluntarily, since they had the option to agree or disagree with their participation. Of the 137 participants, 97 (70.8%) were male, 38 (27.7%) were female, and 2 (1.5%) stated another gender, percentages that are similar to the gender distribution of the department (Table 1). Note, as an engineering department, the IDPE is more preferred by males than by females, so it can be assumed that gender balance was achieved in the sample.

All these students attended the Mechatronics course according to the proposed teaching model (§ Teaching for Mechatronics), and to fulfil the course's learning objectives (§ Learning Objectives of the Mechatronics Course). For this purpose, they formed groups (§ Students Teams), undertook the mechatronics project (§ The Mechatronics Project), and were supported by the didactic team (§ Didactic Team). Finally, after being evaluated (§ Evaluation) for their deliverables (§ Deliverables), they were asked to voluntarily answer the following questionnaire (§ Instrumental Development) regarding the use of the AI tools.

Table 1. Frequencies of participants' gender

1. Gender	Counts	% of Total	Cumulative %
Female	38	27.7%	27.7%
Male	97	70.8%	98.5%
Other	2	1.5%	100.0%

Instrument Development

A questionnaire (§ Appendix I) with 24 items was used to answer the RQs of this research. It included both closed-ended and open-ended questions. Many of the closed-ended questions used a Likert scale to quantify the students' responses, while the open-ended descriptive questions were designed to elicit the students' opinions and feelings about the AI subject.

The research questionnaire – instrument (Table 2) consisted of five parts: i) the demographic data (gender, age, professional status, educational status, etc.), ii) questions about the use of AI by the students related to RQ1, iii) questions about the impact on learning related to RQ2, iv) ethical issues, and v) suggestions and feedback.

Most of the items were measured with a 5-point Likert scale from 1 to 5, and others were measured with a 3-point scale. E.g.

The items Q8.1 – Q8.11, Q10 (Table 2) were measured with a 5-point Likert scale from 1 to 5, where: 1 was "Not at all - I don't know", 2 was "A little", 3 was "Moderate", 4 was "Quite a lot", and 5 was "A lot".

The item Q10 was measured with a 5-point Likert scale from 1 to 5, where 1 was "Not at all", 2 was "A little", 3 was "Moderate", 4 was "Very often", and 5 was "Too much".

Respectively, the items Q19.1 – Q19.6 were measured with a 5-point scale with more relevant answers to the questions: 1- "No – Never", 2- "Rarely", 3- "Sometimes", 4 - "Often", and 5- "Yes –Always".

The items Q14, Q15, Q1, and 8 were measured with a 3-point scale where 1 was "Never", 2 was "Sometimes", and 3 was "Yes", and other items (e.g., Q12, Q16) had a slightly different scale whose answers were more relevant to their questions.

At the end of the Mechatronics course, the students who participated and completed the semester mechatronic project were asked voluntarily to fill out the questionnaire, after completing all the project's deliverables during the 13 weeks.

The full research instrument is listed in Appendix I.

Table 2. The research's instrumental items

Item	Type	Related to
Q1. Gender	Closed-ended	Demographics
Q2. Age	Closed-ended	Demographics
Q3. Which university do you attend?	Closed-ended	Demographics

continued on following page

Table 2. Continued

Item	Type	Related to
Q4. What department are you studying in?	Closed-ended	Demographics
Q5. What academic year are you in?	Closed-ended	Demographics
Q6. Professional status	Closed-ended	Demographics
Q7. If you work, fill in how many hours you work per week.	Open-ended	Demographics
Q8. Which of the following Artificial Intelligence (AI) applications do you use? Select the frequency of use.	Closed-ended	RQ1
Q8.1 ChatGPT	Likert scale	RQ1
Q8.2 DeepSeek	Likert scale	RQ1
Q8.3 Gemini	Likert scale	RQ1
Q8.4 Claude AI	Likert scale	RQ1
Q8.5 Copilot	Likert scale	RQ1
Q8.6 Perplexity AI	Likert scale	RQ1
Q8.7 Meta AI	Likert scale	RQ1
Q8.8 MidJourney	Likert scale	RQ1
Q8.9 DALL·E 3	Likert scale	RQ1
Q8.10 Cursor	Likert scale	RQ1
Q8.11 Sora	Likert scale	RQ1
Q9. What other AI applications not listed above do you use?	Open-ended	RQ1
Q10. How often do you generally use Artificial Intelligence (AI) applications in your daily life?	Likert scale	RQ1
Q11. Why do you use Artificial Intelligence (AI) applications?	Closed-ended	RQ1
Q12. How often do you use Artificial Intelligence (AI) applications when writing your academic papers?	Likert scale	RQ1
Q13. Why do you use Artificial Intelligence (AI) applications when writing your papers?	Closed-ended	RQ1

continued on following page

Table 2. Continued

Item	Type	Related to
Q14. Do you check the answers/results produced by Artificial Intelligence (AI) applications before using them?	Closed-ended	RQ1
Q15. Do you usually edit or improve the responses generated by AI applications before using them?	Closed-ended	RQ1
Q16. Do you think that using Artificial Intelligence (AI) applications helps you understand the subject?	Closed-ended	RQ2
Q17. How do you use Artificial Intelligence (AI) applications when preparing for exams?	Closed-ended	RQ2
Q18. Do you think that using Artificial Intelligence (AI) applications helps you develop your critical thinking skills for problem solving (e.g., in your academic work)?	Closed-ended	RQ2
Q19. Do you think that using Artificial Intelligence (AI) applications helps you with the following?	Closed-ended	RQ2
Q19.1. Developing your critical thinking skills for problem solving (e.g., in your academic work)	Likert scale	RQ2
Q19.2. When faced with a problem, identifying the individual steps required to solve it	Likert scale	RQ2
Q19.3. Identifying similarities or patterns in problems you have solved in the past	Likert scale	RQ2
Q19.4. Plan a series of clear and precise steps to solve a problem	Likert scale	RQ2
Q19.5. Be able to ignore details that are not important and focus on the key elements of a problem	Likert scale	RQ2
Q19.6. In a proposed solution, be able to recognize and correct errors and optimize it	Likert scale	RQ2
Q20. Do you consider the use of Artificial Intelligence (AI) applications to complete your academic work to be ethical?	Closed-ended	General Info
Q21. Have you previously submitted an assignment or exam answer that was created mainly or entirely using Artificial Intelligence (AI) applications?	Closed-ended	General Info
Q22. Has a teacher discussed with you the guidelines for using Artificial Intelligence (AI) applications?	Closed-ended	General Info
Q23. Do you believe that teachers should incorporate the use of Artificial Intelligence (AI) applications into the learning process?	Closed-ended	General Info
Q24. Explain why you answered Yes or No to the question "Should teachers incorporate the use of Artificial Intelligence (AI) applications into the learning process?"	Open-ended	General Info

Data Collection & Analysis

The collection of the research data was limited to quantitative data that was collected online via an online electronic questionnaire form. Participants were informed via this form (questionnaire), where they had to give their consent to continue completing it. The questionnaire had been completed using the Microsoft Forms application, which is in accordance with European Law and the GDPR regulation of the European Union. The questionnaire allowed for anonymous completion; therefore, it did not collect personal information from participants. The researcher did not have access to the IP addresses of participants, and the answers that participants gave to the questionnaires were not visible to other users.

The open-source, free Jamovi ver. 2.6.26.0 SPSS21 statistical software was used for statistical analysis (Jamovi, 2021). The personal data recorded in this study were the age range and gender of the participants in order to ensure their anonymity throughout the research when publishing the results in conferences, scientific journals, etc. Moreover, some variables were coded to increase anonymity.

Limitations

In this pilot case study, several limitations were identified:

First, not all students (137 people participated, out of a total of 188) who attended the Mechatronics course participated in the research. Although there was the possibility that the teaching team could force them to participate, e.g., in the context of completing their deliverables, this option was rejected because there was the possibility of random and/or false answers from the students. The researcher's goal was for the students' answers to the questionnaires to be as honest as possible; for this reason, their voluntary participation was chosen. However, the sample is considered satisfactory.

Second, in the sample, the genders are not represented at the same rate (70.8% male, 27.7% female, 1.5% other). Although in general this sample could be a problem, it is not the case in the present research, which focuses on the subset of the students studying Industrial Design and Production engineering, where the representation of the sample coincides very much with the corresponding distribution of students attending the department.

Third, the research was conducted only in the specific Mechatronics course. It would have more value if it could include all the courses of the IDPE. However, not all the courses are suitable for applying the proposed teaching model (§ Teaching for Mechatronics), as the interdisciplinary nature of Mechatronics is more suitable for applying STEM, CT, and PBL.

Fourth, the control group of the research was absent, since this was a pilot study to evaluate the students' perspectives about the usage of AI tools, their benefits with respect to CT, and their impact on them.

Fifth, the results of the RQ2, that is, if the use of Artificial Intelligence benefits the students in developing their CT, were produced from the students' perspectives and not by a validated tool like Weese's for testing CT (Weese, 2017), but in this case, a control group would be needed, as discussed above in the fourth limitation.

Research Ethics

This case study was approved by UNIWA's Research Ethics Committee, and it was conducted in accordance with the rules of the Helsinki Declaration. Moreover, the data collected from the case study is handled and stored according to the Data Protection Law.

3. RESULTS

In this section, the results of the research on the use of AI tools by the students and their impact on their CT are thoroughly presented. In addition, it presents how students have used AI. Specifically, whether they have used it to easily and quickly write their assignments without delving into the results of their queries, and without trying to understand the generated text of the assignment. Or, whether they have used it as a source of inspiration, to better understand a problem, to obtain some basic guidelines, and proceed to solve the tasks on their own.

This research is the beginning of a series of studies; therefore, at this stage it does not seek to discover any correlations between its variables, which is why it was chosen to analyze the collected data using mostly descriptive statistics to explore the students' means.

A. Demographic profile

Participants were students attending the Mechatronics course in the IDPE department at the Uniwa during the winter semester in 2024 and 2025. A total of 188 students attended the Mechatronics course; however, only 137 (73%) participated voluntarily, since they had the option to agree or disagree with their participation. Of the 137 participants, 97 (70.8%) were male, 38 (27.7%) were female, and 2 (1.5%) stated another gender, percentages that are similar to the gender distribution of the department. Gender balance was achieved in the sample, since the IDPE, as an engineering department, has a similar student gender balance who attend.

Participants aged from less than 21 to 64 years old, with the majority of them (92%) in the age range between ≤21 and 34 (Table 3).

Table 3. Frequencies of participants' age.

2. Age	Counts	% of Total	Cumulative %
less or equal to 21	51	37.2%	37.2%
22-34	75	54.7%	92.0%
35-44	7	5.1%	97.1%
45-54	1	0.7%	97.8%
55-64	3	2.2%	100.0%

Regarding the professional status of the participants, the percentages, 58.4% are working (Employed, 58.4%) and 41.6% not working (Unemployed, 41.6%); therefore, the percentage of Employed is higher (Table 4).

Table 4. Frequencies of participants' professional status

6. Professional status	Counts	% of Total	Cumulative %
Employed	80	58.4%	58.4%
Unemployed	57	41.6%	100.0%

What is of particular interest, however, and may further explain the use of AI tools by students, is the weekly total hours worked by students. While there is a wide distribution (from 12 to 84 hours per week), the largest number of responses (21 counts, 26.9%) indicate 40 hours per week, which is practically equivalent to a full-time job rather than a part-time job.

It is observed that 45% of working students work 40 or more hours per week, while 64.3% of them work 30 (about 6 hours/day) or more (Table 5, Figure 11). This observation is particularly important as the duration of work significantly limits the available time of students for their studies, and it could justify the use of AI as a time-saving tool. For this purpose, the chi-squared test of association, or test for independence, was used below to measure this.

Table 5. Frequencies of participants' working hours per week status

7. If you work, fill in how many hours you work per week.	Counts	% of Total	Cumulative %
12	1	1.3%	1.3%
15	1	1.3%	2.6%
16-24	1	1.3%	3.8%
18	2	2.6%	6.4%

continued on following page

Table 5. Continued

7. If you work, fill in how many hours you work per week.	Counts	% of Total	Cumulative %
19	1	1.3%	7.7%
20	6	7.7%	15.4%
20-30	2	2.6%	17.9%
21	1	1.3%	19.2%
24	5	6.4%	25.6%
25	3	3.8%	29.5%
25-35	1	1.3%	30.8%
26	1	1.3%	32.1%
30	6	7.7%	39.7%
32	4	5.1%	44.9%
32-35	2	2.6%	47.4%
35	1	1.3%	48.7%
36	2	2.6%	51.3%
40	21	26.9%	78.2%
40-44	1	1.3%	79.5%
42	2	2.6%	82.1%
45	3	3.8%	85.9%
46	1	1.3%	87.2%
48	1	1.3%	88.5%
50	2	2.6%	91.0%
6	1	1.3%	92.3%
60-70	1	1.3%	93.6%
8	3	3.8%	97.4%
80	1	1.3%	98.7%
84	1	1.3%	100.0%

Figure 11. The Pareto chart of the students' weekly working hours

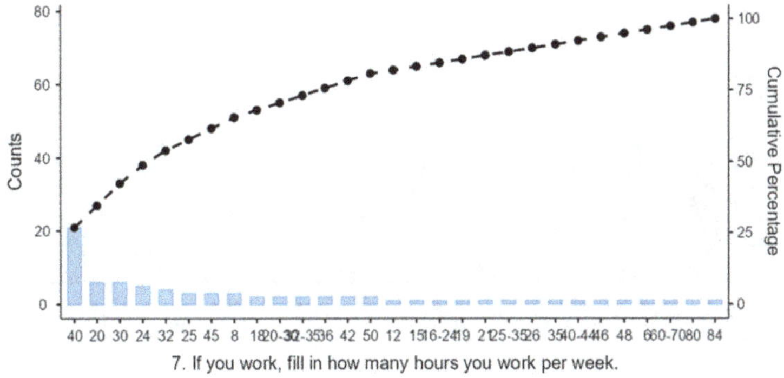

B. Participants' use of AI tools

The first question (RQ1) of the survey that needs to be answered is whether students use AI tools to solve their assignments. To measure this, the multiple responses of the research items Q8.1 – Q8.11 were converted to Yes/No, where the responses "A little, Moderate, Quite a lot, and A lot" were assigned to Yes and the rest (Not at all - I don't know) to No. The results of the survey were extremely enlightening (Figure 12)!

Almost all students (Table 6) use or have used AI tools, especially ChatGPT (Yes: 96.4%, *n* = 132; No: 3.6%, *n* = 5). The next most popular AI tool was Copilot (Yes: 46.7%, *n* = 64; No: 53.3%, *n* = 73), followed by Gemini (Yes: 43.1%, *n* = 59; No: 56.9%, *n* = 78), and DeepSeek (Yes: 40.1%, *n* = 55; No: 59.9%, *n* = 82).

In contrast, the least popular tools were Cursor (Yes: 8.0%, *n* = 11; No: 92.0%, *n* = 126), Sora (Yes: 10.2%, *n* = 14; No: 89.8%, *n* = 123), Claude AI (Yes: 10.9%, *n* = 15; No: 89.1%, *n* = 122), and Perplexity AI (Yes: 12.4%, *n* = 17; No: 87.6%, *n* = 120).

Figure 12. Frequencies of the research's AI tools

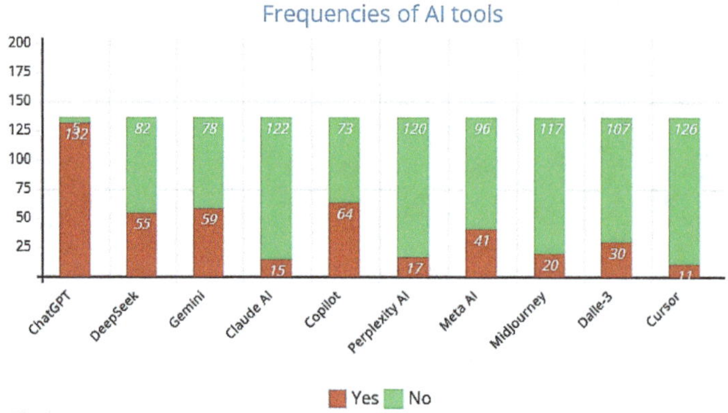

Table 6. Frequencies (Yes/No) of participants' use of AI tools (ChatGPT, DeepSeek, Gemini, Claude AI, Copilot, Perplexity AI, Meta AI, MidJourney, DALL·E 3, Cursor, Sora

Q8.1 ChatGPT	**Counts**	**% of Total**	**Cumulative %**
Yes	132	96.4%	96.4%
No	5	3.6%	100.0%
Q8.2 DeepSeek	**Counts**	**% of Total**	**Cumulative %**
Yes	55	40.1%	40.1%
No	82	59.9%	100.0%
Q8.3 Gemini	**Counts**	**% of Total**	**Cumulative %**
Yes	59	43.1%	43.1%
No	78	56.9%	100.0%
Q8.4 Claude AI	**Counts**	**% of Total**	**Cumulative %**
Yes	15	10.9%	10.9%
No	122	89.1%	100.0%
Q8.5 Copilot	**Counts**	**% of Total**	**Cumulative %**
Yes	64	46.7%	46.7%
No	73	53.3%	100.0%
Q8.6 Perplexity AI	**Counts**	**% of Total**	**Cumulative %**
Yes	17	12.4%	12.4%
No	120	87.6%	100.0%
Q8.7 Meta AI	**Counts**	**% of Total**	**Cumulative %**

continued on following page

Table 6. Continued

Yes	41	29.9%	29.9%
No	96	70.1%	100.0%
Q8.8 MidJourney	**Counts**	**% of Total**	**Cumulative %**
Yes	20	14.6%	14.6%
No	117	85.4%	100.0%
Q8.9 DALL·E 3	**Counts**	**% of Total**	**Cumulative %**
Yes	30	21.9%	21.9%
No	107	78.1%	100.0%
Q8.10 Cursor	**Counts**	**% of Total**	**Cumulative %**
Yes	11	8.0%	8.0%
No	126	92.0%	100.0%
Q8.11 Sora - Yes/No	**Counts**	**% of Total**	**Cumulative %**
Yes	14	10.2%	10.2%
No	123	89.8%	100.0%

This can be explained by looking at the corresponding lines "Not at all – I don't know" in Table 7, where the frequencies of the multiple responses of the AI tools are recorded.

The least popular AI tools, Cursor, Sora, Claude AI, Perplexity AI, etc., are those that students do not know about, and according to Table 7, first is Cursor (91.5%, *n* = 119), followed by, Sora (89.2%, *n* = 116), Perplexity AI (87.0%, *n* = 114), and Claude AI (85.5%, *n* = 116), which are in full correspondence with their usage rate.

Table 7. Frequencies (multiple responses) of participants' use of AI tools (ChatGPT, DeepSeek, Gemini, Claude AI, Copilot, Perplexity AI, Meta AI, MidJourney, DALL·E 3, Cursor, Sora).

8.1 ChatGPT	**Counts**	**% of Total**	**Cumulative %**
Not at all - I don't know	4	2.9%	2.9%
A little	20	14.7%	17.6%
Moderate	32	23.5%	41.2%
Quite a lot	48	35.3%	76.5%
A lot	32	23.5%	100.0%
8.2 DeepSeek	**Counts**	**% of Total**	**Cumulative %**
A little	32	24.4%	24.4%

continued on following page

Table 7. Continued

A lot	2	1.5%	26.0%
Moderate	11	8.4%	34.4%
Not at all - I don't know	76	58.0%	92.4%
Quite a lot	10	7.6%	100.0%
8.3 Gemini	**Counts**	**% of Total**	**Cumulative %**
A little	35	26.7%	26.7%
A lot	4	3.1%	29.8%
Moderate	14	10.7%	40.5%
Not at all - I don't know	72	55.0%	95.4%
Quite a lot	6	4.6%	100.0%
8.4 Claude AI	**Counts**	**% of Total**	**Cumulative %**
A little	10	7.6%	7.6%
A lot	1	0.8%	8.4%
Moderate	3	2.3%	10.7%
Not at all - I don't know	116	88.5%	99.2%
Quite a lot	1	0.8%	100.0%
8.5 Copilot	**Counts**	**% of Total**	**Cumulative %**
A little	35	26.3%	26.3%
A lot	4	3.0%	29.3%
Moderate	18	13.5%	42.9%
Not at all - I don't know	69	51.9%	94.7%
Quite a lot	7	5.3%	100.0%
8.6 Perplexity AI	**Counts**	**% of Total**	**Cumulative %**
A little	10	7.6%	7.6%
Moderate	6	4.6%	12.2%
Not at all - I don't know	114	87.0%	99.2%
Quite a lot	1	0.8%	100.0%
8.7 Meta AI	**Counts**	**% of Total**	**Cumulative %**
A little	31	23.8%	23.8%
Moderate	9	6.9%	30.8%
Not at all - I don't know	89	68.5%	99.2%
Quite a lot	1	0.8%	100.0%
8.8 MidJourney	**Counts**	**% of Total**	**Cumulative %**
A little	16	12.5%	12.5%
A lot	1	0.8%	13.3%

continued on following page

Table 7. Continued

Moderate	2	1.6%	14.8%
Not at all - I don't know	108	84.4%	99.2%
Quite a lot	1	0.8%	100.0%
8.9 DALL·E 3	**Counts**	**% of Total**	**Cumulative %**
A little	15	11.4%	11.4%
A lot	3	2.3%	13.6%
Moderate	8	6.1%	19.7%
Not at all - I don't know	102	77.3%	97.0%
Quite a lot	4	3.0%	100.0%
8.10 Cursor	**Counts**	**% of Total**	**Cumulative %**
A little	8	6.2%	6.2%
A lot	2	1.5%	7.7%
Moderate	1	0.8%	8.5%
Not at all - I don't know	119	91.5%	100.0%
8.11 Sora	**Counts**	**% of Total**	**Cumulative %**
A little	11	8.5%	8.5%
A lot	1	0.8%	9.2%
Moderate	1	0.8%	10.0%
Not at all - I don't know	116	89.2%	99.2%
Quite a lot	1	0.8%	100.0%

Next, a chi-square test of association (or test for independence) was performed to determine if there is a statistically significant relationship between the professional status of the students and the use of ChatGPT (Q8.1). ChatGPT was selected as the pilot AI tool since most of the students use it.

To perform the chi-square test, the four assumptions below had been met (Lund & Lund, 2025):

1. two variables measured at the categorical level,
2. independence of observations,
3. used cross-sectional sampling (also known as naturalistic sampling) when collecting the data, and,
4. all cells should have expected counts greater than or equal to five.

The chi-square test revealed that there was no statistically significant relationship (Table 8). Frequencies between Professional Status (Employed, Unemployed) and the use of ChatGPT by the students, $x^2(4) = 1.26$, $p = 0.869$, Cramer's V 0.096.

This is also visually confirmed in the graph Figure 13, where similar statistical data on ChatGPT usage are observed by student groups, employed, and non-employed.

Table 8a. Contingency tables and x^2 test

	8.1 ChatGPT					
6. Professional status	**Not at all - I don't know**	**A little**	**Moderate**	**Quite a lot**	**A lot**	**Total**
Employed	2	11	17	28	21	79
Unemployed	2	9	15	20	11	57
Total	4	20	32	48	32	136

Table 8b.

χ^2 Tests			
	Value	df	p
χ^2	1.26	4	0.869
N	136		

Table 8c.

Nominal	
	Value
Phi-coefficient	NaN
Cramer's V	0.0962

Figure 13. The use of ChatGPT by employed and non-employed students

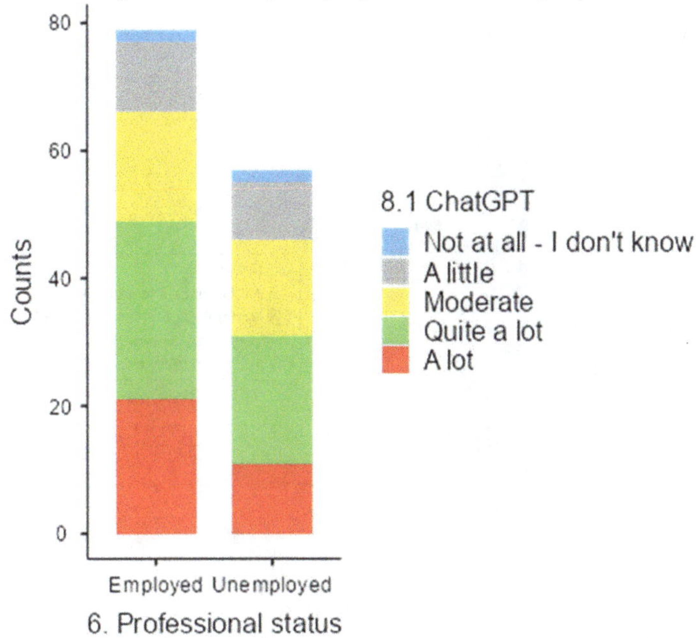

The research item Q9 ("What other AI applications not listed above do you use?") revealed that students also use other AI tools, including Ollama-3, Grok, Mistral AI (Le Chat), Sesame, and Canva.

Regarding the frequency of use of AI tools in students' everyday lives (research item Q10), the research indicates (Table 9) that the AI application use is very common to the students, with over half of them (54.0%) using them at least moderately (a few times a month), and a combined 46.0% reporting daily, weekly, or very frequent use (Figure 14).

Table 9. Frequencies of how often the student use the AI tools in their daily life

10. How often do you generally use Artificial Intelligence (AI) applications in your daily life?	**Counts**	**% of Total**	**Cumulative %**
Not at all	4	2.9%	2.9%
A little (once a month or less)	23	16.8%	19.7%
Moderate (a few times a month)	47	34.3%	54.0%
Very often (several times a week)	34	24.8%	78.8%
Too much (daily or almost daily)	29	21.2%	100.0%

Figure 14. Frequencies of AI use

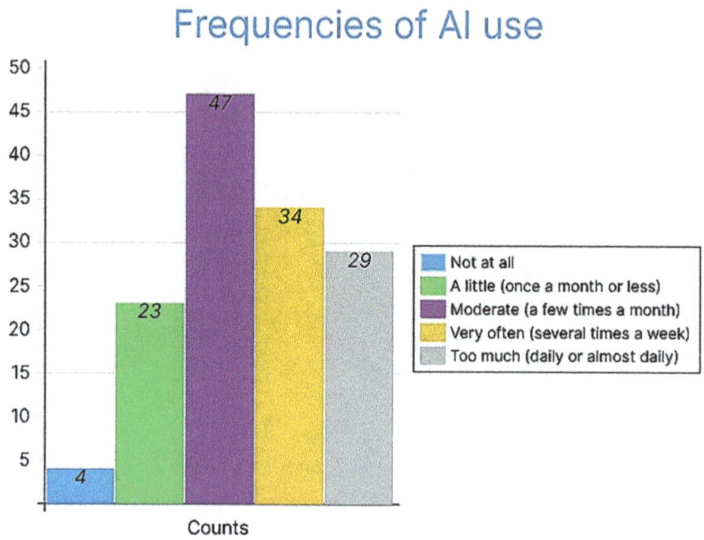

Similar results were also revealed by the question (research item Q12) on how often the students use the AI tools to write their academic papers, with about half of them (46.7%) using them moderately, and a combined 27.0% reporting very often and extremely often use. Frequencies of this item are shown in Table 10, and a relative graph is depicted in Figure 15. So, the vast majority (91.9%) of the students have already used the AI to write their academic papers even once, while 73.7% use them frequently.

Table 10. Frequencies of how often the students use the AI tools when writing their academic papers

12. How often do you use Artificial Intelligence (AI) applications when writing your academic papers?	**Counts**	**% of Total**	**Cumulative %**
Not at all - I have never used AI in writing papers	11	8.0%	8.0%
A little - I have used AI only once	25	18.2%	26.3%
Moderately - I have used AI a few times (less than 10)	64	46.7%	73.0%
Very often - I use AI very often in my papers	31	22.6%	95.6%
Extremely often - I always use AI in my papers	6	4.4%	100.0%

Figure 15. Frequencies of AI use in writing an academic paper

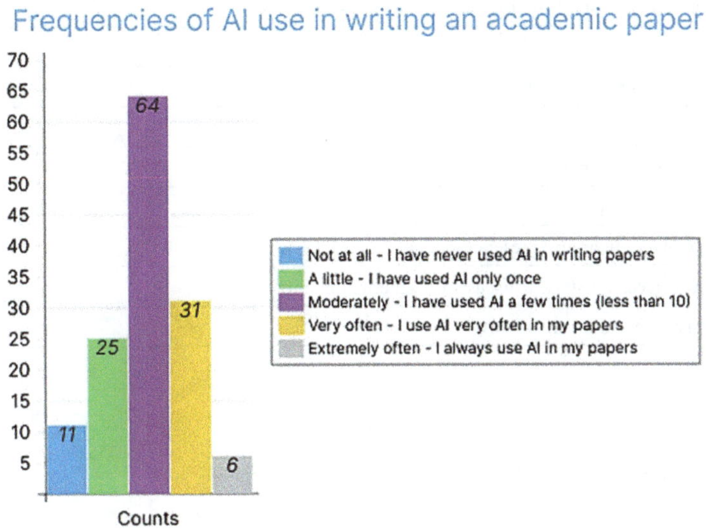

Regarding why the students use AI tools (research item Q11), in this case study, it is clear (Table 11) that students utilize AI tools primarily to facilitate their searches (Q11.A1 *n* = 110). Then they use it to explain and understand difficult concepts in simple terms (Q11.B1 *n* = 73). The third and fourth most popular uses of AI tools by students are code programming (Q11.A3 *n* = 72) and help with the academic work (Q11.B2 *n* = 62), which can be easily explained since this research was implemented in the context of a Mechatronics project assignment to be completed by the students. All uses of the AI tools by the students, with their counts, are depicted in Figure 16.

Table 11. Reasons why students use AI tools

11. Why do you use Artificial Intelligence (AI) applications?	**Counts**
A. Task automation and productivity	50
A1. Information search	110
A2. Text writing	43
A3. Programming (code assistance, algorithm explanation, code debugging)	72
B. Education and learning	59
B1. Explaining and understanding difficult concepts in simple terms	73
B2. Help with academic work (writing papers, generating ideas and inspiration, gathering study material)	62

continued on following page

Table 11. Continued

11. Why do you use Artificial Intelligence (AI) applications?	Counts
B3. Exam preparation	52
B4. Language assistance (conversation practice, translation, grammar)	30
C. Creativity	40
C1. Creating or editing images	42
C2. Creating or editing videos	15
C3. Creating graphics, diagrams, presentations	20
D. Entertainment (ideas for stories, discussions, entertaining responses)	40
E. Personal assistance and organization	53

Figure 16. Reasons why students use AI tools

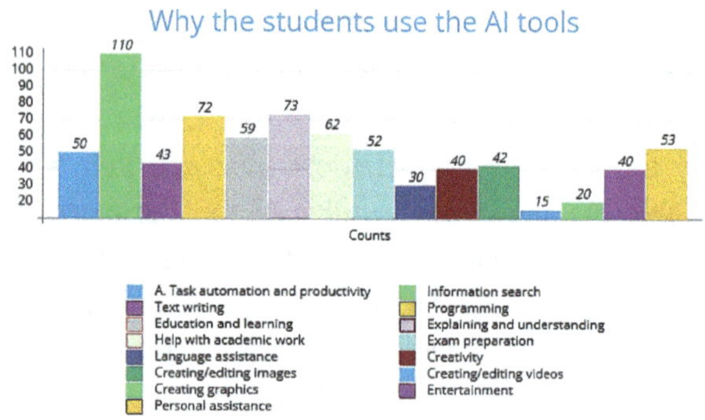

Similar results (Table 12) were obtained from the research item Q13. Why do you use Artificial Intelligence (AI) applications when writing your papers? Students seem to use AI tools mostly to explain and understand difficult concepts (Q13.1 *n* = 86), to facilitate their searches (Q13.7 *n* = 71), for programming and writing code (Q13.3 *n* = 65), to gather study material (Q13.5 *n* = 58), to solve problems (Q13.2 *n* = 48), and to generate/test ideas & inspiration (Q13.4 *n* = 47). All uses of the AI tools by the students when writing their papers, and the counts, are depicted in Figure 17.

Table 12. Reasons why students use AI tools in their assignments

13. Why do you use Artificial Intelligence (AI) applications when writing your papers?	Counts
13.1. To explain and understand difficult concepts	86
13.2. To solve problems, e.g., in mathematics, physics, engineering, etc.	48
13.3. Programming and code writing	65
13.4. Generating and testing ideas, inspiration	47
13.5. Gathering study material	58
13.6. Writing papers	25
13.7. Searching for sources and bibliography	71
13.8. Creating or editing images	20
13.9. Creating or editing videos	7
13.10. Creating graphics, diagrams, presentations	14
13.11. Other	2

Figure 17. Reasons why students use AI tools in their assignments

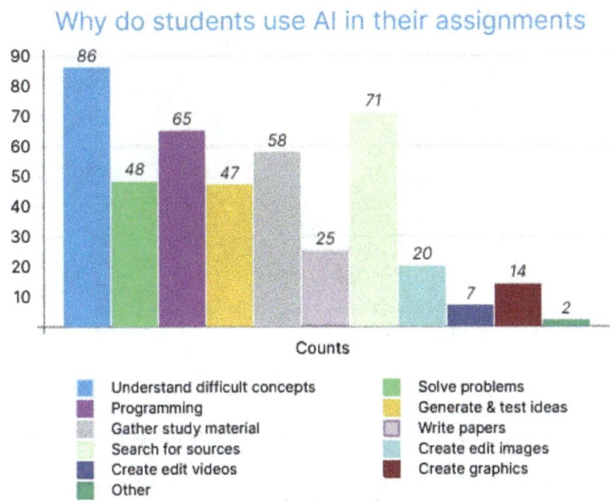

The next critical question related to the reliability of the AI tools is whether students check the answers/results produced by Artificial Intelligence (AI) applications before using them. This is answered by the data of the research item Q14, "Do you check the answers/results produced by Artificial Intelligence (AI) applications before using them?".

The results (Table 13) showed that the vast majority of the students (99.3%, *n* = 134) maintain a responsible attitude and check the results produced, some of whom (68.2%, *n* = 92) always check them. Only a small minority (0.7%, *n* = 1) do not check them at all, as depicted in Figure 18.

Table 13. Frequencies of the Q14. Do you check the answers/results produced by Artificial Intelligence (AI) applications before using them?

	Counts	% of Total	Cumulative %
Never. I use them as they are	1	0.7%	0.7%
Sometimes	42	31.1%	31.9%
Yes, I always check them	92	68.2%	100.0%

Figure 18. Do the students check AI's answers?

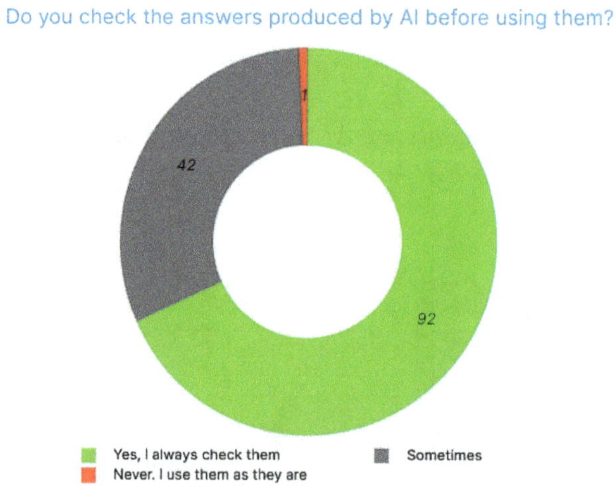

Consequently, the data in Table 14 of the research item Q15, "Do you usually edit or improve the responses generated by AI applications before using them?", showed that the majority of the students (63.0%, *n* = 85) always modify the responses generated by the AI tools. A minority (36.3%, *n* = 49) sometimes modify them, depending on whether they think they need improvement, and only a very small minority (0.7%, *n* = 1) use the AI responses as they are (Figure 19).

Table 14. Frequencies of the Q15. Do you usually edit or improve the responses generated by AI applications before using them?

	Counts	% of Total	Cumulative %
Not at all. I use them as is.	1	0.7%	0.7%
Sometimes, if I think they need correction improvement, I edit them	49	36.3%	37.0%
Yes, I always modify the responses generated by AI applications	85	63.0%	100.0%

Figure 19. Do the students edit or improve the AI's answers?

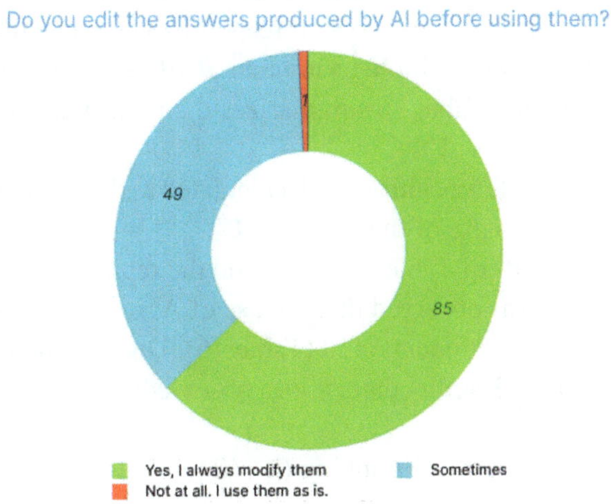

C. Developing participants' CT skills

The next research question to be answered is the impact of AI tools on student learning, and the conclusion on whether the use of Artificial Intelligence tools benefits students in developing their Computational Learning. For this purpose, the research questions Q19.1 – Q19.6 were formed in a way to represent the CT's skills. Specifically:

1. The Q19.1 represents critical thinking.
2. The Q19.2 represents the decomposition or segmentation, i.e., the ability to break a complex problem into smaller, manageable parts.
3. The Q19.3 represents the pattern recognition or generalization, i.e., the ability to recognize known tasks or patterns.

4. The Q19.4 represents the algorithmic thinking, i.e., the ability to create an ordered series of steps to solve a problem.
5. The Q19.5 represents the abstraction, i.e., the ability to focus on the essentials of a problem and remove its unimportant details.
6. The Q19.6 represents the debugging, i.e., the ability to find and improve the errors of the proposed solution.

These research items, were based on the students' perspectives, and used a Likert scale, converted to numerical values ranging from 1 to 5 (Krosnick & Presser, 2010), according to the following range of the scale: 1 for "No – Never", 2 for "Rarely", 3 for "Sometimes", 4 for "Often", and 5 for "Yes –Always".

In this way, the closed-ended students' responses were quantified to calculate their Mean, Median, and Mode. Table 15 summarizes the descriptives of the research items Q19.1 – Q19,6, and Table 16 summarizes their calculated central tendency and dispersion.

A new field, named CT, was introduced, calculated as the mean of these research items, to give an overall sense of the students' CT.

By studying the results of Tables 15 & 16 and the representative Figures 20-25 of the research data, it was observed that the use of AI tools has a neutral effect ($\bar{x}$ = 3.08, SD = 0.91) on the students' CT (Table 16). Digging more into the Q19.1 –Q19.6 -the individual CT skills- data, it was observed:

1. There is no effect on critical thinking ($\bar{x}$ = 2.99, SD = 1.12) on the students' CT,
2. There is no effect on decomposition or segmentation ($\bar{x}$ = 3.25, SD = 1.17).
3. There is no effect on pattern recognition or generalization ($\bar{x}$ = 2.74, SD = 1.18).
4. There is no effect on algorithmic thinking ($\bar{x}$ = 3.27, SD = 1.21).
5. There is no effect on the abstraction ($\bar{x}$ = 2.94, SD = 1.19).
6. There is no effect on the debugging ($\bar{x}$ = 3.32, SD = 1.09).

Table 15. Descriptives of the research items Q19.1 – Q19.6

	Counts	% of Total	Cumulative %
19.1 Developing your critical thinking skills for problem solving (e.g., in your academic work)			
No - Never	16	11.8%	11.8%
Often	38	27.9%	39.7%
Rarely	28	20.6%	60.3%

continued on following page

Table 15. Continued

	Counts	% of Total	Cumulative %
Sometimes	44	32.4%	92.6%
Yes -Always	10	7.4%	100.0%
19.2. When faced with a problem, identifying the individual steps required to solve it			
No - Never	15	11.0%	11.0%
Often	35	25.7%	36.8%
Rarely	13	9.6%	46.3%
Sometimes	52	38.2%	84.6%
Yes -Always	21	15.4%	100.0%
19.3. Identifying similarities or patterns in problems you have solved in the past			
No - Never	23	16.9%	16.9%
Often	30	22.1%	39.0%
Rarely	38	27.9%	66.9%
Sometimes	36	26.5%	93.4%
Yes -Always	9	6.6%	100.0%
19.4. Plan a series of clear and precise steps to solve a problem			
No - Never	15	11.0%	11.0%
Often	41	30.1%	41.2%
Rarely	18	13.2%	54.4%
Sometimes	40	29.4%	83.8%
Yes -Always	22	16.2%	100.0%
19.5. Be able to ignore details that are not important and focus on the key elements of a problem			
No - Never	20	14.7%	14.7%
Often	30	22.1%	36.8%
Rarely	26	19.1%	55.9%
Sometimes	46	33.8%	89.7%
Yes -Always	14	10.3%	100.0%
19.6. In a proposed solution, be able to recognize and correct errors and optimize it			
No - Never	11	8.1%	8.1%
Often	46	34.1%	42.2%
Rarely	15	11.1%	53.3%
Sometimes	46	34.1%	87.4%
Yes -Always	17	12.6%	100.0%

Table 16. Dispersion and central tendency of the transformed research items Q19.1 – Q19.6 and the CT (Computational Thinking)

	Q19.1 Developing your critical thinking skills for problem solving (e.g., in your academic work)	Q19.2. When faced with a problem, identifying the individual steps required to solve it	Q19.3. Identifying similarities or patterns in problems you have solved in the past	Q19.4. Plan a series of clear and precise steps to solve a problem	Q19.5. Be able to ignore details that are not important and focus on the key elements of a problem	Q19.6. In a proposed solution, be able to recognize and correct errors and optimize it	CT
N	136	136	136	136	136	135	135
Missing	1	1	1	1	1	2	2
Mean	2.99	3.25	2.74	3.27	2.94	3.32	3.08
Median	3.00	3.00	3.00	3.00	3.00	3.00	3.17
Mode	3.00	3.00	2.00	4.00	3.00	3.00	3.17
Standard deviation	1.12	1.17	1.18	1.21	1.19	1.09	0.910
Minimum	1	1	1	1	1	1	1.00
Maximum	5	5	5	5	5	5	5.00

More than one mode exists, only the first is reported

Figure 20. Do the students develop their critical thinking skills for problem-solving when using the AI tools?

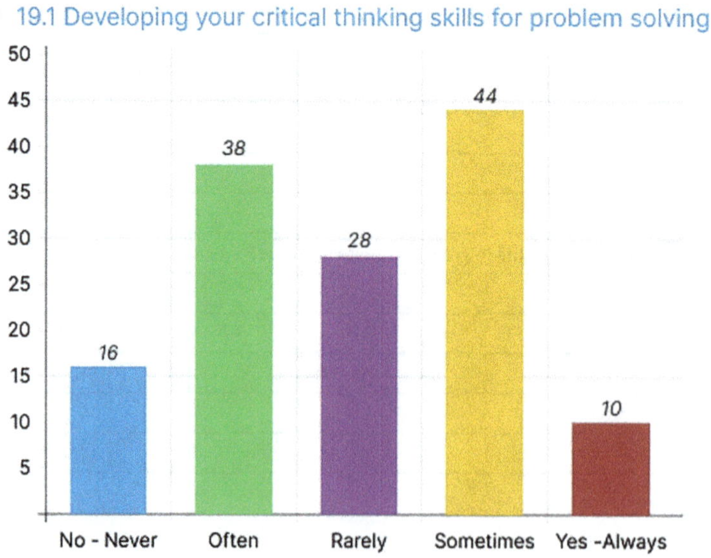

Figure 21. Do the students identify the individual steps required to solve a problem when using the AI tools?

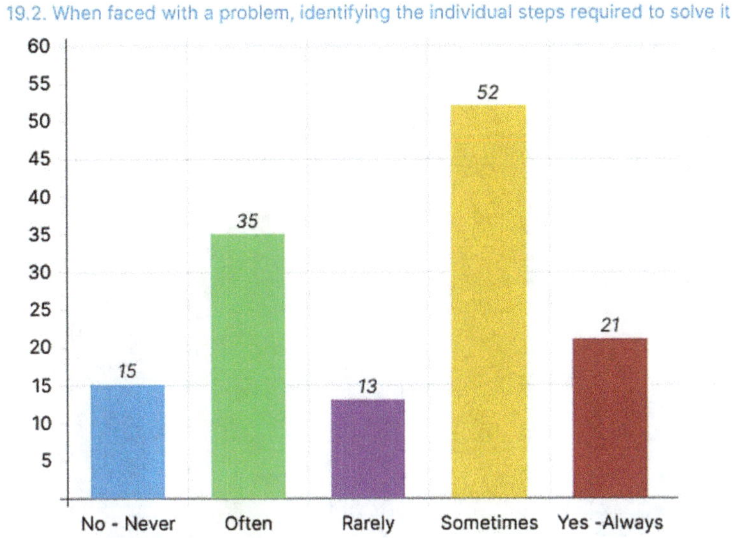

Figure 22. Do the students identify similarities or patterns in problems they have solved in the past when using the AI tools?

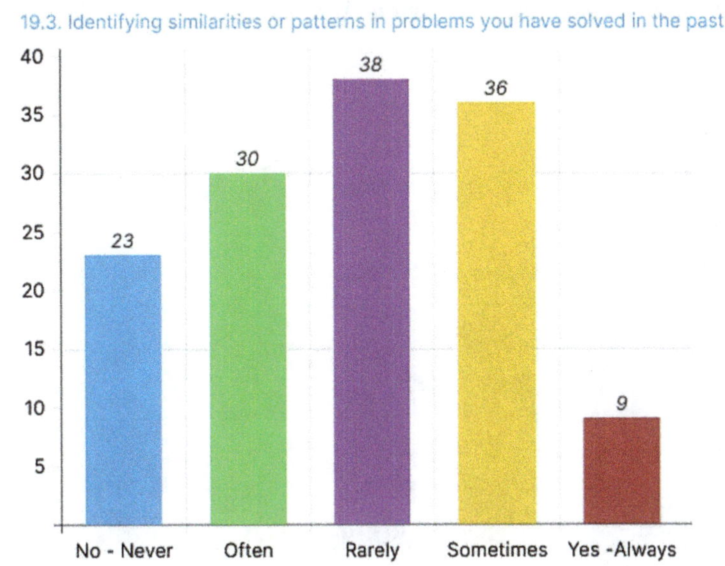

Figure 23. Do the students plan a series of clear and precise steps to solve a problem when using the AI tools?

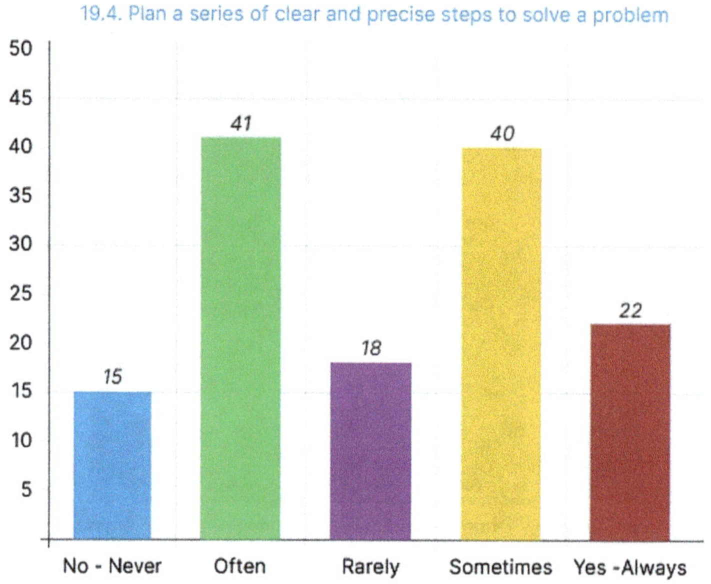

Figure 24. Are the students able to ignore non-important details and focus on the key elements of a problem when using the AI tools?

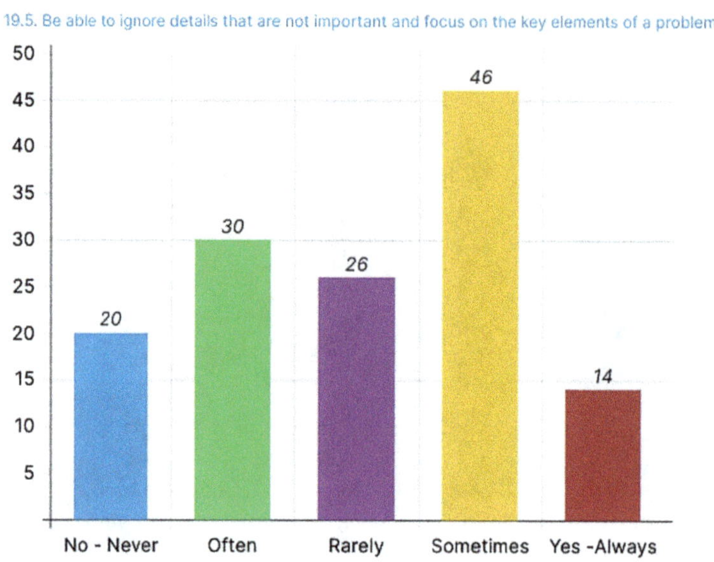

Figure 25. Are the students able to recognize and correct errors and optimize a proposed solution when using the AI tools?

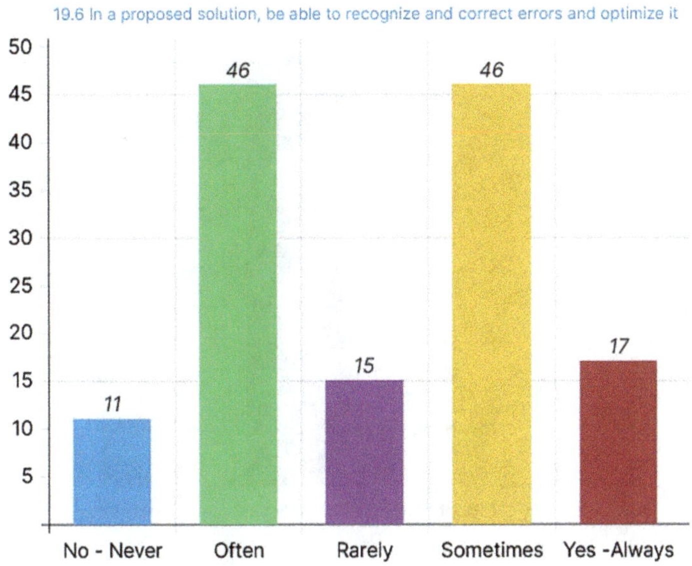

In contrast, with respect to the students' beliefs about the educational value of the AI tools, the vast majority of them (90.4%, *n* = 122) believe that using the AI tools helps them to understand a subject (Table 17, Figure 26).

This in imprinted by the research item Q16, "Do you think that using Artificial Intelligence (AI) applications helps you understand the subject?, where the students responded as following: Absolutely Yes 26.7%, *n* = 36, Probably yes 63.7%, *n* = 86, Probably not 8.9%, *n* = 12, and Absolutely not 0.7%, *n* = 1 (Table 17).

Table 17. Frequency table for the research item Q16, "Do you think that using Artificial Intelligence (AI) applications helps you understand the subject?"

16. Do you think that using Artificial Intelligence (AI) applications helps you understand the subject?	**Counts**	**% of Total**	**Cumulative %**
Absolutely Yes. Using Artificial Intelligence (AI) helps me fully understand the subject I have used it for.	36	26.7%	26.7%
Absolutely not. On the contrary, Artificial Intelligence (AI) makes me rely on it too much.	1	0.7%	27.4%
Probably not. Artificial Intelligence (AI) helps me a little in understanding the subject for which I have used it.	12	8.9%	36.3%
Probably yes. Artificial Intelligence (AI) helps me understand somewhat (or sometimes) the subject for which I have used it.	86	63.7%	100.0%

Figure 26. Students' opinions on whether the use of AI tools helps them understand a topic

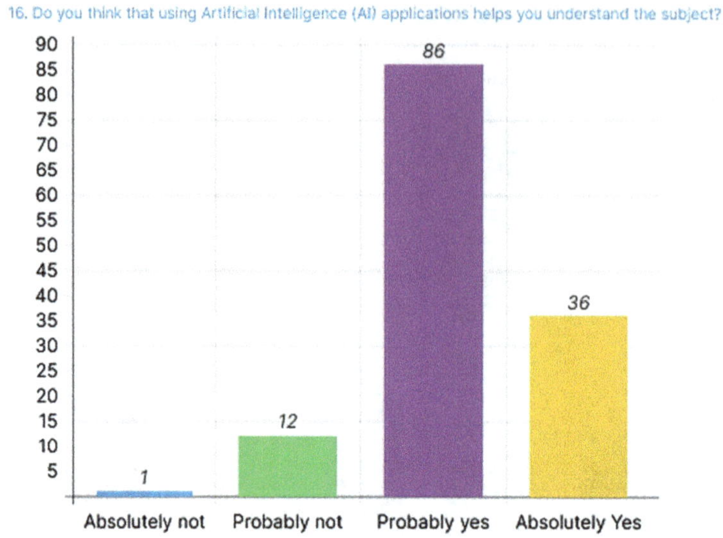

4. DISCUSSION

This pilot study investigated the use and the impact of the GenAI tools among engineering university students in a Mechatronics course, with particular focus on how these tools affect their CT skills development.

Patterns of GenAI tools usage

Initially, the results demonstrate a high adoption of the GenAI tools among the students, with ChatGPT being the dominant platform (96.4% usage rate). This finding aligns with other studies (Almassaad et al., 2024; HEPI, 2025; Malmström et al., 2023; Pavlenko & Syzenko, 2024) conducted in higher education where GenAI is used more and more by the students and mainly ChatGPT.

On the other hand, the significantly lower adoption rates of other GenAI tools, such as Perplexity AI (12.4%), Claude AI (10.9%), Sora (10.2%), and Cursor (8.0%), are mainly due to students' ignorance about them rather than their non-acceptance. This is demonstrated in practice by the very high percentages of the "Not at all - I don't know " responses that they had: Perplexity AI (87.0%), Claude AI (88.5%), Sora (89.2%), and Cursor (91.5%).

The frequency tables (Table 9 & 10) of the participants' responses reveal that, the use of GenAI tools is more than moderate (a few times a month), with over half of the students (54.0%) using them at least moderately in their daily lives, and a total of 73.7% employing them frequently, especially for their academic work, which leads us to the conclusion that these tools are now a key academic aid.

Working students and the use of GenAI as a time-management strategy

Another important finding of this research came from the hypothesis of the correlation between the working hours of working students and their corresponding use of GenAi tools, since an increased proportion of them (58.4%), working 40 or more hours per week (45%). However, the chi-square analysis revealed no statistically significant relationship between professional status and ChatGPT usage, $x^2(4) = 1.26$, $p = 0.869$. This negative finding is itself informative, since it suggests that GenAI adoption is driven by factors beyond time constraints alone, which is evidenced by the similar AI engagement patterns demonstrated by both employed and unemployed students (Table 8).

How engineering students use GenAI tools

Another important finding of this research relates to the usage of GenAI tools by engineering students. The study reveals that the primary use of these tools is to facilitate their searches (80.9%), then to explain and understand difficult concepts (53.7%), and the third and fourth most popular uses are code programming (52.9%) and help with academic work (45.6%), findings that are already confirmed in the literature (HEPI, 2025; Pavlenko & Syzenko, 2024; Reihanian et al., 2025; Wang et al., 2025; Yabaku & Ouhbi, 2024).

Responsible use of GenAI tools

A promising finding of this research regards the students' responsibility in using the GenAI tools. The vast majority of them (99.3%) report that they usually check the responses before use, while 68.2% always do so. Furthermore, the majority of them (63.0%) consistently modify the GenAI outputs rather than accepting them as they are. These findings, already documented in the literature (Aisha Irshad et al., 2025; Hicks, 2025; Yabaku & Ouhbi, 2024), demonstrate that students are concerned about the GenAI outputs, they develop critical evaluation skills, and treat them as starting points for inquiry rather than final principles.

The CT skills paradox

The most remarkable finding of this research is the neutral effect of GenAI tool usage on CT skills development (M = 3.08, SD = 0.91). Across all six measured CT skills, critical thinking (M = 2.99), decomposition (M = 3.25), pattern recognition (M = 2.74), algorithmic thinking (M = 3.27), abstraction (M = 2.94), and debugging (M = 3.32), the students reported neither substantial benefits nor detriments to their CT skills development.

In the literature, few studies have examined the impact of the GenAI tools on students' CT. One of these is (Liao et al., 2024), which proposed an intelligent, scaffolding, programming system using ChatGPT that followed the theoretical framework of CT. It was found that their proposed system improved the students' CT, but they faced the paradox of having a decrease in the students' problem-solving skills. This paradox is aligned with other studies' results in the literature (Aisha Irshad et al., 2025; Kwid et al., 2024; Wang et al., 2025), reveal demonstrate that the excessive use of GenAI tools can lead to negative results for students, hindering the development of their critical analysis, critical thinking, and learning (Freeman, 2025), especially for young learners (Kwid et al., 2024).

However, in the literature, there are also cases with opposite findings. For example, (Ruiz-Rojas et al., 2024) highlighted the potential of GenAI tools to improve critical thinking. Or, in their scoping review (Mahrishi et al., 2024) unveiled cases where GenAI tools, especially ChatGPT, proved to enhance the students' skills and critical thinking. Or, in their study (Sánchez Muñoz et al., 2025), they proposed a practical GenAI-based framework and argued that it promoted computational literacy and critical thinking. In conclusion, the research of (Gervacio, 2024), in correspondence to this research, encountered the CT paradox and wrote it as an argument about the potential impact of the GenAI tools on students' learning, and particularly on critical thinking and problem-solving.

Limitations and Future Directions

This is a pilot study with several limitations, and its findings can't be generalized. It employed a cross-sectional design with self-report measures in a single course (Mechatronics) at one university. While the sample is respectable (n=137), it represents 73% of enrolled students, and the missing 27% may differ systematically from participants. The CT skills measures relied on students' self-assessment rather than objective performance measures; however, they were based on established frameworks. The reliance on Likert-scale responses converted to numerical values assumes interval-level measurement, which may not accurately reflect the nature of the constructs being measured. Additionally, the study cannot prove causality—the neutral CT skills results may reflect, among other things, selection effects, difficulty in understanding the questions, or time factors beyond the study's scope.

Future research could employ longitudinal designs to track students' CT skills development over time. It must incorporate objective performance measures alongside self-reports, and investigate potential variables such as prior academic achievement, specific AI usage strategies, and instructor guidance. In addition, there should be a comparison between two student groups (experimental and control) with common characteristics, comparing their CT skills scores, with and without AI access, or comparing different pedagogical approaches to AI integration. Last but not least, a qualitative investigation into how students actually interact with GenAI tools would be extremely useful, including prompts' examination, outputs' interpretation, and problem-solving workflows' integration.

5. CONCLUSION

This pilot study reveals that engineering students have rapidly and nearly universally adopted GenAI tools, particularly ChatGPT, for daily and academic work. Students demonstrated a responsible pattern of use of these tools since they verify and modify the tools' outputs. However, this study, based on their self-report measures, and despite students' strong beliefs about the educational value of the GenAI tools, measured a neutral impact on their CT skills development.

This may be due to the way the research was conducted and its limitations - it is a pilot study - and reflects a discrepancy between the perceived usefulness of the tools and the development of skills in engineering education.

The conclusion that emerges is that the mere availability and use of GenAI tools does not automatically translate into enhanced learning outcomes. So, educators must move forward, structure learning environments based on GenAI tools and find the correct ways to use them in engineering education, rather than worry if their students use them; after all, they do. The future of engineering education lies in using them in ways that enhance CT skills rather than supplant human cognitive development.

DATA AVAILABILITY

Data analyzed during this case study are available from the author on request.

REFERENCES

Aayushi. (2025). *What is Perplexity AI? A Complete Guide.* https://www.appypieautomate.ai/blog/what-is-perplexity-ai

AIxploria. (2025). *Free AI Tools: The Full List of over 5,000 AI sites.* AIxploria. https://www.aixploria.com/en/free-ai/

Almassaad, A., Alajlan, H., & Alebaikan, R. (2024). Student Perceptions of Generative Artificial Intelligence: Investigating Utilization, Benefits, and Challenges in Higher Education. *Systems*, *12*(10), 16. DOI: 10.3390/systems12100385

Alptekin, S. E., & Freeman, H. J. A. (1996). Mechatronics Education: Model and Implementation. *Proceedings of Mechatronics*, *96*, 13–15.

Andersen, T. O., Hansen, M. R., & Pedersen, J. K. (2003). A Mechatronic Curriculum With Project-Based and Problem-Based Learning: A Dynamic Teaching Approach for the Future. *A Mechatronic Curriculum With Project-Based and Problem-Based Learning: A Dynamic Teaching Approach for the Future.*

Anysphere, I. (2025). *Cursor: The best way to code with AI.* https://cursor.com/

APS. G. (2017). *Science, Technology, Engineering and Mathematics (STEM) Evidence Base. October.* www.gov.scot

Arkin, R. C., Lee, K. M., McGinnis, L. F., & Zhou, C. (1997). Development of a shared interdisciplinary intelligent mechatronics laboratory. *Journal of Engineering Education*, *86*(2), 113–118. DOI: 10.1002/j.2168-9830.1997.tb00273.x

Atmatzidou, S., Demetriadis, S., & Nika, P. (2018). How Does the Degree of Guidance Support Students' Metacognitive and Problem Solving Skills in Educational Robotics? *Journal of Science Education and Technology*, *27*(1), 70–85. DOI: 10.1007/s10956-017-9709-x

Aubry, F. (2024). *Cursor AI: A Guide With 10 Practical Examples.* DataCamp. https://www.datacamp.com/tutorial/cursor-ai-code-editor

Awan, A. A. (2025). *What Is DALL-E?* DataCamp. https://www.datacamp.com/blog/what-is-dall-e

Awtar, S., Bernard, C., Boklund, N., Master, A., Ueda, D., & Craig, K. (2002). Mechatronic design of a ball-on-plate balancing system. *Mechatronics*, *12*(2), 217–228. DOI: 10.1016/S0957-4158(01)00062-9

Bers, M. U., Flannery, L., Kazakoff, E. R., & Sullivan, A. (2014). Computational thinking and tinkering: Exploration of an early childhood robotics curriculum. *Computers & Education*, *72*, 145–157. DOI: 10.1016/j.compedu.2013.10.020

Brennan, K., Chung, M., Martin, W., Cervantes, F., Tally, B., & Resnick, M. (2019). *What is Computational Thinking*. Harvard Graduate School of Education. https://scratched.gse.harvard.edu/ct/defining.html

Brennan, K., & Resnick, M. (2012). *New frameworks for studying and assessing the development of computational thinking*. Annual American Educational Research Association Meeting., https://web.media.mit.edu/~kbrennan/files/Brennan_Resnick_AERA2012_CT.pdf

Brown, N. J., & Brown, O. T. (2002). Mechatronics "a graduate perspective.". *Mechatronics*, *12*(2), 159–167. DOI: 10.1016/S0957-4158(01)00056-3

Bula, I., Hoxha, V., & Hajrizi, E. (2018). Robot from Mechatronics Scrap -Beggar Robot. *IFAC-PapersOnLine*, *51*(30), 216–219. DOI: 10.1016/j.ifacol.2018.11.289

Cardona, M. A., & Rodriguez, R. J. (2024). *Designing for Education with Artificial Intelligence: An Essential Guide for Developers. July*, 1–49. https://tech.ed.gov

Carryer, J. E. (1995). The design of laboratory experiments and projects for mechatronics courses. *Mechatronics*, *5*(7), 787–797. DOI: 10.1016/0957-4158(95)00046-8

Carryer, J. E. (2002). March madness: A mechatronics project theme. *Mechatronics*, *12*(2), 383–391. DOI: 10.1016/S0957-4158(01)00077-0

Chamilothoris, G. (2002). Development of a Mechatronics Curriculum in Greece. *Mechatronics*, (June), 24–26.

Chamilothoris, G. E., & Papoutsidakis, M. G. (2005). Shaping the mechatronics courses for the control curriculum. In *IFAC Proceedings Volumes (IFAC-PapersOnline)* (Vol. 16, Issue 1). IFAC. DOI: 10.3182/20050703-6-CZ-1902.02304

Chan, C. K. Y., & Hu, W. (2023). Students' voices on generative AI: Perceptions, benefits, and challenges in higher education. *International Journal of Educational Technology in Higher Education*, *20*(1), 43. Advance online publication. DOI: 10.1186/s41239-023-00411-8

Chatzopoulos, A., Papoutsidakis, M., Elza, D., Papadakis, S., Kalogiannakis, M., & Psycharis, S. (2021). DuBot: An Open-Source, Low-Cost Robot for STEM and Educational Robotics. In Papadakis, S., & Kalogiannakis, M. (Eds.), *Handbook of Research on Using Educational Robotics to Facilitate Student Learning* (pp. 441–465). IGI Global., DOI: 10.4018/978-1-7998-6717-3.ch018

Chatzopoulos, A., Papoutsidakis, M., Kalogiannakis, M., & Psycharis, S. (2019). Action Research Implementation in Developing an Open Source and Low Cost Robotic Platform for STEM Education. *International Journal of Computer Applications*, *178*(24), 33–46. DOI: 10.5120/ijca2019919039

Chatzopoulos, A., Papoutsidakis, M., Kalogiannakis, M., Psycharis, S., & Papachristos, D. (2020). Measuring the impact on student's Computational Thinking skills through STEM and Educational Robotics projects implementation. In Kalogiannakis, M., & Papadakis, S. J. (Eds.), *Handbook of Research on Tools for Teaching Computational Thinking in P-12 Education* (pp. 234–284). IGI Global., DOI: 10.4018/978-1-7998-4576-8.ch010

Chatzopoulos, A., Tzerachoglou, A., Priniotakis, G., Papoutsidakis, M., Drosos, C., & Symeonaki, E. (2023). Using STEM to Educate Engineers about Sustainability : A Case Study in Mechatronics Teaching and Building a Mobile Robot Using Upcycled and Recycled Materials. *Sustainability (Basel)*, *15*(21), 15187. Advance online publication. DOI: 10.3390/su152115187

Chatzopoulos, A., Xenakis, A., Papoutsidakis, M., Kalovrektis, K., Kalogiannakis, M., & Psycharis, S. (2024). Proposing and Testing an Open - Source and Low - Cost Drone under the Engineering Design Process for Higher Education : The Mechatronics Course Use Case. *2024 IEEE Global Engineering Education Conference (EDUCON)*, 1–7. DOI: 10.1109/EDUCON60312.2024.10578677

Cheville, A. (2014). Defining Engineering Education. *121st ASEE Annual Conference & Exposition.*

CopilotTeam. (2025). *What Is a Copilot and How Does It Work?* Microsoft. https://www.microsoft.com/en-us/microsoft-copilot/copilot-101/what-is-copilot

CoSN. (2025). *2024 State of EdTech District Leadership.*

DeepSeek-AI. Guo, D., Yang, D., Zhang, H., Song, J., Zhang, R., Xu, R., Zhu, Q., Ma, S., Wang, P., Bi, X., Zhang, X., Yu, X., Wu, Y., Wu, Z. F., Gou, Z., Shao, Z., Li, Z., Gao, Z., … Zhang, Z. (2025). *DeepSeek-R1: Incentivizing Reasoning Capability in LLMs via Reinforcement Learning. 500*, 1–22. https://arxiv.org/abs/2501.12948

Diogo, R. A., dos Santos, N., & Loures, E. F. R. (2023). Digital Transformation of Engineering Education for Smart Education: A systematic literature review. In *Reliability Modeling in Industry 4.0* (pp. 407–438). Elsevier. DOI: 10.1016/B978-0-323-99204-6.00002-9

Dotson, M. E., Alvarez, V., Tackett, M., Asturias, G., Leon, I., & Ramanujam, N. (2020). Design Thinking-Based STEM Learning: Preliminary Results on Achieving Scale and Sustainability Through the IGNITE Model. *Frontiers in Education*, *5*(February), 1–10. DOI: 10.3389/feduc.2020.00014

Eghosa, F. (2025). *I used Perplexity AI for one month instead of ChatGPT: here is my review*. https://techpoint.africa/guide/my-perplexity-ai-review/

Francis, D., & Stephens, A. (2018). *English Learners in STEM Subjects: Transforming Classrooms*. Schools, and Lives., DOI: 10.17226/25182

Freeman, J. (2025). Student Generative AI Survey 2025. *Higher Education Policy Institute*, (February), 1–12.

Gardner, J. F. (2002). Two projects for undergraduate mechatronics class: Success and failure. *Mechatronics*, *12*(2), 337–342. DOI: 10.1016/S0957-4158(01)00073-3

Geddam, A. (2003). Mechatronics for Engineering Education: Undergraduate Curriculum. *International Journal of Engineering Education*, *19*(4), 575–580.

Gemini Team. Anil, R., Borgeaud, S., Alayrac, J.-B., Yu, J., Soricut, R., Schalkwyk, J., Dai, A. M., Hauth, A., Millican, K., Silver, D., Johnson, M., Antonoglou, I., Schrittwieser, J., Glaese, A., Chen, J., Pitler, E., Lillicrap, T., Lazaridou, A., … Vinyals, O. (2025). *Gemini: A Family of Highly Capable Multimodal Models*. https://arxiv.org/abs/2312.11805

Gervacio, A. P. (2024). Exploring how generative AI contributes to the motivated engagement and learning production of science-oriented students. *Environment and Social Psychology*, *9*(11), 1–17. DOI: 10.59429/esp.v9i11.3194

Gill, S. S., Xu, M., Patros, P., Wu, H., Kaur, R., Kaur, K., Fuller, S., Singh, M., Arora, P., Parlikad, A. K., Stankovski, V., Abraham, A., Ghosh, S. K., Lutfiyya, H., Kanhere, S. S., Bahsoon, R., Rana, O., Dustdar, S., Sakellariou, R., … Buyya, R. (2024). Transformative effects of ChatGPT on modern education: Emerging Era of AI Chatbots. *Internet of Things and Cyber-Physical Systems*, *4*(November 2022), 19–23. DOI: 10.1016/j.iotcps.2023.06.002

Giurgiutiu, V., Bayoumi, A. M. E., & Nall, G. (2002). Mechatronics and smart structures: Emerging engineering disciplines for the third millennium. *Mechatronics*, *12*(2), 169–181. DOI: 10.1016/S0957-4158(01)00057-5

Google. (2025). *Gemini Models*. Google AI for Developers. https://ai.google.dev/gemini-api/docs/models

Grover, S. (2011). Robotics and engineering for middle and high school students to develop computational thinking. *Annual Meeting of the American Educational Research Association, New Orleans, LA, 650*, 1–15. http://web.stanford.edu/~shuchig/docs/AERA2011-Shuchi Grover-Robotics and Engineering for Middle and High School Students to Develop Computational Thinking.pdf

Gurova, D. (2025). *What is Cursor AI? Everything You Need to Know*. https://uibakery.io/blog/what-is-cursor-a#:~:text=Cursor AI is an AI,explaining codebases in natural language.

Hanna, D. (2023). The Use of Artificial Intelligence Art Generator "Midjourney" in Artistic and Advertising Creativity. *Journal of Design Sciences and Applied Arts*, *4*(2), 42–58. DOI: 10.21608/jdsaa.2023.169144.1231

Harimurti, R., Ekohariadi, , Munoto, , & IGP Asto, B. (2019). The concept of computational thinking toward information and communication technology learning. *IOP Conference Series. Materials Science and Engineering*, *535*(1), 6–13. DOI: 10.1088/1757-899X/535/1/012004

He, R., Cao, J., & Tan, T. (2025). Generative artificial intelligence: A historical perspective. *National Science Review*, *12*(5), nwaf050. Advance online publication. DOI: 10.1093/nsr/nwaf050 PMID: 40191253

HEPI. (2025). *Student Generative AI Survey 2025 - HEPI*. Higher Education Policy Institute. https://www.hepi.ac.uk/reports/student-generative-ai-survey-2025/

Hicks, A. (2025). *Integrating Generative AI into Sustainability Education : The Lorax as a Case Study Integrating Generative AI into Sustainability Education : The Lorax as a Case Study*. 0–12.

IDPE. (2023). *Learning Objectives*. Department of Industrial Design & Production Engineering. https://idpe.uniwa.gr/en/studies/undergraduate/learning-objectives

IDPE. (2024). *Brief Presentation - Department of Industrial Design and Production Engineering*. https://idpe.uniwa.gr/en/department/dep-presentation

IDPE. (2025). *Undergraduate Program - Department of Industrial Design and Production Engineering*. https://idpe.uniwa.gr/en/courses

Ioannidou, A., Bennett, V., Repenning, A., Koh, H., & Basawapatna, A. (2011). Computational Thinking Patterns. *Annual Meeting of the American Educational Research Association (AERA), 2*. http://www.agentsheets.com

Ioannou, M., & Bratitsis, T. (2016). Utilizing Sphero for a speed related STEM activity in Kindergarten. *Hellenic Conference on Innovating STEM Education.*

Irshad, A. (2025). Students' Perspectives on Generative AI's Role in Transforming, Challenging, and Enhancing Higher Education Learning Practices in Education. *Indus Journal of Social Sciences, 3*(3), 253–268. DOI: 10.59075/ijss.v3i3.1897

Jamovi. (2021). *The jamovi project* (1.6). https://www.jamovi.org/

Jiang, H., Liu, Q., Li, R., Ye, S., & Wang, S. (2024). *CursorCore: Assist Programming through Aligning Anything*. https://arxiv.org/abs/2410.07002v1

Kalogiannakis, M., Papakonstantinou, N., & Sotiropoulos, D. (2025). From Support Tool to Learning Partner : A Systematic Review of GenAI Integration in University Science Labs. *Creative Education, 16*(9), 1364–1401. DOI: 10.4236/ce.2025.169083

Kanaki, K., Chatzakis, S., & Kalogiannakis, M. (2025). Fostering Algorithmic Thinking and Environmental Awareness via Bee-Bot Activities in Early Childhood Education. *Sustainability (Basel), 17*(9), 1–19. DOI: 10.3390/su17094208

Kanaki, K., Kalogiannakis, M., Poulakis, E., & Politis, P. (2022). Investigating the Association between Algorithmic Thinking and Performance in Environmental Study. *Sustainability (Basel), 14*(17), 10672. Advance online publication. DOI: 10.3390/su141710672

Kantaros, A., Diegel, O., Piromalis, D., Tsaramirsis, G., Khadidos, A. O., Khadidos, A. O., Khan, F. Q., & Jan, S. (2021). 3D printing: Making an innovative technology widely accessible through makerspaces and outsourced services. *Materials Today: Proceedings, 49*, 2712–2723. DOI: 10.1016/j.matpr.2021.09.074

Karageorgakis, T. (2023). *Best 100 AI apps for Teachers and the Classroom*. Educraft. https://educraft.tech/best-100-ai-apps-for-teachers/

Karageorgakis, T. (2025). *200 AI Tools Reviewed - Here are the Best.* Educraft. https://educraft.tech/best-ai-tools-for-teachers-2024-survey

Karpuzi, M., Georgiou, K., Papoutsidakis, M., & Chatzopoulos, A. (2019). Design of an object identification system with a thermal camera. *International Journal of Engineering Applied Sciences and Technology, 4*(5), 471–477. DOI: 10.33564/IJEAST.2019.v04i05.068

Kelly, A., Sullivan, M., & Strampel, K. (2023). Generative artificial intelligence: University student awareness, experience, and confidence in use across disciplines. *Journal of University Teaching & Learning Practice, 20*(6). Advance online publication. DOI: 10.53761/1.20.6.12

Kember, D. (2005). *Action learning and action research: Improving the quality of teaching & learning*. Taylor & Francis e-Library.

Kharrufa, A., Alghamdi, S., Aziz, A., & Bull, C. (2024). LLMs Integration in Software Engineering Team Projects: Roles, Impact, and a Pedagogical Design Space for AI Tools in Computing Education. *ArXiv*, 1–25. https://arxiv.org/pdf/2410.23069

Koikas, D., Aggelis, P., & Chatzopoulos, A. (2015). Rebuilding a CNC Milling Machine. *International Conference ERA - 10*, 52–58. era.teipir.gr

Krosnick, J. A., & Presser, S. (2010). Question and Questionnaire Design. In *Handbook of Survey Research* (2nd ed.). Emerald Publishing., DOI: 10.1111/j.1432-1033.1976.tb10115.x

Kwid, G., Sarty, N., & Yang, D. (2024). A Review of AI Tools: Definitions, Functions, and Applications for K-12 Education. *AI. Computer Science and Robotics Technology*, *3*(August), 1–22. DOI: 10.5772/acrt.20240048

Lagogiannis, G., & Chatzopoulos, A. (2025). A No-Code Educational Platform for Introducing Internet of Things and Its Application to Agricultural Education. *IoT*, *6*(3), 42. https://doi.org/https://doi.org/10.3390/iot6030042. DOI: 10.3390/iot6030042

Larmer, J., & Mergendoller, J. (2010). *Seven Essentials for Project-Based Learning*. https://www.ascd.org/el/articles/seven-essentials-for-project-based-learning

Carnegie Learning. (2024). *The State of AI in Education Artificial Intelligence in Education 2024 Report*.

Lego, E. (2016). *LEGO Education WeDo 2. 0 - Computational Thinking - Teacher's Guide* (Issue V1, p. 42). LEGO Group. https://le-www-live-s.legocdn.com/sc/media/files/user-guides/wedo-2/computational-thinking-teacher-guides/computational thinkingteacherguide-en-gb-v1-69cd677d61d21b2a44999328c40e7122.pdf

Liao, J., Zhong, L., Zhe, L., Xu, H., Liu, M., & Xie, T. (2024). Scaffolding Computational Thinking With ChatGPT. *IEEE Transactions on Learning Technologies*, *17*, 1668–1682. DOI: 10.1109/TLT.2024.3392896

Lindsey, J., Gurnee, W., Ameisen, E., Chen, B., Pearce, A., Turner, N. L., Citro, C., Abrahams, D., Carter, S., Hosmer, B., Marcus, J., Sklar, M., Templeton, A., Bricken, T., McDougall, C., Cunningham, H., Henighan, T., Jermyn, A., Jones, A., . . . Batson, J. (2025). *On the Biology of a Large Language Model*. Anthropic. https://transformer-circuits.pub/2025/attribution-graphs/biology.html

Liu, Y., Zhang, K., Li, Y., Yan, Z., Gao, C., Chen, R., Yuan, Z., Huang, Y., Sun, H., Gao, J., He, L., & Sun, L. (2024). *Sora: A Review on Background, Technology, Limitations, and Opportunities of Large Vision Models*. https://arxiv.org/abs/2402.17177

Louros, A., Papoutsidakis, M., Chatzopoulos, A., & Drosos, C. (2018). Design of an Innovative Flight Controller for Quadcopter Robust Handling. [JMEST]. *Journal of Multidisciplinary Engineering Science and Technology*, *5*(10), 8968–8972.

Lund, A., & Lund, M. (2025). *Chi-square test of independence in SPSS Statistics*. Laerd Statistics. https://statistics.laerd.com/premium/spss/cstoirxc/chi-square-test-of-independence-rxc-in-spss-3.php

Luo, Y., Chen, E., Liu, H., Riener, K., & Yang, S.-H. (2025). Generative AI in Engineering Education: A Survey of Student and Instructor Usage and Attitudes. *Proceedings of the Human Factors and Ergonomics Society Annual Meeting*, 1–6. DOI: 10.1177/10711813251358792

Lyshevski, S. E. (2002). Mechatronic curriculum - Retrospect and prospect. *Mechatronics, 12*(2), 195–205. DOI: 10.1016/S0957-4158(01)00060-5

Mahrishi, M., Abbas, A., Radovanović, D., & Hosseini, S. (2024). Emerging Dynamics of ChatGPT in Academia: A Scoping Review. *Journal of University Teaching & Learning Practice*, *21*(1). Advance online publication. DOI: 10.53761/b182ws13

Malmström, H., Stöhr, C., & Ou, A. W. (2023). Chatbots and other AI for learning: A survey of use and views among university students in Sweden. *Chalmers Studies in Communication and Learning in Higher Education, 2023*(1).

Meta. (2025a). *AI at Meta*. https://ai.meta.com/

Meta. (2025b). *Introducing the Meta AI App: A New Way to Access Your AI Assistant*. https://about.fb.com/news/2025/04/introducing-meta-ai-app-new-way-access-ai-assistant/

Microsoft. (2025a). *AI in Education A Microsoft Special Report*. DOI: 10.58952/nit20251301053

Microsoft. (2025b). *What is Microsoft 365 Copilot?* Microsoft. https://learn.microsoft.com/en-us/copilot/microsoft-365/microsoft-365-copilot-overview

Minetou, L., Chatzopoulos, A., Tzerachoglou, A., Priniotakis, G., van Hoof, J., Sfyroera, E., Georgiadou, Z., Tyrovola, S., & Drosos, C. (2024). Homing wellness: Can narrative design transform living spaces for people with dementia into engaging environments enabling communication? *Frontiers in Public Health*, *11*, 1198253. Advance online publication. DOI: 10.3389/fpubh.2023.1198253 PMID: 38292379

Morrison, J., & Bartlett, R. V. (2009). *STEM as a Curriculum*. Education Week. papers3://publication/uuid/48C36DF6-30CA-42ED-876D-0D4214A1F890

Ngo, T. T. A. (2023). The Perception by University Students of the Use of ChatGPT in Education. *International Journal of Emerging Technologies in Learning*, *18*(17), 4–19. DOI: 10.3991/ijet.v18i17.39019

Nichols, M., Cator, K., & Torres, M. (2016). *Challenge Based Learning Guide* (Issue March). Digital Promise.

Nolasco, G., & Dicuangco, J. D. (2025). A Review Article – Facebook's Meta AI: A Potential Boon or Doom for Learning? *International Journal of Metaverse*, *3*(1), 1–7. DOI: 10.54536/ijm.v3i1.3845

Open, A. I. (2024). GPT-4 System Card. *OpenAI.Com*, 1–60. https://cdn.openai.com/papers/gpt-4-system-card.pdf

Open, A. I. (2025a). *Explore GPTs*. https://chatgpt.com/gpts?utm_source=chatgpt.com

Open, A. I. (2025b). *Generating videos on Sora | OpenAI Help Center*. https://help.openai.com/en/articles/9957612-generating-videos-on-sora

Open, A. I. (2025c). *Introducing ChatGPT*. https://chatgpt.com/overview?openaicom_referred=true

Open, A. I. (2025d). *Introducing GPT-5*. https://openai.com/index/introducing-gpt-5/

Pageon. (2025). *Transforming Academic Research: How Perplexity's Peer-Review Mode Revolutionizes Scholarly Discovery*. https://www.pageon.ai/blog/perplexity-academic-mode-sources-only-peer-reviewed-papers

Papadakis, S., Kalogiannakis, M., & Zaranis, N. (2016). Developing fundamental programming concepts and computational thinking with ScratchJr in preschool education: A case study. *International Journal of Mobile Learning and Organisation*, *10*(3), 187. DOI: 10.1504/IJMLO.2016.077867

Papert, S. (1996). An exploration in the space of mathematics educations. *International Journal of Computers for Mathematical Learning*, *1*(1), 95–123. DOI: 10.1007/BF00191473

Papoutsidakis, M., Symeonaki, E., Chatzopoulos, A., & Piromalis, D. (2018). Iot Design To Support Wireless Sensor Networks And Data Transmission. [IJESI]. *International Journal of Engineering and Science Invention*, *7*(10), 54–62. www.ijesi.org

Pastrana, M. A., Santana, M. S., Mendoza-Peñaloza, J., Bautista, J., Pinto Lopera, J. E., & Muñoz, D. M. (2025). A Novel Approach to Teaching Theory Control : Integrating STEM Education, Mobile Robot Simulation, and Bio-inspired. *Operations Research Forum (2025)*, *6*(85). DOI: 10.1007/s43069-025-00489-y

Pavlenko, O., & Syzenko, A. (2024). Using ChatGPT as a Learning Tool: A Study of Ukrainian Students' Perceptions. *Arab World English Journal*, *1*(1), 252–264. DOI: 10.24093/awej/ChatGPT.17

Pazur, B. (2025). *What Is Midjourney? Here's What You Need to Know About the AI Image Generator - CNET*. CNET. https://www.cnet.com/tech/services-and-software/what-is-midjourney-heres-what-you-need-to-know-about-the-ai-image-generator/

Perkins, D. (2025). *The 5 Phases Of Project-Based Learning – TeachThought*. https://www.teachthought.com/project-based-learning-posts/phases/

Priniotakis, G., Chronis, I., Chatzopoulos, A., & Louris, E. (2015). Lilipad Arduino platform for a multifunctional garments and wearables laboratory course. *15th AUTEX World Textile Conference 2015*, 10–13.

Priyanshu, A., Maurya, Y., & Hong, Z. (2024). *AI Governance and Accountability: An Analysis of Anthropic's Claude*. https://arxiv.org/abs/2407.01557

Psycharis, S. (2020). The Impact of STEM-based Mobile Apps on learners' Self-efficacy for Computational Thinking Dimensions. *The 13th International Conference on E-Learning in the Workplace*. http://learningideasconf.s3.amazonaws.com/Docs/Past/2020/Papers/Psycharis.pdf

Radiopoulou, D., Kantaros, A., Ganetsos, T., & Zacharia, P. (2025). 3D Printing as a Multimodal STEM Learning Technology: A Survey Study in Second Chance Schools. *Multimodal Technologies and Interaction*, *9*(9), 87. DOI: 10.3390/mti9090087

Reihanian, I., Hou, Y., Chen, Y., & Zheng, Y. (2025). *A Review of Generative AI in Computer Science Education: Challenges and Opportunities in Accuracy, Authenticity, and Assessment. 2142503*. https://arxiv.org/pdf/2507.11543

Rudra, S. (2023). *ChatGPT in Education: Generative AI Pros, Cons & Unknowns*. EdTech Magazie. https://edtechmagazine.com/k12/article/2023/03/chatgpt-in-education-generative-ai-perfcon

Ruiz-Rojas, L. I., Salvador-Ullauri, L., & Acosta-Vargas, P. (2024). Collaborative Working and Critical Thinking: Adoption of Generative Artificial Intelligence Tools in Higher Education. *Sustainability (Basel), 16*(13), 5367. Advance online publication. DOI: 10.3390/su16135367

Sánchez Muñoz, J. A., Flores-Eraña, G., Silva-Campos, J. M., Chavira-Quintero, R., & Olais-Govea, J. M. (2025). GenAI as a cognitive mediator: A critical-constructivist inquiry into computational thinking in pre-university education. *Frontiers in Education, 10*(September), 1597249. Advance online publication. DOI: 10.3389/feduc.2025.1597249

Sattar, F., & Nawaz, M. (2023). Developing Computational Thinking in STEM Education with Drones. *2023 IEEE Global Engineering Education Conference (EDUCON)*, 1–5. DOI: 10.1109/EDUCON54358.2023.10125117

Schoenfeld, A. H. (1992). Learning to think mathematically: Problem solving, metacognition, and sense-making in mathematics. *Handbook for Research on Mathematics Teaching and Learning*, 334–370.

Sigalos, A., Papoutsidakis, M., Chatzopoulos, A., & Piromalis, D. (2019). Design of a flight controller and peripherals for a quadcopter. *International Journal of Engineering Applied Sciences and Technology, 4*(5), 463–470. DOI: 10.33564/IJEAST.2019.v04i05.067

Slack, G. (2023). *What DALL-E Reveals About Human Creativity | Stanford HAI (9_29_2025 1:35:04 PM)*. https://hai.stanford.edu/news/what-dall-e-reveals-about-human-creativity

Slagg, A. (2024). *AI in Education in 2024: Mixed Feelings on The Tech's Future*. EdTech Magazine. https://edtechmagazine.com/k12/article/2024/09/ai-education-2024-educators-express-mixed-feelings-technologys-future-perfcon?utm_source=chatgpt.com

Spinellis, D. (2025). False authorship: An explorative case study around an AI-generated article published under my name. *Research Integrity and Peer Review, 10*(1), 8. Advance online publication. DOI: 10.1186/s41073-025-00165-z PMID: 40420142

Stone, A. (2024). *How Creative Generative AI Can Help Higher Education Institutions*. EdTech Magazine. https://edtechmagazine.com/higher/article/2024/07/how-creative-generative-ai-can-help-higher-education-institutions

Stone, A. (2025). *AI Ethics in Higher Education: How Schools Are Proceeding*. EdTech Magazine. https://edtechmagazine.com/higher/article/2025/03/ai-ethics-higher-education-how-schools-are-proceeding-perfcon

Teamann, A. (2023). *To ChatGPT or Not to ChatGPT, That Is the Question*. EdTech Magazine. https://edtechmagazine.com/k12/article/2023/11/chatgpt-or-not-chatgpt-question

Thananuwong, R. (2015). Learning Science from Toys: A Pathway to Successful Integrated STEM Teaching and Learning in Thai Middle School. *K-12 STEM Education, 1*(2), 75–84. DOI: 10.14456/K12STEMED.2015.22

Tzirides, A. O. (Olnancy), Saini, A., Zapata, G., Searsmith, D., Cope, B., Kalantzis, M., Castro, V., Kourkoulou, T., Jones, J., Abrantes da Silva, R., Whiting, J., & Kastania, N. P. (2023). Generative AI: Implications and Applications for Education. *ArXiv*, 2023. https://doi.org/https://doi.org/10.48550/arXiv.2305.07605

Van Amerongen, J. (2000). The Role of Control in Mechatronics. *Engineering Science and Education Journal*, *9*(3), 105–112. DOI: 10.1049/esej:20000302

Vasquez, J. A., Comer, M., & Sneider, C. (2013). *STEM Lesson Essentials, Grades 3-8: Integrating Science, Technology, Engineering, and Mathematics* (1st editio). Heinemann. https://www.amazon.com/STEM-Lesson-Essentials-Grades-3-8/dp/0325043582

Wan, I., Wan, S. 'Azzam and A., Nur, A., & Pauzi, M. N. (2024). An Overview of the Use of Artificial Intelligence Tools in Higher Education. *Current Research Progress in Agricultural Sciences Vol. 4, 19*(3), 29–42. DOI: 10.9734/bpi/crpas/v4/2280

Wang, K. D., Wu, Z., Tufts, L., Wieman, C., Salehi, S., & Haber, N. (2025). Scaffold or Crutch? Examining College Students' Use and Views of Generative AI Tools for STEM Education. *IEEE Global Engineering Education Conference, EDUCON*, 1–21. DOI: 10.1109/EDUCON62633.2025.11016406

Weese, J. L. (2017). *Bringing Computational Thinking to K-12 and Higher Education*. Kansas State University.

Wiki, A. (2025a). *DALL-E*. https://aiwiki.ai/wiki/DALL-E

Wiki, A. (2025b). *Meta AI*. https://aiwiki.ai/wiki/Meta_AI_%28Company%29

Wiki, A. (2025c). *Meta AI - AI Wiki*. https://aiwiki.ai/wiki/Meta_AI

Wiki, A. (2025d). *Midjourney*. https://aiwiki.ai/wiki/Midjourney

Wikipedia. (2025a). *DALL-E*. https://en.wikipedia.org/wiki/DALL-E

Wikipedia. (2025b). *Perplexity AI*. https://en.wikipedia.org/wiki/Perplexity_AI

Wikipedia. (2025c). *Sora (text-to-video model)*. https://en.wikipedia.org/wiki/Sora_(text-to-video_model)

Wing, J. M. (2006). Computational Thinking. *Communications of the ACM, 49*(3), 33–35. DOI: 10.1145/1118178.1118215

Xatzopoulos, A., Papoutsidakis, M., & Chamilothoris, G. (2013). Mobile Robotic Platforms as Educational Tools in Mechatronics Engineering. *International Scientific Conference ERA – 8*, 41–51. era.teipir.gr

Yabaku, M., & Ouhbi, S. (2024). University Students' Perception and Expectations of Generative AI Tools for Software Engineering. *Software Engineering Education Conference, Proceedings*, 1–5. DOI: 10.1109/CSEET62301.2024.10663035

Yadav, A., Zhou, N., Mayfield, C., Hambrusch, S., & Korb, J. T. (2011). Introducing computational thinking in education courses. *SIGCSE'11 - Proceedings of the 42nd ACM Technical Symposium on Computer Science Education, 2*, 465–470. DOI: 10.1145/1953163.1953297

Zahilah Mohamed Zaki, F., Wong, S. L., & Ridzwan Yaakub, M. (2019). A Review of Common Features inComputational Thinking Frameworks in K-12 Education. *IOP Conference Series. Materials Science and Engineering, 551*(1), 012063. DOI: 10.1088/1757-899X/551/1/012063

KEY TERMS AND DEFINITIONS

Artificial intelligence (AI): Artificial intelligence (AI) is a term to describe a machine-based system that can make predictions, learn through human interaction, make decisions, or recommendations based on users' input. AI is a superset, an umbrella, of technologies including the supervised, unsupervised, reciprocal, and 'deep' learning systems.

Computational Thinking: Computational Thinking is a term to describe a way of thinking, analyzing, and acting to solve problems. It is a set of skills usually referred to as dimensions that includes all these analytical methods for problem solving, including problem decomposition, generalization, algorithmic thinking, evaluation, and abstraction.

Constitutional AI: It is a subset, a framework, of Artificial Intelligence (AI) that bases its results and behavior using embedded ethical principles rather than human feedback, to ensure alignment of the result with predetermined moral principles and values.

Data: From the perspective of AI technologies, data are units of information necessary for the training and use of AI that come from information related to people and/or objects.

Engineering Design Process: Engineering Design Process (EDP) is an engineering design process to describe, think, analyze an engineering problem, and implement, evaluate, and communicate a solution for it. It is a cyclical process where one step leads to another, while there are times when some steps do not bring results, so they are repeated or the process returns to a previous one.

Generative Artificial Intelligence: Generative Artificial Intelligence (GenAI or GAI) is a subset of AI that uses the sophisticated Large Language Models (LLMs) to create new content from scratch from a user text input called a prompt. GenAI can create text, computer code, images, presentations, audio, video, notes, applications, and almost anything. GenAI is distinguished from other AI forms since its novel output and the provided insights that other AI technologies can't provide.

Large Language Model: The Large Language Models (LLM) refer to artificial neural networks that are the foundation models used by GenAI. At a very basic level, these models usually detect statistical relationships between words, if the GenAI's output is text, during their training phase, and use these words to predict the next word to generate, responding to the user's request (prompt).

Machine Learning: Machine learning (ML) is a subset of AI, and includes a range of algorithms that can be used in it. Usually these algorithms identify rules and patterns in the training data without human intervention. Then, based on these data, they build a model for decision making, meaning the discover new rules and patterns.

Mechatronics systems: These are the systems based on and produced by applying Mechatronics. From one perspective, all modern automatic, autonomous systems can be considered mechatronic systems since they incorporate mechanical, electronic, and electrical elements that are controlled by control theories, AI, etc., implemented in information systems.

Mechatronics: Mechatronics is a growing interdisciplinary field that integrates many engineering disciplines, including mechanical, electrical, electronics, computer, control theory, and more, to create intelligent, automated, and/or autonomous systems called mechatronics systems.

STEM: STEM is an acronym for Science, Technology, Engineering, and Mathematics, and usually refers to teaching and learning in or across these disciplines. It should be noted that there are many different approaches to integrating STEM into education, including the disciplinary, multidisciplinary, interdisciplinary, and transdisciplinary approaches.

Training Data: From the perspective of AI technologies, training data are those used to train an AI algorithm or model. They could be human or objects, and were generated in the past. Training data is the most important aspect related to the training of the AI system, since the wrong data could easily lead to systemic biases. Special attention should be paid to training data as algorithms parsed the biases included in them.

APPENDIX: THE QUESTIONNAIRE OF THE RESEARCH "THE USE OF ARTIFICIAL INTELLIGENCE (AI) TOOLS IN EDUCATION"

Table 18. Demographic data

1. Gender	☐ Male ☐ Female ☐ Other
2. Age	☐ less or equal to 21 ☐ 22-34 ☐ 35-44 ☐ 45-54 ☐ 55-64 ☐ equal or more to 65
3. Which university do you attend?	
4. What department are you studying in?	
5. What academic year are you in?	☐ 1st ☐ 2nd ☐ 3rd ☐ 4th ☐ 5th ☐ I have exceeded the normal length of study for my department.
6. Professional status	☐ Unemployed ☐ Employed
7. If you work, fill in how many hours you work per week.	

Table 19. Questions about the Use of Artificial Intelligence

8. Which of the following Artificial Intelligence (AI) applications do you use? Select the frequency of use.					
	Not at all - I don't know	A little	Moderate	Quite a lot	A lot
8.1 ChatGPT					
8.2 DeepSeek					
8.3 Gemini					
8.4 Claude AI					
8.5 Copilot					
8.6 Perplexity AI					
8.7 Meta AI					

continued on following page

Table 19. Continued

8.8 MidJourney					
8.9 DALL·E 3					
8.10 Cursor					
8.11 Sora					
9. What other AI applications not listed above do you use?					
10. How often do you generally use Artificial Intelligence (AI) applications in your daily life?	☐ Not at all ☐ A little (once a month or less) ☐ Moderate (a few times a month) ☐ Very often (several times a week) ☐ Too much (daily or almost daily)				
11. Why do you use Artificial Intelligence (AI) applications? Multiple answers are allowed.	☐ A. Task automation and productivity ☐ A1. Information search ☐ A2. Text writing ☐ A3. Programming (code assistance, algorithm explanation, code debugging) ☐ B. Education and learning ☐ B1. Explaining and understanding difficult concepts in simple terms ☐ B2. Help with academic work (writing papers, generating ideas and inspiration, gathering study material) ☐ B3. Exam preparation ☐ B4. Language assistance (conversation practice, translation, grammar) ☐ C. Creativity ☐ C1. Creating or editing images ☐ C2. Creating or editing videos ☐ C3. Creating graphics, diagrams, presentations ☐ D. Entertainment (ideas for stories, discussions, entertaining responses) ☐ E. Personal assistance and organization ☐ Other				
12. How often do you use Artificial Intelligence (AI) applications when writing your academic papers?	☐ Not at all - I have never used AI in writing papers ☐ A little - I have used AI only once ☐ Moderately - I have used AI a few times (less than 10) ☐ Very often - I use AI very often in my papers ☐ Extremely often - I always use AI in my papers				
13. Why do you use Artificial Intelligence (AI) applications when writing your papers? Multiple answers are allowed.	☐ To explain and understand difficult concepts ☐ To solve problems, e.g., in mathematics, physics, engineering, etc. ☐ Programming and code writing ☐ Generating and testing ideas, inspiration ☐ Gathering study material ☐ Writing papers ☐ Searching for sources and bibliography ☐ Creating or editing images ☐ Creating or editing videos ☐ Creating graphics, diagrams, presentations ☐ Other				

continued on following page

Table 19. Continued

14. Do you check the answers/results produced by Artificial Intelligence (AI) applications before using them?	☐ Never. I use them as they are ☐ Sometimes ☐ Yes, I always check them
15. Do you usually edit or improve the responses generated by AI applications before using them?	☐ Not at all. I use them as they are ☐ Sometimes, if I think they need correction/improvement, I edit them ☐ Yes, I always modify the responses generated by AI applications

Table 20. Impact on Learning

16. Do you think that using Artificial Intelligence (AI) applications helps you understand the subject?	☐ Absolutely not. On the contrary, Artificial Intelligence (AI) makes me rely on it too much. ☐ Probably not. Artificial Intelligence (AI) helps me a little in understanding the subject for which I have used it. ☐ Probably yes. Artificial Intelligence (AI) helps me understand somewhat (or sometimes) the subject for which I have used it. ☐ Absolutely Yes. Using Artificial Intelligence (AI) helps me fully understand the subject I have used it for.
17. How do you use Artificial Intelligence (AI) applications when preparing for exams? Multiple answers are allowed.	☐ To create summaries of key topics ☐ To create sample questions and answers related to the exam material ☐ To understand difficult topics ☐ To solve exam questions ☐ I do not use Artificial Intelligence (AI) applications to prepare for exams ☐ Other
18. Do you think that using Artificial Intelligence (AI) applications helps you develop your critical thinking skills for problem solving (e.g., in your academic work)?	☐ No. It makes me less concerned with solving my problems/assignments. ☐ Sometimes. But I rely heavily on AI applications. ☐ Yes. It helps me conduct more in-depth research and develop my critical thinking skills. ☐ Other

19. Do you think that using Artificial Intelligence (AI) applications helps you with the following?

	No - Never	Rarely	Sometimes	Often	Yes -Always
19.1. Developing your critical thinking skills for problem solving (e.g., in your academic work)					
19.2. When faced with a problem, identifying the individual steps required to solve it					
19.3. Identifying similarities or patterns in problems you have solved in the past					
19.4. Plan a series of clear and precise steps to solve a problem					
19.5. Be able to ignore details that are not important and focus on the key elements of a problem					
19.6. In a proposed solution, be able to recognize and correct errors and optimize it					

Table 21. Ethical Issues

20. Do you consider the use of Artificial Intelligence (AI) applications to complete your academic work to be ethical?	☐ No, it is dishonest ☐ Only if I mention that I used AI applications ☐ Yes, as long as it helps me learn from it ☐ Other
21. Have you previously submitted an assignment or exam answer that was created mainly or entirely using Artificial Intelligence (AI) applications?	☐ No, I do not use Artificial Intelligence (AI) applications in academic work or exams. ☐ No, I use Artificial Intelligence (AI) applications only for learning purposes ☐ Yes, but only occasionally ☐ Yes, frequently ☐ Other
22. Has a teacher discussed with you the guidelines for using Artificial Intelligence (AI) applications?	☐ No, and I'm not sure if there are any rules ☐ No, but I believe there should be guidelines and rules ☐ Yes, I am familiar with the guidelines and rules for using Artificial Intelligence (AI) applications ☐ Other

Table 22. Suggestions and Feedback

23. Do you believe that teachers should incorporate the use of Artificial Intelligence (AI) applications into the learning process?	☐ No ☐ Yes
24. Explain why you answered Yes or No to the question "Should teachers incorporate the use of Artificial Intelligence (AI) applications into the learning process?"	
25. Suggest the ideal way to integrate Artificial Intelligence (AI) into education	
26. Suggest the appropriate limits for the use of Artificial Intelligence (AI) integration in education. In other words, what should be done to maximize the benefits while minimizing the negative aspects of its use?	

Chapter 6
Training in the Age of Generative AI:
Towards Augmented Pedagogy in Higher Education

Saida Ifiss
https://orcid.org/0009-0001-3491-0104
The National School of Business and Management, Mohammed Premier University, Oujda, Morocco

ABSTRACT

This chapter examines the determinants of generative artificial intelligence use by higher education teachers in Morocco utilizing a mixed methodological approach based on multiple linear regression, machine learning models (Random Forest, XGBoost, SVM), and partial least squares structural equations (PLS-SEM). Based on a survey of 252 teachers using a three-part questionnaire, the findings show three primary and converging levers to the adoption of these technologies: participation in continuing education, prior digital experience, and perceived institutional support. The AI models show high predictive performance (F1 > 0.80; AUC > 0.85), and the PLS-SEM model substantiates the theoretical consistency of the conceptual framework (R^2 = 0.61). Socio-demographic variables contributed little. This methodological triangulation allows for the combination of statistical robustness and explanatory richness, and provides concrete recommendations to support pedagogical transformation in the age of generative AI.

DOI: 10.4018/979-8-3373-9074-1.ch006

INTRODUCTION

The emergence of Generative Artificial Intelligence (GAI), via advancements in conversational tools like ChatGPT, Bard, or Copilot, represents a significant technological development with far-reaching implications to many sectors, and higher education is no exception. GAI is able to produce text, visuals or even code autonomously and in relevant context, altering the landscape of knowledge production and human engagement. In higher education, GAI is not an abstraction or a far-off possibility, it's a now, a present opportunity for personalization of learning, developing alternative teaching resources, providing individualized feedback to students, and perhaps even redefining the teacher-learner relationship (Haroud & Saqri, 2025).

While this digital transformation offers an "augmented pedagogy," it also raises significant problems, especially regarding the adaptation of teaching practices and the reflection on how to use these digital tools ethically and responsibly. In Morocco, similar to many other countries, higher education is implementing a modernization of the digital landscape. National initiatives, like as the e-Takwine program of the Ministry of Higher Education (El mustapha & El adnanI, 2022), Scientific Research and Innovation, digital strategies created by each university (UM6P, Université de Mohammed V, Université Ibn Tofaïl), demonstrate a strong will towards their technological revolution. Yet, the reality of achieving these ambitions is met with heterogeneities, in terms of resource availability, a digital maturity of the institution, and of course, the preparation and support to teach the staff (Ismaili, 2024;Abbas, Jam & Khan, 2024).

This chapter proposes to look closely at how Moroccan university teachers perceive and use generative AI tools in their teaching practice. To do this, we aim to identify the key elements that influence the adoption, access and proper use of generative AI tools, based on a large-scale quantitative survey of a numerous academy. We will analyse both the constraints and advantages that exist at the level of use pinging the constraints and possible opportunities and benefits provided by using such tools, while we are also interested in understanding to what extent such tools can contribute to solve the continued problem in education related to quality and massification. In the end we hope to provide some concrete, contextualised recommendations that will address how best to support teachers through this possible transition to AI-powered pedagogy, designed and delivered in ethical, quality and sustainable ways.

1. IN-DEPTH LITERATURE REVIEW

If there is an abundance of research on the application of digital technologies in education, the coming of generative AI creates a new dimension that requires a re-evaluation of currently existing constructions.

1.1 Emerging uses of generative AI in higher education

AI in education has historically developed from intelligent tutor systems to conversational chatbots to adaptive learning systems (Woolf, 2010), with generative AI enormously enhancing the machine's ability. One of the most direct applications of generative AI is the creation of educational content. Teachers can create a course outline, exercises, case studies, or even simulation scenarios in a matter of minutes (Luckin et al., 2022). This innovation enables teachers to divert time to higher value-added activity and differentiate learning content (Molenaar, 2022).

Another primary application... provided by generative AI is the personalization of learning and individual feedback. Generative AI can read their productions and write constructive feedback, unique to their specific context and needs, at a scale that was previously not possible (Baker & Inventado, 2014). In addition to allowing for more robust engagement with their learning and improvements in progress, students can be provided with feedback and support when not being supported or monitored by their teacher.

Developing assessments and creating various exam formats are also promising applications to provide some protection against cheating and offer different forms of assessment (Zawacki-Richter et al., 2019). Finally, generative AI can offer teachers research assistant capabilities such as synthesizing articles, offering bibliographic leads, or assisting in scientific writing (Dwivedi et al., 2023).

1.2 Perceived Impacts: Benefits and Challenges

The potential impacts of IAG are double-edged.

Advantages

- **Personalization and adaptation**: IAG makes it possible to design tailor-made learning paths, adapted to the learning rhythms and styles of each student, promoting truly differentiated pedagogy (Luckin, 2018).
- **Motivation and engagement**: Relevant content and rapid feedback can increase learners' intrinsic motivation.

- **Efficiency and time savings**: Automation of repetitive tasks frees up the teacher for more complex, interactive activities (Selwyn, 2021).
- **Development of new skills**: Interaction with intelligent tutoring systems promotes the development of high-level cognitive skills, as demonstrated by meta-analyses comparing human and artificial tutoring (VanLehn, 2011). This dynamic also applies to contemporary generative AI.

Challenges

- **Learning assessment:** If AI generates sophisticated responses, how do we evaluate the authenticity of student output? This raises deep questions about understanding and learning (Luckin, 2018).
- **Cognitive overload and verification:** The teacher must verify the relevance and accuracy of the content generated, which can paradoxically create a work overload (Williamson, 2017), particularly in a context where educational data is becoming massively algorithmized.
- **Facilitator role:** The automation of some routine elements leads to the re-evaluation of the teacher's role, which now needs to transition towards montage/creating learning experiences and ethically guiding (Holmes et al., 2022).

1.3 Adoption and Integration Factors: A Systemic Perspective

The successful integration of any new technology into education will refer to a process of implementation that extends beyond the digital technology alone and looks at a technical ecosystem.

- **Teacher digital competency and background experience:** Previous studies suggest that teachers with a favourable familiarity and experience with digital tools in the way they best understand use, are more likely to adopt new technologies (Tondeur et al, 2017). Digital competency is not only technical but contains a pedagogical and critical dimension.
- **Ongoing training:** Continuous and targeted training is critical to empower teachers to know the affordances of RTI, but more importantly to create ethical and targeted pedagogical scenarios (UNESCO, 2021).
- **Institutional support and infrastructure:** Quality access to digital infrastructure (internet access, quality hardware, access to tools), technical and qualified technical assistance, and an institutionally developed digital strategy or policy, are minimum prerequisites necessary for meaningful uptake.

Techno-pedagogical governance policies must be established to monitor the use of RTI (OECD, 2021).

- **Discipline and context:** Uptake can differ significantly between disciplines. For example, the uptake of RTI may be more intuitively attended to in environments where text or code generation frequently occurs compared to disciplines that are primarily concerned with physical manipulation or experimentation in laboratory settings.

1.4 Ethical and Responsible Issues

At the core of the discourse around RTI in education are ethical considerations (Holmes et al. 2022; UNESCO, 2021).

- **Accountability and transparency:** Should an error or bias occur in the AI-generated outcome, who is responsible? There needs to be training for educators to engage with AI as a tool and understand its limits and workings. Algorithmic transparency is critical for building trust.
- **Algorithmic biases and fairness:** AI models are executed using massive datasets which may have inherent ideological biases, using these programs and tools can therefore accidentally replicate or exacerbate large inequalities-reliable access and use of these tools is a significant concern.
- **Data protection and privacy:** The use of generative AI in education will require an enormous amount of sensitive data with significant implications (student data, pedagogical output), protecting data with regulation is necessary.
- **Learner autonomy:** Overreliance on AI is likely to hinder how students can cultivate cognitive autonomy and critical thought. Human-centered learning must remain the goal for student.

1.5 Gaps in the Literature and the Study's Contribution

Along with the growing volume of research there are also a number of voids in research that could be explored regarding case studies and reports of empirical studies that examine the adoption and effects of generative AI on the context of Southern countries. In particular, Morocco as an example of a Southern context, is under-researched. The available research is largely based in the Western context which has different infrastructures, higher educational cultures, and resource availability. The study will aim to provide backlog for any future development in education on generative AI through contextualized data and analysis, thereby providing specific insights into Moroccan higher education and how it adapts in response to a new wave of technology.

2. METHODOLOGICAL FRAMEWORK

Our study adopts a quantitative approach to analyze the factors predictively responsible for influencing the decision of higher education teachers in Morocco to adopt and engage with generative AI tools.

2.1 Target Population and Sampling

The study's target population was comprised of teachers at Moroccan higher education institutions, including instructors at the public universities (such as Mohammed V University, Cadi Ayyad, Hassan II; business schools (such as ISCAE, ENCG), and engineering schools (such as EMI, ENSEM). The sample was diversified to include varied geographical and disciplinary representation.

Data collection was through non-probabilistic convenience and snowball sampling because of the challenges in accessing the teaching cohort on a national scale. Invitations to the online survey were shared via university networks, professional email lists and academic social networks, and included colleagues, friends and acquaintances. A total of **252** complete responses were received, providing a good sample size for the planned statistical inquires.

This non-probabilistic sampling approach may limit the representativeness of the results. Nevertheless, nonresponse bias was assessed by comparing early and late respondents, and no significant differences were found. Missing values represented less than 2% of the dataset and were imputed using mean substitution. Participation was voluntary, informed consent was obtained, and responses were treated anonymously to ensure ethical compliance.

2.2 Data Collection Tools: Structured Questionnaire

A structured online questionnaire was designed to be used as the data collection instrument. The structured online questionnaire was based on existing theoretical models of technology acceptance, namely Davis' Technology Acceptance Model (TAM) (1989) and Venkatesh et al.'s Unified Theory of Acceptance and Use of Technology (UTAUT) (2003). These theories tell us more about how individuals adopted technology taking into account constructs such as perceived usefulness, perceived ease of use, social influence and facilitating conditions (access to resources, institutional supports, etc). The structured questionnaire consisted of several sections:

- **Socio-demographic data**: Age, gender, time in higher education, primary teaching discipline (humanities and social sciences, exact and technical sciences, health sciences, arts, etc.), institution of affiliation.

- **Digital literacy and prior technological experience**: Assessed by questions related to the regularity of the use of e-learning platforms (Moodle, Teams), collaborative tools (Google Workspace, Office 365), and prior educational technologies.
- **Usage of generative AI tools**: Frequency of usage (never, rarely, sometimes, often, very often), types of tools used (ChatGPT, Bard, Copilot, Midjourney, etc.), specific pedagogical purposes of the generative AI tools (generation of courses, exercises, lesson plans, feedback, research assistance, etc.). To assess frequency of usage a Likert scale (1= Not at all, 5=Very often) was adopted.
- **Perceptions of the impact of generative AI**: Likert scale (1=Don't agree at all, 5=Strongly agree) was used to assess the impact of generative AI on personalization of learning, student motivation, refer formative assessment, support facilitate content creation, time savings.
- **Barriers and brakes to adoption**: Likert scale to measure concerns of lack of training, ethical issues (plagiarism, authenticity), infrastructure issues (connection, equipment), lack of institutional support, cognitive overload, tool costs.
- **Perceived institutional support**: This was measured on a Likert scale in response to the availability of training, availability of access to resources (guides, tutorials), availability of technical support and access to institutional support for pedagogical innovation.

The validity of the full questionnaire was confirmed with a pilot study with twenty teachers spanning multiple disciplines. This pilot validated the clarity and relevance of the questions, identified ambiguities, estimated response times. This included changes including rewording some formulations, and expanding response options to reflect diversity of practice.

The internal consistency of the scales was assessed using the Cronbach's alpha (α) coefficient, a commonly used statistic within the social sciences to assess the fidelity of attitude or perception scales. A general acceptable threshold is 0.70, with a reading above 0.80 indicating excellent reliability (Hair et al., 2021).

Table 1. Internal reliability of questionnaire subscales

Thematic scale	Number of items	Cronbach's α
Perceptions of the impact of generative AI	6	0.89
Obstacles and brakes to adoption	7	0.85
Perceived institutional support	5	0.87
Digital familiarity and previous technological experience	4	0.82

The results are presented in Table 1, where the coefficients with all above the 0.80 threshold confirming strong homogeneity of responses for each subscale. Therefore, the measures used in this study were considered sufficiently psychometrically robust to guarantee the reliability of the ensuing analyses (Hair et al., 2021; Tavakol & Dennick, 2011).

2.3 Research hypotheses

To guide the statistical analysis and test relationships between variables, the following hypotheses were formulated:

- **H1: Continuing education** On generative AI positively influences the intensity and diversity of teachers' pedagogical uses of these tools.
- **H2:** Teachers' **level of prior digital familiarity** is positively correlated with their adoption and integration of generative AI into their pedagogical practices.
- **H3: Perceived institutional support** (access to infrastructure, technical support, promotion) significantly favors the adoption and use of generative AI by teachers.
- **H4a: Teaching discipline** influences the **specific type of use of** generative AI by teachers.
- **H4b: Teaching discipline** moderates **overall intensity of use of** generative AI by teachers, after controlling for other factors.
- **H5: Positive perceptions of** the impacts of generative AI (personalization, time saving, motivation) are associated with higher adoption and better integration of these tools.
- **H6: Ethical concerns** and **infrastructure constraints** are negatively correlated with the adoption and intensity of use of generative AI.

Inspired by these hypotheses, we built a conceptual model to show the theoretical relationships between main explanatory factors (training; digital familiarity; institutional support; perceptions; brakes) and intensity of use of generative AI (Figure 1). In using the PLS-SEM analysis, this model will be used to empirically test the structural links and the relative contribution of each variable.

Figure 1. PLS-SEM conceptual model of the determinants of generative AI use among higher education teachers

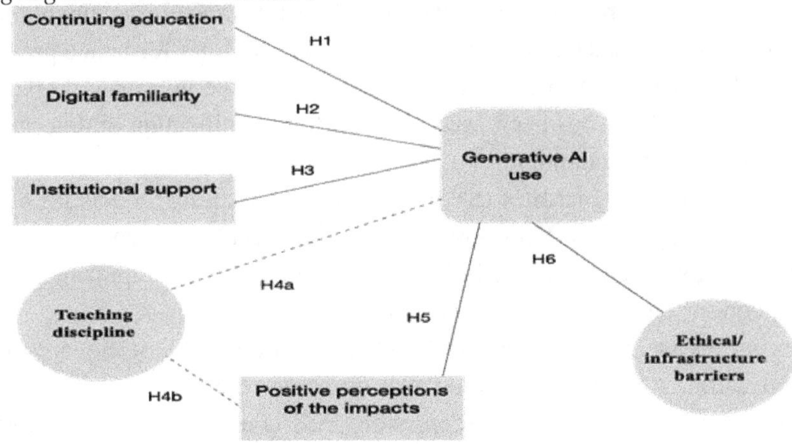

2.4 Data analysis methods

The data from the questionnaire were analyzed through a combination of statistical techniques and machine learning algorithms, so we could explore relationships between variables in-depth, and build both explanatory and predictive models. We wanted to achieve these two aims - identify the influential factors of adopting generative AI technology, and classify typical teacher profiles in order to offer differentiated support.

All analysis was conducted in Python, using scikit-learn (Pedregosa et al., 2011), which provided many modeling and visualization tools that enabled a robust methodological approach. First, we used descriptive statistical analysis (means, standard deviations, frequencies) to characterize the sample, their uses of generative AI tools, and we summarized perceptions and brakes. Pearson correlation tests were then conducted to determine if continuous variables (e.g. digital familiarity, frequency of pedagogical use of AI tools) were linearly linked (Field, 2024).

In order to expand the identification of determinants, a number of machine learning algorithms were enlisted:

- **Random Forest:** An ensemble learning method based on decision trees (Breiman, 2001). Random forests excel at determining the most important variables (feature importance) without requiring strong assumptions about the form of the distribution of the data, and handling non-linearities. It has been used to establish the relative influence of each variable on adoption and intensity of use;

- **XGBoost (Extreme Gradient Boosting):** An advanced implementation of decision trees based on gradient boosting. It is a high-performance prediction algorithm that is robust to noise, and can also handle missing data (Chen & Guestrin, 2016). It has been used to refine the identification of determinants and for their predictability;
- **Support Vector Machines (SVM)**: supervised learning models for classification and regression (Cortes & Vapnik, 1995). SVMs are particularly powerful for non-linear data and in high dimensional spaces, capturing complex interactions between factors of adoption.
- **Partial Least Squares (PLS) Regression**: Partial Least Squares (PLS) Regression: A statistical method that combines features of principal component analysis and multiple regression. PLS is useful when the number of predictors is high and they are highly correlated (multicollinearity), which is often the case in perception surveys. It has been used to explore relationships between sets of latent variables (for example, latent "institutional support" and latent "AI adoption") (Wold et al., 2001).
- Multiple linear regression was also mobilized to model the relationship between a continuous dependent variable (e.g., "Generative AI use intensity score") and several independent variables (training, digital familiarity, institutional support, etc.). This analysis makes it possible not only to quantify the effect of each factor, but also to control for cross-effects that could bias the estimates.
- The general formulation of the model is as follows: Y = Œ≤,ÇÄ + Œ≤,ÇÅX,ÇÅ + Œ≤,ÇÇX,ÇÇ + ... + Œ≤,ÇôX,Çô + Œµ, where Y denotes the dependent variable (intensity of use), Xi the predictor variables (training, familiarity, support, etc.), Œ≤i the estimated coefficients, and Œµ the random error term. This model thus makes it possible to identify the specific and significant contributions of each factor in the effective adoption of generative AI, while ensuring the statistical robustness of the interpretation of the effects.
- Finally, to analyze the diversity of behaviors and perceptions among teachers, an unsupervised cluster analysis was performed. The K-means algorithm, a classification method that partitions observations into K distinct groups according to proximity to their centroid (Lloyd, 1982), was used to identify homogeneous teacher profiles based on their practices and attitudes towards generative AI.

Multiple linear regression was also employed to model the relationship between the dependent variable, which is continuous ("Generative AI use intensity score"), and several independent variables (training, digital familiarity, institutional support, etc.). This analysis allows for estimating not only the magnitude of the effect of each of those factors but also controlling for any cross-effects that may confound any of the estimates.

The general formulation of the model is as follows: $Y = \beta_0 + \beta_1 X_1 + \beta_2 X_2 + ... + \beta X + \varepsilon$, where Y is the dependent variable (intensity of use), Xi are the predictor variables (training, familiarity, support, etc.), βi are the estimated coefficients, and ε is the random error term. The model allows to precise the distinct and significant contributions of factors that play a role in the successful adoption of generative AI, while also preserving the statistical reliability of the interpretation of the effects overall.

Finally, in order to understand the diversity of behaviors and perceptions of teachers, we undertook an unsupervised cluster analysis and K-means, a classification method that groups observations into K distinct groups and measures their proximity to K centroids (Lloyd, 1982), was selected to identify homogeneous groups of teachers by describing their practices and attitudes towards generative AI.

We also employed DBSCAN (Density-Based Spatial Clustering of Applications with Noise), which is able to discover clusters of arbitrary shapes while also identifying outliers, in order to contrast with the clustering done by K-means, and also to better capture any complex structure contained in the data (Ester et al., 1996).

Both techniques were run in Python with the scikit-learn library, which is well known for its robust performance with machine learning methods. The main motivation for selecting this coding environment was that it provides an adequate level of flexibility, optimized processing and additional visualization capabilities. The quality of the clusters was examined using the Silhouette Score (Rousseeuw, 1987) which is a measure of cohesion within clusters and the separation of clusters, as well as by examining the profiles produced.

For these analyses, the results were assessed through relevant criteria: for the regression - Adjusted R^2 and p-values; for the classification models - precision, recall, F1-score and ROC/AUC curve; and for clustering cluster evaluation metrics (silhouette score).

3. RESULTS AND DISCUSSION

In this section, we provide the detailed results from the statistical analyses structured according to the objectives of the study and the hypotheses outlined. Then, we discuss each result in the context of relevant literature, the particulars of adopting technology in Morocco and the local context and implications for practice.

3.1 Sample Characteristics and GenAI Tool Usage Profiles

This work is based on a sample of 252 teachers from a variety of Moroccan public and semi-public higher education institutions, ranging from universities to engineering colleges and management colleges to faculties of art or faculties of medicine. By using a sample from varied institutions, we can appreciate the adoption of generative artificial intelligence (GenAI) in different contexts; including, institutional contexts and disciplinary contexts.

There was reasonable balance of gender with 47% of the respondents being women and 53% being men in our survey, echoing the general situation of university teaching staff in Morocco. The average age of the respondents was 43.1 years with a standard deviation of 9.8 years which may suggest some variation between young and more experienced teachers. The mean length of service in higher education was 15.2 years so we can describe our sample as mature and with a number of waves of pedagogical innovation behind them including implementing digital technology in teaching practices.

There was reasonable balance of gender with 47% of the respondents being women and 53% being men in our survey, echoing the general situation of university teaching staff in Morocco. The average age of the respondents was 43.1 years with a standard deviation of 9.8 years which may suggest some variation between young and more experienced teachers. The mean length of service in higher education was 15.2 years so we can describe our sample as mature and with a number of waves of pedagogical innovation behind them including implementing digital technology in teaching practices.

In terms of disciplinary variation, the survey sample was reasonably distributed across some key fields. Human and social sciences (HSS) (38%) represented the largest group of respondents and was followed closely by exact and technical sciences (37%). Health sciences accounted for 13% of the sample while put together, arts, law and humanities had a share of 12%. The breakdown is summarized in figure 2 and suggests the diversity of the disciplinary nature of the teachers who completed the survey.

Figure 2. Disciplinary profiles of teachers in the sample

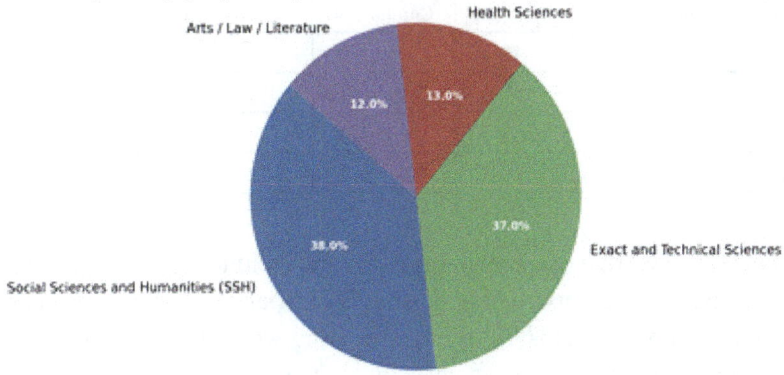

In relation to the use of generative artificial intelligence (GenAI) tools, it is interesting to note that 75% of teachers reported they have used at least one GenAI tool, either for personal use or professional use. Nevertheless, the strictly pedagogical uses of these tools still seemed more limited: only 52% of respondents reported they used the tools "sometimes," "often" or "very often" in relation to their teaching practice.

Of the tools mentioned, ChatGPT is the most commonly reported (68% of respondents reported having used this), followed by Bard (42%) and Copilot (28%), in all combinations of frequency and context. These findings are aligned with worldwide analyses surrounding the development and implementation of GenAI in higher education: the rapid and significant learning that occurred upon the initial release of ChatGPT (November 2022) has transformed educational and pedagogical uses of the tool, both in terms of content and learning support (Baidoo-Anu & Owusu Ansah, 2023).

Table 2 is included to illustrate differences in pedagogical use by disciplines. It provides the percentage of teachers who reported frequent use of these tools for pedagogical purposes (either "often" or "very often"), and an overall usage average (with a Likert scale ranging from 1 to 5). The results demonstrate that there are some variations in use by discipline, with greater use in the sciences than in the arts and humanities. The discipline effects that we observed are consistent with the observations made by Tondeur et al. (2017), who noted that disciplinary differences profoundly influence the integration of digital tools in teaching, and the objectives associated with the resulting pedagogical approaches, teachers' prior practices, etc.

Table 2. Rate of frequent pedagogical use of GenAI tools by discipline

Discipline	ChatGPT (%)	Bard (%)	Copilot (%)	Average pedagogical use (Likert /5)
SHS	62	41	12	3.7
Sciences	78	52	35	4.1
Health	48	29	18	3.2
Arts/ Law	33	18	6	2.8

The data revealed that teachers in the exact and technical sciences had the highest levels of pedagogical use, using these tools in particular for code generation, simulating complex problems, or technical writing when they used the tools pedagogically. While humanities and social sciences teachers reported using GenAI for tasks such as reformulating texts, generating ideas, or making discursive content, the teachers in arts and literature, law, etc drew on it much less in terms of frequency and use in different ways.

These findings corroborate hypothesis H4a, which posited that the discipline being taught significantly influences the specific pedagogical use of generative AI tools but does not necessarily predict the overall intensity of use across all contexts.

3.2 Perceived Impact of Generative AI on Pedagogy

A further analysis of responses from the sample (N = 252) shows that, all things considered, teachers view generative AI as a pedagogical tool that could have some promise, despite some lingering reservations. The results, summarized in Figure 3 below, illustrate the percentage of agreement (% of respondents choosing a score of 4 or 5 on a Likert scale of 1 to 5), as well as the standard deviations associated with those responses, providing an indication of the degree of consensus.

Figure 3. Teachers' perceptions of the impact of generative AI

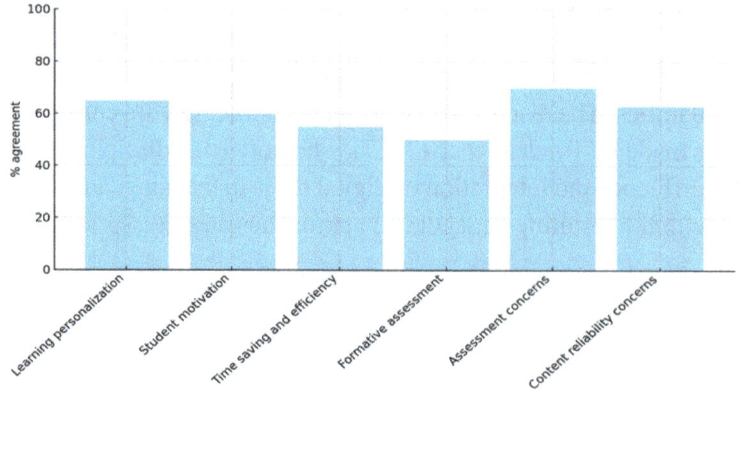

Analysis shows that teachers' overall perceptions of generative AI have an overall disposition suggesting a favorable perception, and regular use of generative AI was more favorably perceived than not. The results are based on 252 teachers' responses to a series of items measuring perceived pedagogical benefits and limitations of these technologies..

A number of dimensions of impact was measured:

- **Personalization of learning**: 65% of teachers indicated that generative AI allows content personalization based on student-specific needs. This suggests that these tools have the potential to individualize education paths (Luckin, 2018; Molenaar, 2022).
- **Student motivation**: 60% report that using AI makes learning more engaging and interactive, which helps increase learner engagement (i.e., Baidoo-Anu & Owusu Ansah, 2023).
- **Time savings and efficiency**: 55% of advanced teachers report a reduction in the time preparing teaching materials, and are able to redirect that time into more pedagogical follow-up, and human interaction.
- **Formative assessment**: 50% reported using AI to generate quick, personalized feedback, further confirmation of the formative aspect of assessment.

However, concerns remain:

- **Assessment validity**: 70% feel there is a lack of ability from AI tools to assess or completely alter outcomes of assessment (i.e., cheating, generating inauthentic responses), as identified by Dwivedi et al. (2023).
- **Content reliability:** 63% are not sure of the quality, accuracy or recency of information created requiring systematic scrutiny (i.e., McGrath et al. 2024).

The results indicate a tension between perceived pedagogical interest, and ethical or methodological apprehension; they somewhat support hypothesis H5 (positive perceptions in favour of use), while making evident the barriers outlined in hypothesis H6..

3.3 Determinants of Generative AI Adoption: Regression Analyses and Machine Learning Models

To test our hypotheses (H1, H2, H3, H5, H6) in a more robust manner, we utilized multiple linear regression and machine learning techniques. The dependent variable we derived was a usage intensity score (normalized sum of usage frequencies for different pedagogical tasks, for a possible range from 0 to 100), a "Generative AI Usage Intensity Score."

3.3.1 Multiple Linear Regression results

The multiple linear regression model was fitted with the key independent variable for our hypotheses.

Table 3. Results of the multiple linear regression model on intensity of use of generative AI

Independent variable	Coefficient (β)	Standard error	t-statistic	p-value
Continuing education IA (H1)	**8.50**	1.50	5.67	< **0.**001*
Previous digital familiarity (H2)	**6.90**	1.30	5.31	< **0.**001*
Perceived institutional support (H3)	**5.20**	1.20	4.33	< **0.**001*
Positive perception of impact (H5)	3.00	1.40	2.14	0.033*
Ethical concerns (H6a)	-4.50	1.25	-3.60	< 0.001***
Infrastructure issues (H6b)	-3.20	1.10	-2.91	0.004**
Discipline (Exact Sciences=1 vs. SHS=0)	2.00	1.45	1.38	0.169
Age	-0.12	0.10	-1.20	0.231
Gender (Male=1 vs. Female=0)	1.00	1.20	0.83	0.406

*Note: p-values: ***p < 0.001, **p < 0.01, *p < 0.05. The adjusted $R^{(2)}$) of the model is 0.58, indicating that 58% of the variance in intensity of use is explained by the variables included in the model.

The outputs of the regression model demonstrate support for many of our hypotheses at a high degree of statistical significance.

- The coefficient for Continuing Education IA is significantly positive (beta = 8.50, p <0.001), constituting strong support for H1. This suggests that for each point increase on the training participation scale, the intensity of use of generative AI goes up by 8.50 points, assuming all else is held equal. This result highlights the indispensable role of training in the appropriation of new technologies, in line with UNESCO recommendations (UNESCO, 2021).
- In the same way, Prior Digital Familiarity has a positive and highly statistically significant (b = 6.90, p < 0.001) coefficient supporting H2. Teachers familiar with digital tools (i.e., Learning Management System, collaborative tools) are most likely to see a natural way forward that enables an easy shift toward generative AI usage which is consistent with Tondeur et al. (2017)

where prior experience was found to be an important explanatory variable with regard to acceptance.

- Similarly, Perceived Institutional Support appears to be an important predictor that is statistically significant and positive ($b = 5.20$, $p < 0.001$) providing support for H3. Institutions that provide support (technical support, resources, and promoting innovation) and infrastructure make adoption and integration of AI easier for teachers and remove the technical implementation barriers.
- Positive perceptions of impact (H5) is also statistically significant and positively associated with increased intensity of use ($b = 3.00$, $p = 0.033$). A teacher that perceives AI as a means of providing better personalization or saving them time is more likely to use it more often.
- For the negative motivators (H6), ethical concerns ($b = -4.50$, $p < 0.001$) and problems related to infrastructure ($b = -3.20$, $p = 0.004$) are all negative and highly statistically significant coefficients. This suggests that concerns about plagiarism or access to a sustained connection or adequate equipment are serious challenges that significantly impede the teacher's ability to use generative AI. These findings confirm the words of Holmes et al. (2022) and Dwivedi et al. (2023) that caution should be exercised with regard to cognitive overload, as well as ethical implications.
- In terms of our hypothesis H4b (on overall intensity of use), the discipline variable (Exact Sciences=1 vs. SHS=0) had a positive coefficient ($b = 2.00$) which was not significant at the 0.05 level ($p = 0.169$) on the overall intensity of use of generative AI. This indicates that, while there may be an observable tendency for teachers in the exact sciences to show numerically higher intensity of use, this difference does not significantly contribute to overall intensity of use once we take into account other more powerful predictors such as training, digital familiarity and institutional support. This therefore complicates our H4b concerning a direct and significant influence of discipline on overall intensity of use.
- However, it is important to bear in mind that, as we found in section 4.1 discipline is highly influential on the kinds of generative AI applications and specific nature of that application (for example, code generation versus text reformulation). Our data therefore shows that H4a is validated on usage type, but that H4 holds up on the intensity of use of generative AI when other levers are utilized. Instead discipline tends to determine how AI is used not whether it is used with specific intensity.
- Socio-demographic variables (age, gender) proved insignificant, indicating their direct impact on usage intensity is negligible once other factors are considered.

3.3.2 Cross-Tabulated Results of Machine Learning and PLS-SEM Models

To triangulate the findings from the multiple linear regression, and extend the understanding of factors dominant in the use of generative AI, two complementary types of model were adopted:

- supervised machine learning models (Random Forest, XGBoost, SVM) that provided a measure of the relative importance of explanatory variables in a predictive logic (Breiman, 2001; Chen & Guestrin, 2016).
- and a partial least squares structural equation model (PLS-SEM); the PLS approach is best suited for causal relationships between latent variables (Hair et al., 2021).

3.3.2.1. Relative Importance of Explanatory Factors

The Random Forest and XGBoost models based on decision trees revealed the variables that had most influence on AI usage intensity. The SVM was opaque in its inner workings, but was qualitatively appraised using a convergence of results.

Table 4. Relative importance of variables according to the RF, XGBoost and SVM models

Factor	Random Forest (%)	XGBoost (%)	SVM (qualitative)
Continuing education IA	29.0	30.5	High
Previous numerical familiarity	22.5	24.0	High
Perceived institutional support	19.0	18.5	Medium to high
Ethical concerns	9.0	8.5	Average
Positive perception of impacts	8.0	7.0	Low to medium
Infrastructure problems	6.0	5.5	Low
Discipline taught	3.0	2.5	Low
Age of teacher	1.5	1.3	Very low
Teaching experience	1.0	1.2	Very low

Note: The importance of variables in the SVM model is derived from a qualitative cross-tabulation, due to the non-interpretable nature of the RBF kernel.

Table 4 shows a significant coherence across the models in terms of determining variables. Each model considers participation in continuing education to be the most important variable, with a relative importance of 29.0% in Random Forest and 30.5% in XGBoost, and a value of "high" in the SVM model. Participation was followed by prior digital familiarity, which had relative importance values of 22.5% (RF) and 24.0% (XGBoost), and also received a value of "high" from the SVM. Perceived institutional support was ranked 3rd in both models, with an importance of 19.0% (RF) and 18.5% (XGBoost) and received a "medium to high" rating in the SVM.

All socio-demographic variables received negligible or very little weight:

- **Age of teacher**: 1.5% (RF), 1.3% (XGBoost), value of "very low" (SVM)
- **Teaching seniority**: 1.0% (RF), 1.2% (XGBoost), value of "very low" (SVM)
- **Discipline taught**: 3.0% (RF), 2.5% (XGBoost), value of "weak" (SVM)

These results corroborate the results of the linear regression and emphasize that the determinants of generative AI use are primarily pedagogical and organizational. Use, therefore, depends above all on digital skills developed, ongoing training, and institutional support, rather than personal attributes like age, discipline, or seniority.

The agreement of the various statistical and algorithmic models strengthens the credence of the reported results, and justifies the recommendations to support a targeted training and support policy. The claims of common observation versus common stories have methodological convergence, and are consistent with several of the recent works that sought to encourage the cross-use of explanation models (e.g., PLS-SEM) and prediction models (ML) in order to enhance our understanding of techno-educational behaviors (Dwivedi et al., 2023; Ferguson et al., 2023).

3.3.2.2 Analysis of latent relationships via PLS-SEM

The PLS-SEM model was activated to explore the structural relationships between the latent factors (training, familiarity, support, perceptions, disincentives) and the use of generative AIs. The path coefficients are significant in general, except for the "discipline" variable validating the conceptual links associated (Hair et al., 2021; Henseler et al., 2015).

Table 5. Path coefficients of the PLS-SEM model

Relationship modeled	Coefficient (β)	p-value	Interpretation
Continuing education → IA use	0.32	< 0.001	Highly significant
Digital familiarity → AI usage	0.29	< 0.001	Highly significant
Institutional support → AI usage	0.25	< 0.001	Highly significant
Positive perceptions → Usage IA	0.18	0.021	Significant
Barriers (ethical/infrastructure) → AI usage	-0.22	< 0.01	Significant negative effect
Discipline → AI usage	0.05	0.210	Not significant

Note: Ethical concerns and infrastructural constraints have been grouped together under a single latent factor entitled *"Impediments (ethical/infrastructural)"*, due to their strong empirical correlation

The PLS-SEM model demonstrates (as shown in Table 5) the strength of the causal relationships from the main transformation levers to the use of generative AIs. The path coefficients are especially strong for continuing education ($\beta = 0.32$, $p < 0.001$), digital familiarity ($\beta = 0.29$, $p < 0.001$), and perceived institutional support ($\beta = 0.25$, $p < 0.001$); all of which indicate direct significant effects on adoption (Hair et al., 2021; Sarstedt et al., 2014). Additionally, their positive perceived affects on impacts are also significant, but are the lesser ($\beta = 0.18$, $p = 0.021$.

In contrast, the brakes factor (ethical/infrastructure) is moderately to highly negative in relation to use ($\beta = -0.22$, $p < 0.01$), emphasizing the importance of eliminating barriers within deployment policies. The discipline variable is not significant ($\beta = 0.05$, $p = 0.210$), which suggests that the impacts we see are across disciplinary fields.

The PLS-SEM model provides empirical support to the structural associations in the theoretical model. The informed levers of training, familiarity, and support are all strongly and significantly associated with the use of AI. The model explains 61% of the variance in usage for generative AI ($R^2 = 0.61$), so we can be confident in the explanatory ability of the model. These results provide empirical support for the proposed conceptual framework and ground the recommendations on a strong scientific structural foundation.

3.3.2.3. Comparative performance of predictive and explanatory models

To bring together the findings from the multiple linear regression analyses and deepen our understanding of factors affecting the use of generative AI, we used two complementary approaches:

- **Supervised machine learning models** (Random Forest, XGBoost and SVM) that predict the level of a teacher's use by means of the most relevant combinations of explanatory variables. The models perform particularly well in identifying complicated non-linear relationships, and assess the relative importance of each predictor in their prediction (Breiman, 2001; Chen & Guestrin, 2016).
- **The PLS-SEM**, which offers both an explanatory and theoretical treatment of causal relationships with multivariate latent variables. This allows us to empirically assess the level of validity of the conceptual framework we proposed and quantify the unique contribution of each lever (training, supporting, perceived, brake ...), to the use of generative AI (Hair et al., 2021; Sarstedt et al., 2014).

This is essentially the same when we consumer level as two families of models: the former quantifies predictive performance and the latter provides deeper analysis of the underlying causal structure.

Table 6. Comparative model performance

Model	F1-average score	AUC ROC	Overall performance
Random Forest	0.83	0.87	Accuracy: 85.0
XGBoost	0.83	0.89	Accuracy: 86.2
SVM (RBF kernel)	0.81	0.89	Accuracy: 84.2
PLS-SEM	-	-	R^2 (IA usage): 0.61

Note: The PLS-SEM model is not a predictive model in the strict sense, but an explanatory tool based on the variance explained (here, 61%).

Three AI models confirm their prediction strength, as shown in Table 6, with F1-score above 0.80 and AUC ROC curve above 0.85 thus confirming they can effectively differentiate levels of generative AI use as a function of explanatory variables. The model's performance demonstrates that both algorithms are able to capture complex non-linear relationships during the adoption behavior including an implicit interaction effect among the individual, educational and institutional dimensions (Dwivedi et al., 2023).

The PLS-SEM model, while not intended for prediction, confirms the reality of the theoretical framework by modeling structural relationships among latent factors. With an R^2 of 0.61, it has strong explanatory power in an educational context that frequently involves multidimensional and interdependent adoption behaviors. Specifically, it allows us to estimate direct and indirect effects of composite variables, such as institutional support and ethical constraints.

Thus, the combination of these two approaches - one predictive, and the other explanatory - provides a triangulated and strengthened vision. It allows us to consider the statistical relevance of the variables alongside the theoretical hypotheses articulated upstream, reinforcing the credibility of the results obtained and transferability to operational recommendations. This methodological complementarity is a significant contribution of the study by effectively combining conceptual depth and empirical strength in analysing the adoption of generative AI.

3.3.2.4. Synthesis

The convergence between the three approaches (regression, machine learning, PLS-SEM) serves as some solid validation of the major results. Three key levers - continuing education, digital familiarity and institutional support - are highlighted as being essential and cross-cutting. Ethical and infrastructural matters represent recurring barriers across each model. Finally, individual characteristics (age, seniority, discipline) are shown to have marginal influence.

This convergence in contrast legitimizes the strategic recommendations made in this chapter and grounds them in statistical rigor, explanatory breadth and external validity.

3.4 Typology of teacher profiles: Clustering analysis

Using clustering analysis (K-means, with K=3 based on the Silhouette Score and interpretability), we identified three profiles among Moroccan higher education teachers based on their posture towards generative AI. Clustering was supplemented and verified by the DBSCAN method, and revealed significant diversity in terms of uses, perceptions and related support needs. (Lloyd, 1982; Hair et al., 2021; Chicco et al., 2021). We called the three profiles: the Innovators, the Cautious and the Technological Rejecters.

Figure 4. Characteristics of teacher profiles concerning generative AI

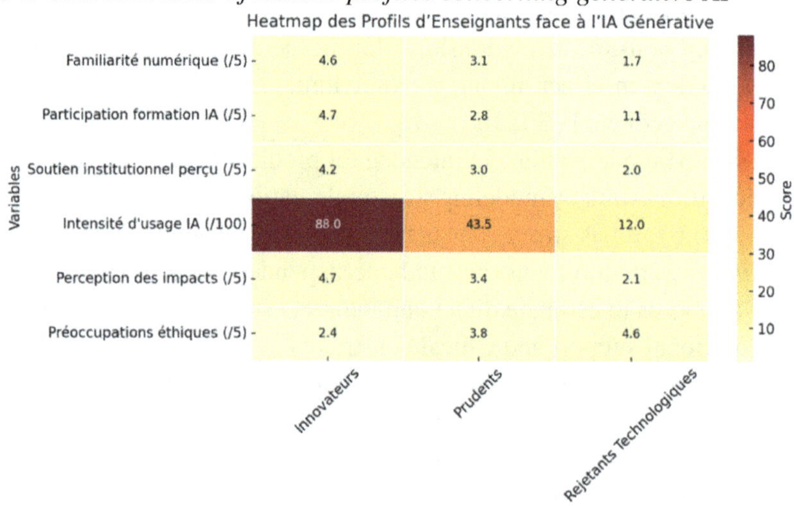

Figure 4 displays differences between the three profiles, based on six dimensions. The following paragraphs describe the characteristics and needs of the three profiles.

- **Innovators** (approx. 18.0%): This group is representative of the farthest fringe of teachers. This group exhibits a very high digital landscape familiarity (Mean = 4.6/5) and have taken AI training courses (Mean = 4.7/5). They view generative AI as a good lever for pedagogy innovation (Impact

Perception Average = 4.7/5) and use these tools in a far more complex way than other groups (Usage Intensity Score = 88.0/100). Their perceived institutional support is also quite high (Mean = 4.2/5), which may reflect their comparatively greater means to seek and leverage the products available. Ethical concerns were evident here, but they appear to be better able to manage these elements in a proactive manner (Mean = 2.4/5). Overall, this profile appears more often in courses where the discipline is on the fringe of technology and/or has a large textual or coding production (e.g., computer sciences, parts of scientific research, communication sciences). This finding is also supportive of our H4a regarding discipline as playing a role in certain modes of preferred use (Zawacki-Richter et al., 2019; Baidoo-Anu & Owusu Ansah, 2023; Khlaif et al., 2024).

- **Prudent (approx. 57.0%):** This category consists of the majority in our sample, with sufficiently moderate digital familiarity (M = 3.1/5), occasional AI training (M = 2.8/5), and modest interest in the possible potentials of generative AI, using it occasionally for related but low-risk specific tasks (usage intensity score = 43.5/100). This group's concern about high ethical integrity issues (M = 3.8/5) and quite variable institutional support (M =3.0/5, M= 3.4/5). This profile is likely to be reflective of subject areas where AI integration is not systematic nor prioritized (e.g. humanities and social sciences that are not communication, basic sciences, management) . For this group the impact of the discipline is evidenced in a more gradual and reflective approach to the technology and a quest for relevant applications for their own contexts, consistent with H4a. For this group, further relevant training, explicit examples of applications in their disciplines, and a more explicit central support, will help them navigate a more systematic and planned approach to use generative AI (Khlaif et al., 2024).
- **Rejecters (approx. 25.0%):** This segment represents the group of teachers who are least likely to embrace generative AI. They had low digital familiarity (Mean = 1.7/5) and no engagement in AI training (Mean = 1.1/5). Their usage intensity score is very low (12.0/100), reflecting anecdotal or low use. Their perceived impacts are either negative or neutral (Mean = 2.1/5). They are characterized by very high ethical concerns (Mean = 4.6/5), typically raise their high levels of ethical concerns with unknown concerns, the fear of plagiarism and/or the dehumanization of teaching, or loss of control of pedagogy, a way of practicing (using "fear" in place of pedagogical or positive cooking). Their perceived institutional support for AI was very low (Mean = 2.0/5), even lower than the Rejected individuals, which contrasts these individuals with previously illustrated their institutions support even for two-thirds of their concern to even consider engaging with AI. This behaviour is

more prevalent in Disciplines of study such as Arts, Humanities, and Masters, where teaching methods are likely to have been more traditional, and the sense of need for use of technology is less asserted that in other disciplines. Here, this discipline, the low digital familiarity, and ethical concerns appear strongly tied to low-intensity use. This helps to explain the importance of the awareness of measuring activity potentially associated with H4a. Awareness-raising actions would be needed for this profile that are fundamental (Van Braak et al., 2004; Al-Kfairy et al., 2024; Khlaif et al., 2024; Baidoo et al., 2023.) actions on AI, to raise awareness of AI based use and clear and ethically framed benefits.

These profiles reveal the diversity of teachers in their engagement with generative AI and reinforce that coaching/training should occur in unique ways. The massification of Moroccan education cannot be solved with AI unless each group of teachers has specific support strategies delineated.

4. COMPLEMENTARY QUALITATIVE STUDY

To further our understanding of the appropriation dynamics of generative artificial intelligence (generative AI) in Moroccan higher education, we also completed a complementary qualitative analysis together with the quantitative analysis. This qualitative study sought to explore the representations, doubts, hopes, and expectations expressed by teachers regarding AI, beyond the numbers.

4.1 Qualitative Interview Methodology

A total of 15 semi-structured interviews were performed with a sub-sample of teachers who were intentionally selected to represent the three generated profiles and the clustering analysis (Innovators, Cautious, Rejecters). The interview guide contained five major areas of reflection: concrete usages of AI, perceived advantages, fears/limitations, needs for support, and representations of the teacher.

The interviews were done either face-to-face or remotely (via videoconference), and had an average duration of 45 minutes each. The semi-structured interview guide was developed to explore the representations, uses, fears and expectations of generative AI in teaching practice. A thematic analysis of the interviews indicated that four main dimensions in the perception of AI were present that often emerged in the teachers' discourse, and were often mentioned with nuances of intensity, and ambivalence. This analysis was conducted through an inductive thematic approach which combined manual coding of verbatim, and cross-validations between researchers to assure inter-coder reliability and consistency of interpretation (Tesch, 1990).

- **Facilitation vs. Deprivation:** A number of teachers identify that AI can facilitate developing lessons, generating exercises, and helping to research. However, a considerable number also express the fear of "detriment" regarding losing valuable pedagogical skills or disrupting the teacher-learner relationship if AI were to take up too much space (Holmes et al., 2022; Williamson, 2017).
- **Ethics in AI and "Pedagogical Responsibility:** Through the discussions there was a deep concern with respect to plagiarism, the veracity of AI-generated information and fairness. Teachers are questioning their "pedagogical responsibility" in light of these challenges, and are searching for outlined frameworks that could help them and the students they teach navigate these kinds of issues (UNESCO, 2021; Holmes et al., 2022).
- **The Need for Support and Structures:** No matter the profile, a strong need was indicated for hands-on training, the clear institutional support and documented technical support. A sense of dislocation or disconnection about the new technologies seemed to be a major barrier for many teachers, clearly pointing to the need for a proactive institutional framework (Selwyn, 2020; OECD, 2020).
- **Redefining the teacher's role:** There emerged a collective awareness within the interviews regarding the need to redefine the teacher's role. Generative AI should not substitute, but should "enhance" pedagogy, using the teacher as a facilitator for complex skills (critical thinking, problem solving), and as an ethical guide in terms of AI. This dimension captures an evolution towards a role less focused on measuring the outcomes of learning experiences and student learning, and more focused on designing learning experiences and providing personalized engagement with students (Luckin, 2018.

These qualitative aspects endorsed and contextualized the quantitative evidence, adding greater understanding of the motivations, fears and needs of teachers and affirming the recommendations made in the conclusion.

Figure 5 below demonstrates the themes, sub-themes/codes and examples of the verbatim that were deduced from the thematic analysis of the interviews (N=15):

4.2 Results of the Thematic Analysis

The thematic analysis of the interviews has highlighted four key dimensions which structure Moroccan higher education teachers' perception of generative AI, and these dimensions consist of recurring sub-themes, fed by significant verbatim excerpts illustrating the differentiated moments of postures according to profiles (Innovators, Cautious, Rejecters). The key contents are summarized in Figure 5.

4.2.1 Facilitation vs. Dispossession: The Central Tension

This first dimension illustrates the duality in perceived benefits of increased efficiency and of concerns of diminished pedagogical agency.

- **Efficiency gains and time savings** Many of the educators interviewed mentioned that they appreciated the usful benefits of generative artificial intelligence tools for their one acutal teaching practice. These technologies are effective facilitators, and capable of speeding up the production of content (such as lesson writing, exercises and learning, obtaining documentary research, but also freeing up a significant amount of time, that was previously spent on repetitive tasks. An "innovator" teacher expresses this efficiency succinctly, stating that "AI has potential for creating exercises and covering a few ground ideas really quickly, which has saved me really meaningful preparation time." In a similar vein, the teacher who is "Cautious", stressed the possibilities of generative AIs to lighten a few of the stages of instructional design: "For documentary research or even the synthesis of a text, it is a really powerful tool that is going to lighten the work." These quotes, shared with other examples, are indicative of a commonly adopted understanding of time-saving and productivity, and pointing to an opportunity to redirect time onto high value-added, multidimensional activities, like following up with students individually or designing more interactive learning experiences.
- **Fear of loss of teaching skills** In leaning towards the potential benefits, a number of entities mentioned a sustained fear of their place within a pedagogical role, as generative AI will perform more of the creative, organizational and editorial functions. This sense of dispossession of the profession or professional precariousness was especially pronounced for the Cautions and Rejecters types, as the automation of teaching may position the educator mostly as a verifier of content, or a supervisor. One of them worried: "I worry that if AI does this all for us, we'll never learn to think, to construct our lessons. Does the teacher becomes only a 'validator'?" (Prudent Teacher). This fear also bears an attachment to the human dimension of teaching as irreplaceable. Another teacher foregrounds this idea: "Human interaction and spontaneous interactions contribute to teaching richness. AI could dehumanize the relationship with students." (Teacher Rejecting). These comments

reveal highlighted a identity tension between technological promise and educational mission rooted in exchange, empathy, and pedagogical intuition.

4.2.2 AI Ethics and Pedagogical Responsibility

The second dimension relates to academic legitimacy and the ethical challenges prompted by the use of AI for both teachers and students.

- **Plagiarism and academic integrity:** The rapid incursion of generative AI tools raises important issues regarding academic integrity. Many teachers are concerned about the risk of cheating, particularly through automated copy-pasting, and especially through the undocumented use of these technologies by students for assignment completion. The urgency of this issue is further heightened, given that current plagiarism detection systems appear to have no way of truly understanding AI-generated content. In the words of one of the teachers in the Rejecters profile: "How can we be certain students are not cheating with AI? Plagiarism is a huge problem, and our systems are often so backwards." Not only is this concern technical, but it suggests that the validity of assessment processes is called into question, as former reliable forms of assessment feel exposed in the new condition. In their own words, teacher four highlights the caution some educators share: "This is all new territory for me but what worries me most is how to maintain the integrity of the work. We absolutely have to find other ways of assessing. These comments show an increasing concern about the need to change assessment, to better reflect the new challenges created by AI, by moving towards process, individual progress and oralization of knowledge.
- **Veracity and biases in the information produced:** In addition to the concerns surrounding cheating, a number of educators want to emphasize that not only are AI tracking tools not infallible, they are not neutral. As many have suggested, there are effective options for AI, but those options may include factual errors, lack citations, provide incorrect information, or present biases associated with the limitations of their databases. Where data has identified an issue or bias it is important to have signals of intellectual integrity. This reflection spurs a conversation of caution and critical vigilance, regarding both personal use and in teaching students. One cautious teacher expresses this position succinctly: "You can't just trust AI with the truth of information. You always have to check, and that is something we must teach our students." For his part, one innovative teacher incorporates his stance: "there's bias in the data for AI and we have to help students to see the bias." These comments converge on the same obligation: to develop a critical literacy of AI in both

teachers and students, which is not confined to technical proficiency, but the opportunity to question, verify and contextualize the generated content.

4.2.3 The need for support and a framework

This third dimension groups together concrete requests: it shows that teachers, in whatever position, want clear reference points and support systems.

- **Practical, contextualized training** Teachers, challenged by the rapid emergence of generative AI, stated a clear desire for relevant and practical training. Many lamented the gap between rhetoric about the innovative use of technology in pedagogy from institutions, and real skills-building opportunities (that work operationally). They want relevant workshops, contextualized for their teaching field, that allow them to play with GenAI tools in realistic, adapted pedagogical scenarios. As one hesitant teacher voiced: "We hear a lot about AI but not adequate, practical training; meaning, we don't know how to integrate it into our course." This expectation was echoed by the more advanced profiles, as one innovative teacher indicated: "I would like to see workshops where we could try out AI using examples from our discipline." These testimonials all show the will for reasoned, thought-out appropriation, based on some logic of supervised experimentation, rather than just promoting use.
- **Clarity of institutional guidelines** A common and frequent concern is no institutional clear guidelines regarding using generative artificial intelligence in higher education. For many teachers, this absence of regulation creates both legal and ethical ambiguity for them and their students. Some noted the particular and urgent need for guidelines that clearly set out what is permissible, recommended, and prohibited in a higher education context. One teacher, in the Rejecters profile, summarized this expectation by stating, "We need clear guidelines from the university on what is and is not allowed with AI, for us and for our students." This need for a framework is not viewed as unnecessary restriction, but rather as a confidence-building lever in encouraging pedagogical experimentation. A view expressed by the cautious teacher, "A clear institutional framework would help comply with many teachers and facilitate experimentation." These comments illustrate a wish to have the use of AI embedded in purposeful academic policy and governance to better ensure innovation, responsibility, and security.

4.2.4 Redefining the role of the teacher

Lastly, the fourth cross-cutting dimension describes a reflection on the change in professional posture relating to the rise of AI.

- **Teacher as facilitator / guide** In the era of generative artificial intelligence many teachers are recognizing a significant change in their professional role. They no longer see themselves as simply transmitters of knowledge; they are more guides or facilitators tasked with guiding student exploration and critical and reasoned usage of AI. This shift in role entails a change in focus to the acquisition of complex cognitive capabilities (e.g., critical thinking, analysis, and distinguishing the relevance of information). This transition is illustrated by one innovative teacher when she remarked, "My role is changing: I'm not just the 'one who gives information', I'm the one who helps them understand the mass of information including the information generated by AI." Similarly, a timid teacher stated, "We need to focus on developing critical skills, complex thinking because AI can't do complex thinking for students." These responses illustrate some commitment to rethinking their teaching posture, not in opposition to AI technology, but in complementarity with AI and looking at students becoming more autonomous, reflective and ethically engaged.
- **AI to "augment" pedagogy** Some teachers, Deskbound Innovators in particular, as well as some Incorporated Cautious profile teachers, openly express an excitingly optimistic view: generative artificial intelligence is seen as a way to "augment" pedagogy, and just like that, it does not threaten teachers; it can also personalize learning, entrusting some of the repetitive or technical tasks to the AI to free up time to support learners in personalized ways. One innovative teacher had made this point before: "AI should not replace the teacher, it should add to the teacher. It could create time to focus on more personalized learning." This kind of pedagogical innovationCartography is also backed up by a Caut'+ve profile teacher who sees it as a lever for renewing practices. "Its an opportunity to tackle rethink our aholpl onceusing_ stimulate more interactive or learner-directed, and solve-real problems." These remarks give a positive and committed account of the possibilities of AI, and it is seen as a point of departure for changing education, perhaps more opportunity for interaction, creativity, or relevance learning paths..

4.3 Schematic representation of results

Figure 5 summarizes the major themes, sub-themes, representative verbatims and teacher profiles most concerned. It illustrates the richness, complexity, and diversity of postures towards generative AI, while also identifies points of convergence.

Figure 5. Themes, Sub-themes/Codes and Verbatim Examples from the thematic analysis

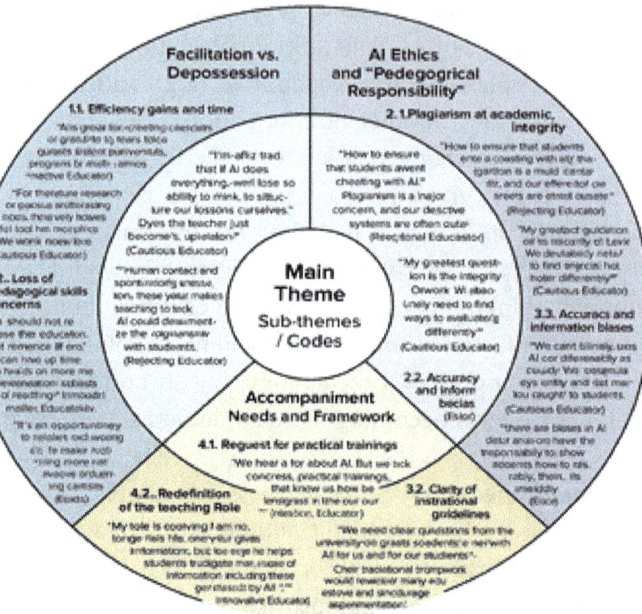

CONCLUSION AND OUTLOOK

The insertion of generative artificial intelligence into Moroccan higher education is more than a technological shift; it is a deep dynamic change in the contour of pedagogy, learning, and research. This study has highlighted the variety of Moroccan teachers' uses and perceptions for this revolution to emphasis, with the trained eye, that the effective and ethical use of generative AI is conditioned by a range of interdependent factors.

From our analyses using regression and machine learning models, we corroborated several important hypotheses. We flagged that continuing education in AI, teachers' prior familiarity with digital involves, and teachers' perceived institutional support are the more powerful predictors of the intensity of use of these tools. At the same time, ethical concerns and infrastructure limitations are key barriers. Teaching discipline also influences usage type, with a more natural adoption for specific tasks in narrower fields, without being the overall main predictor of intensity of use. Finally, the typology being teachers (innovators, cautious, rejectionists) confirms this heterogeneity and layer upon layer calls for tailored support strategies.

The potential of generative AI to change the shape of teaching is significant: it can support the personalization of learning, increase student engagement through customized content, and provide potentially significant time savings for educators performing routine tasks. However, the benefits of generative AImust not undermine major challenges that must be addressed: ongoing training, infrastructure issues, ethical frameworks, and institutional culture that supports responsible innovation.

- **Strategic recommendations for higher education in Morocco:** Based on our work we offer the following recommendations for better supporting Moroccan educators as we move into generative AI:
  - **Develop specific and differentiated continuous education programs:**
    - **For "Innovators":** A program that includes detailed training on prompt engineering for level 1, appropriate use of AI within complex learning settings (LMS, virtual reality) and action research on AI-aided pedagogy; and opportunities for participants' expertise and peer mentoring to be shared.
    - **For the "Prudent":** Design practical training based on real case studies with tangible demonstrations of the direct value of AI for course planning and formative assessment and direct feedback to students. Highlight good ethical (ethical standards) and risk management practices (verification of content generation and plagiarism).
    - **For "Rejecters":** Provide awareness training in basic digital skills, emphasizing the simple, concrete benefits of AI for sharing the workload and improving the engagement of students, stressing the ease-of-use aspect.
  - **Strengthen digital infrastructure and technical support:**
    - Ensure consistent high-speed internet access in all higher education institutions.
    - Provide teachers with proper hardware (high-performance computers, required software), and simplify access to premium versions of generative AI tools, or develop good quality secure institutional versions.

    - Provide responsive tech support services specific to AI to respond to teachers' inquiries and resolve their issues.
- **Develop ethical governance and guidelines to support AI in education:**
    - Create institutional or national charters for responsible use of generative AI; clarify intellectual property issues; student data protection; algorithmic transparency; and teacher accountability.
    - Encourage conversations and research on the ethical issues of AI for pedagogy; embrace a critical and humanistic perspective as per UNESCO (2021).
    - Embed AI ethics training as an essential pillar of all teacher training programs.
- **Promote a culture of experimentation and pedagogical innovation:**
    - Foster local initiatives and pedagogical "laboratories" in which teachers can experiment with AI in a safe and collaborating context.
    - Share and promote instances of good practice through the delivery of seminars, and the publication of internal papers and institutional recognition.
    - Redesign the framework for teachers evaluation to include and recognize pedagogical innovation through AI.

■ **Research implications:** This research while extensive is a starting point for many future directions:

- **Longitudinal studies:** Track the changes made by teachers in their practices and perceptions over time, providing an opportunity to study the long-term implications of generative AI on their pedagogy, learning objectives, and student satisfaction.
- **In-depth qualitative research:** Conduct semi-structured interviews, and case studies with teachers in differing contexts to explore their stories, experiences, challenges and strategies in different prescription of using AI..
- **Impact on student learning:** Offer direct measures of teachers use of AI and its implications for students' learning goals, engagement, agency and critical skills.
- **Develop precise frameworks for assessment:** Design and test assessment for learning approaches to educators that are contextually rooted in the era of generative AI, that can recognize creativity and critical thought beyond mimicking the knowledger.

- **International comparisons:** Conduct comparative studies with like countries in the region to uncover best practices, mistakes and learnings on the use of AI in education.
- **Cost-benefit analysis:** Determine the economic efficiency of incorporating generative AI in higher education, looking at expenditures on infrastructure, training and software versus gains in productivity and added pedagogical value

In summary, teacher training is not simply one factor in technical adoption, it is the foundation of a pedagogical, ethical, and effective transformation. With intentional investment to support its academics, Morocco can not only rise to the challenge of generative AI, but can position its higher education system as an innovative and excellence-driven model for the digital era. A balanced future for AI-enhanced pedagogy remains with a thoughtful synergy between technology, human training and ethical governance.

REFERENCES

Abbas, M., Jam, F. A., & Khan, T. I. (2024). Is it harmful or helpful? Examining the causes and consequences of generative AI usage among university students. *International Journal of Educational Technology in Higher Education*, *21*(1), 10. DOI: 10.1186/s41239-024-00444-7

Al Kfairy, M., Mustafa, D., Kshetri, N., Insiew, M., & Alfandi, O. (2024). Ethical Challenges and Solutions of Generative AI: An Interdisciplinary Perspective. *Informatics (MDPI)*, *11*(3), 58. DOI: 10.3390/informatics11030058

Baidoo-Anu, D., & Owusu Ansah, L. (2023). Education in the Era of Generative Artificial Intelligence (AI): Understanding the Potential Benefits of ChatGPT in Promoting Teaching and Learning. *Journal of AI*, *7*(1), 52–62. DOI: 10.61969/jai.1337500

Baker, R. S., & Inventado, P. S. (2014). *Educational Data Mining and Learning Analytics*. Springer.

Breiman, L. (2001). Random forests. *Machine Learning*, *45*(1), 5–32. DOI: 10.1023/A:1010933404324

Chen, T., & Guestrin, C. (2016). XGBoost: A scalable tree boosting system. In *Proceedings of the 22nd ACM SIGKDD International Conference on Knowledge Discovery and Data Mining* (pp. 785-794).

Chicco, D., Warrens, M. J., & Jurman, G. (2021). The coefficient of determination R^2: Analogies, misconceptions, and some alternatives. *PLoS One*, *16*(9), e0257181. PMID: 34473812

Cortes, C., & Vapnik, V. (1995). Support-vector networks. *Machine Learning*, *20*(3), 273–297. DOI: 10.1023/A:1022627411411

Davis, F. D. (1989). Perceived usefulness, perceived ease of use, and user acceptance of information technology. *Management Information Systems Quarterly*, *13*(3), 319–340. DOI: 10.2307/249008

Dwivedi, Y. K., Kshetri, N., Hughes, L., Slade, E. L., Jeyaraj, A., Kar, A. K., & Papagiannidis, S. (2023). So what if ChatGPT wrote it? Multidisciplinary perspectives on opportunities, challenges and implications of generative conversational AI for research, practice and policy. *International Journal of Information Management*, *71*, 102642. DOI: 10.1016/j.ijinfomgt.2023.102642

EL mustapha, E. A., & EL ADNANI, M. J. (2022). The contribution of e-learning in the professional development of teachers. Revue Marocaine de l'Évaluation et de la Recherche Educative, 8(8), 223-241.

Ester, M., Kriegel, H.-P., Sander, J., & Xu, X. (1996). A density-based algorithm for discovering clusters in large spatial databases with noise. In *Proceedings of the Second International Conference on Knowledge Discovery and Data Mining* (pp. 226-231). AAAI Press.

Ester, M., Kriegel, H. P., Sander, J., & Xu, X. (1996). A density-based algorithm for discovering clusters in large spatial databases. *KDD : Proceedings / International Conference on Knowledge Discovery & Data Mining. International Conference on Knowledge Discovery & Data Mining*, *96*, 226–231.

Ferguson, R.. (2023). *AI and Education: The Reality and the Potential.* OECD Publishing.

Field, A. (2024). Discovering Statistics Using IBM SPSS Statistics. *Sage (Atlanta, Ga.).*

Hair, J. F., Hult, G. T. M., Ringle, C. M., & Sarstedt, M. (2021). *A Primer on Partial Least Squares Structural Equation Modeling (PLS-SEM)* (3rd ed.). SAGE Publications. DOI: 10.1007/978-3-030-80519-7

Haroud, S., & Saqri, N. (2025). Generative AI in Higher Education: Teachers' and Students' Perspectives on Support, Replacement, and Digital Literacy. *Education Sciences*, *15*(4), 396. DOI: 10.3390/educsci15040396

Henseler, J., Ringle, C. M., & Sarstedt, M. (2015). A new criterion for assessing discriminant validity in variance-based structural equation modeling. *Journal of the Academy of Marketing Science*, *43*(1), 115–135. DOI: 10.1007/s11747-014-0403-8

Holmes, W., Persson, J., Chounta, I.-A., Wasson, B., & Dimitrova, V. (2022). *Artificial Intelligence and Education: A Critical View Through the Lens of Human Rights, Democracy and the Rule of Law*. Council of Europe.

Ismaili, Y. (2024). AI Literacy and Adaptive Learning in Moroccan Education: Advancing Critical Thinking and Personalized Learning. Research on Education and Media, 16(2).

Kasneci, E., Sechel, I., & Seidel, K. (2023). Generative AI in Higher Education: Promises and Pitfalls. *Frontiers in Education*, *8*, 117397.

Khlaif, Z. N., Ayyoub, A., Hamamra, B., Bensalem, E., Mitwally, M. A. A., Ayyoub, A., Hattab, M. K., & Shadid, F. (2024). University Teachers' Views on the Adoption and Integration of Generative AI Tools for Student Assessment in Higher Education. *Education Sciences*, *14*(10), 1090. DOI: 10.3390/educsci14101090

Lloyd, S. (1982). Least squares quantization in PCM. *IEEE Transactions on Information Theory*, *28*(2), 129–137. DOI: 10.1109/TIT.1982.1056489

Luckin, R. (2018). *Machine Learning and Human Intelligence: The Future of Education for the 21st Century*. UCL Institute of Education Press.

McGrath, C., Farazouli, A., & Cerratto Pargman, T. (2024). Generative AI chatbots in higher education: A review of an emerging research area. *Higher Education*, *89*(6), 1533–1549. DOI: 10.1007/s10734-024-01288-w

Molenaar, I. (2022). Towards hybrid human-AI learning technologies. *European Journal of Education*, *57*(4), 632–645. DOI: 10.1111/ejed.12527

Organisation for Economic Co-operation and Development (OECD). (2021). *The Future of Education and Skills 2030: Learning Compass 2030*. OECD Publishing.

Pedregosa, F., Varoquaux, G., & Gramfort, A.. (2011). Scikit-learn: Machine learning in Python. *Journal of Machine Learning Research*, *12*, 2825–2830.

Rousseeuw, P. J. (1987). Silhouettes: A graphical aid to the interpretation and validation of cluster analysis. *Journal of Computational and Applied Mathematics*, *20*, 53–65. DOI: 10.1016/0377-0427(87)90125-7

Sarstedt, M., Ringle, C. M., Smith, D., Reams, R., & Hair, J. F.Jr. (2014). Partial least squares structural equation modeling (PLS-SEM): A useful tool for family business researchers. *Journal of Family Business Strategy*, *5*(1), 105–115. DOI: 10.1016/j.jfbs.2014.01.002

Selwyn, N. (2021). *Education and Technology: Key Issues and Debates*. Bloomsbury.

Tavakol, M., & Dennick, R. (2011). Making sense of Cronbach's alpha. *International Journal of Medical Education*, *2*, 53–55. DOI: 10.5116/ijme.4dfb.8dfd PMID: 28029643

Tondeur, J., van Braak, J., Ertmer, P. A., & Ottenbreit-Leftwich, A. (2017). Understanding the relationship between teachers' pedagogical beliefs and technology use in education: A systematic review of qualitative evidence. *Educational Technology Research and Development*, *65*(3), 555–575. DOI: 10.1007/s11423-016-9481-2

UNESCO. (2021). AI and Education: Guidance for Policy-Makers. https://unesdoc.unesco.org/ark:/48223/pf0000376709

VanLehn, K. (2011). The relative effectiveness of human tutoring, intelligent tutoring systems, and other tutoring systems. *Educational Psychologist*, *46*(4), 197–221. DOI: 10.1080/00461520.2011.611369

Venkatesh, V., Morris, M. G., Davis, G. B., & Davis, F. D. (2003). User acceptance of information technology: Toward a unified view. *Management Information Systems Quarterly*, *27*(3), 425–478. DOI: 10.2307/30036540

Williamson, B. (2017). Big Data in Education: The Digital Future of Learning. *Policy & Practice.*

Wold, H., Sjöström, M., & Eriksson, L. (2001). PLS-regression: A basic tool of chemometrics. *Chemometrics and Intelligent Laboratory Systems*, *58*(2), 109–130. DOI: 10.1016/S0169-7439(01)00155-1

Woolf, B. P. (2010). *Building Intelligent Interactive Tutors: Student-Centered Strategies for Revolutionizing e-Learning*. Morgan Kaufmann.

Zawacki-Richter, O.. (2019). Systematic review of AI in higher education. *International Journal of Educational Technology in Higher Education.*

Chapter 7
Teaching Climate Change through the Lens of Generative AI

Zokir Mamadiyarov
Termez University of Economics and Service, Uzbekistan

Artiqova O'g'iljon
Mamun University, Uzbekistan

Temur Eshchanov
Urgench State University, Uzbekistan

Munir Ahmad
https://orcid.org/0000-0003-4836-6151
Survey of Pakistan, Pakistan

ABSTRACT

This chapter explores the transformative role of Generative AI (GenAI) in climate change education, highlighting its ability to personalize learning, visualize complex systems, and foster meaningful engagement. GenAI empowers educators to create interactive, adaptive, and action-oriented content, bridging gaps between scientific data and learner understanding. However, realizing its potential requires strategic integration, educator training, ethical design, and inclusive access. Through multi-stakeholder collaboration, GenAI can help build a more climate-literate, resilient, and empowered generation ready to lead sustainable change.

DOI: 10.4018/979-8-3373-9074-1.ch007

INTRODUCTION

With the climate problem rising even more, including the increase of global temperature, extreme weather, and more, the necessity of climate literacy is more important than ever (Ismail et al., 2024; Puri et al., 2024; Sato & Park, 2025; Yeh et al., 2025). The method of climate education should shift away from providing scientific facts; it should be motivating to think, emotional, and aimed at action. Yet, on the one hand, due to the urgency of the situation, climate education can be insufficient in educating the diversity of students, developing abstract scientific knowledge into an understandable format, or transforming knowledge into practical problem-solving abilities. That lack of capability is often a given when it comes to static textbooks, oftentimes one-size-fits-all lectures, and visual aids that simply are not capable of summing up the magnitude and scope of the climate crisis, as well as all the human consequences at large (Alenda-Demoutiez, 2022; Helbling et al., 2021; Kolenatý et al., 2022; Simpson et al., 2021).

Generative Artificial Intelligence (GenAI) offers an opportunity to change that by changing how we approach these constraints. Dynamic simulations, dynamic simulations, video generation, image synthesis, and highly powerful natural language processing gather understanding of complex climate information and turn it into personalized, interactive, and simple to learn (Atkins et al., 2024; Kanbach et al., 2024; Law, 2024; Yan et al., 2024). It offers teachers the possibility to create visualizations of climate conditions in the future, make real-time simulations of ecological conditions, or collaboratively develop a narrative case that shows local effects of climate change. Machines like ChatGPT, DALL-E, and video generators, including Sora, can cultivate curiosity, boost understanding, and aid in inquiry-based learning both formally and informally.

The chapter addresses the potential of GenAI, which can transform climate education because it fills the gap in academic abstraction and interest among learners. It starts with a contextualization of the technical possibilities of GenAI with regard to education and then proceeds to applications in the classroom and community-based learning. It proceeds to discuss the activities of GenAI in its support of creativity, critical thinking, and climate action amongst learners. Lastly, it focuses on ethical, technical, and pedagogical issues of GenAI integration and how a responsible, inclusive, and future-ready integration can be achieved.

GENERATIVE AI

GenAI is an innovative change in artificial intelligence as a whole. In contrast to the traditional AI systems that either use predetermined instructions or come up with inert datasets to offer a prediction or a classification, GenAI can produce completely new data, i.e., text, images, videos, audio, and simulations, using patterns it has learned in large volumes of data. This source of the generative ability already provides new horizons in areas of education, such as climate change, where it is crucial to comprehend the complexity, to be able to visualize inter-relationships, and encourage participation. The creative and adaptive character of GenAI is close to pedagogical priorities, which are individual learning, visualization of concepts, interactive involvement, and critical thinking (Andersen et al., 2025; Kumar et al., 2025; Law, 2024; Surathunmanun et al., 2024).

Overview of GenAI Tools for Education

The tools of GenAI are quickly changing the pedagogical paradigm that allows creating, visualizing, and interacting with complicated tasks in a different way. The tools present the chance to take the abstract or data-intensive aspects of climate education and render them in a more accessible, active, and even personal way to the learners. There has also development of a variety of GenAI applications that can assist teaching and learning, depending on different functionalities specific to teaching and learning (Law, 2024).

The most notable tool is ChatGPT, a large language model that can interpret and generate human text based on a prompt given by the user. Regarding educational places, ChatGPT works as an immediate tutor, debate companion, or a peace maker (Adeshola & Adepoju, 2024; Lo, 2023). To climate students and educators, it may respond to technical inquiries and interpret scientific terms in everyday language, help write lesson material, or interact as a hypothetical climate scientist to enable students to have a dialogue with him or her. Its language skills also make it suitable to use in role-playing activities, such as a discussion on how to tackle climate policy or look through the eyes of a stakeholder. That can be further enlightened through discussions and reflections.

Another very strong attribute of learning is visual representation, and functions such as those of DALL·E have a great future potential in this regard. DALL·E makes it possible to visualize phenomena in the environment that an educator or a student might not be able to directly capture or visualize, using only text (Küchemann et al., 2025; Temsah et al., 2024). It involves interactive diagrams of such processes as the melting of sea ice, coastal erosion, or the growth of urban heat islands. Creatively, students can use it to dream of hypothetical futures or even solutions, like adopted green city infrastructure or more forested regions, which actively promote scientific knowledge as well as imaginative pursuits.

The tools can be complemented with Sora, a video generation model created by OpenAI that introduces an audiovisual background to the climate storytelling.

Sora can convert text into brief video clips, so learners can see how the effect of the climate is changing over the years or simulate the consequences of various environmental policy decisions (Adetayo et al., 2024; CHEN et al., 2024). For example, the students might design videos where they could compare a situation where there were climate mitigation efforts and one without them, as animated data, the students purposefully choose the emissions, temperature change, or the loss of biodiversity to come to life. This form of immersion not only stimulates better understanding; it assists with an emotional connection, which can help students to engage with the urgency and complexity of climate problems.

In addition to these headline tools, an ecosystem of increasingly specialized GenAI applications is also appearing to facilitate interactive, data-driven learning experiences. Such products are AI-driven systems to learn a 3D model of environmental systems, tools that recreate natural processes or socio-environmental dynamics, and adaptive learning environments where the content is manipulated depending on student performance. With these kinds of tools, traditional classrooms can be converted to interactive labs where students can experiment, visualize, and reflect on climate systems and human-environment interactions in real time.

The combination of the GenAI tools has a multifaceted approach to going green in climate education. Combining capabilities supporting text, image, video, and simulation, they offer novel pedagogical affordances, enabling personalized and engaging learning, based on evidence. Nevertheless, their responsible usage requires a considered combination, ethical control, and teacher readiness that, at least, such potent technologies become the drivers, but not the barriers of high-quality education. Table 1 shows the key pedagogical goals aligned with GenAI functionalities.

Table 1. Pedagogical goals aligned with genAI functionalities

Pedagogical Goal	GenAI Functionality	Example Tool	Climate Education Use Case
Conceptual Visualization	Text-to-image or video generation	DALL·E, Sora	Illustrating coral bleaching or climate migration patterns
Inquiry-Based Learning	Prompt-based exploration, simulation	ChatGPT	Running climate futures scenarios
Differentiated Instruction	Adaptive content creation	ChatGPT	Multi-level texts on greenhouse gases
Emotional Engagement	Storytelling and narrative co-creation	ChatGPT, Sora	Narratives of climate justice

Applications in Content Creation, Personalization, and Storytelling

GenAI provides transformative opportunities in three major climate-education phases: generating content its personalizing, and storytelling. Its capability to push out bigger videotapes on education in less time enables educators to have less to do with the monotonous administration and pay more attention to engaging students (El Saddik et al., 2025; Karpouzis et al., 2024a; Pilaniwala, 2024). The applications of GenAI are rather impressive, as with the help of this solution, educators can create a curriculum on the topic, like climate change mitigation, renewable energy, or the carbon cycle, in a few minutes. The AI can produce reading passages based on the curriculum, make vocabulary lists, develop comprehension questions, and even make suggestions for interactive classroom activities. This capability saves a great deal of time required to design an instruction and, at the same time, makes it relevant and pedagogically coherent.

The other strong GenAI affordance that helps facilitate inclusive and differentiated learning is personalization. Educators can use varying input instructions to come up with relevant content to fit the needs of different students in terms of their level of education, language, and learning patterns. As an example, an ocean acidification lesson can be introduced as a visual narrative to younger learners, as a mass of data-laden excused learners in high schools, and as a research project-like activity to more advanced learners. The GenAI can also be used to convert technical content into local languages or make the reading easier to suit various readers with different types of needs. This degree of responsiveness aids in the closure of learning gaps and facilitates equitable access to climate education, notably where learners have one or more languages and where resources are limited.

One of the most interesting uses of GenAI, perhaps, is its storytelling ability. Storytelling is a way to render climate science concrete by locating knowledge and ideas in emotionally appealing, plot-structured contexts. GenAI is able to create detailed and scientifically explained stories that demonstrate what people and society live through due to climate change. Such as, it can cover the account of a village by the sea reacting to a rise of the oceans or a youthful activist working on getting a polluted city onto green energy. These things are not only informative but also motivating, such that the students can be able to identify themselves as change agents. In addition, GenAI allows students to create their own stories, to co-create, therefore, improving creativity, critical thinking, and empathy. This seminar style of education turns passive reading of text into active discovery inquiry, where students learn to internalize climate problems and envision solutions of specific invention and meaning to the mind and hearts. Table 2 illustrates the breadth of GenAI's instructional applications.

Table 2. Applications of genAI in climate education

Application Area	GenAI Use Case	Example Output	Educational Benefit
Content Generation	Lesson plan drafting, reading comprehension questions	Climate-themed lesson plan for grade 8	Saves time, aligns with learning goals
Personalization	Level-based content adaptation	Simplified vs. advanced versions of a text	Supports differentiated instruction
Storytelling	Narrative generation based on scientific scenarios	Story of a flooded coastal town	Enhances empathy and engagement
Data Visualization	Graph generation, interactive maps	Animated graph of CO_2 trends	Makes data accessible and memorable
Scenario Simulation	Policy impact modeling, "what-if" environments	Emissions vs. afforestation model	Fosters systems thinking
Localized Interpretation	Community-specific narratives and dashboards	Urban heat map for Jakarta	Increases contextual relevance

To conclude, the features of GenAI, such as developing customized content, customization to personal needs of a learner, and the ability to support compelling narratives, make it a diverse instrument in the arsenal of climate education. In the case of thoughtful use, it has the potential to enhance more engaging, inclusive, and effective learning experiences, which go beyond rote learning to encourage better insights about climate challenges and active climate citizenship.

GenAI and Climate Science

Climate science is intrinsically complex, based on the interpretation of vast data and interrelationships between the environmental, social, and economic systems. This complexity may pose big problems to learners, especially those who may not be well-versed with such abstract data or technical models. GenAI can address these limitations by presenting raw data in an engaging, interactive, and emotionally appealing learning experience in a completely new way. Its visualization of data, modeling of dynamic situations, and even production of rich stories make it easier to understand basic climate concepts and become more connected with them in more profound and relevant ways (Cheung et al., 2024; Ferreira, 2025; Kim, 2025; Richards et al., 2024; Suraj Kumar et al., 2024). Figure 1 offers a conceptual overview of how GenAI supports an end-to-end learning journey.

Figure 1. GenAI-enabled learning flow in climate science education

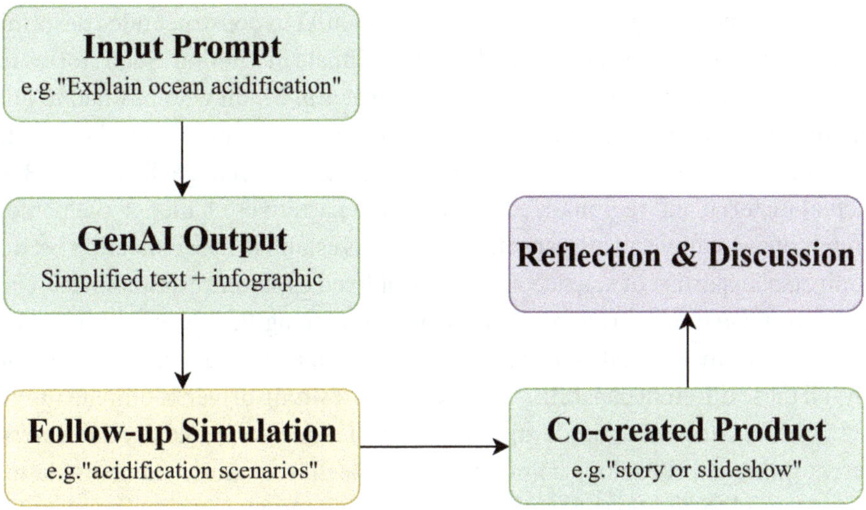

Data visualization is one of the main ways in which GenAI contributes to the field of climate science education. Making numerical data visual by turning them into dynamic data visual models, e.g., animated graphs, thematic maps, or interactive dashboards, GenAI enables students to discover patterns and trends otherwise hidden by data. As an example, students are given an opportunity to access time-lapse representations of the temperature anomalies worldwide, polar ice extents, or monsoon variability on a decade level. These graphical outputs allow scientific evidence to be touched and understood much more easily, and be able to think analytically and reason. Besides, GenAI can be able to simulate numerous datasets at the same interface, which allows learners to discover the connections between events, such as the relationship between the urban heat islands and population density or the connection between CO2 concentration and ocean acidification.

In addition to being visualized, GenAI manages to model climate experience in the form of a simulation. The inputs can be manipulated by the students as a use of fossil fuels, deforestation, or the amount of carbon tax, among others, and the projected outcomes can be seen on temperature increase, economic, or ecological degradation. Such simulated settings contribute to experiential learning because they enable students to perform hypothesis tests, solve problems, and contemplate the long-term impacts of the policies undertaken or changes in behavior. This type of learning, involving such scenario-based learning, is not just reinforcing systems thinking; it is also promoting the sense of agency and responsibility, leading to the exploration of viable solutions in complex systems by the learners.

Most interestingly and importantly, GenAI can provide the much-needed human-friendly nature in climate teaching. Rather than addressing issues and working only with charting and graphs, teachers can employ GenAI to construct tales describing the story of human life and how it is affected by climate disruption. Such stories may capture a variety of voices, such as that of a farmer in Sindh who has had to adapt to unpredictable rainfall, or an Arctic scientist who has been seeing the receding ice, or a coastal young person who has been mobilizing to change the policy. Based on actual material and regionalized contexts, the narratives challenge the personal emotions of sympathy and introspection, as well as establish the connection between the universal expertise of science and the local lived experiences. Students are also enabled to create these narratives, with which they strengthen their communication of complex information and their empowerment to evangelize radical change. Collectively, all these different capabilities make GenAI a strong driver of climate literacy. It embodies intellectual aptitude stimulation, as it reduces complexity and caters to different grading. It develops an emotional connection to stories and simulations, which makes climate impacts real. And it allows autonomy since it allows students to co-create content, ask questions about what-if scenarios, and imagine solutions.

GenAI offers a flexible set of tools and prompts that augment the functionality of the more traditional approaches to teaching climate change as it shifts towards more digitally-supported, learner-centered systems of teaching. Intentionally combined, GenAI would not just make us more effective in teaching climate science: GenAI would help shape how people learn, how they make sense of, and how they connect with one of the most complex issues of our era, and determine how they engage with it.

INTEGRATING GENAI IN CLIMATE CHANGE TEACHING AND LEARNING

With GenAI applied to climate education, the scope of altering the ways of teaching climate concepts, exploring their significance, and performing related actions is rather broad. It can do more than provide content, but it is capable of creating a touchable, learner-driven, and emotionally oriented experience. Applied in traditional classroom environments as well as informal learning contexts, GenAI provides teachers and schools with new resources to create, in the language of climate science, and the spirit of pedagogic invention, effective experiences of climate education to adopt. GenAI takes this a step further to reach the head and heart of students by encouraging the capability to visualize and establish the power to change the climate (Cheung et al., 2024; Kim, 2025; Liu & Château, 2025; Tang, 2024).

GenAI in Formal Education

GenAI promises to revolutionize formal education, especially in ways of improving curriculum development and encouraging active and student-centered learning. In the classroom setting, GenAI applications can provide an immense ability for teachers to augment the way climate education is given to students with an effective individualization of the art. Such tools help teachers achieve the adaptation of complex content, differentiated instructions, and greater participation in the form of interactive pedagogies (Chang & Kidman, 2023; Cooper, 2023; Lane, 2025; Suraj Kumar et al., 2024).

The ability to supplement the curriculum design can be seen as one of the most important contributions GenAI can make to formal education (Khamis et al., 2025; Rutecka et al., 2025). Applications such as ChatGPT enable the development of instructional material, which complies with the requirements of the instructional standard but is still flexible and can be applied in different learning settings. An example of this would be an international scientific organization, such as the United Nations, that is able to have an automatically created report that focuses on climate change being rewritten into easy-to-read language or into a multi-language report to suit students who have different linguistic backgrounds. Such ability to customize the content to the reading level of the students, their background preparation, and their language orientation makes the foundational climate science concepts accessible and inclusive. In addition, GenAI can be used by the teacher to build learning aids like discussion pre-setters, comparison tables, or slides with visual aspects to increase conceptual clarity and discussions around tricky concepts like a carbon budget, feedback, or climate resilience mechanisms.

In addition to creation, GenAI is highly beneficial in terms of lesson planning and instructional design (Karpouzis et al., 2024b; Moundridou et al., 2024). When they identify objectives of the learning process (e.g., learning the greenhouse effect with students in grade eight or introducing students to high school to renewable energy systems), educators may get scaffolded instructions (lesson plans with concise explanations, illustrative examples, active activities, and jogging tests). All these AI-developed lesson items can be quickly modified to the rhythm, form, and theme of a particular classroom. It not only decreases the administrative overhead of teaching staff but also increases instructional accuracy, permitting instructors to devote more time toward encouraging learning as opposed to making learning aids from start to finish.

Lastly, with GenAI, it is possible to support active learning where interactive simulations occur (Borge et al., 2024; Nguyen et al., 2025). In geography and science labs, learners can be able to access GenAI-enabled platforms that imitate climate scenarios and manipulate such variables as CO2 emissions, urban sprawl, or even interventions on policy. It can be assisted by following the ripple effects of such changes within the system, students learn about emission into the atmosphere systematically, i.e., through the rise of sea levels, precipitation alteration, or a reduction in biodiversity. Such practical experiences not only strengthen knowledge in the sciences, but also develop in students critical thinking, hypothesis testing, and teamwork abilities. As one example, students could model the effects of global afforestation over several decades and compare outcomes of different frameworks of climate policies, thus bridging the gap between theoretical and applied decision-making.

GenAI in Informal Education

The role of GenAI in making climate education more pervasive and influential than ever before by going beyond the scope of formal schooling cannot be overestimated. GenAI is helping to create more interactive, collaborative, and self-directed experiences in museums, community workshops, and citizen science activities, where people can come to a better, nuanced knowledge of the climate problems and establish a new level of meaningful interrelationship between science and society.

Science centers and museums are beginning to use GenAI to design current and high-impact exhibits, which react immediately to online input by visitors (Adiba et al., 2025; Hosseini et al., 2025). These fixtures are not merely passive models since they provide individually customized investigations within the climate. As an example, a visitor can specify a hometown and see immediately a GenAI-generated forecast of mean local impacts of climate change, including the likely rise in sea level and rates of heatwaves or distributions of native species. Such individualized, knowledge-based visualizations turn dry mathematical climate models into something personal and familiar based on local geography and raise cognitive comprehension and emotional connection. Visitors can feel more personally interested in the issue of climate change and determined to learn more or act because they can sense how the problem can impact the communities they live in.

In the community, GenAI can be a compelling community-building tool that enables co-authoring stories that provides priority to marginalized people and contextual expertise (De Vos et al., 2025; Radwan et al., 2025). Workshop facilitators can work with participants to create living processes, online artwork, or even Brilliant Education YouTube videos that voice lived experiences of climate change, whether because of drought and flooding scenarios in one area, or changing agricultural patterns, or building patterns in another. Guided prompts and collaborative editing with GenAI allow transforming such experiences into compelling stories that not only develop Cultural identity and regional specificity, but also a sense of agency can be developed when such experiences are transformed into compelling narratives with the help of GenAI through guided prompts and collaborative editing. The process of participatory storytelling would not only foster civic engagement but also support intergenerational transmission of knowledge and enhance the connection of science communication to social justice because it provides space to diverse voices in the discourse of climate change.

GenAI also allows citizen science initiatives to be optimized through the interpretation and visualization of more complicated environmental data. People and groups that can provide observations, e.g., on local temperature, air pollution records, or biodiversity observations, are familiar with the difficulties of making sense out of raw data sets. GenAI can target this gap with synthesized information based on crowd-sourced data and in formats that are easy to digest as visuals, summaries, or interactive dashboards. These products can be used in any specific area or of users, enabling communities to monitor trends, recognize anomalies, and even publish the discoveries with decision-makers. GenAI democratizes data access in such a manner that it empowers non-experts to become active members in the process of monitoring and advocating for climate change. GenAI makes climate science more inclusive and responsive by placing the community in a position to co-create climate knowledge.

All in all, the implementation of GenAI into the environment of informal education promotes climate literacy through immersive, locally relevant, and socially contextualized learning processes. GenAI enables the public to actively participate in contributing towards and being informed change agents whether through their own Morales story in the Museum exhibits, through their own lived stories in the community sense-making process, or even via their care and understanding of data via citizen interpreters, they become not only the recipients of information, but also the ones to deliver, to contribute towards and to be informed change agents. Such a transition is critical towards the development of mass literacy and social movement against the climate crisis on a global scale. To better understand the range and contrast of GenAI's contributions across educational environments, Table 3 outlines its distinct and overlapping roles in formal and informal settings.

Table 3. GenAI applications in formal vs informal climate education settings

Educational Setting	Primary Use of GenAI	Examples	Pedagogical Impact
Formal	Curriculum-aligned instruction and assessment support	AI-generated quizzes on climate systems; ChatGPT explanations of IPCC data	Reinforces conceptual clarity and supports differentiated instruction
Informal	Experiential and creative exploration	Interactive storytelling via ChatGPT; image creation with DALL·E	Enhances curiosity, emotional engagement, and self-guided learning
Formal	Climate simulation and forecasting exercises	Scenario modeling tools predicting sea-level rise under different emissions	Develops systems thinking and applied scientific reasoning
Informal	Community-driven awareness and advocacy	Citizen science reports visualized by GenAI; youth-led video campaigns	Fosters civic engagement and real-world problem-solving

Future Applications Scenarios

An increasing number of practices are demonstrating the potential of GenAI tools in enabling potent pedagogical applications in climate education. Scenario generation of climate futures is one example of such an application, in which students can follow through plausible accounts of various climate trajectories (e.g., stabilizing at 1.5 °C and exceeding 4 °C). When learners are prompted to think about the long-term consequences and ethical trade-offs of climate policy through the process of GenAI, simulating the environmental, economic, and social conditions.

Its other effective use is in climate justice AI storytelling. GenAI can be used by learners to create stories, conversations, or campaigns on social media that would help shed light on the way minorities are disproportionately impacted by climate change. Through responding to cues like telling a story about a smallholder farmer who is affected term or imagining a future in which indigenous knowledge helped prevent an environmental tragedy, students perceive the human aspect of climate defenselessness, strength, and demonstration. These stories create empathy and awareness and propagate an interdisciplinary way of thinking that occurs at the cross where science, society, and ethics meet.

Also, GenAI can be used as part of an assessment and feedback event. Image generators such as DALL·E or other tools can provide visual feedback to react to projects made by students. An example here is the individual visual understanding of a lesson plan after taking a climate action plan or a written reflection; the student can get a visualization of their idea, an infographic about their mitigation plan, or an image that symbolizes their theme of discussion. This form of multimodal response enhances learning and strengthens the mental fortification via dual coding (verbalized and visual).

Transforming Climate Learning Ecosystems

With these various applications, GenAI liberates both teachers and students to leave behind the conventional and linear models of classroom instruction in favor of vibrant, participatory, and interdisciplinary learning models of climate education. It is accessible to learners in visualizing the future, challenging ethical issues, investigating systemic connections, and experiencing a mixture of both the emotional and intellectual aspects involved in one of the most pressing problems of our era. To show how GenAI operates across diverse learning environments, Figure 2 maps GenAI's ecosystem-wide roles, spanning schools, museums, community workshops, and citizen science.

Figure 2. GenAI integration across climate learning ecosystems

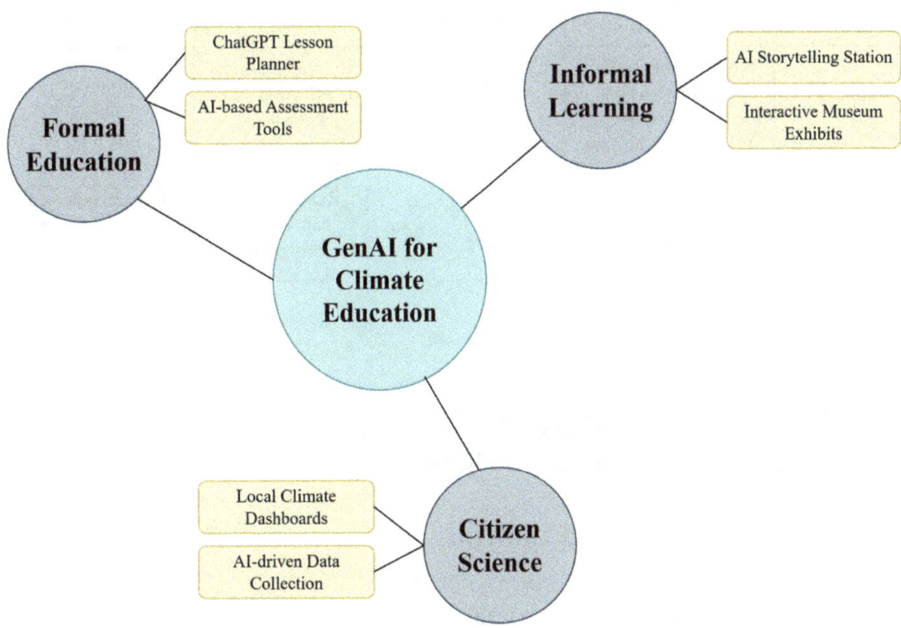

GenAI is a potential game-changer in climate literacy, a creative and nimble, participatory and responsive tool that can be practiced and applied in schools, museums, citizen science networks, and community facilities. GenAI can educate a whole new generation of people to not just be aware of climate change but inspired and ready to take climate action by combining technology, pedagogical knowledge, and human-centered storytelling processes. Table 4 summarizes key GenAI-supported use cases in climate education, linking each with its educational objective, example activity, and the expected learner outcome.

Table 4. Pedagogical use cases of genAI in climate education

Use Case	Description	Example Prompt/ Activity	Learning Objective	Expected Outcome
Scenario generation	Producing alternative climate futures under various emission levels	"Simulate Earth's climate at +4°C"	Explore the cause-and-effect of climate change scenarios	Ability to evaluate climate mitigation options
Climate justice storytelling	Co-creating narratives around marginalized experiences in climate contexts	"Narrate the journey of a climate migrant."	Understand climate justice through lived perspectives	Develop empathy and socio-environmental awareness
Visual feedback generation	Producing AI-created visuals to represent student ideas or climate solutions	"Create a symbolic image of my solution to drought."	Translate abstract ideas into expressive visual media	Strengthen communication and creativity
Reflective dialogue	Supporting self-explanation and metacognition via AI-facilitated questions	"What did I learn about CO_2 and oceans today?"	Reinforce critical reflection and knowledge integration	Enhanced retention and conceptual clarity
Data personalization	Tailoring data visualizations or summaries to the learner context	"Show me CO_2 trends in my city"	Relate climate data to local experience	Deepen personal relevance and motivation

FOSTERING ENGAGEMENT, CRITICAL THINKING, AND CLIMATE ACTION

Enhancing Inquiry-Based Learning

GenAI renews inquiry-based and project-based learning paradigms as it provides an interactive, data-dense, and discovery-based environment. The pedagogical methods are desperately needed in the climate education process because climate problems are dynamic, complex issues that demand critical questioning, hypothesis, inquiry, and action from the students. GenAI allows learners to address the question of what-if that has never been explored before. As an example, when a student requests a question about the impact of rising global temperatures on agriculture in the area he or she lives in, AI tools can provide the simulated data, create images of the trend of climate variations, and provide a description of the situation through scenarios. Such ability to make rapid visualizations of climate trends or interpret local records makes abstract learning real and context-based discovery.

In project-based environments, GenAI helps generate a sense of ownership by being creative and logistical back-up assistance. Students may want to create climate communication campaigns using AI-aided scripts or create multilingual content used in awareness events, or play out interventions by simulating policy effects. The activities promote 21st-century skills, especially cooperation, digital elements, design thinking, and scientific communication. In this way, GenAI gives classroom assignments a major overhaul so that they can be a living, breathing format by which students discover the reality of climate problems in the real world. To clarify the pedagogical distinctions and synergies, Table 5 compares how GenAI supports both inquiry-based and project-based climate learning approaches across cognitive, technical, and creative dimensions.

Table 5. GenAI applications in inquiry-based vs project-based climate learning

Learning Approach	Role of GenAI	Example Activities	Skills Cultivated	Pedagogical Outcome
Inquiry-Based	Facilitates question formation, explanation, and exploration	Using ChatGPT to probe "Why are Arctic temperatures rising faster?"	Critical thinking, scientific inquiry, and conceptual reasoning	Deepened understanding of climate systems and inquiry processes
Project-Based	Co-develops artifacts and visual aids for climate solutions	Creating climate action posters with DALL·E; simulating outcomes with Sora	Collaboration, design thinking, problem-solving	Real-world engagement and creative solution development
Inquiry-Based	Aids in hypothesis testing and interpreting data	Summarizing CO_2 trend data using GenAI and proposing explanations	Data interpretation, analytical reasoning	Evidence-based reasoning and hypothesis refinement
Project-Based	Assists in structuring multi-phase student-led investigations	Using GenAI to outline steps for a local climate adaptation plan	Project planning, iterative refinement	Ownership of learning and sustained inquiry

Promoting Systems Thinking Through AI-Generated Scenarios

Climate change cannot be thought of as an independent issue; rather, it exists as a part of complex systems of ecological, economic, technological, and sociopolitical relations. Climate literacy, therefore, requires systems thinking or the skills to identify and analyze interconnections or feedback loops. GenAI helps it by allowing students to emulate and investigate multidimensional climate conditions. It is capable of producing models in which one cause, such as deforestation, can produce several different effects, such as loss of biodiversity, displacement of the indigenous, the amount of CO2 in the atmosphere, and even economic stability. Figure 3 demonstrates how students can visualize interconnections in climate systems using GenAI tools. This kind of map helps uncover direct and indirect consequences of environmental decisions.

Figure 3. Systems thinking map generated with genAI

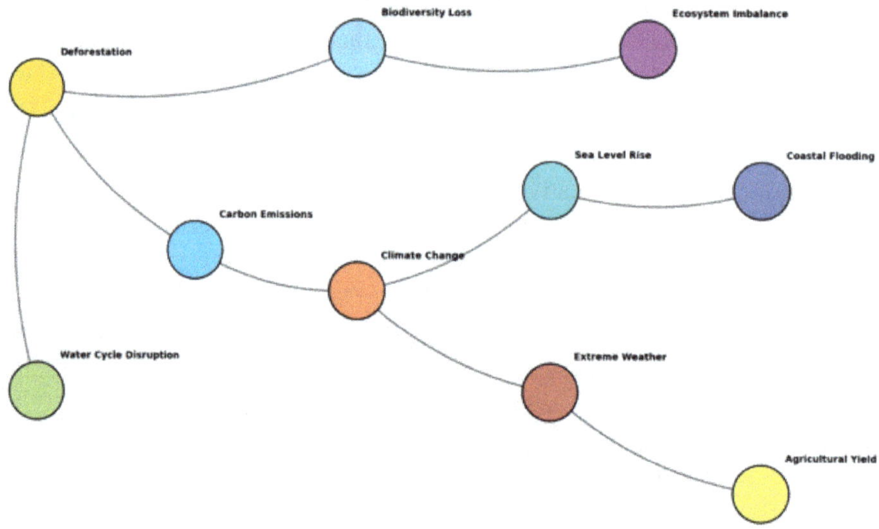

As another example, the students may investigate the influence of renewable energy transition on freshwater consumption, carbon emissions, labor markets, or geopolitical coalitions. Such AI-based scenarios favor integrated analysis and comparative slanting. What is more important, they provide the replies in the form of trade-offs and unintended consequences of environmental decisions. As such, simulations are reviewed with the help of the instructor, and learners start understanding the global systems as dynamic and non-linear, which can allow them to assess policy solutions, expect cascading effects, and develop wholesome, sustainable futures.

Facilitating Student Co-Creation with AI

Generative AI promotes the transition to active co-creation of information instead of passive information consumption as students create content in collaboration with AI systems. It starts by prompting the students with their questions, hypotheses, or situations that are then elaborated upon by the AI into written or graphic form, or visualizations of the information. A descriptive narrative, visual representation, visual representation as well as risk maps can be obtained with a prompt like "Envision a coastal village in Bangladesh under various IPCC climate models". Learners do not have to take these outputs unquestioningly; instead, they criticize, re-prompt, and revise them, comparing the replies of AI to the reliable scientific resources and the reality in their locality.

This cyclic procedure creates metacognitive consciousness, with students coming to learn how to think about the construction of knowledge, and its determination by context of input, limitation in data, and bias-suggestible assumptions. It develops digital acumen and scientific cynicism, too, which are important in a time of falsehoods. Above all, student-AI co-creation creates agency and involvement, with students realizing that they are not only the consumers of climate information but also a part of climate discourse and the solution to climate problems. To highlight the transition from awareness to action, Table 6 summarizes common student-led initiatives empowered by GenAI, along with tools used and intended outcomes.

Table 6. GenAI-supported student climate actions

Student Action	AI Tool/Function Used	Educational Outcome	Community Impact Example	Student Action
Drafting climate speeches	ChatGPT	Communication skills	Presentation at school assembly	Drafting climate speeches
Designing digital posters	DALL·E	Creative expression	Public outreach campaign	Designing digital posters
Modeling emissions scenarios	ChatGPT + Code Interpreter	Systems thinking	City council climate proposal	Modeling emissions scenarios
Creating explainer videos	Sora + Script from ChatGPT	Multimedia literacy	YouTube awareness series on climate action	Creating explainer videos
Developing climate trivia games	ChatGPT + Python game generator	Engagement through gamification	School-wide climate literacy challenge	Developing climate trivia games
Writing op-eds or blog posts	ChatGPT	Persuasive writing	Local newspaper climate awareness column	Writing op-eds or blog posts
Mapping local heat islands	ChatGPT + GIS tool assistance	Spatial analysis skills	Urban greening proposal to the municipality	Mapping local heat islands

GenAI as a Catalyst for Climate Engagement

Climate education is also to awaken people. Its end purpose is not just vision but to transform. GenAI has the potential to form a potent pathway between awareness and civic and environmental action, as students can create and implement relevant projects. AI has the potential to help write an effective speech, generate policy letters, plan environmentally-friendly campaigns, or create tools like a carbon footprint calculator. As an example, a lesson could be given where a class tries to model local emission patterns using GenAI and afterward provide custom recommendations to individual mitigation, such as tree planting measures, through to plastic reduction campaigns.

The uses of AI in storytelling are particularly useful in promoting emotional intimacy and a feeling of unity on a global scale. GenAI enables students to learn the lived experience of vulnerability, resilience, and justice by creating stories about communities on the frontline of climate change, like Pacific Island countries or inner-city impoverished communities. These narratives may be used as the motivating forces of student-led activism, determining the outcome of community presentations, social media campaigns, or cross-school climatic campaigns. Moreover, one can leverage GenAI on such activities as service-learning and citizen science and apply AI-generated ideas to practical decision-making. Such incorporation not only makes scientific learning stronger, but also reminds an individual of some purpose and makes education a stepping stone into participatory change.

The use of GenAI in climate education can prompt climate activism, as this can help students move beyond knowledge into action. The GenAI tools have the potential to become more emotive and locally relevant to the climate crisis in order to incite empathy, urgency, and purpose. As an example, a student can create a set of climate scenarios on the possibilities of future climates with AI and then present it to the school, a social media campaign, or to local policymakers. It can also help create logos, slogans, or even posters of environmental initiatives, which should equip the students with the tools to make their voices heard and their fellow students mobilized. GenAI can facilitate action-based learning, which transcends the classroom, to improve civic engagement and create a spirit of international citizenship.

Facilitating participation and inculcating systems thinking and making effective action possible, GenAI can contribute to raising a generation of climate-literate, yet climate-resilient and climate-responsible learners. It creates the cognitive, emotional, and ethical background to enable the students to bring valuable input to one of the most burning issues of our era.

Ethics, Misinformation and Bias

One of the vital ethical issues to address when introducing the use of GenAI in learning is to make AI-generated information trustworthy, balanced, and scientifically accurate. GenAI models are educated using a massive amount of data scraped off the internet that, in most cases, might be culturally biased or lack historical details or even political leanings. This may be expressed through climate education, which ignores the voices of Indigenous communities or places the blame on emissions on them, presents climate change in an apolitical context, or is too technical to ignore issues of justice.

In addition, GenAI is, by nature, probabilistic and capable of creating outputs that sound authoritative, whereas being factually incorrect or misleading, particularly in covering provocative or speculative areas. To illustrate this situation, in case of asking about the issue or technique of climate geoengineering or carbon market mechanisms, AI chatbot responses could simplify the heated discussions of some controversial researchers or refer to a study that is not current. This poses a danger that students will take this content with no criticism. To overcome this, the teacher should also learn to be a critical assessor of AI products, so they can have a culture of checking in the classroom. It makes it crucial to teach students to challenge AI-generated work by cross-checking it with reliable scientific data, such as that found in an IPCC report, peer-reviewed publications, or governmental databases, in short, to triangulate.

Privacy, Consent, and Data Protection

Because GenAI tools are used on a large scale, students and data security concerns become legitimate issues to be concerned with. Most AI platforms operate using cloud-based operations, which keep data (including identifiers of the user, geographical data, or behavioral indicators) that can be entered by the user, particularly in cases where the students are using the AI platforms interactively. This brings in dangers of illegal data mining or unintentional violation of trust, especially in case the data is utilized to train further versions of the model without express authorization.

Schools and institutions that use the internet, especially in their learning environments, have to institute high levels of protection in their schools since, in most cases, the internet users are children and, in most cases, minors. This involves, among other things, that any AI tools adapt to the applicable data protection legislation, e.g., GDPR in the EU, COPPA in the U.S., or similar at the local level. The usage of the data by the educational facilities should be clear, and students should be well informed on the way their data is accessed, maintained, and preserved.

Also, teachers are advised not to resort to tools that are not sufficiently moderated or allow the creation of unacceptable, emotionally stimulating, or politically biased content, which is not filtered.

Scientific Rigor and Pedagogical Alignment

Preservation of scientific accuracy in AI-produced educational material is both a pedagogical requirement and a practical difficulty. GenAI does an excellent job of digesting masses of data to present it in consumable story formats, but it cannot, in principle, assert what is scientifically sound, speculative, outdated, or conflicting with curriculum requirements. As an example, an AI could generate an aesthetically interesting summary of global warming that reduces the feedback effects or misses the complexity of tipping points, resulting in over-simplified or distorted learning.

In order to reduce this risk, GenAI tools should be creatively and curatively applied. To teach the use of AI, the teachers need to pre-screen the AI-based content before using it in classroom settings and complement it with authoritative one to promote accuracy. It is also important to put AI-derived outputs into context with the development stage of the students and their cognitive abilities. In line with younger learners, analogies need to be carefully used in a simplified approach without strengthening false beliefs, whereas older students can be posed a critical question of how AI-generated models should be considered against the framework of climate science. GenAI should be treated as an addition to the science-based reasoning and critical investigation rather than its replacement.

Building Educator Capacity and Student AI Literacy

Responsible and effective use of GenAI in the classroom will be dependent on ensuring the teacher can gain the skills and confidence to put these tools to meaningful use. A large number of teachers might not be acquainted with GenAI technologies or even show little or no assurance of their abilities, or be concerned with the dangers imminent to them. This requires thorough professional growth schemes concerning not only technical but also ethical abilities. Such areas must include:

Developing teacher capacity in the ethical, responsible use of GenAI in climate education needs highly developed knowledge in four inseparable areas: prompt engineering, tool evaluation, ethical frameworks, and content validation. These competencies can enable teachers to utilize AI technologies effectively without limiting scientific accuracy, ethics, or pedagogy coherence.

Prompt engineering can be understood as the capability of setting up the questions in a way that delivers pertinent, precise, and educationally sensitive outputs of the GenAI-based tools. The teachers can have to study the impact of the structure, concreteness, and clarity of a prompt that may affect the answer given by the AI. When considering climate education, the prompts should take the form of context-sensitive and well-developed questions, including those that stipulate the target age group, regional perspectives, or the conceptual aspect of the study. As an example, such a question as the description of the impact of sea level rise on agriculture in Bangladesh at the level of a high school student has more chances to provide a piece of valuable learning than a pure request. Incremental refinement, constraints, and prompting that are specific to roles enable teachers to direct GenAI systems to generate results that are scientifically sound as well as pedagogically applicable. To ensure meaningful integration of GenAI into classrooms, educators require interdisciplinary skills across four critical domains, outlined in Table 7.

Table 7. Educator capacity-building domains for ethical genAI use

Domain	Core Competencies	Example Practices	Relevance to Climate Education
Prompt Engineering	Craft effective prompts	Tailor queries by age, context	Increases clarity and relevance
Tool Evaluation	Assess platform biases	Compare training data sources	Ensures equity and accuracy
Ethical Frameworks	Identify bias/inclusion gaps	Critique AI-generated stories	Builds critical awareness
Content Validation	Verify AI outputs	Cross-check with IPCC reports	Maintains scientific rigor

The extent to which GenAI tools could be estimated in terms of technical design and education-related appropriateness is of equal importance. Different platforms do not use the same data and are not optimized for the same tasks. Some can use resources on the academic repositories, and some will scrape data off the open web, further making the content quality inconsistent. The educators need to know about the variance among the tools regarding transparency, handling of bias, privacy policies, and content measures that should be applied. The possibility to evaluate strengths and weaknesses of a certain tool can enable educators to choose the ones that should be best used to provide climate instructions, and both accuracy and inclusivity can be maintained. Moreover, the awareness of the platform-specific functionality, e.g., accessibility, interface usability, or the characteristics of integration, can also contribute to a better learning process and reduce the risks of barriers to different learners.

The ethical aspects of using GenAI should also play a key role in training the educators. GenAI tools do not exist in a vacuum; any social, political, and cultural biases in the training data are reflected, and in a few cases, given further power.

Teachers should be able to foster equality and non-discrimination through the critical sampling of the materials produced with the help of such instruments. This involves asking when a particular voice or geographic area is not being used as much in the climate movement and in discourse, doubting how industrial or governmental actors will be depicted, and making sure that students do not hear discriminatory or incorrect opinions. The integration of ethical constructs in the classroom can inspire students to think critically about how technology has been used to shape the perception of climate change by the masses and enable them to become good digital citizens.

Teachers should consider cultivating effective validations of the GenAI-produced content. Since AI models tend to provide information that is fluent yet sometimes inaccurate or, in some cases, outdated, they have to be checked against reputable sources in order to ascertain scientific claims. Educators must be careful to compare the results provided by AI with the work of such organizations as the Intergovernmental Panel on Climate Change (IPCC), the United Nations Environment Programme (UNEP), or peer-reviewed science-related journals. This procedure does not just protect the integrity of the teaching material but also provides a good example of critical questioning to the students. As soon as learners are encouraged to take part in such a validation process, e.g., by comparing AI-based summations with primary sources, it will not only improve their climate literacy but also their knowledge construction and evaluation awareness in a digital age.

The same value should be given to the problem of promoting literacy in AI among the students. The learners should not only be taught how to use GenAI but also learn to critically interpret the outputs of GenAI. This involves knowing how the models are trained, and whether there are possible biases in the narratives that AI provide, and why the authority of the material posted is unreliable. Within climate education, where information is pervasively distorted and much of the climate discussion polarized, fostering these important digital literacies is one of the ways of educating people who are well-informed and empowered to act on climate issues.

CONCLUSION

The growing speed and complexity of the climate crisis require dynamic and innovative responses in education as well. As has been shown in this chapter, GenAI can be of immeasurable value when it comes to the intersection of climate change education and making it more actionable, interactive, and personalized. Ranging through the production of adaptive lesson content and immersive simulation, co-authoring climatic narratives and visualizing complex environmental systems, GenAI is opening the door to introducing climatic phenomena in an experientially scientific and emotionally personal manner. It reconciles the divide between knowledge and information, progress and simplicity, consciousness and performance.

In order to realize this potential in full, a number of strategic recommendations have to be taken into consideration. In the case of educators, GenAI should be incorporated into learning so that it is not part of sound pedagogy, replacing it, but is an add-on to aid inquiry, creativity, and systems thinking. Teachers' ought to be put through formal education on GenAI instruments, such as timely design, content analysis, and morality integration into their classroom implementation. To the policymakers, updated curricular design, investment in digital infrastructure, and the provision of clear guidelines on the use of AI in education that focus on the scientific integrity and safety of learners are to be ensured. In the meantime, developers and technology vendors need to create GenAI tools that are pedagogically sound, culturally diverse, and have transparency capabilities, e.g., citing the sources it uses, alerting about the bias, and setting up control over what you want to see.

One of the most significant priorities going forward is to pay attention to the equity and accessibility of GenAI-based climate education. Unless proactive measures are taken, the technology-driven trends will enhance the current levels of imbalances in education, especially in ill-equipped schools, rural areas, and underrepresented groups. It will be necessary to make the solutions accessible, smartphone-friendly, multilingual content generators, and offline capabilities. Simultaneously, a future vision of learning has to be rooted in adaptive ecosystems that are in a position to react to changes in reality in the climate, learner requirements, and emerging technologies. GenAI is an exclusive possibility to develop dynamic learner-centered, data-based, and real-world responsive learning environments.

The issue of GenAI-powered climate literacy requires a multi-stakeholder partnership with school teachers, students, AI developers, policy-makers, scientists, non-governmental organizations, and local leaders. The development of responsible, inclusive, honest solutions in GenAI applications as part of climate education is the responsibility not of any individual but a joint initiative based on shared responsibility and vision. The stakeholders need to collectively develop an educational model in which technological innovation is used towards the common good to provide learners not only the capacity to know about the climate crisis but also to think about new futures, to envision, to design, and to lead change.

GenAI is not just a technological piece, which can be summed up by a pedagogical catalyst. With forethought, it can be used to help power a generation of climate-aware students who are knowledgeable, motivated, and enabled to change. Our future must be the responsible, innovative, and dedicated use of this technology so that every learner has a chance to become an agent of action in overcoming climate crises and in restoring environmental justice in an ever-changing world.

REFERENCES

Adeshola, I., & Adepoju, A. P. (2024). The opportunities and challenges of ChatGPT in education. *Interactive Learning Environments, 32*(10), 6159–6172. DOI: 10.1080/10494820.2023.2253858

Adetayo, A. J., Enamudu, A. I., Lawal, F. M., & Odunewu, A. O. (2024). From text to video with AI: The rise and potential of Sora in education and libraries. *Library Hi Tech News*. Advance online publication. DOI: 10.1108/LHTN-02-2024-0028

Adiba, S. Febriyanto, & Rahmawati, N. S. (2025). Exploring GenAI's Role in Digital Cultural Memory at Museums and Art Galleries in Indonesia: AR and VR Perspectives. *Lecture Notes in Computer Science (Including Subseries Lecture Notes in Artificial Intelligence and Lecture Notes in Bioinformatics), 15493 LNCS*, 198–211. DOI: 10.1007/978-981-96-0865-2_16

Alenda-Demoutiez, J. (2022). Climate change literacy in Africa: The main role of experiences. *The International Journal of Environmental Studies, 79*(6), 981–997. Advance online publication. DOI: 10.1080/00207233.2021.1987059

Andersen, J. P., Degn, L., Fishberg, R., Graversen, E. K., Horbach, S. P. J. M., Schmidt, E. K., Schneider, J. W., & Sørensen, M. P. (2025). Generative Artificial Intelligence (GenAI) in the research process – A survey of researchers' practices and perceptions. *Technology in Society, 81*, 102813. DOI: 10.1016/j.techsoc.2025.102813

Atkins, C., Girgente, G., Shirzaei, M., & Kim, J. (2024). Generative AI tools can enhance climate literacy but must be checked for biases and inaccuracies. *Communications Earth & Environment, 5*(1), 1–8. DOI: 10.1038/s43247-024-01392-w

Borge, M., Smith, B. K., & Aldemir, T. (2024). Using generative ai as a simulation to support higher-order thinking. *International Journal of Computer-Supported Collaborative Learning, 19*(4), 479–532. DOI: 10.1007/s11412-024-09437-0

Chang, C. H., & Kidman, G. (2023). The rise of generative artificial intelligence (AI) language models - challenges and opportunities for geographical and environmental education. *International Research in Geographical and Environmental Education, 32*(2), 85–89. DOI: 10.1080/10382046.2023.2194036

CHEN, C.-C., LI, C., & WANG, Y.-F. (2024). Text-To-Video Model Sora for Education and Teaching: Opportunities and Challenges. *Modern Educational Technology, 34*(5), 27–34. DOI: 10.3969/J.ISSN.1009-8097.2024.05.003

Cheung, K. K. C., Pun, J. K. H., & Li, W. (2024). Students' Holistic Reading of Socio-Scientific Texts on Climate Change in a ChatGPT Scenario. *Research in Science Education, 54*(5), 957–976. DOI: 10.1007/s11165-024-10177-2

Cooper, G. (2023). Examining Science Education in ChatGPT: An Exploratory Study of Generative Artificial Intelligence. *Journal of Science Education and Technology, 32*(3), 444–452. DOI: 10.1007/s10956-023-10039-y

De Vos, E., Schneider, L., Baccarne, B., De Marez, L., & Emmanouil, M. (2025). The reservoir effect: The role of GenAI based conversational agents in participatory futures. *Digital Creativity (Exeter), 36*(3), 193–222. Advance online publication. DOI: 10.1080/14626268.2025.2512773

El Saddik, A., Ahmad, J., Khan, M., Abouzahir, S., & Gueaieb, W. (2025). Unleashing Creativity in the Metaverse: Generative AI and Multimodal Content. *ACM Transactions on Multimedia Computing Communications and Applications, 21*(7), 1–43. Advance online publication. DOI: 10.1145/3713075

Ferreira, R. (2025). Creative intra-actions: Co-creating with generative AI in the age of climate change. *Learning, Media and Technology, 50*(3), 1–14. DOI: 10.1080/17439884.2025.2532550

Helbling, M., Auer, D., Meierrieks, D., Mistry, M., & Schaub, M. (2021). Climate change literacy and migration potential: Micro-level evidence from Africa. *Climatic Change, 169*(1–2), 9. Advance online publication. DOI: 10.1007/s10584-021-03241-7

Hosseini, M., Horbach, S. P. J. M., Holmes, K., & Ross-Hellauer, T. (2025). Open Science at the generative AI turn: An exploratory analysis of challenges and opportunities. *Quantitative Science Studies, 6*, 22–45. DOI: 10.1162/qss_a_00337 PMID: 40124128

Ismail, S., Ali, F., & Yasukawa, S. (2024). *Advancing Climate Risk Governance and Education Through UNESCO*. 221–239. DOI: 10.1007/978-981-97-5987-3_13

Kanbach, D. K., Heiduk, L., Blueher, G., Schreiter, M., & Lahmann, A. (2024). The GenAI is out of the bottle: generative artificial intelligence from a business model innovation perspective. In *Review of Managerial Science* (Vol. 18, Issue 4). DOI: 10.1007/s11846-023-00696-z

Karpouzis, K., Pantazatos, D., Taouki, J., & Meli, K. (2024a). Tailoring Education with GenAI: A New Horizon in Lesson Planning. *IEEE Global Engineering Education Conference, EDUCON*. DOI: 10.1109/EDUCON60312.2024.10578690

Karpouzis, K., Pantazatos, D., Taouki, J., & Meli, K. (2024b). Tailoring Education with GenAI: A New Horizon in Lesson Planning. *IEEE Global Engineering Education Conference, EDUCON*. DOI: 10.1109/EDUCON60312.2024.10578690

Khamis, N., Chen, B., Egan, C., Gaglani, S., & Tackett, S. (2025). More intelligent faculty development: Integrating GenAI in curriculum development programs. *Medical Teacher*, *47*(11), 1739–1741. Advance online publication. DOI: 10.1080/0142159X.2025.2473606 PMID: 40029714

Kim, W. J. (2025). Teachers' Use of Generative Artificial Intelligence for Designing Science Lessons in Support of Environmental Science Agency. *Research in Science Education*, •••, 1–20. DOI: 10.1007/s11165-025-10262-0

Kolenatý, M., Kroufek, R., & Činčera, J. (2022). What Triggers Climate Action: The Impact of a Climate Change Education Program on Students' Climate Literacy and Their Willingness to Act. *Sustainability (Basel)*, *14*(16), 10365. Advance online publication. DOI: 10.3390/su141610365

Küchemann, S., Steinert, S., Avila, K. E., & Kuhn, J. (2025). Enhancing students' critical thinking skills through the use of DALL-E. *The Physics Teacher*, *63*(2), 138–139. DOI: 10.1119/5.0253990

Kumar, A., Shankar, A., Hollebeek, L. D., Behl, A., & Lim, W. M. (2025). Generative artificial intelligence (GenAI) revolution: A deep dive into GenAI adoption. *Journal of Business Research*, *189*, 115160. DOI: 10.1016/j.jbusres.2024.115160

Lane, R. (2025). Mitigating risks, embracing potential: A framework for integrating generative artificial intelligence in geographical and environmental education. *International Research in Geographical and Environmental Education*, 1–18. Advance online publication. DOI: 10.1080/10382046.2025.2458561

Law, L. (2024). Application of generative artificial intelligence (GenAI) in language teaching and learning: A scoping literature review. *Computers and Education Open*, *6*, 100174. DOI: 10.1016/j.caeo.2024.100174

Liu, S. C., & Château, P. A. (2025). Fostering Hope and Action on Climate Change among University Students: Impact of a Futures-Oriented Teaching Module with Generative AI Integration. *Journal of Science Education and Technology*, *34*(6), 1–16. DOI: 10.1007/s10956-025-10229-w

Lo, C. K. (2023). What Is the Impact of ChatGPT on Education? A Rapid Review of the Literature. *Education Sciences*, *13*(4), 410. DOI: 10.3390/educsci13040410

Moundridou, M., Matzakos, N., & Doukakis, S. (2024). Generative AI tools as educators' assistants: Designing and implementing inquiry-based lesson plans. *Computers and Education: Artificial Intelligence*, *7*, 100277. DOI: 10.1016/j.caeai.2024.100277

Nguyen, A., Gul, F., Dang, B., Huynh, L., & Tuunanen, T. (2025). Designing embodied generative artificial intelligence in mixed reality for active learning in higher education. *Innovations in Education and Teaching International*, *62*(5), 1632–1647. Advance online publication. DOI: 10.1080/14703297.2025.2499177

Pilaniwala, P. (2024). Artificial Intelligence in Product Management: Enhancing User Experience Personalization through GenAI. *3rd International Conference on Automation, Computing and Renewable Systems, ICACRS 2024 - Proceedings*, 1135–1140. DOI: 10.1109/ICACRS62842.2024.10841633

Puri, R., Ghosh, A., & Ketkar, S. (2024). The Role of the G20 Countries in Embedding Climate Literacy in Education: From Knowing to Doing. *HAPSc Policy Briefs Series*, *5*(1), 104–112. DOI: 10.12681/hapscpbs.38975

Radwan, A. Y., Alasmari, K. M., Abdulbagi, O. A., & Alghamdi, E. A. (2025). SARD: A Human-AI Collaborative Story Generation. *Lecture Notes in Computer Science (Including Subseries Lecture Notes in Artificial Intelligence and Lecture Notes in Bioinformatics), 15375 LNCS*, 94–105. DOI: 10.1007/978-3-031-76806-4_7

Richards, D., Worden, D., Song, X. P., & Lavorel, S. (2024). Harnessing generative artificial intelligence to support nature-based solutions. *People and Nature*, *6*(2), 882–893. DOI: 10.1002/pan3.10622

Rutecka, P., Cicha, K., Rizun, M., & Strzelecki, A. (2025). Generative AI in Curriculum Design: Empirical Insights into Model Performance and Educational Constraints. *IEEE Transactions on Learning Technologies*, *18*, 757–768. Advance online publication. DOI: 10.1109/TLT.2025.3587081

Sato, F. E., & Park, J. (2025). A systematic review of climate change literacy assessment methods. *The Journal of Environmental Education*, *56*(1), 65–83. DOI: 10.1080/00958964.2024.2385333

Simpson, N. P., Andrews, T. M., Krönke, M., Lennard, C., Odoulami, R. C., Ouweneel, B., Steynor, A., & Trisos, C. H. (2021). Climate change literacy in Africa. *Nature Climate Change*, *11*(11), 937–944. Advance online publication. DOI: 10.1038/s41558-021-01171-x

Suraj Kumar, S., Chatterjee, K., Ramchandra Reddy, S., Praveen Kumar, R., Sachin, A., Abhinav Vardhan Reddy, T., & Sriya Reddy, M. (2024). GenAI: Transforming Climate Science Education in the Digital Age. *Studies in Computational Intelligence*, *1177*, 355–372. DOI: 10.1007/978-981-97-8460-8_16

Surathunmanun, S., Ongsakul, W., & Singh, J. G. (2024). Exploring the Role of Generative Artificial Intelligence in the Energy Sector: A Comprehensive Literature Review. *Proceedings of the 2024 International Conference on Sustainable Energy: Energy Transition and Net-Zero Climate Future, ICUE 2024*. DOI: 10.1109/ICUE63019.2024.10795598

Tang, K. S. (2024). Informing research on generative artificial intelligence from a language and literacy perspective: A meta-synthesis of studies in science education. *Science Education*, *108*(5), 1329–1355. DOI: 10.1002/sce.21875

Temsah, M. H., Alhuzaimi, A. N., Almansour, M., Aljamaan, F., Alhasan, K., Batarfi, M. A., Altamimi, I., Alharbi, A., Alsuhaibani, A. A., Alwakeel, L., Alzahrani, A. A., Alsulaim, K. B., Jamal, A., Khayat, A., Alghamdi, M. H., Halwani, R., Khan, M. K., Al-Eyadhy, A., & Nazer, R. (2024). Art or Artifact: Evaluating the Accuracy, Appeal, and Educational Value of AI-Generated Imagery in DALL·E 3 for Illustrating Congenital Heart Diseases. *Journal of Medical Systems*, *48*(1), 1–13. DOI: 10.1007/s10916-024-02072-0 PMID: 38780839

Yan, L., Greiff, S., Teuber, Z., & Gašević, D. (2024). Promises and challenges of generative artificial intelligence for human learning. *Nature Human Behaviour*, *8*(10), 1839–1850. DOI: 10.1038/s41562-024-02004-5 PMID: 39438686

Yeh, S. C., Chen, Y. H., Van Velzen, R., & Lin, P. H. (2025). The climate change literacy of public officials in Taiwan: Implications and strategies for global adaptation. *Policy Studies*, *46*(2), 168–201. Advance online publication. DOI: 10.1080/01442872.2024.2304086

Chapter 8

Innovating Sustainable Climate Change Education in STEM With Generative Artificial Intelligence

Sachin Sharma
https://orcid.org/0000-0002-7821-3685
Amity University Punjab, Mohali, India

ABSTRACT

The developing criticalness of tending to climate alter requires inventive approaches to instruction, especially within the areas of Science, Technology, Engineering, and Mathematics (STEM). Generative Artificial Intelligence (GenAI) offers interesting openings to upgrade educating and learning in these spaces, advertising energetic, personalized, and adaptable arrangements for climate alter instruction. This chapter investigates the potential of GenAI to revolutionize STEM instruction by giving versatile learning situations, real-time information investigation, and inventive arrangements for climate-related challenges. By joining GenAI into climate alter instruction, we will engage the another era of researchers, engineers, and pioneers to contribute seriously to climate activity and supportability. This chapter talks about the integration of GenAI tools in educational module, their potential benefits, and challenges, and offers a vision for the future of climate alter instruction inside STEM disciplines

DOI: 10.4018/979-8-3373-9074-1.ch008

1. INTRODUCTION

Climate alter is one of the foremost squeezing worldwide challenges of our time, requesting critical and maintainable arrangements. Science, Technology, Engineering, and Mathematics (STEM) instruction plays a significant part in preparing understudies with the information and aptitudes vital to get it and address climate-related issues. In any case, conventional educating techniques frequently battle to keep pace with the fast headways in climate science and the developing complexity of maintainability challenges. In reaction, joining generative artificial intelligence (AI) into STEM instruction presents a transformative opportunity to improve climate alter education, cultivate inventive problem-solving abilities, and develop a modern era of naturally cognizant pioneers.

Generative AI, a subset of fake insights that makes unused substance based on existing information, is revolutionizing different areas, counting instruction. By leveraging AI-powered devices such as natural language processing (NLP) models, machine learning calculations, and intelligently simulations, teachers can give students with immersive, energetic, and personalized learning encounters. Within the setting of climate alter instruction, generative AI can encourage Data-driven Experiences where AI models can prepare endless sums of climate information, create prescient examinations, and show discoveries in an open way, making a difference understudies get a handle on complex natural concepts. AI-powered reenactments and virtual labs empower understudies to explore with climate models, analyze real-time natural information, and investigate the potential impacts of different climate approaches. Adaptive learning stages utilizing AI can tailor instructive substance to person learning paces, guaranteeing understudies completely get it crucial climate alter concepts some time recently advancing to progressed themes. AI-generated narrating, intuitively case thinks about, and gamification components can make climate instruction more locks in and relatable, cultivating more profound understudy inclusion. Generative AI offers a few imaginative approaches to improving climate alter instruction in STEM areas (Sharma et al., 2025). One of the essential challenges in climate instruction is translating complex environmental forms into reasonable groups. AI-driven climate models permit understudies to imagine worldwide warming scenarios, predict the affect of human exercises on environments, and investigate potential moderation procedures. These models utilize authentic climate information and progressed machine learning calculations to produce real-time estimates, empowering understudies to analyze patterns and try with arrangements. AI-based coaching frameworks give personalized instruction in climate science by adjusting to each student's learning fashion and pace. These cleverly mentors can answer questions, propose extra assets, and evaluate students' understanding through intelligently tests and real-time feedback. By leveraging NLP and AI-generated clarifications, understudies can get customized support tailored to their needs (Agarwal et al., 2024).

Generative AI can make climate-related instructive materials, counting reading material, articles, and intelligently instructional exercises. These AI-generated assets can be persistently overhauled with the most recent logical discoveries, guaranteeing that understudies get the foremost up-to-date data (Sharma et al., 2024). Additionally, AI can create multilingual substance, making climate instruction more available to assorted gatherings of people around the world. AI-driven virtual and augmented reality (VR/AR) applications permit understudies to investigate climate alter impacts in an immersive way. For case, VR reenactments can transport understudies to dissolving ice sheets, deforested scenes, or coastal zones debilitated by rising ocean levels. By encountering these scenarios firsthand, understudies can create a more profound passionate and intellectual association to climate issues. Understudies can lock in in real-world climate inquire about by analyzing huge datasets utilizing AI-powered instruments. Generative AI can help in recognizing designs, foreseeing climate patterns, and recommending possible interventions (Sharma et al., 2024). Moreover, AI-driven citizen science stages empower understudies to contribute to worldwide climate investigate by collecting and analyzing natural information from their neighborhood communities. Whereas generative AI presents various openings for progressing climate alter instruction, it too raises moral contemplations that must be tended to. AI-driven instructive apparatuses ought to be planned to be comprehensive and open to all understudies, notwithstanding of financial foundation or geographic area. Securing students' individual information and guaranteeing moral AI sending in instructive settings must be prioritized. AI should complement, instead of supplant, human teachers. The integration of AI should upgrade teachers' capacity to provide compelling climate instruction whereas protecting the human component of mentorship and direction.

The integration of generative AI into STEM instruction offers a promising pathway to revolutionizing climate alter learning (Sharma et al., 2024). By leveraging AI-powered simulations, personalized mentoring, and immersive encounters, understudies can create a more profound understanding of natural challenges and develop the basic considering abilities required to address them. To maximize the potential of AI-driven climate instruction, teachers, policymakers, and innovation engineers must collaborate to guarantee the ethical, inclusive, and effective usage of AI devices. By doing so, able to engage future eras with the information, aptitudes, and inspiration to drive sustainable arrangements to climate alter and make a more flexible world. Generative AI speaks to a capable device for changing climate alter instruction in STEM fields (Bhatt et al., 2024). By saddling its capabilities, able to prepare understudies with the insights and advancements required to tackle the climate emergency, cultivating a feasible and educated worldwide community. The future of climate instruction lies within the collaboration between progressed AI innovations and human-driven instructive techniques, clearing the way for a more economical and naturally cognizant society.

2. LITERATURE REVIEW

Nedungadi et al. (2024) study methodicallly audits existing writing to recognize and analyze the competences that are cultivated in higher instruction courses centered on maintainability or Education for Sustainable Development (ESD). The review points to contribute to a much better understanding of how higher instruction educate are planning understudies to address supportability challenges. Henriksen et al. (2024) examines existing investigate to understand how climate alter instruction and communication methodologies impact person and collective behaviors towards supportability. It points to distinguish viable strategies and approaches for advancing pro-environmental behaviors. Skowronek et al. (2021) examine how instruction can contribute to building versatile capacity and cultivating versatility within the face of climate alter impacts. It emphasizes that instruction isn't almost conferring information, but moreover almost creating aptitudes, values, and states of mind that empower people and communities to adjust. Baskara (2024) investigates how GAI can be utilized to progress the objectives of maintainable instruction by making more personalized, locks in, and successful learning encounters. It examines the different ways GAI can back teachers and learners in tending to supportability challenges. Nixon et al. (2024) aims to supply a system to direct teachers and educate within the dependable and viable integration of GAI into instructing and learning. It emphasizes the have to be adjust the potential benefits of GAI with the moral and academic challenges it presents. Adnan et al. (2024) explores how Generative AI (GenAI) can change instruction towards supportability objectives. It emphasizes GenAI's potential for personalized learning, information examination, and making locks in instructive substance. In any case, it too highlights moral concerns like algorithmic predisposition and information protection. The creators contend that GenAI can be a powerful device for advancing supportability instruction, but its execution requires cautious thought of moral suggestions and capable utilize. Future investigate should center on creating systems that ensure evenhanded and compelling GenAI integration in instructive settings. Relmasira et al. (2023) explores the significance of integrating Artificial Intelligence (AI) education into early instruction, particularly in STEAM subjects. It emphasizes that with the rise of generative AI advances, understudies must be prepared with the abilities to get it, make, and fundamentally assess AI frameworks. The paper advocates for educational program change to incorporate AI principles, fostering an understanding of AI's potential, risks, and ethical considerations. The article also highlights the require for teacher professional improvement and interdisciplinary approaches to bolster AI instruction in elementary schools. Ruiz-Rojas et al. (2024) discusses the integration of generative AI devices into higher instruction, especially centering on cultivating collaborative work and basic considering. It highlights the potential of AI apparatuses to upgrade learning encounters by empowering understudies to collaborate more viably, engage in complex problem-solving, and create basic considering abilities. The paper emphasizes the significance of adjusting instructive hones to incorporate AI, guaranteeing that understudies are arranged to work nearby these advances. Moreover, it investigates the suggestions of AI on academic methodologies and the require for teachers to remain educated almost AI headways to direct their understudies fittingly. Carmona-Galindo et al. (2025) explores how virtual reality (VR) can be utilized as an instructive instrument to cultivate a deeper understanding of climate alter. By immersing people in simulated situations, VR offers a special way to imagine both nearby and worldwide climate impacts, making a difference clients get a handle on the criticalness and scope of the issue. The study highlights VR's potential in advancing natural awareness and encouraging a more comprehensive point of view on climate change, pointing to lock in clients emotionally and cognitively. This approach energizes dynamic learning and worldwide collaboration, subsequently contributing to more successful climate alter instruction and activity.

3. STEM

STEM, which stands for Science, Technology, Engineering, and Mathematics, is an intrigue approach to instruction that coordinating these four areas to cultivate problem-solving, basic considering, and advancement. STEM instruction is fundamental for planning understudies to explore an increasingly complex world driven by innovation and logical progressions. STEM instruction is significant for a few reasons. STEM careers drive innovative development, driving to financial advancement and work creation. Countries with solid STEM instruction programs lead in logical inquire about and mechanical headways. STEM information makes a difference create economical arrangements to worldwide challenges such as climate alter, renewable vitality, and asset preservation. STEM instruction prepares understudies with the abilities required within the advanced work showcase, counting information investigation, coding, and building plan. STEM instruction emphasizes intrigue learning by interfacing distinctive subjects to unravel real-world issues. This approach empowers understudies to think inventively, apply logical standards, and create imaginative arrangements. As AI, mechanization, and rising innovations proceed to shape the world, STEM instruction must advance to incorporate computerized proficiency, morals in innovation, and intrigue collaboration. By cultivating interest and advancement, STEM instruction will proceed to be a driving drive in forming a feasible and innovatively progressed future.

4. SUSTAINABLE CLIMATE CHANGE EDUCATION

Climate change is one of the foremost basic worldwide issues of the 21st century, influencing biological systems, economies, and social orders around the world. As natural challenges proceed to heighten, the part of instruction in cultivating economical arrangements has gotten to be progressively imperative. Sustainable climate change education (SCCE) seeks to enable understudies with the information, aptitudes, and values essential to address climate-related issues successfully. By joining supportability standards into STEM (Science, Technology, Engineering, and Mathematics) education, SCCE gives a establishment for creating ecologically cognizant people who can drive important alter. SCCE plays a significant part in preparing people and communities with the instruments to moderate and adjust to climate alter. The key benefits of economical climate instruction incorporate raising awareness by understanding the causes, impacts, and potential arrangements to climate alter is fundamental for fostering global awareness and environmental responsibility. SCCE advances logical request, information investigation, and evidence-based decision-making, empowering understudies to survey natural challenges and investigate imaginative arrangements. Instruction empowers individuals and communities to require proactive measures, advocate for approach changes, and contribute to feasible hones. Climate alter arrangements require interdisciplinary collaboration, coordination information from areas such as science, financial matters, approach, and designing. As the request for supportability experts develops, SCCE plans understudies for careers in renewable vitality, natural science, conservation, and feasible improvement. SCCE includes a few key components that improve its adequacy in cultivating natural proficiency and activity. A fundamental aspect of SCCE is giving understudies with a strong understanding of climate science. This incorporates nursery impact, worldwide warming, climate designs, extraordinary weather events, carbon impressions and their affect on the environment. The part of biodiversity in climate flexibility by joining hands-on tests, climate models, and real-world case thinks about, teachers can offer assistance understudies grasp the logical components behind climate alter. Beyond scientific knowledge, SCCE emphasizes the moral and social duties of people and organizations in moderating climate alter. This incorporates Corporate social responsibility (CSR) and sustainability activities affect of climate change on vulnerable populations. Students are energized to reflect on their claim ecological footprints and adopt sustainable lifestyles that contribute to long-term natural well-being. Understanding climate arrangements, worldwide assentions, and government directions is pivotal for successful climate activity. The Paris Assention, worldwide climate arrangements, National and neighborhood climate activity plans, Carbon estimating and outflows exchanging frameworks. The part of non-governmental organizations (NGOs) in climate promotion analyzes case considers of effective climate approaches, understudies can gain experiences into the part of administration in driving sustainable solutions. SCCE empowers understudies to investigate inventive arrangements for relieving climate alter and adjusting to its impacts. This incorporates renewable vitality sources (solar, wind, hydro, geothermal), carbon capture, capacity advances, maintainable horticulture, reforestation endeavours, smart city activities and economical urban arranging by coordination project-based learning and problem-solving exercises, understudies can effectively engage in creating climate arrangements. STEM instruction gives a capable system for inserting SCCE into educational module. By leveraging logical and innovative progressions, understudies can create commonsense arrangements for natural challenges. The integration of SCCE in STEM incorporates Engineering Sustainable Solutions by planning eco-friendly advances, renewable vitality frameworks, and strong framework. Science for Climate Analysis utilize factual models to analyze climate patterns, foresee natural changes, and optimize asset utilization. Innovation and AI in Climate Science leverages counterfeit insights, machine learning, and enormous information analytics to make strides climate determining and supportability endeavors. Hands-On Experiments and Fieldwork conduct tests related to carbon emanations, renewable vitality effectiveness, and environment wellbeing evaluations. Despite the benefits of SCCE, a few challenges prevent its far reaching execution. Climate instruction changes over districts, driving to crevices in information and awareness. Constrained financing and get to to instructive materials can prevent compelling climate instruction. A few teach may be moderate to receive sustainability-focused educational module due to political, financial, or ideological components.

Climate change could be a multifaceted issue that requires intrigue collaboration, making it challenging to educate comprehensively. To address these challenges, policymakers, teachers, and partners must work together to coordinated SCCE into national instruction approaches, apportion subsidizing for climate programs, and create instructor preparing activities. Artificial intelligence (AI) is revolutionizing instruction, and its potential in SCCE is noteworthy. AI-driven devices can upgrade climate information investigation. AI models can handle tremendous climate datasets, identify patterns, and generate predictive insights. Adaptive learning stages can tailor climate instruction to individual student needs. Virtual reality (VR) and augmented reality (AR) can give understudies with immersive encounters, such as investigating environments or mimicking climate alter scenarios. AI can produce intelligently reading material, climate reports, and multilingual instructive materials. By integrating AI into SCCE, educators can give understudies with cutting-edge assets that improve learning and engagement. Governments ought to command climate instruction in school educational module and distribute subsidizing for supportability programs. Teachers ought to get proficient improvement in climate science, sustainability, and interdisciplinary instructing strategies. Schools should collaborate with nearby communities, businesses, and NGOs to actualize climate activity ventures. SCCE should coordinated science, innovation, arrangement, and ethics to supply a comprehensive understanding of climate change.

AI, VR, and computerized stages ought to be utilized to upgrade climate instruction and engagement. Feasible Climate Alter Instruction is fundamental for building a future where people are prepared to handle natural challenges with information and advancement. By integrating SCCE into STEM instruction, cultivating intrigue collaboration, and utilizing rising innovations, able to engage future eras to lead the way in climate activity. Governments, teachers, and communities must work together to guarantee SCCE becomes a crucial component of global instruction frameworks, clearing the way for a more feasible and flexible world.

5. GENERATIVE ARTIFICIAL INTELLIGENCE

Generative AI, the field committed to making modern information occasions that take after preparing information, depends on a diverse set of calculations. These calculations, each with interesting qualities and applications, empower the era of images, content, sound, and indeed code. Figure 1 explores the models of GAI.

Figure 1. Models of GAI

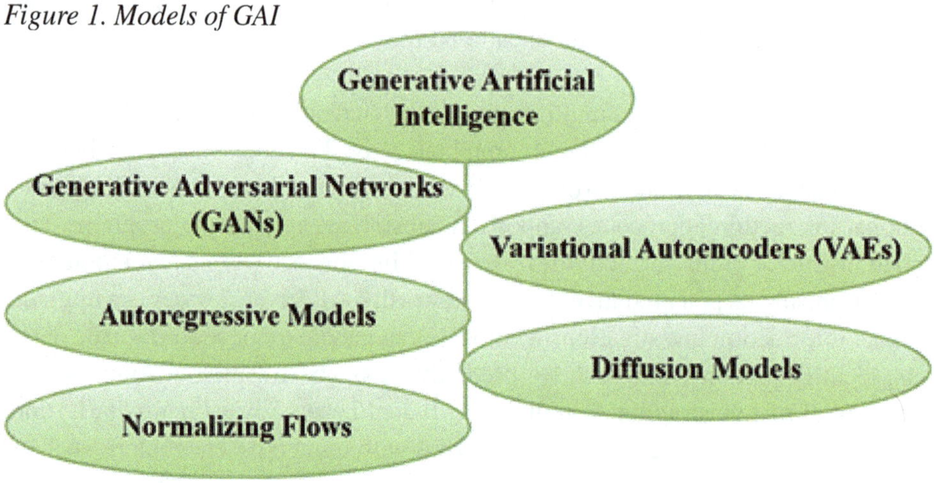

- Generative Adversarial Networks (GANs): GANs comprise of two neural systems, a generator and a discriminator, bolted in an adversarial amusement. The generator points to deliver reasonable information, whereas the discriminator tries to recognize between genuine and produced information. The generator takes arbitrary clamor as input and yields a manufactured information test (Bhatt et al., 2024). The discriminator gets both genuine information from the preparing set and produced information from the generator. The discriminator yields a likelihood showing whether the input is genuine or fake. The generator's objective is to trick the discriminator, whereas the discriminator's objective is to accurately recognize fakes. Through iterative preparing, the generator learns to create progressively practical information. Deep Convolutional GANs (DCGANs) utilize convolutional neural systems, exceeding expectations in image era. Conditional GANs (CGANs) permit control over the generated output by providing additional information (e.g., labels). StyleGANs focus on disentangling style and substance in image generation, empowering fine-grained control. CycleGANs enable image-to-image interpretation without paired preparing information. This procedure is utilized for Image synthesis, fashion exchange, super-resolution, and video era.
- Variational Autoencoders (VAEs): VAEs are probabilistic generative models that learn an inactive representation of the information. They encode input information into a probability distribution in a lower-dimensional latent space and then decode from that space to generate new data (Pandey et al., 2024). An encoder organizes maps the input data to a distribution in the idle space (typically a Gaussian distribution). A decoder network maps tests from the idle space back to the initial information space. The VAE is trained to play down the reconstruction error and the Kullback-Leibler (KL) divergence between the latent distribution and a prior distribution. VAEs are known for their stable preparing and ability to learn smooth latent spaces, which allows for important introduction and control of produced information. This strategy is utilized for Image generation, information compression, and anomaly detection.
- Autoregressive Models: Autoregressive models create information consecutively, foreseeing each component based on the going before components. Recurrent Neural Networks (RNNs), Long Short-Term Memory (LSTM) and Gated Recurrent Unit (GRU) systems, are utilized for producing consecutive information like content and music. Transformers initially outlined for characteristic language preparing, transformers have been adjusted for generative assignments, like image and music creation. PixelRNN/PixelCNN models produce images pixel by pixel, conditioning each pixel's esteem on

the already created pixels. The demonstrate learns the probability dissemination of each component given the past components. To generate new data, the model tests elements sequentially, using the anticipated probabilities. Autoregressive models can capture complex conditions in consecutive information. This procedure is utilized for Text generation, music composition, and image generation. Large Language Models (LLMs) are a type of transformer based autoregressive model.

- Diffusion Models: Diffusion models work by slowly including noise to the preparing information until it gets to be pure noise, and then learning to invert this handle to produce modern information. A forward dissemination handle slowly includes Gaussian noise to the information, changing it into a noise dispersion. A reverse dissemination prepare learns to denoise the information, beginning from the noise distribution and slowly recouping the initial information. The reverse process is conditioned to generate outputs that take after the preparing information. Diffusion models have illustrated state-of-the-art execution in image era, creating high-quality and different tests. This method is utilized for Image era, image altering, and video era.
- Normalizing Flows: Normalizing streams change a simple likelihood dissemination (e.g., Gaussian) into a complex distribution by applying a arrangement of invertible changes. The show learns a series of invertible changes that outline the input information to a basic dispersion. To produce modern information, the show tests from the basic dispersion and applies the reverse changes. Normalizing streams permit for correct probability computation and productive inspecting. This procedure is utilized for Image era, thickness estimation, and audio era.

The quality and diversity of the preparing information are vital for the execution of generative models. Assessing generative models can be challenging, and different measurements are utilized to survey the quality and differences of generated information (Kohli et al., 2023). Training large generative models requires critical computational assets. Generative AI raises ethical concerns almost deepfakes, misinformation, and bias. These calculations are always advancing, with progressing investigations pushing the boundaries of what generative AI can accomplish. Their ability to generate realistic and diverse information has opened up unused possibilities in different fields, from art and entertainment to scientific discovery and drug development.

6. ASSESSMENT PARAMETERS

Evaluating the specialized parameters for enhancing feasible climate change instruction in STEM with generative AI requires a multifaceted approach, centering on both the AI's capabilities and its educational viability. Here's a detailed breakdown of key specialized parameters:

- Dataset Precision: Survey the exactness and unwavering quality of the climate alter information utilized to prepare the generative AI. This incorporates assessing information sources, recognizing potential inclinations, and guaranteeing information keenness.
- Domain Specificity: The AI must produce substance important to STEM disciplines and adjusted with climate alter instruction destinations. Assess the model's capacity to deliver experimentally precise and educationally sound yields.
- Information Differences: Guarantee the preparing information includes assorted climate alter scenarios, territorial varieties, and logical points of view to maintain a strategic distance from one-sided or constrained yields.
- Content Generation Quality: Assess the quality of generated content, images, recreations, and other media. This incorporates surveying genuine exactness, coherence, imagination, and engagement.
- Customization and Personalization: Survey the AI's capacity to create personalized learning encounters based on person understudy needs and learning styles. This includes assessing the model's flexibility and responsiveness to client input.
- Interactive Simulation and Visualization: Assess the AI's capacity to create intelligently recreations and visualizations that successfully outline complex climate alter concepts. This incorporates surveying the authenticity, interactivity, and instructive esteem of the created reenactments.
- Multimodal Output: The AI ought to be able to create a wide cluster of substance. Assess the capacity of the show to generate content, sound, pictures, and video, and the quality of each.
- Computational Efficiency: Survey the computational assets required to prepare and deploy the generative AI show. This incorporates assessing preparing time, deduction speed, and memory utilization.
- Adaptability: Assess the model's capacity to handle a huge number of clients and generate substance for different instructive settings.
- API and Integration: Evaluate the ease of coordination the generative AI demonstrate with existing learning management systems (LMS) and instructive stages.

- Information Acquisition: Assess the viability of AI-generated substance in advancing information securing and understanding of climate alter concepts. This may be surveyed through pre- and post-tests, tests, and other evaluation instruments.
- Critical Thinking and Problem-Solving: Evaluate the AI's capacity to cultivate basic considering and problem-solving skills related to climate alter. This could be assessed through case thinks about, reenactments, and project-based appraisals.
- Engagement and Motivation: Assess the AI's capacity to lock in and motivate understudies in climate alter instruction. This could be evaluated through studies, criticism shapes, and observational thinks about.
- Educational Plan: Guarantee that AI-generated substance adjusts with existing STEM educational program and climate alter instruction measures.
- Accessibility and Inclusivity: Assess the AI's capacity to supply available and comprehensive learning encounters for understudies with differing needs and foundations.
- Teacher Support and Integration: Evaluate the AI's capacity to support instructors in conveying compelling climate alter instruction. This incorporates assessing the ease of utilize, preparing assets, and specialized bolster.
- Inclination and Decency: Assess the potential for predisposition in AI-generated substance and guarantee reasonableness in learning results.
- Information Security and Security: It guarantee that understudy information is secured and utilized responsibly (Sharma et al., 2024).
- Transparency and Explainability: It survey the transparency and explainability of the AI's decision-making prepare. Understudies and teachers should be able to get it how the AI creates substance and makes proposals.
- Misinformation and Deepfakes: Climate alter related deception is wild. Asses the AI's capacity to anticipate and relieve the creation of wrong or deceiving data.
- Cloud Computing: It assess the require for cloud computing assets to bolster the preparing and sending of the generative AI demonstrate.
- Hardware Determinations: It decide the equipment determinations required for ideal execution, counting preparing control, memory, and capacity.
- Software Conditions: Distinguish and address any computer program conditions required for the generative AI show.
- Transfer speed Necessities: It evaluate the transfer speed prerequisites for conveying AI-generated substance to understudies and teachers.
- Inactivity and Unwavering quality: Guarantee that the arrange association is dependable and has low inactivity to supply a consistent learning involvement.

- Information Capacity Capacity: Decide the information capacity required to store preparing information, created substance, and understudy information.
- Information Reinforcement and Recuperation: Execute information reinforcement and recuperation methods to guarantee information security and avoid information misfortune.

7. TOOLS FOR ASSESSMENT

Fig. 2 illustrates the tools for assessment.

Figure 2. Tools for assessment

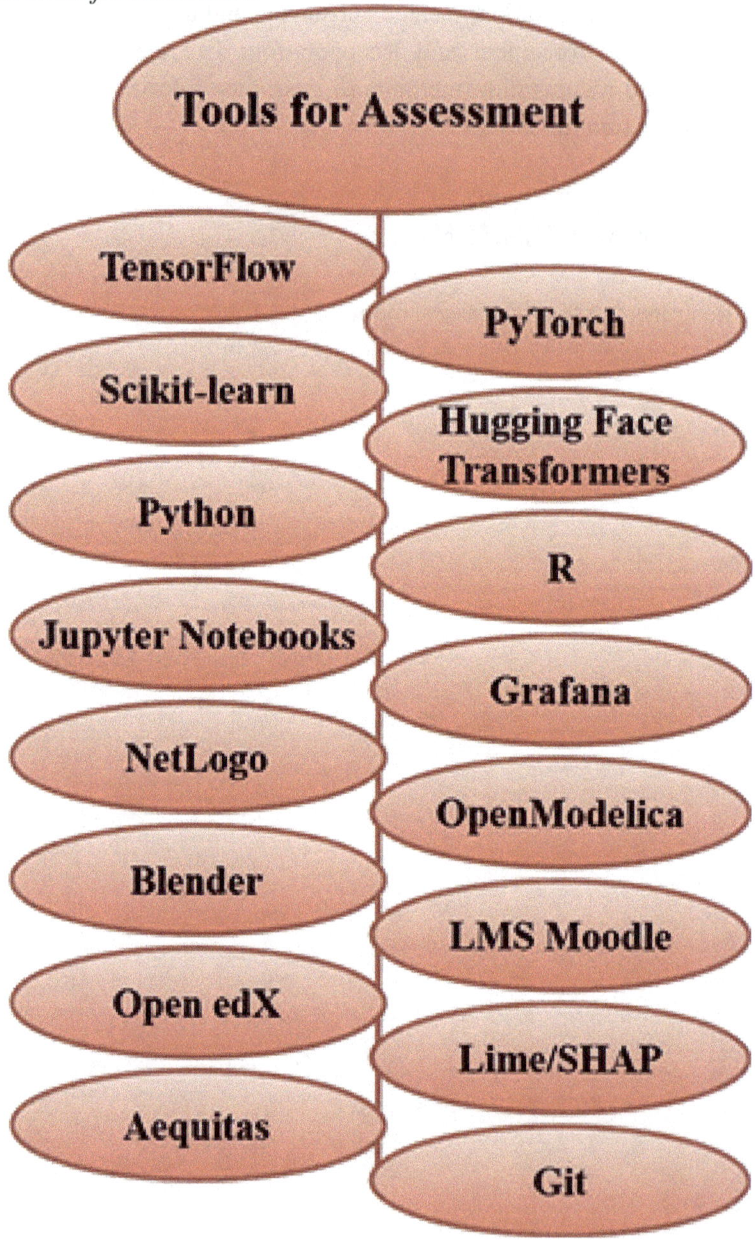

- TensorFlow: A flexible system for building and preparing machine learning models, counting generative AI models.

- PyTorch: Another prevalent system known for its adaptability and ease of utilize in investigate and improvement.
- Scikit-learn: A comprehensive library for machine learning errands, counting information preprocessing, show assessment, and visualization.
- Hugging Face Transformers: A library giving pre-trained models and instruments for common dialect preparing, significant for content era and investigation.
- Python (Pandas, NumPy, Matplotlib, Seaborn): Effective libraries for information control, examination, and visualization, fundamental for assessing learning analytics and AI show execution.
- R: A measurable computing dialect with broad libraries for information investigation and visualization.
- Jupyter Notebooks: An interactive environment for information investigation, coding, and documentation, encouraging collaborative investigate and improvement.
- Grafana: For the creation of dashboards that can show genuine time information from different sources.
- NetLogo: A multi-agent programmable modeling environment for recreating complex frameworks, appropriate for modeling climate alter scenarios.
- OpenModelica: An open-source modeling and recreation environment for physical frameworks, valuable for making climate models.
- Blender: A 3D creation suite, valuable for making 3D models of climate alter occasions, or geological information.
- Learning Management Systems (LMS) Moodle: A broadly utilized open-source LMS that can be customized to coordinated AI-powered learning instruments.
- Open edX: An open-source stage for making and conveying online courses, advertising adaptability for joining AI-driven highlights.
- Lime/SHAP: Libraries that offer assistance clarify the yields of machine learning models, making a difference with predisposition discovery, and expanding demonstrate straightforwardness.
- Aequitas: An open-source predisposition and reasonableness review toolkit.
- Git: Fundamental for collaborative advancement and form control of code and information.

8. POSSIBLE SOLUTION USING ANCIENT INDIAN KNOWLEDGE SYSTEM

It is vital to approach the concept of "civilization collapse" with nuance. Civilizations once in a while vanish completely; or maybe, they regularly experience changes, shifts in population centers, and changes in socio-political structures. With that in intellect, here's a center on how climate alter has associating with authentic occasions within the Indian subcontinent, with the understanding that these are complex intelligent:

- Indus Valley Civilization (Harappan Civilization): Typically the foremost well-documented case. Around 3900-3000 a long time prior, shifts within the Indian rainstorm driven to diminished precipitation, drying of streams, and agrarian decrease. This brought about within the deserting of urban centers and a move towards littler, more scattered settlements. The "4.2-kiloyear occasion" is heavely linked to this decay.
- Impacts on Post-Harappan Cultures: Taking after the decline of the Indus Valley Civilization, changes in precipitation designs proceeded to impact settlement designs and rural process within the locale. Vacillations within the rainstorm have generally driven to periods of dry season and flooding, which have affected agrarian social orders all through the subcontinent.
- Impact on Regional Kingdoms: All through Indian history, periods of drought and starvation have driven to social turmoil, movements, and the debilitating of territorial kingdoms. Whereas not continuously the sole cause of collapse, climate inconstancy has regularly exacerbated existing vulnerabilities.
- Historical Droughts and Famines: India encompasses a long history of droughts and famines, a few of which have had obliterating results. These events have frequently been connected to varieties within the storm framework. In spite of the fact that these events are more show within the more recent chronicled record, the likely hood of these occasions happening has been show for all of the past 10,000 a long time.
- Shifting River Systems: Changes in waterway courses, impacted by tectonic movement and climate change, have also affected settlement designs and rural efficiency. The Saraswati River, said in ancient texts, could be a subject of progressing debate, with a few analysts suggesting that changes in its course may have been connected to climatic shifts. It's vital to recognize that climate alter is regularly one calculate among numerous that contribute to societal alter. Social, financial, and political variables moreover play noteworthy parts. Investigate in paleoclimatology is continuous, and our understanding of the relationship between climate and chronicled events proceeds to advance.

- Coordination the Old Indian Information Framework (AIKS) with generative AI for sustainable climate change instruction in STEM offers a unique and effective approach (Gautam et al., 2024). AIKS, profoundly established in all encompassing considering, biological adjust, and maintainable living, gives important bits of knowledge that can complement and upgrade cutting edge logical understanding.
- Panchamahabhutas (Five Elements): AI can be prepared on datasets that reflect the interconnecting of the five components (earth, water, fire, air, and space) as portrayed in AIKS. Generative AI can make recreations and visualizations that illustrate the affect of human exercises on these components and their sensitive adjust. For case, AI seem create recreations appearing how deforestation influences soil erosion (earth), water cycles (water), and atmospheric temperatures (fire and air).
- Ayurveda and Ecological Balance: Ayurvedic standards emphasize the significance of keeping up agreement between the person and the environment. AI can analyze information on conventional rural hones, timberland administration, and asset utilization from an Ayurvedic viewpoint. Generative AI can at that point create instructive substance that highlights the economical viewpoints of these hones and their significance to advanced climate challenges.
- Vrikshayurveda (Science of Plant Life): AIKS incorporates a wealthy convention of information around plant life, counting soil wellbeing, bother control, and maintainable agribusiness. AI can be utilized to analyze old writings and conventional information to distinguish maintainable agrarian hones. Generative AI can make intuitively recreations that illustrate the benefits of these practices, such as natural pest control and soil enrichment.
- Yoga and Mindfulness: Yoga and mindfulness hones advance a sense of interconnecting with nature and empower capable natural stewardship. AI can be utilized to develop virtual reality (VR) or augmented reality (AR) encounters that drench understudies in common situations and advance mindfulness. Generative AI can make personalized mindfulness works out that offer assistance understudies interface with nature and create a more profound understanding of their part in natural supportability.
- AI-Generated Simulations and Visualizations: Create intuitively simulations that illustrate the affect of climate alter on particular biological systems, coordination AIKS standards of interconnecting. Create visualizations that grandstand the impacts of conventional feasible hones, such as water collecting and natural cultivating, on climate flexibility. Create virtual field trips to ancient Indian locales that illustrate feasible engineering and asset administration
- AI-Powered Language Translation and Interpretation: Utilize AI to translate and interpret ancient Indian texts related to environmental science and fea-

sible living. Create AI-powered chatbots that can reply students' questions approximately AIKS concepts and their pertinence to present day climate challenges. Make instructive materials that bridge the crevice between antiquated shrewdness and cutting edge logical understanding.

- AI-Driven Personalized Learning: Create AI-powered learning stages that personalize climate alter instruction based on students' learning styles and interface. Utilize AI to analyze understudy execution and give personalized criticism and suggestions. Create customized learning ways that coordinated AIKS concepts with present day STEM educational module.
- AI-Assisted Investigate and Information Analysis: Utilize AI to analyze expansive datasets of conventional environmental information and recognize designs and bits of knowledge. Create AI-powered devices that offer assistance analysts analyze the affect of climate alter on conventional agricultural practices. Make AI-driven stages that encourage collaboration between researchers, teachers, and conventional information holders.
- AI for generating culturally relevant content: AI can produce stories, poems, and art that reflect the social setting of AIKS and its relevance to climate alter. This makes a difference to form the subject more relatable and locks in for understudies from different foundations. AI can make localized substance, reflecting the particular climate challenges and conventional information of diverse locales inside India.
- Integration with STEM Curriculum: Science Integrate AIKS concepts into lessons on environment, biodiversity, and climate science. Utilize AI-generated recreations to illustrate the standards of biological adjust and interconnecting. Investigate the logical premise of conventional hones, such as Ayurvedic medication and Vrikshayurveda. Innovation makes a difference to create AI-powered instruments and stages for climate alter instruction. It utilize VR and AR innovations to make immersive learning encounters. It investigates the utilize of AI for information examination and modeling in climate investigate. Designing makes a difference to plan feasible building arrangements based on AIKS standards of asset preservation and biological adjust. It develop AI-powered frameworks for checking and overseeing natural assets. It investigate the utilize of conventional building materials and strategies in present day engineering. Science utilize numerical models to analyze and measure the affect of climate alter on environments. It create AI-powered instruments for information investigation and visualization. It investigates the scientific standards fundamental conventional Indian cosmic and environmental information
- Regard for Traditional Information: It guarantee that conventional information is utilized morally and with regard for its social centrality. It get educated

assent from conventional information holders some time recently utilizing their information in AI-powered instructive instruments. It recognize and credit the sources of conventional information.

- Information Protection and Security: It ensure the security of understudy information and guarantee that AI-powered instructive devices are secure. It execute information encryption and access control measures to avoid unauthorized access.
- Bias Mitigation: It address potential inclinations in AI models and datasets to guarantee reasonableness and inclusivity. It utilize assorted datasets that speak to the complete extend of conventional information and viewpoints. It give instructors with preparing and bolster on how to coordinated AIKS concepts and AI-powered devices into their instructing. It create assets and materials that offer assistance instructors bridge the crevice between antiquated shrewdness and present day STEM educational program.
- Community Engagement: It lock in with neighborhood communities and conventional information holders within the improvement and usage of AI-powered instructive programs. It make openings for understudies to memorize from and interact with conventional information holders. By keenly coordination AIKS with generative AI, able to make a effective and socially pertinent approach to maintainable climate alter instruction, cultivating a more profound understanding of our interconnecting with nature and motivating future eras to gotten to be mindful stewards of the planet.
- Holistic View of Nature: AIKS emphasizes the interconnecting of all components (Panchamahabhutas). This viewpoint highlights that changes in one component can affect the whole framework. This adjusts with advanced climate science's understanding of complex input circles within the Earth's climate.
- Emphasis on Balance (Rita): The concept of "Rita" in Vedic writing alludes to the characteristic arrange and enormous balance. Disturbances to this adjust were seen as having negative results. This resounds with the cutting edge understanding of how human exercises can disturb the Earth's common frameworks, driving to climate alter.
- Feasible Practices: Ancient Indian texts and practices illustrate a strong emphasis on feasible asset administration, especially in agribusiness and water preservation. Vrikshayurveda incorporates the science of plant life, which incorporates information of soil wellbeing, pest control, and sustainable agriculture. Water management incorporates advanced frameworks of water collecting and water system were created. It is critical to respect for woodlands and biodiversity. The perceptions of common phenomena incorporates the Ancient Indian astronomers and researchers made detailed perceptions of

celestial phenomena, counting climate designs and regular changes. These perceptions contributed to a deep understanding of common cycles and their impact on climate.

- Impact of Climate on Civilizations: Later inquire about is progressively highlighting the part of climate in forming the history of Indian civilizations. Studies that investigate paleoclimate records, such as those determined from dust examination, are uncovering how changes within the Indian Summer Rainstorm have impacted vegetation designs, human relocations, and the rise and drop of dynasties. One case of typically, inquire about done on the Ganga plain, that appears how climate driven vegetation changes affected human history over the past 2000 a long time. AIKS offers important experiences into economical hones that can be adjusted to address cutting edge climate challenges. Conventional information of natural agribusiness, water preservation, and environment administration can contribute to creating climate-resilient arrangements.
- Ethical Framework: The moral standards inserted in AIKS, such as regard for nature and the significance of adjust, can give a system for responsible natural stewardship.
- Understanding Climate Variability: The historical observations and information contained in AIKS can contribute to a deeper understanding of long-term climate changeability within the Indian subcontinent. By examining AIKS, we can pick up a wealthier understanding of the chronicled relationship between people and climate, and draw profitable lessons for tending to the climate challenges of nowadays.

9. ADVANTAGES

The direness of addressing climate alter requests inventive instructive approaches, especially inside STEM areas. Generative Artificial Intelligence (GAI) offers a transformative toolkit to revolutionize Sustainable Climate Change Education (SCCE), cultivating deeper understanding, basic considering, and proactive engagement. Here's an broad investigation of the preferences:

- Custom fitted Learning Pathways: GAI can analyze person understudy learning styles, qualities, and shortcomings, making personalized learning ways. This guarantees that understudies get substance custom-made to their particular needs, upgrading comprehension and maintenance. Versatile learning stages fueled by GAI can alter the trouble and pace of learning based on understudy execution, giving a energetic and responsive instructive encounter.

- Interactive Simulations and Virtual Labs: GAI can produce reasonable and interactive simulations of climate frameworks, permitting understudies to investigate complex marvels in a secure and locks in environment. Virtual labs can be made to conduct tests that would be unreasonable or inconceivable in a conventional classroom setting, such as modeling the impacts of rising ocean levels or deforestation. These reenactments can visualize theoretical concepts, making them more available and reasonable, cultivating a more profound understanding of climate science.
- Gamified Learning Experiences: GAI can make gamified learning encounters that make climate alter instruction more locks in and propelling. Intelligently recreations and simulations can challenge understudies to fathom real-world climate issues, advancing basic considering and problem-solving abilities. Gamification can increment understudy inspiration and engagement, making learning more agreeable and successful.
- Personalized Criticism and Evaluation: GAI can give personalized input on understudy work, distinguishing zones for advancement and advertising focused on direction. Computerized evaluation apparatuses can analyze understudy execution information to recognize designs and patterns, giving teachers with important experiences into understudy learning. This permits for more effective and viable appraisal, liberating up teachers to center on giving individualized back.
- Upgrading Climate Information Investigation and Modeling: Climate alter investigate creates enormous sums of information, counting partisan symbolism, climate records, and oceanographic information. GAI can prepare and analyze these tremendous datasets, recognizing designs and patterns that would be troublesome for people to perceive. This permits for more precise and comprehensive understanding of climate alter phenomena.
- Producing Progressed Climate Models: AI can be utilized to develop modern climate models that can foresee future climate scenarios with more prominent exactness. These models can join complex intuitive between different natural variables, giving a more all encompassing see of climate alter. Moved forward climate models can educate arrangement choices and direct the advancement of relief and adjustment procedures.
- Visualizing Complex Information: GAI can create intelligently visualizations of climate information, making it less demanding for understudies and the open to get it complex logical data. Visualizations can incorporate maps, charts, and 3D models that outline the impacts of climate alter, such as rising ocean levels, extraordinary climate occasions, and changes in biodiversity. This upgrades communication and understanding of climate related data.

- Fostering Innovation and Problem-Solving: GAI can be utilized to create novel arrangements to climate alter challenges, such as creating modern maintainable innovations and hones. It can analyze existing information and recognize potential zones for development, quickening the improvement of climate arrangements. For case, GAI can create modern chemical combinations for carbon capture, or unused plans for wind turbine edges.
- Simulating and Assessing Arrangements: GAI can recreate the potential impacts of diverse climate arrangements, permitting for the assessment of their viability and possibility. This could offer assistance recognize the foremost promising arrangements and prioritize inquire about and improvement endeavors. This incorporates reenacting the impacts of diverse arrangements, or diverse designing ventures.
- Advancing Collaborative Problem-Solving: GAI-powered stages can encourage collaborative problem-solving, interfacing understudies and analysts from around the world to work together on climate alter challenges. These stages can give get to to shared information and instruments, empowering collaborative inquire about and development. This will permit for a more extensive run of thoughts, and more differing arrangements.
- Extending Accessibility and Inclusivity: GAI-powered interpretation apparatuses can break down language barriers, making climate alter instruction available to a more extensive gathering of people. Instructive materials can be interpreted into different languages, guaranteeing that everybody has access to critical data.
- Addressing Accessibility Needs: GAI can generate alternative substance groups for understudies with incapacities, such as sound portrayals, sign dialect interpretations, and text-to-speech apparatuses. This guarantees that all understudies have rise to access to climate alter instruction.
- Reaching Remote and Underserved Communities: GAI-powered online learning stages can reach inaccessible and underserved communities, giving access to high-quality climate alter instruction. This will offer assistance bridge the instructive hole and ensure that everybody has the opportunity to memorize approximately climate alter.
- Supporting Teachers and Curriculum Improvement: GAI can help teachers in making locks in and up-to-date educational materials, such as lesson plans, introductions, and intelligently works out. This may spare teachers time and exertion, permitting them to center on giving individualized bolster to understudies.
- Developing Customized Curriculum Modules: GAI can offer assistance create customized educational programs modules custom-made to particular learning destinations and student needs. This permits for more adaptable and

responsive educational programs improvement, guaranteeing that understudies get the foremost significant and viable instruction.

- Providing Real-Time Feedback and Experiences: GAI-powered stages can give teachers with real-time input on understudy execution and engagement. This permits teachers to recognize ranges where understudies require extra bolster and alter their educating procedures appropriately. This permits for much quicker reactions to issues, and for a much more energetic instructing environment.
- Assisting within the creation of up to date data: Climate science is quickly advancing. GAI can be utilized to continually upgrade instructive materials with the latest research discoveries. This guarantees that students are learning the foremost current and exact data almost climate alter.
- Ethical Considerations and Challenges: GAI calculations can acquire inclinations from the information they are prepared on, possibly driving to unjustifiable or discriminatory outcomes. It is pivotal to address these inclinations and guarantee that GAI is utilized in a reasonable and evenhanded way.
- Data Privacy and Security: The utilize of GAI in instruction includes the collection and investigation of understudy information, raising concerns around protection and security. It is basic to execute strong information security measures to protect understudy protection (Sharma et al., 2024).
- Responsible Utilize and Transparency: It is significant to advance mindful and moral utilize of GAI in instruction, guaranteeing that it is utilized to upgrade learning and not to supplant human interaction. Transparency in how GAI is utilized, and how choices are made, is crucial.
- Digital Divide: Unequal access to innovation can compound existing disparities. It is basic to guarantee impartial get to GAI-powered instruction.
- Over-reliance on AI: It is imperative that AI is utilized as a device to expand human insights, and not to supplant it. Critical considering and human interaction are still key.

10. CHALLENGES

Whereas the potential of Generative Artificial Intelligence (GAI) to revolutionize Sustainable Climate Change Education (SCCE) in STEM is verifiable, its execution is full with challenges. Exploring these obstacles is vital to guarantee that GAI serves as a capable apparatus for positive alter, instead of compounding existing disparities or making modern issues.

- Information Limitations and Quality: Climate alter impacts shift essentially over locales. GAI models regularly require tremendous datasets, and information shortage for particular geographic zones or climate marvels can constrain the precision and significance of created substance. For illustration, point by point information on microclimate varieties in inaccessible hilly locales or particular localized impacts of sea fermentation may be missing.
- Information Inclination and Representativeness: AI models are prepared on existing information, which may reflect chronicled predispositions. In case the information is skewed towards certain locales, populaces, or viewpoints, the created substance may perpetuate these inclinations. This may result in wrong or deficient representations of climate alter impacts, especially for marginalized communities.
- Information Quality and Reliability: Climate information can be loud, fragmented, or conflicting. Guaranteeing the quality and unwavering quality of information utilized to prepare GAI models is fundamental for creating exact and reliable instructive substance. Obsolete information can too be an expansive issue, as climate science is an ever advancing field.
- Algorithmic Inclination and Moral Concerns: GAI calculations can incidentally fortify existing imbalances in the event that they are trained on information that reflects societal predispositions. For illustration, in the event that climate alter instruction materials produced by GAI basically center on the encounters of created countries, they may ignore the unbalanced impacts on helpless communities in creating nations. Numerous GAI models work as "black boxes," making it troublesome to get it how they arrive at their yields. This need of straightforwardness can raise concerns almost the legitimacy and unwavering quality of produced substance. This need of explainability moreover makes it difficult to rectify predisposition, and to get it the restrictions of the AI. GAI can generate reasonable but possibly misleading substance, such as deepfakes or created climate information. Shields are needed to anticipate the abuse of GAI for spreading deception or controlling open opinion on climate alter. Who possesses the substance that's generated by AI? Typically a legal gray area, and has to be tended to.
- Mechanical Foundation and Access: Access to GAI-powered instruction requires dependable web network and computerized gadgets. The advanced partition can compound existing imbalances, restricting get to high-quality climate alter instruction for understudies in underserved communities. This is often a gigantic issue in creating countries, and in rustic regions. Creating and executing GAI-based instructive apparatuses requires critical computational assets and skill. Numerous instructive teach, especially in creating nations, may need the essential framework and capacity. The computer program

required to run progressed GAI frameworks is regularly costly, and requires an extraordinary bargain of specialized information.

- Educational and Execution Challenges: Coordination GAI-powered apparatuses into existing STEM curricula requires careful arranging and coordination. Teachers need to be trained on how to viably utilize these devices and adjust their teaching practices appropriately. Teachers have to be create modern aptitudes and competencies to successfully utilize GAI within the classroom. This incorporates understanding how GAI calculations work, assessing the quality of produced substance, and adjusting their instructing procedures to use the qualities of GAI. Whereas GAI can improve learning, it is basic to preserve human association and basic considering abilities. Teachers must guarantee that GAI is utilized as a instrument to expand human insights, not to supplant it. Understudies must still be instructed to address data, and to think fundamentally almost information. How do you evaluate the quality and exactness of substance created by AI? This is a difficult issue, and requires unused evaluation methods. It is imperative to preserve an adjust, and to not over depend on AI.
- Interdisciplinary Collaboration and Approach Considerations: Effective usage of GAI in SCCE requires collaboration between AI specialists, climate researchers, teachers, and policymakers. Bridging the crevice between these disciplines is fundamental for creating important and successful instructive instruments. Clear moral rules and arrangements are required to oversee the utilize of GAI in education. These arrangements ought to address issues such as information protection, algorithmic predisposition, and capable utilize of AI. Significant investment is required to support the improvement and execution of GAI-powered SCCE initiatives. Subsidizing ought to be designated to investigate, advancement, teacher preparing, and infrastructure development. Climate alter could be a worldwide issue, and requires global participation. Sharing of information, technology, and best practices is basic.

11. CASE STUDY

Next Generation Science Standards (NGSS) play a critical part in forming climate alter instruction within the U.S. These measures emphasize inquiry-based learning and energize understudies to explore real-world wonders, counting climate alter. This system empowers teachers to coordinated climate science over different STEM disciplines. Numerous inventive programs prioritize hands-on, project-based learning encounters. Understudies lock in in exercises such as Collecting, analyzing neighborhood climate information, Planning and building maintainable innovations, and Taking part in community-based natural ventures. Hands on work and open air instruction are also progressively joined to supply understudies with coordinate presentation to natural frameworks. Integration of Innovation plays a vital part in improving climate alter instruction. This incorporates utilizing information visualization devices to investigate climate information, utilizing reenactments and modeling program to get it climate frameworks, and utilizing GIS (Geographic Information Systems) to analyze spatial information related to climate alter. There's a developing acknowledgment of the significance of tending to natural equity in climate alter instruction. Programs are progressively centering on highlighting the unbalanced impacts of climate alter on marginalized communities, enabling understudies to advocate for natural equity and including understudies in community-based ventures that address nearby natural issues. National Science Foundation (NSF) plays a imperative part in financing inquire about and instructive programs related to climate alter. Activities just like the Innovations in Graduate Education (IGE) program bolster ventures that get ready the following era of STEM experts to address natural challenges. The NSF underpins different ventures that center on immersive field encounters, stakeholder-driven maintainable improvement, and transdisciplinary inquire about. These programs point to prepare understudies with the essential aptitudes to handle complex climate issues. For illustration, programs centering on elevated inquire about, or those centering on sun powered vitality advancement. Numerous school locale and educational organizations are creating their claim climate alter instruction programs. These programs frequently include organizations with nearby colleges, natural organizations, and community bunches. The adequacy of climate alter instruction depends on giving understudies with exact and up-to-date data. It's too vital to cultivate basic thinking skills and engage understudies to require action. Tending to the computerized isolate and guaranteeing impartial get to to innovation are fundamental for giving all understudies with quality climate alter instruction. By centering on these key patterns and activities, the U.S. is working to plan the another era of STEM experts to address the challenges of climate alter. Analyzing Sustainable Climate Change Education (SCCE) advancement in STEM inside China uncovers a special setting molded by national approaches and needs. National Policy Alignment with China's commitment to environmental civilization and its national climate objectives intensely impact instructive activities. Climate alter instruction is regularly coordinates inside broader endeavors to advance feasible improvement. The government plays a noteworthy part in directing educational modules improvement and instructive needs. Emphasis on STEM and Innovative Arrangements Given China's center on innovative advancement, STEM instruction related to climate alter frequently emphasizes creating arrangements. This incorporates Renewable vitality advances, Natural observing, information examination, and Maintainable designing hones where it could be a solid thrust to prepare understudies with the specialized abilities required to contribute to a green economy. Climate alter instruction is frequently coordinates with broader natural instruction activities. This incorporates raising mindfulness almost Discuss and water contamination, Asset preservation, and Biological security. The colleges are progressively playing a part in climate alter instruction and investigate. There's a developing accentuation on intrigue programs that address the complex challenges of climate alter. Inquire about has appeared that particular climate alter courses inside Chinese colleges, have appeared critical changes in student's convictions almost the anthropogenic causes of climate alter.

Like all expansive instructive framework, there are challenges in guaranteeing reliable usage of climate alter instruction over different districts. Adjusting the accentuation on innovative arrangements with a broader understanding of social and moral measurements of climate alter is additionally a key thought. China's approach to SCCE is closely tied to its national improvement objectives. There's a solid accentuation on down to earth abilities and mechanical advancement. The part of government in forming educational priorities is noteworthy. To urge a more profound understanding, it is imperative to look at the work being wiped out chinese colleges, additionally to see at the way natural science is being coordinates into the typical school educational modules.

In Australia, the integration of Sustainable Climate Change Education (SCCE) inside STEM is picking up force, driven by a developing mindfulness of the nation's powerlessness to climate impacts. The Australian Educational modules plays a significant part, with expanding accentuation on joining supportability and climate alter concepts over different STEM subjects. This points to guarantee that understudies create a foundational understanding of climate science and its suggestions. There's a solid accentuation on interfacing STEM learning to real-world challenges, especially those related to Australia's special environment. This incorporates ventures centering on Bushfire versatility, Water asset administration, Renewable vitality innovations, Marine biological system security. Progressively, there's a acknowledgment of the esteem of joining Inborn information and points of view into climate alter instruction. This recognizes the long history of Innate Australians in overseeing the arrive and their profound understanding of natural frameworks. Community and Industry Organizations for numerous inventive programs include organizations with nearby communities, natural organizations, and industry partners. This gives understudies with openings to engage in authentic ventures and create commonsense abilities. Mechanical Integration with Australian schools and instructive programs are joining innovation into climate alter instruction, counting Information investigation and visualization instruments i.e. Geographic Information Systems (GIS). GIS makes a difference in renewable vitality innovation exhibits. Given Australia's differing environments, hands on work could be a critical component of numerous climate alter instruction programs. This permits understudies to specifically watch and study natural changes. Numerous schools are actualizing economical practices on their campuses, such as Introducing sun oriented boards, Executing water preservation measures, and Building up school gardens. These activities serve as instructive apparatuses and advance a culture of supportability. Like other countries, Australia faces challenges in guaranteeing steady execution of climate alter instruction over differing districts. There's too an continuous discourse around how to best adjust the educating of climate science with tending to potential tensions among understudies. Australia's approach to SCCE is characterized by a solid accentuation on commonsense abilities, real-world applications, and the integration of Indigenous information.

When looking at the scene of imaginative Sustainable Climate Change Education (SCCE) in STEM inside Britain, a few key patterns and activities develop. The UK's national educational modules is progressively consolidating perspectives of climate alter and maintainability over STEM subjects. This points to supply understudies with a foundational understanding of climate science and its suggestions. There's a solid thrust for hands-on, project-based learning encounters that interface understudies to real-world natural challenges. This incorporates exercises such as Information collection and examination of nearby natural conditions, Plan and execution of feasible arrangements, Interest in citizen science ventures, and College and School Organizations. Collaborations between colleges and schools are playing a crucial part in improving SCCE. These organizations regularly include Giving understudies with get to to cutting-edge investigate and mastery, Creating imaginative instructive assets and programs, Encouraging hands on work and experiential learning openings. There's a developing accentuation on preparing understudies with the "green aptitudes" required to flourish in a economical economy. This incorporates abilities related to Renewable vitality advances, Maintainable designing, Natural administration, and Tending to Climate Uneasiness that recognize the developing concern around climate alter among youthful individuals, teachers are progressively centering on Giving exact and adjusted data, Cultivating a sense of organization and strengthening, Advancing mental well-being. Many UK colleges are effectively included in outreach programs that bring climate alter instruction to schools. For Illustration, Newcastle college has worked on programs counting economical waste frameworks. Organizations like "Learning through Landscapes" provide support and resources for schools to enhance outdoor learning and natural instruction. The utilize of information visualization instruments, recreations, and online assets is getting to be progressively common in climate alter instruction. Britain's approach to SCCE in STEM is characterized by a center on viable learning, collaboration, and the improvement of aptitudes required for a feasible future.

Improving Sustainable Climate Change Education (SCCE) in STEM in India presents a complex and significant undertaking, given the nation's powerlessness to climate alter impacts. India's commitment to maintainable improvement and its national climate activity plans impact instructive activities. There's an expanding accentuation on joining natural instruction into the educational programs. The National Education Policy (NEP) 2020 emphasizes the significance of natural mindfulness and supportability. Given the different natural challenges over India, there's a developing drift toward viable, community-based learning. This incorporates Ventures related to water preservation, Squander administration, Renewable vitality, and Nearby environment thinks about. India's solid center on innovation drives the integration of advanced apparatuses into SCCE. This includes Utilizing information examination and visualization apparatuses, Utilizing farther detecting and GIS innovations, Creating instructive apps and online assets. Climate alter impacts change essentially over India, from coastal flooding to dry season and heatwaves. Instructive activities are progressively custom-made to address territorial vulnerabilities. Activities from UNICEF are working to include climate alter instruction into school security programs, and educational modules in numerous of the indian states. Guaranteeing steady usage over a tremendous and different instructive framework could be a critical challenge. Access to assets and innovation can be uneven, especially in country zones. Instructor preparing and capacity building are significant for compelling SCCE. India's approach to SCCE is closely adjusted with its national advancement objectives and needs. There's a developing acknowledgment of the significance of tending to territorial vulnerabilities. Community engagement and down to earth learning are emphasized. Organizations such as the India STEM establishment are working to bring STEM instruction centered on supportability to a more extensive gathering of people. Organizations like UNICEF are working to include climate alter instruction into the as of now existing school frameworks. It's critical to recognize that SCCE in India is an advancing field, with continuous endeavors to improve its viability and reach .

Sustainable Climate Change Education (SCCE) in STEM in South Africa is exploring a unique scene, checked by both significant challenges and inventive approaches. South Africa is profoundly powerless to climate alter impacts, counting water shortage, extraordinary climate occasions, and biodiversity misfortune. Instructive activities are progressively centered on tending to these particular challenges. This implies that educational modules must be pertinent to the neighborhood climate issues. There's a developing acknowledgment of the significance of consolidating Indigenous knowledge systems (IKS) into SCCE. IKS offers important experiences into economical arrive administration hones and conventional environmental information. The point is to make a more all encompassing and socially pertinent approach to climate alter instruction. Numerous programs emphasize hands-on, commonsense aptitudes advancement and community-based ventures. This incorporates exercises such as Water preservation ventures, Maintainable farming activities, and Renewable vitality exhibits. This moreover makes a difference to construct a sense of community possession of climate arrangements. Like numerous creating countries, South Africa faces challenges related to asset availability, particularly in under-resourced schools. This will restrain access to innovation and instructive materials. Educator preparing is additionally a key issue. Endeavors are underway to coordinated climate alter instruction into the national educational programs. Be that as it may, challenges stay in guaranteeing reliable usage over the nation. The "Keep It Cool" extend could be a awesome illustration of work being done. This extend is centered on getting climate alter instruction into secondary schools. It works on approach, additionally on instructor preparing, and educational modules advancement. South Africa's approach to SCCE is characterized by a solid accentuation on tending to nearby vulnerabilities and coordination Indigenous information. Community engagement and commonsense aptitudes improvement are key components of imaginative programs. Tending to asset limitations and guaranteeing reliable execution are continuous challenges. In substance, South Africa is working to construct a climate-resilient future by engaging its youth with the information and abilities required to address the challenges of climate alter.

In Canada, improving Sustainable Climate Change Education (SCCE) in STEM could be a multifaceted endeavor, reflecting the country's different environments and its commitment to tending to climate alter. Canada's instruction framework is decentralized, meaning that each territory and domain has its possess educational programs. This leads to varieties in how climate alter instruction is actualized. In any case, there's a common slant toward consolidating climate alter concepts over STEM subjects. Given Canada's tremendous common assets, there's a solid accentuation on experiential and open air learning. This incorporates Field thinks about in woodlands, wetlands, and coastal locales, Hands-on ventures related to nearby natural issues. Integration of Innate information and viewpoints. Recognizing the significance of Inborn information in understanding and tending to climate alter, there's a developing exertion to coordinated Inborn points of view into SCCE. This includes collaborating with Innate communities and joining conventional biological information. Numerous programs emphasize creating arrangements to climate alter, such as Renewable vitality advances, Maintainable horticulture hones, and Climate alter adjustment methodologies. There's an expanding mindfulness of the affect of climate alter on students' mental wellbeing. Instructive activities are centering on Giving exact data, Cultivating a sense of office, and Advancing mental well-being. E-STEM Approach demonstrates the developing utilize of the E-STEM approach (Environment, Science, Technology, Engineering, and Mathematics). This intrigue demonstrate is demonstrating viable in enhancing environmental awareness. It is being appeared that by combining natural ponders with standard STEM hones, that understudies pick up a much more profound understanding of climate related issues. Community-Based Ventures i.e. Numerous schools and organizations are executing community-based ventures that lock in understudies in tending to nearby climate alter challenges. These ventures frequently include associations with nearby governments, natural organizations, and Innate communities. Considers that analyze the Canadian educational modules have appeared that whereas climate alter points are show, there are holes in consistency and profundity. There's a solid thrust from student led bunches to extend the sum of climate alter instruction inside the educational programs. There's a solid development to utilize issue fathoming approaches inside the instruction framework. This permits understudies to work on genuine world climate issues, and to come up with potential solutions. Ensuring equitable get to to SCCE over Canada's assorted regions could be a vital challenge. Instructor preparing and proficient improvement are basic for successful usage. Proceeded collaboration between teachers, analysts, and community partners is imperative. Canada is taking steps to prepare its youth with the information and skills required to address the challenges of climate alter.

Innovating Sustainable Climate Change Education (SCCE) in STEM over South America presents a special set of openings and challenges. The region's assorted environments, coupled with shifting levels of financial improvement, make a complex scene for instructive activities. Given South America's wealthy biodiversity, numerous instructive programs center on understanding and ensuring biological systems, especially the Amazon rainforest. There's a solid accentuation on interfacing climate alter instruction to nearby natural issues. Integration of Inborn Information by Recognizing the imperative part of Innate communities in natural stewardship, there's a developing exertion to coordinated Innate information into SCCE. This includes esteeming conventional environmental information and advancing intercultural discourse. Center on Down to earth and Community-Based Learning empowers Numerous programs prioritize hands-on, community-based ventures that address nearby climate alter challenges. This incorporates activities related to Maintainable farming, Water asset administration, and Reforestation. Whereas there's a developing utilize of innovation in SCCE, access to computerized assets remains uneven over the locale. Activities are working to bridge the advanced isolate and give get to to online learning instruments. Colleges play a significant part in climate alter inquire about and instruction. There's a developing accentuation on intrigue programs and collaborations with investigate teach. Organizations like UNESCO IESALC, are working to extend territorial collaboration, and to spread best hones with respect to economical instruction. Climate alter instruction must address the financial imbalances that compound defenselessness to climate impacts. Programs ought to engage marginalized communities and advance natural equity.

Contributing in educator preparing is significant for compelling usage of SCCE. Teachers have to be be prepared with the information and abilities to instruct climate alter concepts successfully. Reinforcing national and territorial policies related to climate alter instruction is fundamental. Educational module ought to be upgraded to reflect the most recent logical understanding and address nearby natural challenges. South America's approach to SCCE is characterized by a solid accentuation on biodiversity, Inborn information, and community engagement. Addressing financial disparities and guaranteeing evenhanded get to instruction are key needs. Territorial collaboration is exceptionally critical. By tending to these contemplations, South American countries can enable their youth to gotten to be specialists of alter in building an economical future.

12. FUTURE PERSPECTIVE

The future of Sustainable Climate Change Education (SCCE) in STEM, joined with Generative Artificial Intelligence (GAI), holds remarkable guarantee. As GAI innovation develops and its integration into instructive systems extends, able to imagine a transformative scene where learning is more personalized, locks in, and impactful. Here's a see at the potential future points of view:

- AI-Driven Learning Companions: Envision AI-powered learning companions that act as personalized mentors, adjusting to each student's learning fashion, pace, and interface. These companions might give real-time input, produce customized learning materials, and direct understudies through complex climate science concepts. These companions may too track understudy advance and recognize ranges where they require extra bolster, giving focused on mediations and assets.
- Dynamic Educational programs Adaptation: GAI will empower the creation of dynamic educational module that adjust to real-time changes in climate science, rising advances, and societal needs. Instructive substance will be persistently overhauled with the most recent inquire about discoveries, guaranteeing that understudies are learning the foremost current and important data.
- Neuro-Adaptive Learning: Future GAI frameworks may incorporate neuro-adaptive advances that screen understudy brain movement to optimize learning encounters. This seem include altering the trouble, pacing, and presentation of content based on real-time neural input.
- Metaverse-Based Climate Recreations: The metaverse might give immersive and intelligently situations for investigating climate alter scenarios.

Understudies may for all intents and purposes involvement the impacts of rising ocean levels, deforestation, or extraordinary climate occasions, cultivating a more profound understanding of these complex marvels. These recreations may moreover permit understudies to explore with distinctive climate arrangements and watch their potential impacts.

- Augmented Reality (AR) and Virtual Reality (VR) Integration: AR and VR innovations, fueled by GAI, seem overlay real-world situations with climate information and visualizations. Understudies seem utilize AR to investigate the biodiversity of a neighborhood environment or utilize VR to travel to inaccessible areas and watch the impacts of climate alter firsthand.
- Haptic Feedback and Sensory Experiences: Future GAI frameworks may join haptic criticism and other sensory experiences to improve learning. Understudies seem feel the surface of distinctive soil sorts, encounter the constrain of a typhoon, or scent the fragrance of a rainforest, making a more immersive and locks in learning involvement.
- AI-Facilitated Global Collaboration: GAI-powered stages seem interface understudies and analysts from around the world to collaborate on climate alter ventures. These stages seem give access to shared information, devices, and mastery, cultivating a worldwide community of climate alter problem-solvers.
- AI-Driven Language Translation and Cultural Exchange: Advanced language translation devices might break down language obstructions, empowering understudies from assorted social foundations to collaborate and learn from each other. GAI may moreover encourage social trade by giving experiences into distinctive viewpoints on climate alter.
- Citizen Science Integration: GAI can be utilized to analyze information collected by citizen researchers, engaging people to contribute to climate alter inquire about. This seem include analyzing information from climate stations, natural life cameras, or natural sensors.
- Real-Time Climate Information Visualization and Investigation: GAI will empower the creation of real-time climate information visualization and examination apparatuses, permitting understudies and analysts to investigate energetic climate designs. These devices may give experiences into the interconnecting of different climate components and the potential impacts of future climate scenarios.
- AI-Powered Climate Risk Assessment: GAI may well be utilized to develop advanced climate risk evaluation models that can foresee the probability and seriousness of future climate impacts. These models may advise approach choices and direct the improvement of climate adjustment methodologies.
- Generative Design for Sustainable Technologies: GAI might be utilized to produce novel plans for economical advances, such as carbon capture frame-

works, renewable vitality gadgets, and eco-friendly materials. This will radically increment the speed of development.

- Bias Mitigation and Fairness: Future GAI frameworks will join progressed predisposition moderation methods to guarantee decency and value in climate alter instruction. This will include creating calculations that are prepared on differing and agent datasets.
- Transparency and Explainability: GAI models will gotten to be more transparent and reasonable, permitting clients to get it how they arrive at their yields. This will construct believe in GAI-powered instructive devices and advance mindful utilize.
- AI Ethics Instruction: Climate alter instruction will join AI ethics modules, educating understudies almost the moral suggestions of AI and the significance of mindful AI improvement. This will make an era of AI clients that get it the impediments, and conceivable threats of the innovation.
- Decentralized AI frameworks: Decentralized AI frameworks, and decentralized information capacity will permit for more prominent information security, and avoid single focuses of disappointment, or control (Rawat et al., 2024).
- AI-Driven Policy Examination: GAI may well be utilized to analyze the adequacy of distinctive climate alter policies, giving evidence-based bits of knowledge to policymakers. This will permit for quicker and way better educated arrangement choices.
- Personalized Climate Action Recommendations: AI frameworks seem provide personalized proposals for climate activity, enabling people to create feasible choices in their every day lives. This seem include giving data on energy-efficient machines, maintainable transportation options, and eco-friendly customer items.
- AI-Facilitated Community Engagement: AI can be utilized to facilitate community engagement in climate alter activities, giving stages for dialogue, collaboration, and activity. Long run of SCCE with GAI isn't close to innovation; it's around engaging people and communities to require proprietorship of their climate future. By cultivating basic considering, imagination, and collaboration, GAI can offer assistance us construct a more maintainable and strong world.

13. CONCLUSION

The integration of Generative Artificial Intelligence (GAI) into Sustainable Climate Change Education (SCCE) inside STEM areas speaks to a worldview move with gigantic potential. Whereas challenges exist, the preferences advertised by GAI—personalized learning, upgraded information examination, imaginative problem-solving, and expanded accessibility—are transformative. The key takeaway is that GAI isn't a substitution for human teachers or basic considering, but or maybe a capable instrument to increase and upgrade the learning involvement. By leveraging GAI's capabilities, able to make energetic, locks in, and significant instructive substance that engages understudies to get it and address the complexities of climate alter. Be that as it may, the effective usage of GAI in SCCE requires cautious thought of ethical implications, including algorithmic inclination, information security, and capable utilize. Addressing the advanced partition and guaranteeing evenhanded access to technology are also vital to anticipate compounding existing imbalances. Looking ahead, the longer term of SCCE with GAI holds exciting possibilities, counting hyper-personalized learning environments, immersive virtual environments, and collaborative worldwide systems. By cultivating interdisciplinary collaboration, creating moral rules, and contributing in investigate and foundation, we will saddle the complete potential of GAI to form a more viable, engaging, and impactful climate alter instruction framework. Eventually, this development will prepare future eras with the information, aptitudes, and inspiration required to construct a feasible and flexible future for all.

REFERENCES

Adnan, M., Xiao, B., Ali, M. U., Bibi, S., Yu, H., Xiao, P., Zhao, P., Wang, H., & An, X. (2024). Human inventions and its environmental challenges, especially artificial intelligence: New challenges require new thinking. *Environmental Challenges, 16*, 100976. DOI: 10.1016/j.envc.2024.100976

Agarwal, P., Sharma, S., & Agarwal, J. (2024). ADDMS: Advanced Driver Digital Monitoring System for Efficient Intelligent Traffic Management. *In 2024 1st International Conference on Advanced Computing and Emerging Technologies (ACET)* (pp. 1–6). DOI: 10.1109/ACET61898.2024.10730566

Baskara, F. R. (2024). Generative AI as an enabler of sustainable education: Theoretical perspectives and future directions. *British Journal of Teacher Education and Pedagogy, 3*(3), 122–134. DOI: 10.32996/bjtep.2024.3.3.9

Bhatt, S., & Sharma, S. (2024). Quantum Cryptography Using Blockchain for 6G Enabled Internet of Vehicles. *In 2024 1st International Conference on Advanced Computing and Emerging Technologies (ACET)* (pp. 1–6). DOI: 10.1109/ACET61898.2024.10730580

Bhatt, S., Sharma, S., & Bhadula, S. (2024). NeuroAI: Emerging Artificial Intelligence and Image Processing Techniques in Neuroscience for Enhanced Medical Diagnosis of Brain Tumor. *In 2024 First International Conference on Pioneering Developments in Computer Science & Digital Technologies (IC2SDT)* (pp. 204–209). DOI: 10.1109/IC2SDT62152.2024.10696499

Carmona-Galindo, V. D., Velado-Cano, M. A., & Groat-Carmona, A. M. (2025). The ecology of climate Change: Using virtual reality to share, experience, and cultivate local and global perspectives. *Education Sciences, 15*(3), 290. DOI: 10.3390/educsci15030290

Gautam, A., & Sharma, S. (2024). Artificial Narrow Intelligence Inspired Neuromorphic Computing for Logic Operations in Healthcare Appliances. *In 2024 7th International Conference on Circuit Power and Computing Technologies (ICCPCT)* (pp. 714–719). DOI: 10.1109/ICCPCT61902.2024.10672744

Henriksen, D., Mishra, P., & Stern, R. (2024). Creative learning for sustainability in a world of AI: Action, mindset, values. *Sustainability (Basel), 16*(11), 4451. DOI: 10.3390/su16114451

Kohli, P., & Sharma, S. (2023). Security and Privacy Aware Blockchain Technique for 6G Driven Vehicular Communication Network. *In 2023 IEEE Fifth International Conference on Advances in Electronics, Computers and Communications (ICAECC)*, 1–6. DOI: 10.1109/ICAECC59324.2023.10560325

Nedungadi, P., Tang, K., & Raman, R. (2024). The transformative power of generative artificial intelligence for achieving the sustainable development goal of quality education. *Sustainability (Basel), 16*(22), 9779. DOI: 10.3390/su16229779

Nixon, N., Lin, Y., & Snow, L. (2024). Catalyzing equity in STEM teams: Harnessing generative AI for inclusion and diversity. *Policy Insights from the Behavioral and Brain Sciences, 11*(1), 85–92. DOI: 10.1177/23727322231220356 PMID: 38516055

Pandey, C., Sharma, S., & Bhadula, S. (2024). Artificial Intelligence Technique in Next Generation Healthcare Systems. *In 2024 IEEE International Conference on Communication, Computing and Signal Processing (IICCCS)* (pp. 1–6). DOI: 10.1109/IICCCS61609.2024.10763570

Rawat, R., Goyal, H. R., & Sharma, S. (2024). Hofstede's Cultural Dimension Driven Artificial Narrow Intelligence IDFIS for Industry 5.0 Empowered Digital Society. *Recent Patents on Engineering, 19*. Advance online publication. DOI: 10.2174/01 18722121334543241001050846

Relmasira, S. C., Lai, Y. C., & Donaldson, J. P. (2023). Fostering AI literacy in Elementary Science, Technology, Engineering, Art, and Mathematics (STEAM) education in the age of generative AI. *Sustainability (Basel), 15*(18), 13595. DOI: 10.3390/su151813595

Ruiz-Rojas, L. I., Salvador-Ullauri, L., & Acosta-Vargas, P. (2024). Collaborative working and critical Thinking: Adoption of generative artificial intelligence tools in higher education. *Sustainability (Basel), 16*(13), 5367. DOI: 10.3390/su16135367

Sharma, S., Gautam, A., & Tyagi, R. (2024). Artificial Intelligence and Cyber Security Driven Social Innovations in Digital Adventure Tourism. *In 2024 First International Conference on Pioneering Developments in Computer Science & Digital Technologies (IC2SDT)*, 1–6. DOI: 10.1109/IC2SDT62152.2024.10696759

Sharma, S., Gupta, A., & Tyagi, R. (2024). Artificial Intelligence, Cyber Security and Vedic Scripture Integrated Sustainable Global Youth Leadership Development. *In 2024 IEEE International Conference on Communication, Computing and Signal Processing (IICCCS)* (pp. 1–6). DOI: 10.1109/IICCCS61609.2024.10763618

Sharma, S., Tyagi, R., & Mohan, S. (2024). Artificial intelligence and green 6G network-enabled architectures, scenarios, and applications for autonomous connected vehicles. In *River Publishers eBooks* (pp. 187–212). DOI: 10.1201/9781003515920-9

Sharma, S., Tyagi, R., & Mohan, S. (2024). Generative Artificial Intelligence-Enabled climate change and Deep-Sea food webs. In *Advances in environmental engineering and green technologies book series* (pp. 199–224). DOI: 10.4018/979-8-3693-6670-7.ch009

Sharma, S., Tyagi, R., & Mohan, S. (2025). Artificial intelligence and optimized computational modelling against climate crisis. In *Elsevier eBooks* (pp. 1–14). DOI: 10.1016/B978-0-443-21905-4.00006-7

Skowronek, M., Gilberti, R. M., Petro, M., Sancomb, C., Maddern, S., & Jankovic, J. (2021). Inclusive STEAM education in diverse disciplines of sustainable energy and AI. *Energy and AI*, *7*, 100124. DOI: 10.1016/j.egyai.2021.100124

Compilation of References

Aayushi. (2025). *What is Perplexity AI? A Complete Guide.* https://www.appypieautomate.ai/blog/what-is-perplexity-ai

Abbas, M., Jam, F. A., & Khan, T. I. (2024). Is it harmful or helpful? Examining the causes and consequences of generative AI usage among university students. *International Journal of Educational Technology in Higher Education*, *21*(1), 10. DOI: 10.1186/s41239-024-00444-7

Adeshola, I., & Adepoju, A. P. (2024). The opportunities and challenges of ChatGPT in education. *Interactive Learning Environments*, *32*(10), 6159–6172. DOI: 10.1080/10494820.2023.2253858

Adetayo, A. J., Enamudu, A. I., Lawal, F. M., & Odunewu, A. O. (2024). From text to video with AI: The rise and potential of Sora in education and libraries. *Library Hi Tech News*. Advance online publication. DOI: 10.1108/LHTN-02-2024-0028

Adiba, S. Febriyanto, & Rahmawati, N. S. (2025). Exploring GenAI's Role in Digital Cultural Memory at Museums and Art Galleries in Indonesia: AR and VR Perspectives. *Lecture Notes in Computer Science (Including Subseries Lecture Notes in Artificial Intelligence and Lecture Notes in Bioinformatics), 15493 LNCS*, 198–211. DOI: 10.1007/978-981-96-0865-2_16

Adnan, M., Xiao, B., Ali, M. U., Bibi, S., Yu, H., Xiao, P., Zhao, P., Wang, H., & An, X. (2024). Human inventions and its environmental challenges, especially artificial intelligence: New challenges require new thinking. *Environmental Challenges*, *16*, 100976. DOI: 10.1016/j.envc.2024.100976

Agarwal, P., Sharma, S., & Agarwal, J. (2024). ADDMS: Advanced Driver Digital Monitoring System for Efficient Intelligent Traffic Management. *In 2024 1st International Conference on Advanced Computing and Emerging Technologies (ACET)* (pp. 1–6). DOI: 10.1109/ACET61898.2024.10730566

Agnese, A., De Donato, R., Palmieri, G., Pellegrino, M. A., Petta, A., Scarano, V., & Serra, L. (2020). Visual storytelling by novelette. In *2020 24th International Conference Information Visualisation* (Vol. IV, pp. 723–728). IEEE. https://doi.org/ DOI: 10.1109/IV51561.2020.0012

Agnoli, S., Vanucci, M., Pelagatti, C., & Corazza, G. E. (2018). Exploring the link between mind wandering, mindfulness, and creativity: A multidimensional approach. *Creativity Research Journal, 30*(1), 41–53. DOI: 10.1080/10400419.2018.1411423

AIxploria. (2025). *Free AI Tools: The Full List of over 5,000 AI sites*. AIxploria. https://www.aixploria.com/en/free-ai/

Akçadağ, T. (2010). Öğretmenlerin ilköğretim programındaki yöntem, teknik ölçme ve değerlendirme konularına ilişkin eğitim ihtiyaçları [Training needs of teachers regarding methods, techniques, measurement, and evaluation in the primary education curriculum]. *Ahmet Yesevi Üniversitesi Mütevelli Heyet Başkanlığı, 53*, 29–50.

Akgün, S., & Greenhow, C. (2022). Artificial Intelligence in education: Addressing ethical challenges in K 12 settings. *AI and Ethics, 2*(3), 431–440. DOI: 10.1007/s43681-021-00096-7

Akşin-Yavuz, E., & Zembat, R. (2016). Dinamik değerlendirme yaklaşımı ve okul öncesi eğitimde kullanımı [Dynamic assessment approach and its use in preschool education]. *Eğitim Kuram ve Uygulama Araştırmaları Dergisi, 2*(2), 12–22.

Aktulun, Ö. U., Gözüm, A. İ. C., Kaya, Ü. Ü., Papadakis, S., & Kalogiannakis, M. (2024). Storybooks as a scaffolding tool in teacher–child interaction: The mediating role of vocabulary and receptive language in the investigation of the relationship between teacher attitude and children's language skills. In Papadakis, S., & Kalogiannakis, M. (Eds.), *Education, development and intervention* (pp. 25–48). Springer., DOI: 10.1007/978-3-031-60713-4_2

Akyel, Y., & Tur, E. (2024). Yapay zekanın potansiyelinin ve eğitim bilimlerindeki uygulamalarının araştırılması ve araştırmalarda beklentiler, zorluklar ve gelecek yönelimleri [Investigation of the potential of artificial intelligence and its applications in educational sciences, and expectations, challenges, and future trends in research]. *Ahi Evran Üniversitesi Kırşehir Eğitim Fakültesi Dergisi, 25*(1), 1–1. DOI: 10.29299/kefad.1322341

Al Darayseh, A., & Mersin, N. (2025). Integrating generative AI into STEM education: Insights from science and mathematics teachers. *International Electronic Journal of Mathematics Education, 20*(3), em0832.

Al Kfairy, M., Mustafa, D., Kshetri, N., Insiew, M., & Alfandi, O. (2024). Ethical Challenges and Solutions of Generative AI: An Interdisciplinary Perspective. *Informatics (MDPI), 11*(3), 58. DOI: 10.3390/informatics11030058

Al-Amri, H. M. (2020). Digital storytelling as a communicative language teaching-based method in EFL classrooms. *Arab World English Journal, 11*(1), 270–281. DOI: 10.24093/awej/vol11no1.20

Alan, S. (2019). Comparative ınvestigation of entrepreneurship and ınnovation perceptions of preservice teachers. International Journal of Education in Mathematics. *Science and Technology, 7*(4), 311–318.

Alenda-Demoutiez, J. (2022). Climate change literacy in Africa: The main role of experiences. *The International Journal of Environmental Studies, 79*(6), 981–997. Advance online publication. DOI: 10.1080/00207233.2021.1987059

Alexander, B. (2011). *The new digital storytelling: Creating narratives with new media*. Praeger. DOI: 10.5040/9798216979456

Allen, S. F. (2007). Assessing the development of young children in child care: A research of formal assessment practices. *Early Childhood Education Journal, 34*(6), 455–465. DOI: 10.1007/s10643-007-0153-z

Almassaad, A., Alajlan, H., & Alebaikan, R. (2024). Student Perceptions of Generative Artificial Intelligence: Investigating Utilization, Benefits, and Challenges in Higher Education. *Systems, 12*(10), 16. DOI: 10.3390/systems12100385

Alptekin, S. E., & Freeman, H. J. A. (1996). Mechatronics Education: Model and Implementation. *Proceedings of Mechatronics, 96*, 13–15.

Andersen, T. O., Hansen, M. R., & Pedersen, J. K. (2003). A Mechatronic Curriculum With Project-Based and Problem-Based Learning: A Dynamic Teaching Approach for the Future. *A Mechatronic Curriculum With Project-Based and Problem-Based Learning: A Dynamic Teaching Approach for the Future.*

Andersen, J. P., Degn, L., Fishberg, R., Graversen, E. K., Horbach, S. P. J. M., Schmidt, E. K., Schneider, J. W., & Sørensen, M. P. (2025). Generative Artificial Intelligence (GenAI) in the research process – A survey of researchers' practices and perceptions. *Technology in Society, 81*, 102813. DOI: 10.1016/j.techsoc.2025.102813

Anderson, T., & Shattuck, J. (2012). Design-based research: A decade of progress in education research? *Educational Researcher, 41*(1), 16–25. DOI: 10.3102/0013189X11428813

Ansari, A. N., Ahmad, S., & Bhutta, S. M. (2024). Mapping the global evidence around the use of ChatGPT in higher education: A systematic scoping review. *Education and Information Technologies, 29*(9), 11281–11321. DOI: 10.1007/s10639-023-12223-4

Anysphere, I. (2025). *Cursor: The best way to code with AI.* https://cursor.com/

APS. G. (2017). *Science, Technology, Engineering and Mathematics (STEM) Evidence Base. October.* www.gov.scot

Aria, M., & Cuccurullo, C. (2017). bibliometrix: An R-tool for comprehensive science mapping analysis. *Journal of Informetrics, 11*(4), 959–975. DOI: 10.1016/j.joi.2017.08.007

Arı, S. (2024). Sınıf öğretmenlerinin yapay zekâ kaygılarının farklı değişkenler açısından incelenmesi. *Nevşehir Hacı Bektaş Veli Üniversitesi SBE Dergisi, 14*(4), 2393–2405. DOI: 10.30783/nevsosbilen.1519636

Arkin, R. C., Lee, K. M., McGinnis, L. F., & Zhou, C. (1997). Development of a shared interdisciplinary intelligent mechatronics laboratory. *Journal of Engineering Education, 86*(2), 113–118. DOI: 10.1002/j.2168-9830.1997.tb00273.x

Arnold, D. H., Zeljo, A., Doctoroff, G. L., & Ortiz, C. (2008). Parent involvement in preschool: Predictors and the relation of involvement to preliteracy development. *School Psychology Review, 37*(1), 74–90. DOI: 10.1080/02796015.2008.12087910

Arora, S. D., & Chakraborty, A. (2021). Intellectual structure of consumer complaining behavior (CCB) research: A bibliometric analysis. *Journal of Business Research, 122*, 60–74. DOI: 10.1016/j.jbusres.2020.08.043

Arslan, K. (2020). Eğitimde yapay zekâ ve uygulamaları [Artificial intelligence in education and its applications]. *Batı Anadolu Eğitim Bilimleri Dergisi, 11*(1), 71–88.

Aşık, F., Yıldız, A., Kılınç, S., Aytekin, N., Adalı, R., & Kurnaz, K. (2023). Yapay zekânın eğitime etkileri [The effects of artificial intelligence on education]. *International Journal of Social Humanities Siiences Research, 10*(98), 2100–2107. DOI: 10.5281/zenodo.8307107

Ateş, S. K., Kaleci, F., & Erdoğan, A. (2025). Artificial intelligence in education: A bibliometric analysis. *Ahmet Keleşoğlu Eğitim Fakültesi Dergisi, 7*(1), 14–36.

Atkins, C., Girgente, G., Shirzaei, M., & Kim, J. (2024). Generative AI tools can enhance climate literacy but must be checked for biases and inaccuracies. *Communications Earth & Environment, 5*(1), 1–8. DOI: 10.1038/s43247-024-01392-w

Atmatzidou, S., Demetriadis, S., & Nika, P. (2018). How Does the Degree of Guidance Support Students' Metacognitive and Problem Solving Skills in Educational Robotics? *Journal of Science Education and Technology*, *27*(1), 70–85. DOI: 10.1007/s10956-017-9709-x

Aubry, F. (2024). *Cursor AI: A Guide With 10 Practical Examples*. DataCamp. https://www.datacamp.com/tutorial/cursor-ai-code-editor

Autry, M. M., Lee, J., & Fox, J. (2009). Developing a data-driven assessment for early childhood candidates. *Journal of Early Childhood Teacher Education*, *30*(2), 138–149. DOI: 10.1080/10901020902885695

Awan, A. A. (2025). *What Is DALL-E?* DataCamp. https://www.datacamp.com/blog/what-is-dall-e

Awtar, S., Bernard, C., Boklund, N., Master, A., Ueda, D., & Craig, K. (2002). Mechatronic design of a ball-on-plate balancing system. *Mechatronics*, *12*(2), 217–228. DOI: 10.1016/S0957-4158(01)00062-9

Ay, Y., Anagün, Ş. S., & Demir, Z. M. (2015). Sınıf öğretmeni adaylarının fen öğretiminde okul dışı öğrenme hakkındaki görüşleri [Preservice primary teachers' views on out-of-school learning in science teaching]. *Electronic Turkish Studies*, *10*(15), 1109–1135. DOI: 10.7827/TurkishStudies.8702

Ayyıldız, P., & Yılmaz, A. (2021). 'Moving the kaleidoscope' to see the effect of creative personality traits on creative thinking dispositions of pre-service teachers: The mediating effect of creative learning environments and teachers' creativity fostering behavior. *Thinking Skills and Creativity*, *41*(100879), 1–10. DOI: 10.1016/j.tsc.2021.100879

Baer, J., & Kaufman, J. C. (2008). Gender differences in creativity. *The Journal of Creative Behavior*, *42*(2), 75–105. DOI: 10.1002/j.2162-6057.2008.tb01289.x

Baidoo-Anu, D., & Owusu Ansah, L. (2023). Education in the Era of Generative Artificial Intelligence (AI): Understanding the Potential Benefits of ChatGPT in Promoting Teaching and Learning. *Journal of AI*, *7*(1), 52–62. DOI: 10.61969/jai.1337500

Baker, T., Anissa, N., & Smith, L. (2019). *Educ-AI-tion rebooted? Exploring the future of artificial intelligence in schools and colleges*. Nesta Foundation. https://media.nesta.org.uk/documents/Future_of_AI_and_education_v5_WEB.pdf

Baker, R. S., & Inventado, P. S. (2014). *Educational Data Mining and Learning Analytics*. Springer.

Balcı, A., & Tezel-Şahin, F. (2021). Okul öncesi öğretmenlerinin portfolyoya ilişkin görüşlerinin incelenmesi [Examination of preschool teachers' views on portfolios]. e-Kafkas. *The Journal of Educational Research*, *8*(1), 21–44. DOI: 10.30900/kafkasegt.880423

Baskara, F. R. (2024). Generative AI as an enabler of sustainable education: Theoretical perspectives and future directions. *British Journal of Teacher Education and Pedagogy*, *3*(3), 122–134. DOI: 10.32996/bjtep.2024.3.3.9

Bayram, K., & Çelik, H. (2023). Yapay zekâ konusunda muhakeme ve girişimcilik becerileriyle bütünleştirilmiş sosyo-bilim etkinliği: Fen bilgisi öğretmen adaylarının görüşleri. *Fen Bilimleri Öğretimi Dergisi*, *11*(1), 41–78. DOI: 10.56423/fbod.1241946

Belda-Medina, J., & Goddard, M. B. (2024). AI-driven digital storytelling: A strategy for creating English as a foreign language (EFL) materials. *International Journal of Linguistics Studies*, *4*(1), 40–49. DOI: 10.32996/ijls.2024.4.1.4

Bers, M. U., Flannery, L., Kazakoff, E. R., & Sullivan, A. (2014). Computational thinking and tinkering: Exploration of an early childhood robotics curriculum. *Computers & Education*, *72*, 145–157. DOI: 10.1016/j.compedu.2013.10.020

Berson, I. R., Berson, M. J., & Luo, W. (2025). Innovating responsibly: Ethical considerations for AI in early childhood education. *AI Brain Child*, *1*(2), 2. Advance online publication. DOI: 10.1007/s44436-025-00003-5

Bhatt, S., & Sharma, S. (2024). Quantum Cryptography Using Blockchain for 6G Enabled Internet of Vehicles. *In 2024 1st International Conference on Advanced Computing and Emerging Technologies (ACET)* (pp. 1–6). DOI: 10.1109/ACET61898.2024.10730580

Bhatt, S., Sharma, S., & Bhadula, S. (2024). NeuroAI: Emerging Artificial Intelligence and Image Processing Techniques in Neuroscience for Enhanced Medical Diagnosis of Brain Tumor. *In 2024 First International Conference on Pioneering Developments in Computer Science & Digital Technologies (IC2SDT)* (pp. 204–209). DOI: 10.1109/IC2SDT62152.2024.10696499

Bibri, S. E., & Jagatheesaperumal, S. K. (2023). Harnessing the potential of the metaverse and artificial intelligence for the internet of city things: Cost-effective XReality and synergistic AIoT technologies. *Smart Cities*, *6*(5), 2397–2429. DOI: 10.3390/smartcities6050109

Biddulph, F., & Osborne, R. (1984). Pupils' ideas about floating and sinking. *Research in Science Education*, *14*(1), 114–124. DOI: 10.1007/BF02356797

Borge, M., Smith, B. K., & Aldemir, T. (2024). Using generative ai as a simulation to support higher-order thinking. *International Journal of Computer-Supported Collaborative Learning*, *19*(4), 479–532. DOI: 10.1007/s11412-024-09437-0

Bozdoğan, A. E. (2017). (207). Fen eğitiminde informal öğrenme ortamları dersine yönelik öğretmen adaylarının görüşleri [Pre-service teachers' views on the informal learning environments course in science education]. *Uluslararası Türk Eğitim Bilimleri Dergisi*, (8), 1–17.

Braun, V., & Clarke, V. (2006). Using thematic analysis in psychology. *Qualitative Research in Psychology*, *3*(2), 77–101. DOI: 10.1191/1478088706qp063oa

Breiman, L. (2001). Random forests. *Machine Learning*, *45*(1), 5–32. DOI: 10.1023/A:1010933404324

Brennan, K., Chung, M., Martin, W., Cervantes, F., Tally, B., & Resnick, M. (2019). *What is Computational Thinking*. Harvard Graduate School of Education. https://scratched.gse.harvard.edu/ct/defining.html

Brennan, K., & Resnick, M. (2012). *New frameworks for studying and assessing the development of computational thinking*. Annual American Educational Research Association Meeting., https://web.media.mit.edu/~kbrennan/files/Brennan_Resnick_AERA2012_CT.pdf

British Council. (n.d.). *AI in education: How to navigate the opportunities and challenges*. https://internationalschools.britishcouncil.org/blog/ai-in-education-how-to-navigate-the-opportunities-and-challenges

Brown, N. J., & Brown, O. T. (2002). Mechatronics "a graduate perspective.". *Mechatronics*, *12*(2), 159–167. DOI: 10.1016/S0957-4158(01)00056-3

Bruner, J. S. (2003). *Making stories: Law, literature, life*. Harvard University Press.

Bula, I., Hoxha, V., & Hajrizi, E. (2018). Robot from Mechatronics Scrap -Beggar Robot. *IFAC-PapersOnLine*, *51*(30), 216–219. DOI: 10.1016/j.ifacol.2018.11.289

Buolamwini, J., & Gebru, T. (2018, January). Gender shades: Intersectional accuracy disparities in commercial gender classification. In *Conference on fairness, accountability and transparency* (pp. 77–91). PMLR.

Bura, C., & Myakala, P. K. (2024). Advancing transformative education: Generative AI as a catalyst for equity and innovation (No. arXiv:2411.15971). *arXiv*. https://doi.org//arXiv.2411.15971DOI: 10.48550

Burgsteiner, H., Kandlhofer, M., & Steinbauer, G. (2016). Irobot: Teaching the basics of artificial intelligence in high schools. *Proceedings of the AAAI Conference on Artificial Intelligence*, *30*(1), 4126–4127. DOI: 10.1609/aaai.v30i1.9864

Cardona, M. A., & Rodriguez, R. J. (2024). *Designing for Education with Artificial Intelligence: An Essential Guide for Developers. July*, 1–49. https://tech.ed.gov

Carey, S. (1991). Knowledge acquisition: Enrichment or conceptual change? İçinde S. Carey & R. Gelman (Ed.), The epigenesis of mind: Essays on biology and cognition (s. 257-291). Hillsdale.

Carmona-Galindo, V. D., Velado-Cano, M. A., & Groat-Carmona, A. M. (2025). The ecology of climate Change: Using virtual reality to share, experience, and cultivate local and global perspectives. *Education Sciences*, *15*(3), 290. DOI: 10.3390/educsci15030290

Carnegie Learning. (2024). *The State of AI in Education Artificial Intelligence in Education 2024 Report.*

Carryer, J. E. (1995). The design of laboratory experiments and projects for mechatronics courses. *Mechatronics*, *5*(7), 787–797. DOI: 10.1016/0957-4158(95)00046-8

Carryer, J. E. (2002). March madness: A mechatronics project theme. *Mechatronics*, *12*(2), 383–391. DOI: 10.1016/S0957-4158(01)00077-0

Casal-Otero, L., Catala, A., Fernández-Morante, C., Taboada, M., Cebreiro, B., & Barro, S. (2023). AI literacy in K-12: A systematic literature review. *International Journal of STEM Education*, *10*(1), 29. DOI: 10.1186/s40594-023-00418-7

Çepni, S., & Çoruhlu, T. Ş. (2010). Alternatif ölçme ve değerlendirme tekniklerine yönelik hazırlanan hizmet içi eğitim kursundan öğretime yansımalar [Reflections on teaching from an in-service training course on alternative measurement and evaluation techniques]. *Pamukkale Üniversitesi Eğitim Fakültesi Dergisi*, *28*, 117–128.

Çevik, M., & Senturk, C. (2019). Multidimensional 21st century skills scale: Validity and reliability study. *Cypriot Journal of Educational Sciences*, *14*(1), 11–28. DOI: 10.18844/cjes.v14i1.3506

Cha, K., & Park, J. (2025). Automated analysis of preschoolers' play and social behaviors using multi-object tracking technology: An exploratory approach. *Educación XX1, 28*(2). https://doi.org/DOI: 10.5944/vol28n2a206

Chamilothoris, G. E., & Papoutsidakis, M. G. (2005). Shaping the mechatronics courses for the control curriculum. In *IFAC Proceedings Volumes (IFAC-PapersOnline)* (Vol. 16, Issue 1). IFAC. DOI: 10.3182/20050703-6-CZ-1902.02304

Chamilothoris, G. (2002). Development of a Mechatronics Curriculum in Greece. *Mechatronics*, (June), 24–26.

Chan, C. K. Y., & Hu, W. (2023). Students' voices on generative AI: Perceptions, benefits, and challenges in higher education. *International Journal of Educational Technology in Higher Education, 20*(1), 1–18. DOI: 10.1186/s41239-023-00411-8

Chang, C. H., & Kidman, G. (2023). The rise of generative artificial intelligence (AI) language models - challenges and opportunities for geographical and environmental education. *International Research in Geographical and Environmental Education, 32*(2), 85–89. DOI: 10.1080/10382046.2023.2194036

Chan, S., & Yuen, M. (2014). Personal and environmental factors affecting teachers' creativity-fostering practices in Hong Kong. *Thinking Skills and Creativity, 12*, 69–77. DOI: 10.1016/j.tsc.2014.02.003

Chatzopoulos, A., Papoutsidakis, M., Elza, D., Papadakis, S., Kalogiannakis, M., & Psycharis, S. (2021). DuBot: An Open-Source, Low-Cost Robot for STEM and Educational Robotics. In Papadakis, S., & Kalogiannakis, M. (Eds.), *Handbook of Research on Using Educational Robotics to Facilitate Student Learning* (pp. 441–465). IGI Global., DOI: 10.4018/978-1-7998-6717-3.ch018

Chatzopoulos, A., Papoutsidakis, M., Kalogiannakis, M., & Psycharis, S. (2019). Action Research Implementation in Developing an Open Source and Low Cost Robotic Platform for STEM Education. *International Journal of Computer Applications, 178*(24), 33–46. DOI: 10.5120/ijca2019919039

Chatzopoulos, A., Papoutsidakis, M., Kalogiannakis, M., Psycharis, S., & Papachristos, D. (2020). Measuring the impact on student's Computational Thinking skills through STEM and Educational Robotics projects implementation. In Kalogiannakis, M., & Papadakis, S. J. (Eds.), *Handbook of Research on Tools for Teaching Computational Thinking in P-12 Education* (pp. 234–284). IGI Global., DOI: 10.4018/978-1-7998-4576-8.ch010

Chatzopoulos, A., Tzerachoglou, A., Priniotakis, G., Papoutsidakis, M., Drosos, C., & Symeonaki, E. (2023). Using STEM to Educate Engineers about Sustainability : A Case Study in Mechatronics Teaching and Building a Mobile Robot Using Upcycled and Recycled Materials. *Sustainability (Basel), 15*(21), 15187. Advance online publication. DOI: 10.3390/su152115187

Chatzopoulos, A., Xenakis, A., Papoutsidakis, M., Kalovrektis, K., Kalogiannakis, M., & Psycharis, S. (2024). Proposing and Testing an Open - Source and Low - Cost Drone under the Engineering Design Process for Higher Education : The Mechatronics Course Use Case. *2024 IEEE Global Engineering Education Conference (EDUCON)*, 1–7. DOI: 10.1109/EDUCON60312.2024.10578677

CHEN, C.-C., LI, C., & WANG, Y.-F. (2024). Text-To-Video Model Sora for Education and Teaching: Opportunities and Challenges. *Modern Educational Technology, 34*(5), 27–34. DOI: 10.3969/J.ISSN.1009-8097.2024.05.003

Cheng, Y., Pedaste, M., Bardone, E., & Huang, Y. (Eds.). (2024). *Innovative technologies and learning: 7th International Conference, ICITL 2024, Tartu, Estonia, August 14–16, 2024, Proceedings, Part I* (Vol. 14785). Springer Nature.

Chen, G. (2024). The impacts of AI-driven storytelling applications on language acquisition and literacy development in early childhood education: A systematic review. *Asian Journal of Advanced Research and Reports, 18*(10), 1–12. DOI: 10.9734/ajarr/2024/v18i11770

Chen, J. J., & Li, H. (2025). *AI and the developing child: Ethical and conceptual considerations, and practical frameworks for early childhood education.* AI, Brain and Child., DOI: 10.1007/s44436-025-00016-0

Chen, L., Chen, P., & Lin, Z. (2020). Artificial intelligence in education: A review. *IEEE Access : Practical Innovations, Open Solutions, 8*, 75264–75278. DOI: 10.1109/ACCESS.2020.2988510

Chen, L., & Lee, J. (2023). The effect of digital storytelling on secondary school students' perception of environmental behaviour and affective dispositions. *Research in Science Education, 54*(2), 89–105.

Chen, S. Y. (2023). Generative AI, learning and new literacies. *Journal of Educational Technology Development and Exchange, 16*(2), 1–19. DOI: 10.18785/jetde.1602.01

Chen, T., & Guestrin, C. (2016). XGBoost: A scalable tree boosting system. In *Proceedings of the 22nd ACM SIGKDD International Conference on Knowledge Discovery and Data Mining* (pp. 785-794).

Cheung, K. K. C., Pun, J. K. H., & Li, W. (2024). Students' Holistic Reading of Socio-Scientific Texts on Climate Change in a ChatGPT Scenario. *Research in Science Education, 54*(5), 957–976. DOI: 10.1007/s11165-024-10177-2

Cheung, L. M. E., & Shi, E. (2025). Co-creating stories with generative AI: Reflections from undergraduate students of a storytelling service-learning subject in Hong Kong. *Australian Review of Applied Linguistics*, *47*(4), 259–283. Advance online publication. DOI: 10.1075/aral.24101.che

Cheville, A. (2014). Defining Engineering Education. *121st ASEE Annual Conference & Exposition.*

Chicco, D., Warrens, M. J., & Jurman, G. (2021). The coefficient of determination R^2: Analogies, misconceptions, and some alternatives. *PLoS One*, *16*(9), e0257181. PMID: 34473812

Chiu, T. K. F. (2024). Future research recommendations for transforming higher education with generative AI. *Computers and Education: Artificial Intelligence*, *6*, 100197. DOI: 10.1016/j.caeai.2023.100197

Chiu, T., Meng, H., Chai, C., King, I., Wong, S., & Yam, Y. (2022). Creation and evaluation of a pretertiary artificial intelligence (AI) curriculum. *IEEE Transactions on Education*, *65*(1), 30–39. DOI: 10.1109/TE.2021.3085878

Churchill, N. (2016). Digital storytelling as a means of supporting digital literacy learning in an upper-primary-school English language classroom (Doctoral dissertation). Edith Cowan University. https://ro.ecu.edu.au/theses/1774

Çığrık, E., & Özkan, M. (2016). Bilim merkezi'nde yürütülen öğrenme etkinliklerin öğrencilerin fen bilimleri dersindeki akademik başarılarına etkisi ve motivasyon düzeyleriyle ilişkisi [The effect of learning activities conducted in a science center on students' academic achievement in science lessons and its relation to their motivation levels]. *Uludağ Üniversitesi Eğitim Fakültesi Dergisi*, *29*(2), 279–301.

Cooper, G. (2023). Examining Science Education in ChatGPT: An Exploratory Study of Generative Artificial Intelligence. *Journal of Science Education and Technology*, *32*(3), 444–452. DOI: 10.1007/s10956-023-10039-y

CopilotTeam. (2025). *What Is a Copilot and How Does It Work?* Microsoft. https://www.microsoft.com/en-us/microsoft-copilot/copilot-101/what-is-copilot

Cordero, J., Torres-Zambrano, J., & Cordero-Castillo, A. (2025). Integration of generative artificial intelligence in higher education: Best practices. *Education Sciences*, *15*(1), 32. DOI: 10.3390/educsci15010032

Cortes, C., & Vapnik, V. (1995). Support-vector networks. *Machine Learning*, *20*(3), 273–297. DOI: 10.1023/A:1022627411411

Çoruhlu, Ş. T., Nas, E. S., & Çepni, S. (2009). Fen ve teknoloji öğretmenlerinin alternatif ölçme değerlendirme tekniklerini kullanmada karşılaştıkları problemler: Trabzon örneği [Problems encountered by science and technology teachers in using alternative measurement and evaluation techniques: The case of Trabzon]. Yüzüncü yıl Üniversitesi Eğitim Fakültesi Dergisi, 6(1), 122-141.

Çoruhlu, Ş. T., Nas, E. S., & Çepni, S. (2008). Fen ve teknoloji öğretmenlerinin alternatif ölçme değerlendirme tekniklerini kullanmada karşılaştıkları problemler: Trabzon örneği [Problems encountered by science and technology teachers in using alternative measurement and evaluation techniques: The case of Trabzon] [EFMED]. *Necatibey Eğitim Fakültesi Elektronik Fen ve Matematik Eğitimi Dergisi*, *2*(2), 1–22.

CoSN. (2025). *2024 State of EdTech District Leadership.*

Cotton, D. R., Cotton, P. A., & Shipway, J. R. (2024). Chatting and cheating: Ensuring academic integrity in the era of ChatGPT. *Innovations in Education and Teaching International*, *61*(2), 228–239. DOI: 10.1080/14703297.2023.2190148

Dao, L. T., Tran, T., Van Le, H., Nguyen, G. N., & Trinh, T. P. T. (2023). A bibliometric analysis of Research on Education 4.0 during the 2017–2021 period. *Education and Information Technologies*, *28*(3), 2437–2453. DOI: 10.1007/s10639-022-11211-4

Davis, F. D. (1989). Perceived usefulness, perceived ease of use, and user acceptance of information technology. *Management Information Systems Quarterly*, *13*(3), 319–340. DOI: 10.2307/249008

De Vos, E., Schneider, L., Baccarne, B., De Marez, L., & Emmanouil, M. (2025). The reservoir effect: The role of GenAI based conversational agents in participatory futures. *Digital Creativity (Exeter)*, *36*(3), 193–222. Advance online publication. DOI: 10.1080/14626268.2025.2512773

Dede, C. (2010). Comparing frameworks for 21st century skills. İçinde J. Bellenca & R. Brandt (Ed.), 21st century skills: Rethinking how students. Solution Tree Press.

Dede, C. (2010). Technological supports for acquiring 21st century skills. *International Encyclopedia Of Education*, *3*, 158–166. DOI: 10.1016/B978-0-08-044894-7.00739-9

DeepSeek-AI. Guo, D., Yang, D., Zhang, H., Song, J., Zhang, R., Xu, R., Zhu, Q., Ma, S., Wang, P., Bi, X., Zhang, X., Yu, X., Wu, Y., Wu, Z. F., Gou, Z., Shao, Z., Li, Z., Gao, Z., … Zhang, Z. (2025). *DeepSeek-R1: Incentivizing Reasoning Capability in LLMs via Reinforcement Learning. 500*, 1–22. https://arxiv.org/abs/2501.12948

Demir, İ. C. (2023). Ortaokul 6. sınıf "Dolaşım Sistemi" konusunun öğretiminde interaktif dijital öyküleme kullanımının öğrencilerin akademik başarı ve tutumlarına etkisi [Unpublished master's thesis]. Ordu University.

Demircioğlu, E., & Demir, B. (2024). Yapay zekâ destekli matematik eğitimi: Bir içerik analizi. [JSHSR]. *International Journal of Social and Humanities Sciences Research, 11*(106), 771–785.

Design-Based Research Collective. (2003). Design-based research: An emerging paradigm for educational inquiry. *Educational Researcher, 32*(1), 5–8. DOI: 10.3102/0013189X032001005

Di Blas, N., Paolini, P., & Sabiescu, A. (2010). Collective digital storytelling at school as a whole-class interaction. In *Proceedings of the 9th International Conference on Interaction Design and Children* (pp. 11–19). ACM. DOI: 10.1145/1810543.1810546

Diogo, R. A., dos Santos, N., & Loures, E. F. R. (2023). Digital Transformation of Engineering Education for Smart Education: A systematic literature review. In *Reliability Modeling in Industry 4.0* (pp. 407–438). Elsevier. DOI: 10.1016/B978-0-323-99204-6.00002-9

Donthu, N., Kumar, S., Mukherjee, D., Pandey, N., & Lim, W. M. (2021). How to conduct a bibliometric analysis: An overview and guidelines. *Journal of Business Research, 133*, 285–296. DOI: 10.1016/j.jbusres.2021.04.070

Dotson, M. E., Alvarez, V., Tackett, M., Asturias, G., Leon, I., & Ramanujam, N. (2020). Design Thinking-Based STEM Learning: Preliminary Results on Achieving Scale and Sustainability Through the IGNITE Model. *Frontiers in Education, 5*(February), 1–10. DOI: 10.3389/feduc.2020.00014

Doymaz, C., & Gözüm, A. İ. C. (2025). Okul öncesi öğretmenlerinin dijital içerik üretme yeterliklerinin incelenmesi: Kullanım senaryoları temelli bir uygulama [Examination of preschool teachers' digital content creation competencies: A scenario-based implementation]. In Karademir, A., Demirel, B., & Yılmaz Tam, H. B. (Eds.), *Proceedings of the 18th National Preschool Teacher Education Student Congress* (p. 25). Muş, Türkiye.

Drigas, A., & Ioannidou, R. (2013). A review on artificial intelligence in special education. In *Information Systems, E-learning, and Knowledge Management Research, Communications in Computer and Information Science*. Springer., DOI: 10.1007/978-3-642-35879-1_46

Druga, S., & Ko, A. J. (2021). How do children's perceptions of machine intelligence change when training and coding smart programs? In *Interaction design and children* (pp. 49–61). DOI: 10.1145/3459990.3460712

Druga, S., Vu, S., Likhith, E., Oh, L., Qui, T., & Breazeal, C. (2018). *Cognimates.* http://cognimates.me/home

Druga, S., Vu, S., Likhith, E., & Qiu, T. (2019). Inclusive AI literacy for kids around. the world. *Proceedings of the FabLearn,* 104–111. DOI: 10.1145/3311890.3311904

Duralar, B. (2024). *Matematik eğitiminde yapay zekâ araştırmaları: Sistematik bir inceleme.* Balıkesir Üniversitesi Fen Bilimleri Enstitüsü.

Dwivedi, Y. K., Kshetri, N., Hughes, L., Slade, E. L., Jeyaraj, A., Kar, A. K., & Papagiannidis, S. (2023). So what if ChatGPT wrote it? Multidisciplinary perspectives on opportunities, challenges and implications of generative conversational AI for research, practice and policy. *International Journal of Information Management, 71*, 102642. DOI: 10.1016/j.ijinfomgt.2023.102642

Edwards, S. (2023). Early childhood education and care, artificial intelligence and the postdigital. *Australasian Journal of Early Childhood, 48*(3), 179–181. DOI: 10.1177/18369391231198910

Eghosa, F. (2025). *I used Perplexity AI for one month instead of ChatGPT: here is my review.* https://techpoint.africa/guide/my-perplexity-ai-review/

Eguchi, A., Okada, H., & Muto, Y. (2021). Contextualizing AI education for K-12 students to enhance their learning of AI literacy through culturally responsive approaches. *KI- Künstliche Intelligenz,* 35(2), 153–161.

El Fathi, T., Saad, A., Larhzil, H., Lamri, D., & Al Ibrahmi, E. M. (2025). Integrating generative AI into STEM education: Enhancing conceptual understanding, addressing misconceptions, and assessing student acceptance. *Disciplinary and Interdisciplinary Science Education Research, 7*(1), 6. DOI: 10.1186/s43031-025-00125-z

EL mustapha, E. A., & EL ADNANI, M. J. (2022). The contribution of e-learning in the professional development of teachers. Revue Marocaine de l'Évaluation et de la Recherche Educative, 8(8), 223-241.

El Saddik, A., Ahmad, J., Khan, M., Abouzahir, S., & Gueaieb, W. (2025). Unleashing Creativity in the Metaverse: Generative AI and Multimodal Content. *ACM Transactions on Multimedia Computing Communications and Applications, 21*(7), 1–43. Advance online publication. DOI: 10.1145/3713075

Elbanna, S., & Armstrong, L. (2024). Exploring the integration of ChatGPT in education: Adapting for the future. *Management & Sustainability: An Arab Review, 3*(1), 16–29. DOI: 10.1108/MSAR-03-2023-0016

Ersoy, M., & Gürgen, L. (2021). Eğitim teknolojileri ile ilgili makalelerin incelenmesi. *E-Uluslararası Eğitim Araştırmaları Dergisi, 12*(2), 1–16.

Erstad, O. (2011). Digital storytelling in education: Creative expression, narrative, and technology. *Learning, Media and Technology, 36*(2), 157–162. DOI: 10.1080/17439884.2011.579000

Ester, M., Kriegel, H. P., Sander, J., & Xu, X. (1996). A density-based algorithm for discovering clusters in large spatial databases. *KDD : Proceedings / International Conference on Knowledge Discovery & Data Mining. International Conference on Knowledge Discovery & Data Mining, 96*, 226–231.

Ester, M., Kriegel, H.-P., Sander, J., & Xu, X. (1996). A density-based algorithm for discovering clusters in large spatial databases with noise. In *Proceedings of the Second International Conference on Knowledge Discovery and Data Mining* (pp. 226-231). AAAI Press.

Fang, X., Ng, D. T. K., Leung, J. K. L., & Chu, S. K. W. A. (2023). Systematic review of artificial intelligence technologies used for story writing. *Education and Information Technologies, 28*(11), 1–37. DOI: 10.1007/s10639-023-11741-5

Farrokhnia, M., Banihashem, S. K., Noroozi, O., & Wals, A. (2024). A SWOT analysis of ChatGPT: Implications for educational practice and research. *Innovations in Education and Teaching International, 61*(3), 460–474. DOI: 10.1080/14703297.2023.2195846

Ferguson, R.. (2023). *AI and Education: The Reality and the Potential*. OECD Publishing.

Ferreira, R. (2025). Creative intra-actions: Co-creating with generative AI in the age of climate change. *Learning, Media and Technology, 50*(3), 1–14. DOI: 10.1080/17439884.2025.2532550

Field, A. (2024). Discovering Statistics Using IBM SPSS Statistics. *Sage (Atlanta, Ga.)*.

Firat, M. (2023). What ChatGPT means for universities: Perceptions of scholars and students. *Journal of Applied Learning and Teaching, 6*(1), 57–63. DOI: 10.37074/jalt.2023.6.1.22

Francis, D., & Stephens, A. (2018). *English Learners in STEM Subjects: Transforming Classrooms*. Schools, and Lives., DOI: 10.17226/25182

Freeman, J. (2025). Student Generative AI Survey 2025. *Higher Education Policy Institute*, (February), 1–12.

García-Peñalvo, F. J., Llorens Largo, F., & Vidal, J. (n.d.). The new reality of education in the face of advances in generative artificial intelligence. *Revista Iberoamericana De Educación a Distancia*, *27*(1), 9–39. DOI: 10.5944/ried.27.1.37716

Gardner, J. F. (2002). Two projects for undergraduate mechatronics class: Success and failure. *Mechatronics*, *12*(2), 337–342. DOI: 10.1016/S0957-4158(01)00073-3

Gaube, S., Suresh, H., Raue, M., Merritt, A., Berkowitz, S. J., Lermer, E., Couhlin, J., Guttang, J., Colak, E., & Ghassemi, M. (2021). Do as AI say: Susceptibility in deployment of clinical decision-aids. *NPJ Digital Medicine*, *4*(1), 1–8. DOI: 10.1038/s41746-021-00385-9 PMID: 33608629

Gautam, A., & Sharma, S. (2024). Artificial Narrow Intelligence Inspired Neuromorphic Computing for Logic Operations in Healthcare Appliances. *In 2024 7th International Conference on Circuit Power and Computing Technologies (ICCPCT)* (pp. 714–719). DOI: 10.1109/ICCPCT61902.2024.10672744

Ge, D., Wang, X., & Liu, J. (2021). A teaching quality evaluation model for preschool teachers based on deep learning. *International Journal of Emerging Technologies in Learning*, *16*(3), 127–143. DOI: 10.3991/ijet.v16i03.20471

Geddam, A. (2003). Mechatronics for Engineering Education: Undergraduate Curriculum. *International Journal of Engineering Education*, *19*(4), 575–580.

Gemini Team. Anil, R., Borgeaud, S., Alayrac, J.-B., Yu, J., Soricut, R., Schalkwyk, J., Dai, A. M., Hauth, A., Millican, K., Silver, D., Johnson, M., Antonoglou, I., Schrittwieser, J., Glaese, A., Chen, J., Pitler, E., Lillicrap, T., Lazaridou, A., … Vinyals, O. (2025). *Gemini: A Family of Highly Capable Multimodal Models*. https://arxiv.org/abs/2312.11805

Gervacio, A. P. (2024). Exploring how generative AI contributes to the motivated engagement and learning production of science-oriented students. *Environment and Social Psychology*, *9*(11), 1–17. DOI: 10.59429/esp.v9i11.3194

Gill, S. S., Xu, M., Patros, P., Wu, H., Kaur, R., Kaur, K., Fuller, S., Singh, M., Arora, P., Parlikad, A. K., Stankovski, V., Abraham, A., Ghosh, S. K., Lutfiyya, H., Kanhere, S. S., Bahsoon, R., Rana, O., Dustdar, S., Sakellariou, R., … Buyya, R. (2024). Transformative effects of ChatGPT on modern education: Emerging Era of AI Chatbots. *Internet of Things and Cyber-Physical Systems, 4*(November 2022), 19–23. DOI: 10.1016/j.iotcps.2023.06.002

Giurgiutiu, V., Bayoumi, A. M. E., & Nall, G. (2002). Mechatronics and smart structures: Emerging engineering disciplines for the third millennium. *Mechatronics, 12*(2), 169–181. DOI: 10.1016/S0957-4158(01)00057-5

Gömleksiz, M. N., & Bulut, İ. (2007). Yeni fen ve teknoloji dersi öğretim programının uygulamadaki etkililiğinin değerlendirilmesi [Evaluation of the effectiveness of the new science and technology curriculum in practice]. *Hacettepe Üniversitesi Eğitim Fakültesi Dergisi, 32*, 76–88.

Google. (2025). *Gemini Models.* Google AI for Developers. https://ai.google.dev/gemini-api/docs/models

Gözüm, A. İ. C. (2022). Digital games for STEM in early childhood education: Active co-playing parental mediation and educational content examination. In Papadakis, S., & Kalogiannakis, M. (Eds.), *STEM, robotics, mobile apps in early childhood and primary education* (pp. 355–375). Springer., DOI: 10.1007/978-981-19-0568-1_21

Gözüm, A. İ. C., & Kandır, A. (2021). Digital games pre-schoolers play: Parental mediation and examination of educational content. *Education and Information Technologies, 26*(3), 3293–3326. DOI: 10.1007/s10639-020-10382-2

Grassini, S. (2023). Shaping the future of education: Exploring the potential and consequences of AI and ChatGPT in educational settings. *Education Sciences, 13*(7), 692. DOI: 10.3390/educsci13070692

Grover, S. (2011). Robotics and engineering for middle and high school students to develop computational thinking. *Annual Meeting of the American Educational Research Association, New Orleans, LA, 650*, 1–15. http://web.stanford.edu/~shuchig/docs/AERA2011-Shuchi Grover-Robotics and Engineering for Middle and High School Students to Develop Computational Thinking.pdf

Guettala, M., Bourekkache, S., Kazar, O., & Harous, S. (2024). Generative artificial intelligence in education: Advancing adaptive and personalized learning. *Acta Informatica Pragensia, 13*(3), 460–489. DOI: 10.18267/j.aip.235

Gülbahar, Y., & Kalelioğlu, F. (2018). Bilişim Teknolojileri ve Bilgisayar Bilimi: Öğretim Programi Güncelleme Süreci. *Millî Eğitim Dergisi, 47*(217), 5–23.

Gurova, D. (2025). *What is Cursor AI? Everything You Need to Know*. https://uibakery.io/blog/what-is-cursor-a#:~:text=Cursor AI is an AI,explaining codebases in natural language.

Güven, G., & Yumugan, S. (2025). Artificial intelligence in preschool education: Personalized assessment and evaluation with artificial intelligence. [IJSSER]. *International Journal of Social Sciences and Education Research*, *7*(12), 161–190. DOI: 10.5281/zenodo.14936787

Hair, J. F., Hult, G. T. M., Ringle, C. M., & Sarstedt, M. (2021). *A Primer on Partial Least Squares Structural Equation Modeling (PLS-SEM)* (3rd ed.). SAGE Publications. DOI: 10.1007/978-3-030-80519-7

Han, A., & Cai, Z. (2023). Design implications of generative AI systems for visual storytelling for young learners. In *Proceedings of the 22nd Annual ACM Interaction Design and Children Conference* (pp. 470–474). Chicago, IL, USA. DOI: 10.1145/3585088.3593867

Han, A., Zhou, X., Cai, Z., Han, S., Ko, R., Corrigan, S., & Peppler, K. (2024). Teachers, parents, and students' perspectives on integrating generative AI into elementary literacy education. In *Proceedings of the CHI Conference on Human Factors in Computing Systems*. ACM. DOI: 10.1145/3613904.3642438

Hanna, D. (2023). The Use of Artificial Intelligence Art Generator "Midjourney" in Artistic and Advertising Creativity. *Journal of Design Sciences and Applied Arts*, *4*(2), 42–58. DOI: 10.21608/jdsaa.2023.169144.1231

Harimurti, R., Ekohariadi, , Munoto, , & IGP Asto, B. (2019). The concept of computational thinking toward information and communication technology learning. *IOP Conference Series. Materials Science and Engineering*, *535*(1), 6–13. DOI: 10.1088/1757-899X/535/1/012004

Harji, B. M., & Gheitanchian, M. (2017). Effects of multimedia task-based teaching and learning approach on EFL learners' accuracy, fluency and complexity of oral production. *The Turkish Online Journal of Educational Technology*, *16*(2), 25–34.

Haroud, S., & Saqri, N. (2025). Generative AI in Higher Education: Teachers' and Students' Perspectives on Support, Replacement, and Digital Literacy. *Education Sciences*, *15*(4), 396. DOI: 10.3390/educsci15040396

Harrison, R., & Shazaad, K. (2025). Generative AI in early childhood education: Designing culturally responsive curriculums with ChatGPT. DOI: 10.13140/RG.2.2.15237.26082

Hashmi, N., & Bal, S. (2024). Generative AI in higher education and beyond. *Business Horizons*, *67*(5), 607–614. DOI: 10.1016/j.bushor.2024.05.005

Hasib, K. M., Rahman, F., Hasnat, R., & Alam, M. G. R. (2022, January). A machine learning and explainable AI approach for predicting secondary school student performance. In 2022 *IEEE 12th Annual computing and communication workshop and conference* (CCWC) (pp. 399–405). IEEE. DOI: 10.1109/CCWC54503.2022.9720806

Hazzan-Bishara, A., Kol, O., & Levy, S. (2025). The factors affecting teachers' adoption of AI technologies: A unified model of external and internal determinants. *Education and Information Technologies*, *30*(11), 15043–15069. Advance online publication. DOI: 10.1007/s10639-025-13393-z

Helbling, M., Auer, D., Meierrieks, D., Mistry, M., & Schaub, M. (2021). Climate change literacy and migration potential: Micro-level evidence from Africa. *Climatic Change*, *169*(1–2), 9. Advance online publication. DOI: 10.1007/s10584-021-03241-7

Henriksen, D., Mishra, P., & Stern, R. (2024). Creative learning for sustainability in a world of AI: Action, mindset, values. *Sustainability (Basel)*, *16*(11), 4451. DOI: 10.3390/su16114451

Henseler, J., Ringle, C. M., & Sarstedt, M. (2015). A new criterion for assessing discriminant validity in variance-based structural equation modeling. *Journal of the Academy of Marketing Science*, *43*(1), 115–135. DOI: 10.1007/s11747-014-0403-8

HEPI. (2025). *Student Generative AI Survey 2025 - HEPI*. Higher Education Policy Institute. https://www.hepi.ac.uk/reports/student-generative-ai-survey-2025/

He, R., Cao, J., & Tan, T. (2025). Generative artificial intelligence: A historical perspective. *National Science Review*, *12*(5), nwaf050. Advance online publication. DOI: 10.1093/nsr/nwaf050 PMID: 40191253

Hicks, A. (2025). *Integrating Generative AI into Sustainability Education : The Lorax as a Case Study Integrating Generative AI into Sustainability Education : The Lorax as a Case Study*. 0–12.

Hobbs, R. (2017). *Create to learn: Introduction to digital literacy*. John Wiley & Sons. DOI: 10.1002/9781394260201

Holmes, W., Bialik, M., & Fadel, C. (2019). *Artificial intelligence in education promises and implications for teaching and learning*. Center for Curriculum Redesign.

Holmes, W., Persson, J., Chounta, I.-A., Wasson, B., & Dimitrova, V. (2022). *Artificial Intelligence and Education: A Critical View Through the Lens of Human Rights, Democracy and the Rule of Law*. Council of Europe.

Holmes, W., Porayska-Pomsta, K., Holstein, K., Sutherland, E., Baker, T., Shum, S., Santos, O., Rodrigo, M., Cukurova, M., Bittencourt, I., & Koedinger, K. (2022). Ethics of AI in education: Towards a community-wide framework. *International Journal of Artificial Intelligence in Education, 32*(3), 504–526. DOI: 10.1007/s40593-021-00239-1

Hooda, M., Rana, C., Dahiya, O., Shet, J. P., & Singh, B. K. (2022). Integrating LA and EDM for improving students success in higher education using FCN algorithm. *Mathematical Problems in Engineering, 2022*(1), 7690103. DOI: 10.1155/2022/7690103

Hosseini, M., Horbach, S. P. J. M., Holmes, K., & Ross-Hellauer, T. (2025). Open Science at the generative AI turn: An exploratory analysis of challenges and opportunities. *Quantitative Science Studies, 6*, 22–45. DOI: 10.1162/qss_a_00337 PMID: 40124128

Huang, A. Y., Lu, O. H., & Yang, S. J. (2023). Effects of artificial intelligence-enabled personalized recommendations on learners' learning engagement, motivation, and outcomes in a flipped classroom. *Computers & Education, 194*, 104684. DOI: 10.1016/j.compedu.2022.104684

Huang, R. H. (2018). The integration of artificial intelligence in education: A learner-centered approach. *International Journal of Artificial Intelligence in Education, 28*(2), 289–291.

Husaini, R., Ikhsan, Z., & Toran, H. (2019). A comprehensive 21st century child development through scientific process in early science. *Creative Education, 10*(12), 3202–3214. DOI: 10.4236/ce.2019.1012205

Hwang, G.-J., Xie, H., Wah, B. W., & Gašević, D. (2020). Vision, challenges, roles and research issues of Artificial Intelligence in Education. İçinde *Computers and Education: Artificial Intelligence* (C. 1, s. 100001). Elsevier.

IDPE. (2023). *Learning Objectives*. Department of Industrial Design & Production Engineering. https://idpe.uniwa.gr/en/studies/undergraduate/learning-objectives

IDPE. (2024). *Brief Presentation - Department of Industrial Design and Production Engineering*. https://idpe.uniwa.gr/en/department/dep-presentation

IDPE. (2025). *Undergraduate Program - Department of Industrial Design and Production Engineering*. https://idpe.uniwa.gr/en/courses

Ioannidou, A., Bennett, V., Repenning, A., Koh, H., & Basawapatna, A. (2011). Computational Thinking Patterns. *Annual Meeting of the American Educational Research Association (AERA), 2*. http://www.agentsheets.com

Ioannou, M., & Bratitsis, T. (2016). Utilizing Sphero for a speed related STEM activity in Kindergarten. *Hellenic Conference on Innovating STEM Education.*

Irshad, A. (2025). Students' Perspectives on Generative AI's Role in Transforming, Challenging, and Enhancing Higher Education Learning Practices in Education. *Indus Journal of Social Sciences, 3*(3), 253–268. DOI: 10.59075/ijss.v3i3.1897

Isaacs, M., Tondeur, J., Howard, S., Claro, M., & Braak, J. (2024). Digital storytelling as a strategy for developing 21st-century skills: A systematic review of qualitative evidence. *Technology, Pedagogy and Education, 33*(5), 573–593. DOI: 10.1080/1475939X.2024.2343929

İşler, B., & Kılıç, M. (2021). Eğitimde yapay zekâ kullanimi ve gelişimi. *Yeni Medya Elektronik Dergisi, 5*(1), 1–11.

Ismail, S., Ali, F., & Yasukawa, S. (2024). *Advancing Climate Risk Governance and Education Through UNESCO*. 221–239. DOI: 10.1007/978-981-97-5987-3_13

Ismaili, Y. (2024). AI Literacy and Adaptive Learning in Moroccan Education: Advancing Critical Thinking and Personalized Learning. Research on Education and Media, 16(2).

Jamovi. (2021). *The jamovi project* (1.6). https://www.jamovi.org/

Jiang, H., Liu, Q., Li, R., Ye, S., & Wang, S. (2024). *CursorCore: Assist Programming through Aligning Anything*. https://arxiv.org/abs/2410.07002v1

Jin, L. (2019). Investigation on potential application of artificial intelligence in preschool children's education. In *The 5th annual international conference on network and information systems for computers* (ICNISC2019). DOI: 10.1088/1742-6596/1288/1/012072

Kafai, Y. B., & Burke, Q. (2014). *Connected code: Why children need to learn programming*. Mit Press. DOI: 10.7551/mitpress/9992.001.0001

Kalantari, S., Rubegni, E., Benton, L., & Vasalou, A. (2023). "When I'm writing a story, I am really good": Exploring the use of digital storytelling technology at home. *International Journal of Child-Computer Interaction, 38*, 100613. DOI: 10.1016/j.ijcci.2023.100613

Kalogiannakis, M., Papakonstantinou, N., & Sotiropoulos, D. (2025). From Support Tool to Learning Partner : A Systematic Review of GenAI Integration in University Science Labs. *Creative Education, 16*(9), 1364–1401. DOI: 10.4236/ce.2025.169083

Kanaki, K., Chatzakis, S., & Kalogiannakis, M. (2025). Fostering Algorithmic Thinking and Environmental Awareness via Bee-Bot Activities in Early Childhood Education. *Sustainability (Basel)*, *17*(9), 1–19. DOI: 10.3390/su17094208

Kanaki, K., Kalogiannakis, M., Poulakis, E., & Politis, P. (2022). Investigating the Association between Algorithmic Thinking and Performance in Environmental Study. *Sustainability (Basel)*, *14*(17), 10672. Advance online publication. DOI: 10.3390/su141710672

Kanbach, D. K., Heiduk, L., Blueher, G., Schreiter, M., & Lahmann, A. (2024). The GenAI is out of the bottle: generative artificial intelligence from a business model innovation perspective. In *Review of Managerial Science* (Vol. 18, Issue 4). DOI: 10.1007/s11846-023-00696-z

Kanders, K., Stupple-Harris, L., Smith, L., & Gibson, J. L. (2024). Perspectives on the impact of generative AI on early-childhood development and education. *Infant and Child Development*, *33*(4), e2514. DOI: 10.1002/icd.2514

KANDIR, A., & TEMEL, M. (2025). OKUL ÖNCESİ DÖNEMDE YAPAY ZEKÂ OKURYAZARLIĞI EĞİTİMİNE İLİŞKİN ÖĞRETMEN GÖRÜŞLERİNİN İNCELENMESİ. *Journal of History School*, *18*(LXXIV), 1–21.

Kandlhofer, M., Steinbauer, G., Hirschmugl-Gaisch, S., & Huber, P. (2016). Artificial intelligence and computer science in education: From kindergarten to university. In *2016 IEEE frontiers in education conference* (FIE) (pp. 1–9). IEEE.

Kantaros, A., Diegel, O., Piromalis, D., Tsaramirsis, G., Khadidos, A. O., Khadidos, A. O., Khan, F. Q., & Jan, S. (2021). 3D printing: Making an innovative technology widely accessible through makerspaces and outsourced services. *Materials Today: Proceedings*, *49*, 2712–2723. DOI: 10.1016/j.matpr.2021.09.074

Kapoor, K. K., Tamilmani, K., Rana, N. P., Patil, P., Dwivedi, Y. K., & Nerur, S. (2018). Advances in social media research: Past, present and future. *Information Systems Frontiers*, *20*(3), 531–558. DOI: 10.1007/s10796-017-9810-y

Kaptan, E., & Cakir, R. (2025). The effect of digital storytelling on digital literacy, 21st century skills and achievement. *Education and Information Technologies*, *30*(8), 11047–11071. DOI: 10.1007/s10639-024-13287-6

Karageorgakis, T. (2023). *Best 100 AI apps for Teachers and the Classroom*. Educraft. https://educraft.tech/best-100-ai-apps-for-teachers/

Karageorgakis, T. (2025). *200 AI Tools Reviewed - Here are the Best*. Educraft. https://educraft.tech/best-ai-tools-for-teachers-2024-survey

Karpouzis, K., Pantazatos, D., Taouki, J., & Meli, K. (2024a). Tailoring Education with GenAI: A New Horizon in Lesson Planning. *IEEE Global Engineering Education Conference, EDUCON*. DOI: 10.1109/EDUCON60312.2024.10578690

Karpuzi, M., Georgiou, K., Papoutsidakis, M., & Chatzopoulos, A. (2019). Design of an object identification system with a thermal camera. *International Journal of Engineering Applied Sciences and Technology*, *4*(5), 471–477. DOI: 10.33564/IJEAST.2019.v04i05.068

Kasneci, E., Sechel, I., & Seidel, K. (2023). Generative AI in Higher Education: Promises and Pitfalls. *Frontiers in Education*, *8*, 117397.

Kaya, A., & Yılmaz, R. (2022). The effect of digital story applications on academic achievement in science education. *International Journal of Educational Research*, *11*(3), 112–130.

Kelly, A., Sullivan, M., & Strampel, K. (2023). Generative artificial intelligence: University student awareness, experience, and confidence in use across disciplines. *Journal of University Teaching & Learning Practice*, *20*(6). Advance online publication. DOI: 10.53761/1.20.6.12

Kember, D. (2005). *Action learning and action research: Improving the quality of teaching & learning*. Taylor & Francis e-Library.

Kewalramani, S., Kidman, G., & Palaiologou, I. (2021). Using artificial intelligence (AI)- interfaced robotic toys in early childhood settings: A case for children's inquiry literacy. *European Early Childhood Education Research Journal*, *29*(5), 652–668. DOI: 10.1080/1350293X.2021.1968458

Kewalramani, S., Palaiologou, I., Dardanou, M., Phillipson, S., & Yang, Y. (2021). Using robotic toys in early childhood education to support children's social and emotional competencies. *Australasian Journal of Early Childhood*, *46*(4), 355–369. DOI: 10.1177/18369391211056668

Khamis, N., Chen, B., Egan, C., Gaglani, S., & Tackett, S. (2025). More intelligent faculty development: Integrating GenAI in curriculum development programs. *Medical Teacher*, *47*(11), 1739–1741. Advance online publication. DOI: 10.1080/0142159X.2025.2473606 PMID: 40029714

Kharrufa, A., Alghamdi, S., Aziz, A., & Bull, C. (2024). LLMs Integration in Software Engineering Team Projects: Roles, Impact, and a Pedagogical Design Space for AI Tools in Computing Education. *ArXiv*, 1–25. https://arxiv.org/pdf/2410.23069

Khlaif, Z. N., Ayyoub, A., Hamamra, B., Bensalem, E., Mitwally, M. A. A., Ayyoub, A., Hattab, M. K., & Shadid, F. (2024). University Teachers' Views on the Adoption and Integration of Generative AI Tools for Student Assessment in Higher Education. *Education Sciences*, *14*(10), 1090. DOI: 10.3390/educsci14101090

Kim, S., Jang, Y., Kim, W., Choi, S., Jung, H., Kim, S., & Kim, H. (2021, May). Why and what to teach: AI curriculum for elementary school. *Proceedings of the AAAI Conference on Artificial Intelligence*, *35*(17), 15569–15576. DOI: 10.1609/aaai.v35i17.17833

Kim, W. J. (2025). Teachers' Use of Generative Artificial Intelligence for Designing Science Lessons in Support of Environmental Science Agency. *Research in Science Education*, •••, 1–20. DOI: 10.1007/s11165-025-10262-0

Knapp, S. (2006). *Artificial intelligence: Past, present, and future.* VOX of Dartmouth.

Kocaarslan, M. (2012). Tanılayıcı dallanmış ağaç tekniği ve ilköğretim 5. Sınıf fen ve teknoloji dersi maddenin değişimi ve tanınması adlı ünitede kullanımı [Diagnostic branched tree technique and its use in the 'change and recognition of matter' unit of 5th grade science and technology class]. *Mustafa Kemal Üniversitesi Sosyal Bilimler Enstitüsü Dergisi*, *9*(18), 269–279.

Kohli, P., & Sharma, S. (2023). Security and Privacy Aware Blockchain Technique for 6G Driven Vehicular Communication Network. *In 2023 IEEE Fifth International Conference on Advances in Electronics, Computers and Communications (ICAECC)*, 1–6. DOI: 10.1109/ICAECC59324.2023.10560325

Koikas, D., Aggelis, P., & Chatzopoulos, A. (2015). Rebuilding a CNC Milling Machine. *International Conference ERA - 10*, 52–58. era.teipir.gr

Kolenatý, M., Kroufek, R., & Činčera, J. (2022). What Triggers Climate Action: The Impact of a Climate Change Education Program on Students' Climate Literacy and Their Willingness to Act. *Sustainability (Basel)*, *14*(16), 10365. Advance online publication. DOI: 10.3390/su141610365

Kong, S. C., Cheung, W. M. Y., & Zhang, G. (2021). Evaluation of an artificial intelligencE literacy course for university students with diverse study backgrounds. *Computers & Education. Artificial Intelligence*, *2*, 100026.

Kong, S. C., Cheung, W. M. Y., & Zhang, G. (2022). Evaluating artificial intelligence literacy courses for fostering conceptual learning, literacy and empowerment in university students: Refocusing to conceptual building. *Computers in Human Behavior Reports*, *7*, 100223. DOI: 10.1016/j.chbr.2022.100223

Kong, S. C., Cheung, W. M. Y., & Zhang, G. (2023). Evaluating an artificial intelligence literacy programme for developing university students' conceptual understanding, literacy, empowerment and ethical awareness. *Journal of Educational Technology & Society, 26*(1), 16–30.

Kong, S. C., & Yang, Y. (2024). A human-centred learning and teaching framework using generative artificial intelligence for self-regulated learning development through domain knowledge learning in K–12 settings. *IEEE Transactions on Learning Technologies, 17*, 1588–1599. DOI: 10.1109/TLT.2024.3392830

Krosnick, J. A., & Presser, S. (2010). Question and Questionnaire Design. In *Handbook of Survey Research* (2nd ed.). Emerald Publishing., DOI: 10.1111/j.1432-1033.1976.tb10115.x

Küchemann, S., Steinert, S., Avila, K. E., & Kuhn, J. (2025). Enhancing students' critical thinking skills through the use of DALL-E. *The Physics Teacher, 63*(2), 138–139. DOI: 10.1119/5.0253990

Kumar, A., Shankar, A., Hollebeek, L. D., Behl, A., & Lim, W. M. (2025). Generative artificial intelligence (GenAI) revolution: A deep dive into GenAI adoption. *Journal of Business Research, 189*, 115160. DOI: 10.1016/j.jbusres.2024.115160

Kurniah, N., Agustriana, N., & Sapri, J. (2023). Integration of scientific literacy and technology in designing early childhood learning. *Indonesian Journal of Early Childhood Education Studies, 12*(2), 204–210. DOI: 10.15294/ijeces.v12i2.75634

Kutlucan, E., & Seferoğlu, S. S. (2024). Eğitimde yapay zekâ kullanımı: ChatGPT'nin KEFE ve PEST analizi. *Türk Eğitim Bilimleri Dergisi, 22*(2), 1059–1083. DOI: 10.37217/tebd.1368821

Kwid, G., Sarty, N., & Yang, D. (2024). A Review of AI Tools: Definitions, Functions, and Applications for K-12 Education. *AI. Computer Science and Robotics Technology, 3*(August), 1–22. DOI: 10.5772/acrt.20240048

Labadze, L., Grigolia, M., & Machaidze, L. (2023). Role of AI chatbots in education: Systematic literature review. *International Journal of Educational Technology in Higher Education, 20*(1), 56. DOI: 10.1186/s41239-023-00426-1

Lagogiannis, G., & Chatzopoulos, A. (2025). A No-Code Educational Platform for Introducing Internet of Things and Its Application to Agricultural Education. *IoT, 6*(3), 42. https://doi.org/https://doi.org/10.3390/iot6030042. DOI: 10.3390/iot6030042

Lambert, J. (2013). *Digital storytelling: Capturing lives, creating community.* Routledge. DOI: 10.4324/9780203102329

Landis, J. R., & Koch, G. G. (1977). The measurement of observer agreement for categorical data. *Biometrics, 33*(1), 159–174. DOI: 10.2307/2529310

Lane, R. (2025). Mitigating risks, embracing potential: A framework for integrating generative artificial intelligence in geographical and environmental education. *International Research in Geographical and Environmental Education*, 1–18. Advance online publication. DOI: 10.1080/10382046.2025.2458561

Larmer, J., & Mergendoller, J. (2010). *Seven Essentials for Project-Based Learning*. https://www.ascd.org/el/articles/seven-essentials-for-project-based-learning

Law, L. (2024). Application of generative artificial intelligence (GenAI) in language teaching and learning: A scoping literature review. *Computers and Education Open, 6*, 100174. DOI: 10.1016/j.caeo.2024.100174

Lego, E. (2016). *LEGO Education WeDo 2. 0 - Computational Thinking - Teacher's Guide* (Issue V1, p. 42). LEGO Group. https://le-www-live-s.legocdn.com/sc/media/files/user-guides/wedo-2/computational-thinking-teacher-guides/computational thinkingteacherguide-en-gb-v1-69cd677d61d21b2a44999328c40e7122.pdf

Liao, J., Zhong, L., Zhe, L., Xu, H., Liu, M., & Xie, T. (2024). Scaffolding Computational Thinking With ChatGPT. *IEEE Transactions on Learning Technologies, 17*, 1668–1682. DOI: 10.1109/TLT.2024.3392896

Liaqat, A., Axtell, B., & Munteanu, C. (2021). Participatory design for intergenerational culture exchange in immigrant families: How collaborative narration and creation fosters democratic engagement. In *Proceedings of the ACM on Human-Computer Interaction, 5*, 1–40. CSCW1. DOI: 10.1145/3449172

Limatahu, I., Wasis, W., Sutoyo, S., & Prahani, B. K. (2018). Development of CCDSR teaching model to improve science process skills of pre-service physics teachers. *Journal of Baltic Science Education, 17*(5), 812–827. DOI: 10.33225/jbse/18.17.812

Lim, W. M., Gunasekara, A., Pallant, J. L., Pallant, J. I., & Pechenkina, E. (2023). Generative AI and the future of education: Ragnar¨ok or reformation? A paradoxical perspective from management educators. *International Journal of Management Education, 21*(2), 100790. Advance online publication. DOI: 10.1016/j.ijme.2023.100790

Lin, Y., & Weintrop, D. (2021). The landscape of Block-based programming: Characteristics of block-based environments and how they support the transition to text-based programming. *Journal of Computer Languages,* 67, Article 101075.

Lin, C.-J., Lee, H.-Y., Wang, W.-S., Huang, Y.-M., & Wu, T.-T. (2025). Enhancing reflective thinking in STEM education through experiential learning: The role of generative AI as a learning aid. *Education and Information Technologies, 30*(5), 6315–6337. DOI: 10.1007/s10639-024-13072-5

Lincoln, Y. S., & Guba, E. G. (1985). *Naturalistic inquiry*. Sage Publications. DOI: 10.1016/0147-1767(85)90062-8

Lindsey, J., Gurnee, W., Ameisen, E., Chen, B., Pearce, A., Turner, N. L., Citro, C., Abrahams, D., Carter, S., Hosmer, B., Marcus, J., Sklar, M., Templeton, A., Bricken, T., McDougall, C., Cunningham, H., Henighan, T., Jermyn, A., Jones, A., . . . Batson, J. (2025). *On the Biology of a Large Language Model*. Anthropic. https://transformer-circuits.pub/2025/attribution-graphs/biology.html

Lin, P., Van Brummelen, J., Lukin, G., Williams, R., & Breazeal, C. (2020). Zhorai: Designing a conversational agent for children to explore machine learning concepts. *Proceedings of the AAAI Conference on Artificial Intelligence, 34*(9), 13381–13388. DOI: 10.1609/aaai.v34i09.7061

Liu, J., Chen, M., He, H., Liu, H., Luo, W., & Li, H. (2025). *Forms and functions innovation: A scoping review of digital and intelligence technologies in early childhood education practice*. AI. *Brain and Child, 1*(1), 8. Advance online publication. DOI: 10.1007/s44436-025-00010-6

Liu, K. P., Tai, S. J. D., & Liu, C. C. (2018). Enhancing language learning through creation: The effect of digital storytelling on student learning motivation and performance in a school English course. *Educational Technology Research and Development, 66*(4), 913–935. DOI: 10.1007/s11423-018-9592-z

Liu, S. C., & Château, P. A. (2025). Fostering Hope and Action on Climate Change among University Students: Impact of a Futures-Oriented Teaching Module with Generative AI Integration. *Journal of Science Education and Technology, 34*(6), 1–16. DOI: 10.1007/s10956-025-10229-w

Liu, Y., Zhang, K., Li, Y., Yan, Z., Gao, C., Chen, R., Yuan, Z., Huang, Y., Sun, H., Gao, J., He, L., & Sun, L. (2024). *Sora: A Review on Background, Technology, Limitations, and Opportunities of Large Vision Models*. https://arxiv.org/abs/2402.17177

Li, Y., Wang, K., Xiao, Y., & Froyd, J. E. (2020). Research and trends in STEM education: A systematic review of journal publications. *International Journal of STEM Education, 7*(1), 1–16. DOI: 10.1186/2196-7822-1-1

Lloyd, S. (1982). Least squares quantization in PCM. *IEEE Transactions on Information Theory, 28*(2), 129–137. DOI: 10.1109/TIT.1982.1056489

Lo, C. K. (2023). What Is the Impact of ChatGPT on Education? A Rapid Review of the Literature. *Education Sciences, 13*(4), 410. DOI: 10.3390/educsci13040410

Long, D., & Magerko, B. (2020). What is AI literacy? Competencies and design considerations. In *Proceedings of the 2020 CHI conference on human factors in computing systems* (pp. 1–16). DOI: 10.1145/3313831.3376727

Louros, A., Papoutsidakis, M., Chatzopoulos, A., & Drosos, C. (2018). Design of an Innovative Flight Controller for Quadcopter Robust Handling. [JMEST]. *Journal of Multidisciplinary Engineering Science and Technology, 5*(10), 8968–8972.

Loverude, M. E., Kautz, C. H., & Heron, P. R. L. (2003). Helping students develop an understanding of Archimedes' principle. I. Research on student understanding. *American Journal of Physics, 71*(11), 1178–1187. DOI: 10.1119/1.1607335

Luckin, R. (2017). Towards artificial intelligence-based assessment systems. *Nature Human Behaviour, 1*(3), 0028. DOI: 10.1038/s41562-016-0028

Luckin, R. (2018). *Machine Learning and Human Intelligence: The Future of Education for the 21st Century*. UCL Institute of Education Press.

Lund, A., & Lund, M. (2025). *Chi-square test of independence in SPSS Statistics*. Laerd Statistics. https://statistics.laerd.com/premium/spss/cstoirxc/chi-square-test-of-independence-rxc-in-spss-3.php

Luo, W., He, H., Liu, J., Berson, I. R., Berson, M. J., Zhou, Y., & Li, H. (2024). Aladdin's genie or Pandora's box for early childhood education? Experts chat on the roles, challenges, and developments of ChatGPT. *Early Education and Development, 35*(1), 96–113. DOI: 10.1080/10409289.2023.2214181

Luo, Y., Chen, E., Liu, H., Riener, K., & Yang, S.-H. (2025). Generative AI in Engineering Education: A Survey of Student and Instructor Usage and Attitudes. *Proceedings of the Human Factors and Ergonomics Society Annual Meeting*, 1–6. DOI: 10.1177/10711813251358792

Lyshevski, S. E. (2002). Mechatronic curriculum - Retrospect and prospect. *Mechatronics, 12*(2), 195–205. DOI: 10.1016/S0957-4158(01)00060-5

Mahrishi, M., Abbas, A., Radovanović, D., & Hosseini, S. (2024). Emerging Dynamics of ChatGPT in Academia: A Scoping Review. *Journal of University Teaching & Learning Practice, 21*(1). Advance online publication. DOI: 10.53761/b182ws13

Malmström, H., Stöhr, C., & Ou, A. W. (2023). Chatbots and other AI for learning: A survey of use and views among university students in Sweden. *Chalmers Studies in Communication and Learning in Higher Education, 2023*(1).

Manzini, T., Lim, Y. C., Tsvetkov, Y., & Black, A. W. (2019). Black is to criminal as caucasian is to police: Detecting and removing multiclass bias in word embeddings. *arXiv Preprint arXiv:1904.04047.* DOI: 10.18653/v1/N19-1062

Maraisane, L., Jita, L., & Jita, T. (2024). Engagement of science process skills for teaching science concepts in early childhood. Journal of Childhood. *Education & Society*, *5*(2), 283–293. DOI: 10.37291/2717638X.202452387

McGrath, C., Farazouli, A., & Cerratto Pargman, T. (2024). Generative AI chatbots in higher education: A review of an emerging research area. *Higher Education*, *89*(6), 1533–1549. DOI: 10.1007/s10734-024-01288-w

Memarian, B., & Doleck, T. (2023). A review of assessment for learning with artificial intelligence. *Computers in Human Behavior: Artificial Humans*, *1*(1), 100040. Advance online publication. DOI: 10.1016/j.chbah.2023.100040

Mena-Guacas, A. F., Urueña Rodríguez, J. A., Santana Trujillo, D. M., Gómez-Galán, J., & López-Meneses, E. (2023). Collaborative learning and skill development for educational growth of artificial intelligence: A systematic review. *Contemporary Educational Technology*, *15*(3), ep428. DOI: 10.30935/cedtech/13123

Meta. (2025a). *AI at Meta.* https://ai.meta.com/

Meta. (2025b). *Introducing the Meta AI App: A New Way to Access Your AI Assistant.* https://about.fb.com/news/2025/04/introducing-meta-ai-app-new-way-access-ai-assistant/

Microsoft. (2025a). *AI in Education A Microsoft Special Report.* DOI: 10.58952/nit20251301053

Microsoft. (2025b). *What is Microsoft 365 Copilot?* Microsoft. https://learn.microsoft.com/en-us/copilot/microsoft-365/microsoft-365-copilot-overview

Miles, M. B., & Huberman, A. M. (1994). *Qualitative data analysis: An expanded sourcebook* (2nd ed.). Sage Publications.

Minetou, L., Chatzopoulos, A., Tzerachoglou, A., Priniotakis, G., van Hoof, J., Sfyroera, E., Georgiadou, Z., Tyrovola, S., & Drosos, C. (2024). Homing wellness: Can narrative design transform living spaces for people with dementia into engaging environments enabling communication? *Frontiers in Public Health*, *11*, 1198253. Advance online publication. DOI: 10.3389/fpubh.2023.1198253 PMID: 38292379

Molenaar, I. (2022). Towards hybrid human-AI learning technologies. *European Journal of Education, 57*(4), 632–645. DOI: 10.1111/ejed.12527

Morrison, J., & Bartlett, R. V. (2009). *STEM as a Curriculum*. Education Week. papers3://publication/uuid/48C36DF6-30CA-42ED-876D-0D4214A1F890

Moundridou, M., Matzakos, N., & Doukakis, S. (2024). Generative AI tools as educators' assistants: Designing and implementing inquiry-based lesson plans. *Computers and Education: Artificial Intelligence, 7*, 100277. DOI: 10.1016/j.caeai.2024.100277

Moya, B., Badías, A., González, D., Chinesta, F., & Cueto, E. (2023). Computational sensing, understanding, and reasoning: An artificial intelligence approach to physics-informed world modeling. *Archives of Computational Methods in Engineering, 31*(4), 1897–1914. DOI: 10.1007/s11831-023-10033-y

Muller, M., Chilton, L. B., Kantosalo, A., Maher, M. L., Martin, C. P., & Walsh, G. (2022). GenAICHI: Generative AI and HCI. *Conference on Human Factors in Computing Systems - Proceedings*. DOI: 10.1145/3491101.3503719

Murray, J. T. (2024). *Interactive storytelling*. Springer Nature.

Nan, J. (2020). Research of application of artificial intelligence in. Preschool education. In *The 2020 international symposium on electronic information technology and communication engineering*. Jinan, China.

Nazaretsky, T., Dori, Y. J., & Hazzan, O. (2022). AI-based assessment tools in education: A systematic review. *Educational Technology Research and Development, 70*(1), 123–147.

Nedungadi, P., Tang, K., & Raman, R. (2024). The transformative power of generative artificial intelligence for achieving the sustainable development goal of quality education. *Sustainability (Basel), 16*(22), 9779. DOI: 10.3390/su16229779

Ng, D. T. K., Lee, M., Tan, R. J. Y., Hu, X., Downie, J. S., & Chu, S. K. W. (2022c). A review of AI teaching and learning from 2000 to 2020. *Education and Information Technologies, 28*(7), 8445–8501. DOI: 10.1007/s10639-022-11491-w

Ng, D. T. K., Leung, J. K. L., Chu, K. W. S., & Qiao, M. S. (2021a). AI literacy: Definition, teaching, evaluation and ethical issues. *Proceedings of the Association for Information Science and Technology, 58*(1), 504–509. DOI: 10.1002/pra2.487

Ng, D. T. K., Leung, J. K. L., Chu, S. K. W., & Qiao, M. S. (2021b). Conceptualizing AI literacy: An exploratory review. *Computers & Education. Artificial Intelligence, 2*, 100041.

Ng, D. T. K., Leung, J. K. L., Su, M. J., Yim, I. H. Y., Qiao, M. S., & Chu, S. K. W. (2022b). AI Literacy Education in Early Childhood Education. In *AI Literacy in K-16 Classrooms* (pp. 63–74). Springer International Publishing. DOI: 10.1007/978-3-031-18880-0_5

Ng, D. T. K., Luo, W., Chan, H. M. Y., & Chu, S. K. W. (2022). Using digital story writing as a pedagogy to develop AI literacy among primary students. *Computers and Education: Artificial Intelligence, 3*, 100054. DOI: 10.1016/j.caeai.2022.100054

Ng, D. T., Leung, J. K., Su, J., Ng, R. C., & Chu, S. K. (2023). Teachers' AI digital competencies and twenty- first-century skills in the post-pandemic world. *Educational Technology Research and Development, 71*(1), 137–161. DOI: 10.1007/s11423-023-10203-6 PMID: 36844361

Ngo, T. T. A. (2023). The Perception by University Students of the Use of ChatGPT in Education. *International Journal of Emerging Technologies in Learning, 18*(17), 4–19. DOI: 10.3991/ijet.v18i17.39019

Nguyen, H., Pham, V., Tran, D., & Le, T. (2019). Intelligent tutoring chatbot for solving mathematical problems in high school. *2019 11th International Conference on Knowledge and Systems Engineering*, 1–6. DOI: 10.1109/KSE.2019.8919396

Nguyen, A., Gul, F., Dang, B., Huynh, L., & Tuunanen, T. (2025). Designing embodied generative artificial intelligence in mixed reality for active learning in higher education. *Innovations in Education and Teaching International, 62*(5), 1632–1647. Advance online publication. DOI: 10.1080/14703297.2025.2499177

Nichols, M., Cator, K., & Torres, M. (2016). *Challenge Based Learning Guide* (Issue March). Digital Promise.

Niemi, H., Niu, S. J., Li, B., & Vivitsou, M. (2019). Supporting student learning toward 21st-century skills through digital storytelling. In Yu, S., Niemi, H., & Mason, J. (Eds.), *Shaping future schools with digital technology* (pp. 95–112). Springer., DOI: 10.1007/978-981-13-9439-3_6

Nixon, N., Lin, Y., & Snow, L. (2024). Catalyzing equity in STEM teams: Harnessing generative AI for inclusion and diversity. *Policy Insights from the Behavioral and Brain Sciences, 11*(1), 85–92. DOI: 10.1177/23727322231220356 PMID: 38516055

Nolasco, G., & Dicuangco, J. D. (2025). A Review Article – Facebook's Meta AI: A Potential Boon or Doom for Learning? *International Journal of Metaverse, 3*(1), 1–7. DOI: 10.54536/ijm.v3i1.3845

Nurlaela, M., Ilham, J., & Lisabe, C. M. (2022). The effects of Storyjumper on narrative writing ability of EFL learners in higher education. *Journal of Education, 8*(14), 1641–1647.

Oliveira, A. (2017). *Mentes digitais, a ciência redefinindo a humanidade*. IST Press.

Open, A. I. (2024). GPT-4 System Card. *OpenAI.Com*, 1–60. https://cdn.openai.com/papers/gpt-4-system-card.pdf

Open, A. I. (2025a). *Explore GPTs*. https://chatgpt.com/gpts?utm_source=chatgpt.com

Open, A. I. (2025b). *Generating videos on Sora | OpenAI Help Center*. https://help.openai.com/en/articles/9957612-generating-videos-on-sora

Open, A. I. (2025c). *Introducing ChatGPT*. https://chatgpt.com/overview?openaicom_referred=true

Open, A. I. (2025d). *Introducing GPT-5*. https://openai.com/index/introducing-gpt-5/

Organisation for Economic Co-operation and Development (OECD). (2021). *The Future of Education and Skills 2030: Learning Compass 2030*. OECD Publishing.

Ouyang, F., Dinh, T. A., & Xu, W. (2023). A systematic review of AI-driven educational assessment in STEM education. *Journal for STEM Education Research, 6*(3), 408–426. DOI: 10.1007/s41979-023-00112-x

Özsevgeç, T., & Çepni, S. (2006). Farklı sınıflardaki öğrencilerin yüzme ve batma kavramlarını anlama düzeyleri [Understanding levels of students in different grades regarding the concepts of floating and sinking]. *Milli Eğitim Dergisi, 172*, 297–311.

Pageon. (2025). *Transforming Academic Research: How Perplexity's Peer-Review Mode Revolutionizes Scholarly Discovery*. https://www.pageon.ai/blog/perplexity-academic-mode-sources-only-peer-reviewed-papers

Pahl, K. (2011). My family, my story: Representing identities in time and space through digital storytelling. *Teachers College Record, 113*(13), 17–39. DOI: 10.1177/016146811111301302

Pandey, C., Sharma, S., & Bhadula, S. (2024). Artificial Intelligence Technique in Next Generation Healthcare Systems. *In 2024 IEEE International Conference on Communication, Computing and Signal Processing (IICCCS)* (pp. 1–6). DOI: 10.1109/IICCCS61609.2024.10763570

Papadakis, S., Kalogiannakis, M., & Zaranis, N. (2016). Developing fundamental programming concepts and computational thinking with ScratchJr in preschool education: A case study. *International Journal of Mobile Learning and Organisation, 10*(3), 187. DOI: 10.1504/IJMLO.2016.077867

Papert, S. (1996). An exploration in the space of mathematics educations. *International Journal of Computers for Mathematical Learning, 1*(1), 95–123. DOI: 10.1007/BF00191473

Papoutsidakis, M., Symeonaki, E., Chatzopoulos, A., & Piromalis, D. (2018). Iot Design To Support Wireless Sensor Networks And Data Transmission. [IJESI]. *International Journal of Engineering and Science Invention, 7*(10), 54–62. www.ijesi.org

Pastrana, M. A., Santana, M. S., Mendoza-Peñaloza, J., Bautista, J., Pinto Lopera, J. E., & Muñoz, D. M. (2025). A Novel Approach to Teaching Theory Control : Integrating STEM Education, Mobile Robot Simulation, and Bio-inspired. *Operations Research Forum (2025), 6*(85). DOI: 10.1007/s43069-025-00489-y

Patton, M. Q. (2015). *Qualitative research & evaluation methods* (4th ed.). Sage Publications.

Pavlenko, O., & Syzenko, A. (2024). Using ChatGPT as a Learning Tool: A Study of Ukrainian Students' Perceptions. *Arab World English Journal, 1*(1), 252–264. DOI: 10.24093/awej/ChatGPT.17

Pazur, B. (2025). *What Is Midjourney? Here's What You Need to Know About the AI Image Generator - CNET*. CNET. https://www.cnet.com/tech/services-and-software/what-is-midjourney-heres-what-you-need-to-know-about-the-ai-image-generator/

Pedregosa, F., Varoquaux, G., & Gramfort, A.. (2011). Scikit-learn: Machine learning in Python. *Journal of Machine Learning Research, 12*, 2825–2830.

Penny, A. R., & Coe, R. (2004). Effectiveness of consultation on student ratings feedback: A meta-analysis. *Review of Educational Research, 74*(2), 215–253. DOI: 10.3102/00346543074002215

Perkins, D. (2025). *The 5 Phases Of Project-Based Learning – TeachThought*. https://www.teachthought.com/project-based-learning-posts/phases/

Peterson, G., & Elam, E. (2020). Observation and assessment in early childhood education (Version 1.0). College of the Canyons. https://www.canyons.edu/_resources/documents/academics/earlychildhoodeducation/oer/ObservationandAssessmentinEarlyChildhoodEducation.pdf

Pilaniwala, P. (2024). Artificial Intelligence in Product Management: Enhancing User Experience Personalization through GenAI. *3rd International Conference on Automation, Computing and Renewable Systems, ICACRS 2024 - Proceedings*, 1135–1140. DOI: 10.1109/ICACRS62842.2024.10841633

Poonsawad, A., Srisomphan, J., & Sanrach, C. (2022). Synthesis of problem-based interactive digital storytelling learning model under gamification environment promotes students' problem-solving skills. [iJET]. *International Journal of Emerging Technologies in Learning*, *17*(5), 103–119. DOI: 10.3991/ijet.v17i05.28181

Preface. (2021). *The ultimate guide for artificial intelligence (AI) for kids.* https://www.preface.ai/blog/kids-learning/ai-for-kids

Prentzas, J. (2013). Artificial intelligence methods in early childhood education. In *Artificial Intelligence, evolutionary computing and metaheuristics* (pp. 169–199). Springer. DOI: 10.1007/978-3-642-29694-9_8

Priniotakis, G., Chronis, I., Chatzopoulos, A., & Louris, E. (2015). Lilipad Arduino platform for a multifunctional garments and wearables laboratory course. *15th AUTEX World Textile Conference 2015*, 10–13.

Priyanshu, A., Maurya, Y., & Hong, Z. (2024). *AI Governance and Accountability: An Analysis of Anthropic's Claude*. https://arxiv.org/abs/2407.01557

Psycharis, S. (2020). The Impact of STEM-based Mobile Apps on learners' Self-efficacy for Computational Thinking Dimensions. *The 13th International Conference on E-Learning in the Workplace*. http://learningideasconf.s3.amazonaws.com/Docs/Past/2020/Papers/Psycharis.pdf

Puri, R., Ghosh, A., & Ketkar, S. (2024). The Role of the G20 Countries in Embedding Climate Literacy in Education: From Knowing to Doing. *HAPSc Policy Briefs Series*, *5*(1), 104–112. DOI: 10.12681/hapscpbs.38975

Radiopoulou, D., Kantaros, A., Ganetsos, T., & Zacharia, P. (2025). 3D Printing as a Multimodal STEM Learning Technology: A Survey Study in Second Chance Schools. *Multimodal Technologies and Interaction*, *9*(9), 87. DOI: 10.3390/mti9090087

Radwan, A. Y., Alasmari, K. M., Abdulbagi, O. A., & Alghamdi, E. A. (2025). SARD: A Human-AI Collaborative Story Generation. *Lecture Notes in Computer Science (Including Subseries Lecture Notes in Artificial Intelligence and Lecture Notes in Bioinformatics), 15375 LNCS*, 94–105. DOI: 10.1007/978-3-031-76806-4_7

Raffone, A. (2022). Gamifying English language learning through interactive storytelling and MALL technologies. *Language Teaching Research*. Advance online publication. DOI: 10.1177/13621688221102

Rawat, R., Goyal, H. R., & Sharma, S. (2024). Hofstede's Cultural Dimension Driven Artificial Narrow Intelligence IDFIS for Industry 5.0 Empowered Digital Society. *Recent Patents on Engineering, 19*. Advance online publication. DOI: 10.2174/0118722121334543241001050846

Reihanian, I., Hou, Y., Chen, Y., & Zheng, Y. (2025). *A Review of Generative AI in Computer Science Education: Challenges and Opportunities in Accuracy, Authenticity, and Assessment. 2142503*. https://arxiv.org/pdf/2507.11543

Rejeb, A., Abdollahi, A., Rejeb, K., & Treiblmaier, H. (2022). Drones in agriculture: A review and bibliometric analysis. *Computers and Electronics in Agriculture, 198*, 107017. DOI: 10.1016/j.compag.2022.107017

Relmasira, S. C., Lai, Y. C., & Donaldson, J. P. (2023). Fostering AI literacy in Elementary Science, Technology, Engineering, Art, and Mathematics (STEAM) education in the age of generative AI. *Sustainability (Basel), 15*(18), 13595. DOI: 10.3390/su151813595

Richards, D., Worden, D., Song, X. P., & Lavorel, S. (2024). Harnessing generative artificial intelligence to support nature-based solutions. *People and Nature, 6*(2), 882–893. DOI: 10.1002/pan3.10622

Roberts, P. (2021). Follow the leader: Child-led inquiries to develop science learning of young children. Journal of Childhood. *Education & Society, 2*(3), 303–313. DOI: 10.37291/2717638X.202123120

Rousseeuw, P. J. (1987). Silhouettes: A graphical aid to the interpretation and validation of cluster analysis. *Journal of Computational and Applied Mathematics, 20*, 53–65. DOI: 10.1016/0377-0427(87)90125-7

Rubegni, E., & Landoni, M. (2014). Fiabot!: Design and evaluation of a mobile storytelling application for schools. In *Proceedings of the 2014 conference on Interaction Design and Children* (pp. 165–174). DOI: 10.1145/2593968.2593979

Rudra, S. (2023). *ChatGPT in Education: Generative AI Pros, Cons & Unknowns*. EdTech Magazie. https://edtechmagazine.com/k12/article/2023/03/chatgpt-in-education-generative-ai-perfcon

Ruiz-Rojas, L. I., Salvador-Ullauri, L., & Acosta-Vargas, P. (2024). Collaborative Working and Critical Thinking: Adoption of Generative Artificial Intelligence Tools in Higher Education. *Sustainability (Basel), 16*(13), 5367. Advance online publication. DOI: 10.3390/su16135367

Russell, S., & Norvig, P. (2002). *Artificial intelligence: A modern approach*. https://storage.googleapis.com/pub-tools-public-publication-data/pdf/27702.pdf

Russell, S. J., & Norvig, P. (2010). *Artificial intelligence a modern approach.*

Rutecka, P., Cicha, K., Rizun, M., & Strzelecki, A. (2025). Generative AI in Curriculum Design: Empirical Insights into Model Performance and Educational Constraints. *IEEE Transactions on Learning Technologies*, *18*, 757–768. Advance online publication. DOI: 10.1109/TLT.2025.3587081

Rutta, C. B., Schiavo, G., Zancanaro, M., & Rubegni, E. (2020). Collaborative comic-based digital storytelling with primary school children. In *Proceedings of the Interaction Design and Children Conference* (pp. 426–437). DOI: 10.1145/3392063.3394433

Sánchez Muñoz, J. A., Flores-Eraña, G., Silva-Campos, J. M., Chavira-Quintero, R., & Olais-Govea, J. M. (2025). GenAI as a cognitive mediator: A critical-constructivist inquiry into computational thinking in pre-university education. *Frontiers in Education*, *10*(September), 1597249. Advance online publication. DOI: 10.3389/feduc.2025.1597249

Sarstedt, M., Ringle, C. M., Smith, D., Reams, R., & Hair, J. F.Jr. (2014). Partial least squares structural equation modeling (PLS-SEM): A useful tool for family business researchers. *Journal of Family Business Strategy*, *5*(1), 105–115. DOI: 10.1016/j.jfbs.2014.01.002

Sato, F. E., & Park, J. (2025). A systematic review of climate change literacy assessment methods. *The Journal of Environmental Education*, *56*(1), 65–83. DOI: 10.1080/00958964.2024.2385333

Sattar, F., & Nawaz, M. (2023). Developing Computational Thinking in STEM Education with Drones. *2023 IEEE Global Engineering Education Conference (EDUCON)*, 1–5. DOI: 10.1109/EDUCON54358.2023.10125117

Schoenfeld, A. H. (1992). Learning to think mathematically: Problem solving, metacognition, and sense-making in mathematics. *Handbook for Research on Mathematics Teaching and Learning*, 334–370.

Selwyn, N. (2021). *Education and Technology: Key Issues and Debates*. Bloomsbury.

Sevgi, M., & Yılmaz, A. (2023). Yükseköğretimde dijital dönüşüm ve metaverse [Digital transformation and metaverse in higher education]. İçinde Y. Doğan & N. Şen Ersoy (Ed.), Eğitimde metaverse kuram ve uygulamalar [Metaverse in education: Theory and applications] (s.71-86). Efe Akademi Yayınları.

Sevgi, M., Ayyıldız, P., & Yılmaz, A. (2023). Eğitim bilimleri alanında yapay zekâ uygulamaları ve uygulamaların alana yansımaları [Artificial intelligence applications in the field of educational sciences and their reflections on the field]. İçinde Ö. Baltacı (Ed.). Eğitim bilimleri araştırmaları-IV [Educational sciences research-IV] (ss.1-18). Özgür Yayınları.

Sharma, S., Gautam, A., & Tyagi, R. (2024). Artificial Intelligence and Cyber Security Driven Social Innovations in Digital Adventure Tourism. *In 2024 First International Conference on Pioneering Developments in Computer Science & Digital Technologies (IC2SDT)*, 1–6. DOI: 10.1109/IC2SDT62152.2024.10696759

Sharma, S., Tyagi, R., & Mohan, S. (2024). Artificial intelligence and green 6G network-enabled architectures, scenarios, and applications for autonomous connected vehicles. In *River Publishers eBooks* (pp. 187–212). DOI: 10.1201/9781003515920-9

Sharma, S., Tyagi, R., & Mohan, S. (2024). Generative Artificial Intelligence-Enabled climate change and Deep-Sea food webs. In *Advances in environmental engineering and green technologies book series* (pp. 199–224). DOI: 10.4018/979-8-3693-6670-7.ch009

Sharma, S., Tyagi, R., & Mohan, S. (2025). Artificial intelligence and optimized computational modelling against climate crisis. In *Elsevier eBooks* (pp. 1–14). DOI: 10.1016/B978-0-443-21905-4.00006-7

Sharma, S., Gupta, A., & Tyagi, R. (2024). Artificial Intelligence, Cyber Security and Vedic Scripture Integrated Sustainable Global Youth Leadership Development. *In 2024 IEEE International Conference on Communication, Computing and Signal Processing (IICCCS)* (pp. 1–6). DOI: 10.1109/IICCCS61609.2024.10763618

Shelton, C. C., Warren, A. E., & Archambault, L. M. (2016). Exploring the use of interactive digital storytelling video: Promoting student engagement and learning in a university hybrid course. *TechTrends*, *60*(5), 465–474. DOI: 10.1007/s11528-016-0082-z

Sigalos, A., Papoutsidakis, M., Chatzopoulos, A., & Piromalis, D. (2019). Design of a flight controller and peripherals for a quadcopter. *International Journal of Engineering Applied Sciences and Technology*, *4*(5), 463–470. DOI: 10.33564/IJEAST.2019.v04i05.067

Simpson, N. P., Andrews, T. M., Krönke, M., Lennard, C., Odoulami, R. C., Ouweneel, B., Steynor, A., & Trisos, C. H. (2021). Climate change literacy in Africa. *Nature Climate Change*, *11*(11), 937–944. Advance online publication. DOI: 10.1038/s41558-021-01171-x

Skowronek, M., Gilberti, R. M., Petro, M., Sancomb, C., Maddern, S., & Jankovic, J. (2021). Inclusive STEAM education in diverse disciplines of sustainable energy and AI. *Energy and AI*, *7*, 100124. DOI: 10.1016/j.egyai.2021.100124

Slack, G. (2023). *What DALL-E Reveals About Human Creativity | Stanford HAI (9_29_2025 1:35:04 PM)*. https://hai.stanford.edu/news/what-dall-e-reveals-about-human-creativity

Slade, S., & Prinsloo, P. (2013). Learning Analytics: Ethical Issues and Dilemmas. *The American Behavioral Scientist*, *57*(10), 1510–1529. DOI: 10.1177/0002764213479366

Slagg, A. (2024). *AI in Education in 2024: Mixed Feelings on The Tech's Future*. EdTech Magazine. https://edtechmagazine.com/k12/article/2024/09/ai-education-2024-educators-express-mixed-feelings-technologys-future-perfcon?utm_source=chatgpt.com

Smith, B. C. (2019). *The promise of artificial intelligence: Reckoning and judgment*. Mit Press. DOI: 10.7551/mitpress/12385.001.0001

Smith, C., Carey, S., & Wiser, M. (1985). On differentiation: A case study of the development of the concepts of size, weight, and density. *Cognition*, *21*(3), 177–237. DOI: 10.1016/0010-0277(85)90025-3

Solanki, S. L., Pandrowala, S., Nayak, A., Bhandare, M., Ambulkar, R. P., & Shrikhande, S. V. (2021). Artificial intelligence in perioperative management of major gastrointestinal surgeries. *World Journal of Gastroenterology*, *27*(21), 2758–2770. DOI: 10.3748/wjg.v27.i21.2758 PMID: 34135552

Solek, P., Nurfitri, E., Sahril, I., Prasetya, T., Rizqiamuti, A. F., Rachmawati, I., & Gunawan, K. (2025). The role of artificial intelligence for early diagnostic tools of autism spectrum disorder: A systematic review. *Turkish Archives of Pediatrics*, *60*(2), 126–140. DOI: 10.5152/TurkArchPediatr.2025.24183

Song, Y., Chen, X., Hao, T., Liu, Z., & Lan, Z. (2019). Exploring two decades of research on classroom dialogue by using bibliometric analysis. *Computers & Education*, *137*, 12–31. DOI: 10.1016/j.compedu.2019.04.002

Spinellis, D. (2025). False authorship: An explorative case study around an AI-generated article published under my name. *Research Integrity and Peer Review*, *10*(1), 8. Advance online publication. DOI: 10.1186/s41073-025-00165-z PMID: 40420142

Steinbauer, G., Kandlhofer, M., Chklovski, T., Heintz, F., & Koenig, S. (2021). A differentiated discussion about AI education K-12. *Kunstliche Intelligenz*, *35*(2), 131–137. DOI: 10.1007/s13218-021-00724-8 PMID: 34007103

Stone, A. (2024). *How Creative Generative AI Can Help Higher Education Institutions*. EdTech Magazine. https://edtechmagazine.com/higher/article/2024/07/how-creative-generative-ai-can-help-higher-education-institutions

Stone, A. (2025). *AI Ethics in Higher Education: How Schools Are Proceeding*. EdTech Magazine. https://edtechmagazine.com/higher/article/2025/03/ai-ethics-higher-education-how-schools-are-proceeding-perfcon

Su, J., Yu, C., & Ng, D. T. K. (2022). A meta-review of literature on educational approaches for teaching AI at the K-12 levels in the Asia-Pacific region. *Computers and Education: Artificial Intelligence,* Article 100065.

Su, G. (2018). Unemployment in the AI Age. *AI Matters*, *3*(4), 35–43. DOI: 10.1145/3175502.3175511

Su, J., Ng, D. T. K., & Chu, S. K. W. (2023). Artificial intelligence (AI) literacy in early childhood education: The challenges and opportunities. *Computers and Education: Artificial Intelligence*, *4*, 100124. DOI: 10.1016/j.caeai.2023.100124

Su, J., & Yang, W. (2022). Artificial intelligence in early childhood education: A scoping review. *Computers and Education: Artificial Intelligence*, *3*, 100049. DOI: 10.1016/j.caeai.2022.100049

Sun, N., & Saleh, S. (2024). Mapping the Landscape of AI Implementation in STEM and STEAM Education: A Bibliometric Analysis. *International Conference on Technology in Education*, 99-111. DOI: 10.1007/978-981-96-0205-6_7

Sun, Y., Chen, J., Yao, B., Liu, J., Wang, D., Ma, X., & He, L. (2024). Exploring parents' needs for children-centered AI to support preschoolers' interactive storytelling and reading activities. *Proceedings of the ACM on Human-Computer Interaction, 8*(CSCW2), 1–25.

Suraj Kumar, S., Chatterjee, K., Ramchandra Reddy, S., Praveen Kumar, R., Sachin, A., Abhinav Vardhan Reddy, T., & Sriya Reddy, M. (2024). GenAI: Transforming Climate Science Education in the Digital Age. *Studies in Computational Intelligence*, *1177*, 355–372. DOI: 10.1007/978-981-97-8460-8_16

Surathunmanun, S., Ongsakul, W., & Singh, J. G. (2024). Exploring the Role of Generative Artificial Intelligence in the Energy Sector: A Comprehensive Literature Review. *Proceedings of the 2024 International Conference on Sustainable Energy: Energy Transition and Net-Zero Climate Future, ICUE 2024*. DOI: 10.1109/ICUE63019.2024.10795598

Tang, K. S. (2024). Informing research on generative artificial intelligence from a language and literacy perspective: A meta-synthesis of studies in science education. *Science Education, 108*(5), 1329–1355. DOI: 10.1002/sce.21875

Tavakol, M., & Dennick, R. (2011). Making sense of Cronbach's alpha. *International Journal of Medical Education, 2*, 53–55. DOI: 10.5116/ijme.4dfb.8dfd PMID: 28029643

Teamann, A. (2023). *To ChatGPT or Not to ChatGPT, That Is the Question*. EdTech Magazine. https://edtechmagazine.com/k12/article/2023/11/chatgpt-or-not-chatgpt-question

Temsah, M. H., Alhuzaimi, A. N., Almansour, M., Aljamaan, F., Alhasan, K., Batarfi, M. A., Altamimi, I., Alharbi, A., Alsuhaibani, A. A., Alwakeel, L., Alzahrani, A. A., Alsulaim, K. B., Jamal, A., Khayat, A., Alghamdi, M. H., Halwani, R., Khan, M. K., Al-Eyadhy, A., & Nazer, R. (2024). Art or Artifact: Evaluating the Accuracy, Appeal, and Educational Value of AI-Generated Imagery in DALL·E 3 for Illustrating Congenital Heart Diseases. *Journal of Medical Systems, 48*(1), 1–13. DOI: 10.1007/s10916-024-02072-0 PMID: 38780839

Temur, S. (2025). 2000-2024 Yılları Arasında Eğitim Alanında Yapılan Yapay Zekâ Konulu Lisansüstü Çalışmaların İncelenmesi. *Dokuz Eylül Üniversitesi Buca Eğitim Fakültesi Dergisi, 63*, 1162–1199.

Thananuwong, R. (2015). Learning Science from Toys: A Pathway to Successful Integrated STEM Teaching and Learning in Thai Middle School. *K-12 STEM Education, 1*(2), 75–84. DOI: 10.14456/K12STEMED.2015.22

Thornton-Lang, K. M. (2012). Observation as a formal assessment tool in early childhood classrooms: A professional development module (Graduate Research Paper, University of Northern Iowa). UNI ScholarWorks. https://scholarworks.uni.edu/grp/238

Tırpan, C. (2024). *The ethical issues in generative artificial intelligence: A systematic review*. bmij, 12(4), 729–747.

Tondeur, J., van Braak, J., Ertmer, P. A., & Ottenbreit-Leftwich, A. (2017). Understanding the relationship between teachers' pedagogical beliefs and technology use in education: A systematic review of qualitative evidence. *Educational Technology Research and Development, 65*(3), 555–575. DOI: 10.1007/s11423-016-9481-2

Touretzky, D. S. (2017). *Computational thinking and mental models: From Kodu to Calypso. In 2017 IEEE blocks and beyond workshop (B&B)*. IEEE.

Touretzky, D., Gardner-McCune, C., Martin, F., & Seehorn, D. (2019). Envisioning AI for K-12: What should every child know about AI? *Proceedings of the AAAI Conference on Artificial Intelligence*, *33*(1), 9795–9799. DOI: 10.1609/aaai.v33i01.33019795

Tzirides, A. O. (Olnancy), Saini, A., Zapata, G., Searsmith, D., Cope, B., Kalantzis, M., Castro, V., Kourkoulou, T., Jones, J., Abrantes da Silva, R., Whiting, J., & Kastania, N. P. (2023). Generative AI: Implications and Applications for Education. *ArXiv*, 2023. https://doi.org/https://doi.org/10.48550/arXiv.2305.07605

Uğraş, H., & Uğraş, M. (2025). ChatGPT in early childhood STEM education: Can it be an innovative tool to overcome challenges? *Education and Information Technologies*, *30*(4), 4277–4305. DOI: 10.1007/s10639-024-12960-0

Uğraş, H., Uğraş, M., Papadakis, S., & Kalogiannakis, M. (2024). ChatGPT-supported education in primary schools: The potential of ChatGPT for sustainable practices. *Sustainability (Basel)*, *16*(22), 9855. DOI: 10.3390/su16229855

Uğraş, M. (2024). Evaluation of ChatGPT Usage in Preschool Education: Teacher Perspectives. *Eğitim Ve İnsani Bilimler Dergisi: Teori Ve Uygulama*, *15*(30), 387–414.

Uğraş, M., Çakır, Z., Zacharis, G., & Kalogiannakis, M. (2025). ChatGPT in Early Childhood Science Education: Can It Offer Innovative Effective Solutions to Overcome Challenges? *Computers*, *14*(9), 368. DOI: 10.3390/computers14090368

Ünal, M., & Aral, N. (2014). Deney yöntemine dayalı eğitim programının 6 yaş çocuklarının problem çözme becerilerine etkisinin incelenmesi [Examination of the effect of an experiment-based education program on the problem-solving skills of 6-year-old children]. *Eğitim ve Bilim*, *39*(176), 279–291. DOI: 10.15390/EB.2014.3592

UNESCO. (2021). AI and Education: Guidance for Policy-Makers. https://unesdoc.unesco.org/ark:/48223/pf0000376709

UNICEF. (2022). *AI for children.* https://www.unicef.org/globalinsight/featured-projects/ai-children

Valtonen, T., López-Pernas, S., Saqr, M., Vartiainen, H., Sointu, E. T., & Tedre, M. (2022). The nature and building blocks of educational technology research. *Computers in Human Behavior*, *128*, 107123. DOI: 10.1016/j.chb.2021.107123

Van Amerongen, J. (2000). The Role of Control in Mechatronics. *Engineering Science and Education Journal*, *9*(3), 105–112. DOI: 10.1049/esej:20000302

Van Keulen, H. (2018). STEM in early childhood education. *European Journal of STEM Education, 3*(3), 06.

VanLehn, K. (2011). The relative effectiveness of human tutoring, intelligent tutoring systems, and other tutoring systems. *Educational Psychologist, 46*(4), 197–221. DOI: 10.1080/00461520.2011.611369

Vartiainen, H., Tedre, M., & Valtonen, T. (2020). Learning machine learning with very young children: Who is teaching whom? *International Journal of Child-Computer Interaction, 25*, 100182. DOI: 10.1016/j.ijcci.2020.100182

Vasalou, A., Kalantari, S., Kucirkova, N., & Vezzoli, Y. (2020a). Designing for oral storytelling practices at home: A parental perspective. *International Journal of Child-Computer Interaction, 26*, 100214. Advance online publication. DOI: 10.1016/j.ijcci.2020.100214

Vasconcelos, M. A. R., & dos Santos, R. P. (2023). Enhancing STEM learning with ChatGPT and Bing Chat as objects to think with: A case study. *Eurasia Journal of Mathematics, Science and Technology Education, 19*(7), em2296. Advance online publication. DOI: 10.29333/ejmste/13313

Vasquez, J. A., Comer, M., & Sneider, C. (2013). *STEM Lesson Essentials, Grades 3-8: Integrating Science, Technology, Engineering, and Mathematics* (1st editio). Heinemann. https://www.amazon.com/STEM-Lesson-Essentials-Grades-3-8/dp/0325043582

Venkatesh, V., Morris, M. G., Davis, G. B., & Davis, F. D. (2003). User acceptance of information technology: Toward a unified view. *Management Information Systems Quarterly, 27*(3), 425–478. DOI: 10.2307/30036540

Vezzoli, Y., Kalantari, S., Kucirkova, N., & Vasalou, A. (2020b). Exploring the design space for parent-child reading. In *Proceedings of the 2020 CHI Conference on Human Factors in Computing Systems* (pp. 1–12). DOI: 10.1145/3313831.3376696

Vincent-Lancrin, S., J. Urgel, S. Kar, and G. Jacotin (2019), *Measuring Innovation in Education 2019: What Has Changed in the Classroom?* Educational Research and Innovation, OECD Publishing. DOI: 10.1787/9789264311671-en

Vincent-Lancrin, S., & van der Vlies, R. (2020). *Trustworthy artificial intelligence (AI) in education: Promises and challenges.* OECD Publishing., DOI: 10.1787/a6c90fa9-

Wan, I., Wan, S. 'Azzam and A., Nur, A., & Pauzi, M. N. (2024). An Overview of the Use of Artificial Intelligence Tools in Higher Education. *Current Research Progress in Agricultural Sciences Vol. 4, 19*(3), 29–42. DOI: 10.9734/bpi/crpas/v4/2280

Wang, H. (2023). Formation Mechanism and Practice Path Model of Teachers' Intelligent Literacy in the Context of Artificial Intelligence. *2023 2nd International Conference on Artificial Intelligence and Computer Information Technology (AICIT)*, 1-6.

Wang, K. D., Wu, Z., Tufts, L., Wieman, C., Salehi, S., & Haber, N. (2025). Scaffold or Crutch? Examining College Students' Use and Views of Generative AI Tools for STEM Education. *IEEE Global Engineering Education Conference, EDUCON*, 1–21. DOI: 10.1109/EDUCON62633.2025.11016406

Wang, F., & Hannafin, M. J. (2005). Design-based research and technology-enhanced learning environments. *Educational Technology Research and Development, 53*(4), 5–23. DOI: 10.1007/BF02504682

Weese, J. L. (2017). *Bringing Computational Thinking to K-12 and Higher Education*. Kansas State University.

Weintrop, D., Beheshti, E., Horn, M., Orton, K., Jona, K., Trouille, L., & Wilensky, U. (2016). Defining computational thinking for mathematics and science classrooms. *Journal of Science Education and Technology, 25*(1), 127–147. DOI: 10.1007/s10956-015-9581-5

Weintrop, D., & Wilensky, U. (2015). To block or not to block, that is the question: Students' perceptions of blocks-based programming. In *Proceedings of the 14th international conference on interaction design and children* (pp. 199–208). DOI: 10.1145/2771839.2771860

Wiki, A. (2025b). *Meta AI*. https://aiwiki.ai/wiki/Meta_AI_%28Company%29

Wiki, A. (2025c). *Meta AI - AI Wiki*. https://aiwiki.ai/wiki/Meta_AI

Wiki, A. (2025a). *DALL-E*. https://aiwiki.ai/wiki/DALL-E

Wiki, A. (2025d). *Midjourney*. https://aiwiki.ai/wiki/Midjourney

Wikipedia. (2025a). *DALL-E*. https://en.wikipedia.org/wiki/DALL-E

Wikipedia. (2025b). *Perplexity AI*. https://en.wikipedia.org/wiki/Perplexity_AI

Wikipedia. (2025c). *Sora (text-to-video model)*. https://en.wikipedia.org/wiki/Sora_(text-to-video_model)

Williams, R. (2018). *PopBots: Leveraging social robots to aid preschool children's artificial intelligence education* (Doctoral dissertation, Massachusetts Institute of Technology). Massachusetts Institute of Technology.

Williamson, B. (2017). Big Data in Education: The Digital Future of Learning. *Policy & Practice.*

Williams, R., Park, H. W., & Breazeal, C. (2019, May). A is for artificial intelligence: The impact of artificial intelligence activities on young children's perceptions of robots. In *Proceedings of the 2019 CHI Conference on Human Factors in Computing Systems* (s. 1–11). DOI: 10.1145/3290605.3300677

Williams, R., Park, H. W., Oh, L., & Breazeal, C. (2019a). Popbots: Designing an artificial intelligence curriculum for early childhood education. In *Proceedings of the AAAI Conference on Artificial Intelligence,* 33 pp. 9729–9736), 1. DOI: 10.1609/aaai.v33i01.33019729

Williyan, A., Fitriati, S. W., Pratama, H., & Sakhiyya, Z. (2024). AI as co-creator: Exploring Indonesian EFL teachers' collaboration with AI in content development. *Teaching English with Technology, 24*(2), 5–21. DOI: 10.56297/vaca6841/LRDX3699/RZOH5366

Wing, J. M. (2006). Computational thinking. *Communications of the ACM, 49*(3), 33–35. DOI: 10.1145/1118178.1118215

Wold, H., Sjöström, M., & Eriksson, L. (2001). PLS-regression: A basic tool of chemometrics. *Chemometrics and Intelligent Laboratory Systems, 58*(2), 109–130. DOI: 10.1016/S0169-7439(01)00155-1

Wong, G. K., Ma, X., Dillenbourg, P., & Huan, J. (2020). Broadening artificial intelligence education in K-12: Where to start? *ACM Inroads, 11*(1), 20–29. DOI: 10.1145/3381884

Woolf, B. P. (2010). *Building Intelligent Interactive Tutors: Student-Centered Strategies for Revolutionizing e-Learning*. Morgan Kaufmann.

Wu, L. (2021). Construction of STEM Interdisciplinary Integration Model Supported by Educational Artificial Intelligence. *2021 IEEE 2nd International Conference on Big Data, Artificial Intelligence and Internet of Things Engineering (ICBAIE),* 769-772.

Wu, J., & Chen, D. T. V. (2020). A systematic review of educational digital storytelling. *Computers & Education, 147,* 103786. DOI: 10.1016/j.compedu.2019.103786

Wu, Y. (2024). Is early childhood education prepared for artificial intelligence?: A global and US policy framework literature review. *Open Journal of Social Sciences, 12*(8), 127–143. DOI: 10.4236/jss.2024.128010

Xatzopoulos, A., Papoutsidakis, M., & Chamilothoris, G. (2013). Mobile Robotic Platforms as Educational Tools in Mechatronics Engineering. *International Scientific Conference ERA – 8*, 41–51. era.teipir.gr

Xu, W., & Ouyang, F. (2022). The application of AI technologies in STEM education: A systematic review from 2011 to 2021. *International Journal of STEM Education, 9*(1), 59. DOI: 10.1186/s40594-022-00377-5

Yabaku, M., & Ouhbi, S. (2024). University Students' Perception and Expectations of Generative AI Tools for Software Engineering. *Software Engineering Education Conference, Proceedings*, 1–5. DOI: 10.1109/CSEET62301.2024.10663035

Yadav, A., Zhou, N., Mayfield, C., Hambrusch, S., & Korb, J. T. (2011). Introducing computational thinking in education courses. *SIGCSE'11 - Proceedings of the 42nd ACM Technical Symposium on Computer Science Education, 2*, 465–470. DOI: 10.1145/1953163.1953297

Yang, W. (2022). Artificial Intelligence education for young children: Why, what, and how in curriculum design and implementation. *Computers & Education. Artificial Intelligence*, •••, 100061.

Yang, W. (2022). Artificial intelligence education for young children: Why, what, and how in curriculum design and implementation. *Computers and Education: Artificial Intelligence, 3*, 100061. DOI: 10.1016/j.caeai.2022.100061

Yang, Y. T. C., Chen, Y. C., & Hung, H. T. (2020). Digital storytelling as an interdisciplinary project to improve students' English speaking and creative thinking. *Computer Assisted Language Learning, 35*(4), 840–862. DOI: 10.1080/09588221.2020.1750431

Yan, L., Greiff, S., Teuber, Z., & Gašević, D. (2024). Promises and challenges of generative artificial intelligence for human learning. *Nature Human Behaviour, 8*(10), 1839–1850. DOI: 10.1038/s41562-024-02004-5 PMID: 39438686

Yeh, S. C., Chen, Y. H., Van Velzen, R., & Lin, P. H. (2025). The climate change literacy of public officials in Taiwan: Implications and strategies for global adaptation. *Policy Studies, 46*(2), 168–201. Advance online publication. DOI: 10.1080/01442872.2024.2304086

Yen, K., Chen, Y., Cheng, Y., Chen, S., Chen, Y.-Y., Ni, Y., & Hiniker, A. (2018). Joint media engagement between parents and preschoolers in the U.S., China, and Taiwan. *Proceedings of the ACM on Human-Computer Interaction, 2*(CSCW), 1–19. DOI: 10.1145/3274461

Yıldırım, A., & Şimşek, H. (2013). *Sosyal bilimlerde nitel araştırma yöntemleri* (9. Baskı). Seçkin Yayıncılık.

Yılmaz, A. (2023). Fen bilimleri eğitiminde dijital uygulamalar, yapay zekâ ve akıllı yazılımlar: Tehditler ve fırsatlar. A. Akpınar. *Matematik ve Fen Bilimleri Üzerine Araştırmalar-II*, 1-20.

Yin, Y., Tomita, M. K., & Shavelson, R. J. (2008). Diagnosing and dealing with student misconceptions: Floating and sinking. *Science Scope, 31*(8), 34–39.

Yu, H., & Guo, Y. (2023). Generative artificial intelligence empowers educational reform: Current status, issues, and prospects. *Frontiers in Education, 8*, 1183162. DOI: 10.3389/feduc.2023.1183162

Yu, S., Hou, Y., & Li, H. (2025). Suitability of Chinese GenAI platforms for early childhood education: A multifaceted evaluation. https://doi.org/DOI: 10.21203/rs.3.rs-6300153/v1

Zahilah Mohamed Zaki, F., Wong, S. L., & Ridzwan Yaakub, M. (2019). A Review of Common Features inComputational Thinking Frameworks in K-12 Education. *IOP Conference Series. Materials Science and Engineering, 551*(1), 012063. DOI: 10.1088/1757-899X/551/1/012063

Zawacki-Richter, O.. (2019). Systematic review of AI in higher education. *International Journal of Educational Technology in Higher Education.*

Zawacki-Richter, O., Marín, V., Bond, M., & Gouverneur, F. (2019). Systematic review of research on artificial intelligence applications in higher education: Where are the educators? *International Journal of Educational Technology in Higher Education, 16*(1), 9. Advance online publication. DOI: 10.1186/s41239-019-0171-0

Zeidan, A. H., & Jayosi, M. R. (2015). Science process skills and attitudes toward science among Palestinian secondary school students. *World Journal of Education, 5*(1), 13–24. DOI: 10.5430/wje.v5n1p13

Zhai, X., Chu, X., Chai, C. S., Jong, M. S. Y., Istenic, A., Spector, M., Liu, J.-B., Yuan, J., & Li, Y. (2021). A Review of Artificial Intelligence (AI) in Education from 2010 to 2020. *Complexity, 2021*(1), 1–18. DOI: 10.1155/2021/8812542

Zhao, Y., Yusof, S. M., Hou, M., & Li, Z. (2024). How can generative artificial intelligence help teachers in early childhood education with their teaching? Analyses from the perspective of teaching methods. *International Journal of Academic Research in Progressive Education and Development, 13*(1). Advance online publication. DOI: 10.6007/IJARPED/v13-i1/20958

Zhu, H. (2020). Big data and artificial intelligence modeling for drug discovery. *Annual Review of Pharmacology and Toxicology, 60*(1), 573–589. DOI: 10.1146/annurev-pharmtox-010919-023324

Zupic, I., & Čater, T. (2015). Bibliometric methods in management and organization. *Organizational Research Methods, 18*(3), 429–472. DOI: 10.1177/1094428114562629

About the Contributors

Michail Kalogiannakis is a Professor at the Department of Special Education of the University of Thessaly in Greece and an Associate Tutor at the School of Humanities at the Hellenic Open University. He graduated from the Physics Department of the University of Crete and continued his post-graduate studies at the University Paris 7-Denis Diderot (D.E.A. in Didactic of Physics), University Paris 5-René Descartes-Sorbonne (D.E.A. in Science Education) and received his PhD degree at the University Paris 5-René Descartes-Sorbonne (PhD in Science Education). His research interests include: science education, STEM Education, mobile learning for science education, GenAI in science education, distant learning and science education, and computational thinking in science education. He has published over 180 articles in international conferences and journals and has served on the program committees of numerous international conferences.

Dimitrios Sotiropoulos is a member of the teaching laboratory staff of the Department of Special Education of the University of Thessaly. His qualifications include a PhD on the use of digital technology in science education (University of Athens), a Master's Degree (M.Sc.) in Science Education (University of Athens) and a Bachelor's Degree (B.A.) in Physics (AUTh). He has extensive experience in teaching at all levels of education and in training teachers in the use of new technologies in educational practice. He has taught computing and science at primary, secondary and post-secondary levels. At the tertiary level, for several years he has taught numerous courses on the pedagogical use of digital technology. He has also supervised students in the preparation of their postgraduate theses. He has also participated in a variety of European education programmes, including Erasmus+, Horizon 2020 and previous initiatives. His postdoctoral thesis concerned the design and implementation of a functional, user-friendly and useful web platform for teachers and students. His research interests focus on the scientific disciplines and the use of new technologies in education. In particular, his recent academic research focuses on the pedagogical integration of emerging technologies, especially Generative Artificial Intelligence (GenAI), in STEM and STEAM education. He has presented his research at numerous academic conferences, journals and forums in Greece and abroad.

***

Munir Ahmad is a seasoned professional in the realm of Spatial Data Infrastructure (SDI), Geo-Information Productions, Information Systems, and Information Governance, boasting over 25 years of dedicated experience in the field. With a PhD in Computer Science, Dr. Ahmad's expertise spans Spatial Data Production, Management, Processing, Analysis, Visualization, and Quality Control. Throughout his career, Dr. Ahmad has been deeply involved in the development and deployment of SDI systems specially in the context of Pakistan, leveraging his proficiency in Spatial Database Design, Web, Mobile & Desktop GIS, and Geo Web Services Architecture. His contributions to Volunteered Geographic Information (VGI) and Open Source Geoportal & Metadata Portal have significantly enriched the geospatial community. As a trainer and researcher, Dr. Ahmad has authored over 50 publications, advancing the industry's knowledge base and fostering innovation in Geo-Tech, Data Governance, and Information Infrastructure, and Emerging Technologies. His commitment to Research and Development (R&D) is evident in his role as a dedicated educator and mentor in the field.

Avraam Chatzopoulos is an Assistant Professor at the Department of Industrial Design and Production Engineering at the University of West Attica. He holds a BSc in Automation Engineering, an MSc in Telematics Management, an MSc in Information and Communication Technologies for Education, and a Ph.D. He has taught for several years in many educational institutions, with special experience in adult education, and holds an adult educator certification. He has worked as a freelancer in a significant number of IT and automation projects, especially in the design of applications based on microcontrollers and the development of web applications. He has written educational books and articles in new technology magazines. He founded the Robotics Academy of the Uniwa for training and research in Educational Robotics - STEM Education and the development of educational robots for use in primary and secondary education. Since 2000, he has been involved in the development of Mechatron (an educational robotics platform for university education), while in 2005, he was a member of the research team that received a patent on “Self-propelled polymorphic test base for laboratory training in robotics and micro-controllers” from the Industrial Property Organization.

Cansel Doymaz is an early childhood education specialist who completed her undergraduate studies in Preschool Education at Ankara University. She is currently pursuing a Master's degree (Thesis Track) in Early Childhood Education at Kafkas University, focusing on developmental assessment, scientific process skills, and play-based learning. Her academic interests include early childhood STEM education, early literacy, observational assessment, digital game–based learning, and the integration of artificial intelligence into early learning environments. She is committed to creating developmentally appropriate, inquiry-driven classrooms that foster children's creativity and problem-solving skills. Doymaz aims to contribute to national and international research efforts supporting innovation, digital transformation, and high-quality practices in early childhood education.

Ali İbrahim Can Gözüm is an internationally active researcher specializing in early childhood science and technology education. He received the Faculty Honor Certificate as the top performing student at Kafkas University (2005–2009) and later earned a Publication Incentive Award from TÜBİTAK for his internationally recognized research contributions. Currently, Dr. Gözüm serves as an Associate Professor in Early Childhood Education at Kafkas University. He completed his doctoral studies through a joint program in Early Childhood Education (Gazi University) and Science Education (Ondokuz Mayıs University), focusing on children's scientific thinking, digital learning environments, and technology-supported assessment. His research interests include STEM in early childhood, AI-supported assessment, digital learning applications, parental mediation, and teacher professional development.

Zokir Mamadiyarov is working in the Department of Finance and Tourism at Termez University of Economics and Service, Termez, Uzbekistan.

Nalan Özbey is an asst prof. in the Department of Educational Sciences, Department of Curriculum and Instruction at Kafkas University. She completed her doctorate and master's degrees in Curriculum and Instruction, and her bachelor's degree in Computer and Instructional Technologies. Therefore, she conducts studies by integrating educational technologies into educational sciences by blending two separate programs.

Sachin Sharma is currently working as a Professor, Amity School of Engineering and Technology, Amity University Punjab, Mohali, India. He also worked as Associate Dean, International Affairs and Professor, Department of Computer Science and Engineering at Graphic Era Deemed to be University, Dehradun, Uttarakhand, India. He has experience of 15+ years in industry and academia. He is also Co-founder and Chief Technology officer (CTO) of IntelliNexus

LLC, Arkansas, USA based company. He also worked as a Senior Systems Engineer at Belkin International, Inc., Irvine, California, USA. He received his Philosophy of Doctorate (Ph.D.) degree in Engineering Science and Systems specialization in Systems Engineering from University of Arkansas at Little Rock, USA with 4.0 out 4.0 GPA and M.S. degree in Systems engineering from University of Arkansas at Little Rock with 4.0 out 4.0 GPA. Dr. Sharma has authored/coauthored over 300+ publications in the form of books, patents, and papers in refereed journals and conference proceedings. He holds 100+ US, Indian and international patents in the area of IoT, wireless communication and AI. He has also served as a Guest Reviewer for several Special issues of IEEE/ACM Transactions. His research interests include 6G wireless communication networks, Cloud Computing, Artificial Intelligence, Quantum Computing, IoT, Vehicular ad hoc networking and Cyber security.

Mustafa Uğraş is a professor at the Department of Early Childhood Education, Faculty of Education, Fırat University. His academic work focuses on science education in early childhood, STEM education in early childhood, the integration of productive artificial intelligence tools into the teaching process, and teacher education. Prof. Dr. Mustafa Uğraş particularly focuses on the integration of productive artificial intelligence tools such as ChatGPT into the teaching practices of teacher candidates. Her recent work centres on the role of digital innovations in achieving sustainable education goals and the development of artificial intelligence literacy among teacher candidates. She has published numerous peer-reviewed articles, written book chapters, and presented papers at international scientific conferences on STEM education in early childhood and teacher training in the digital age.

Index

A

B

C

D

E

G

H

I

L

M

P

S

www.ingramcontent.com/pod-product-compliance
Lightning Source LLC
LaVergne TN
LVHW080907300926
849162LV00003B/591